Exploring Time, Tense and Aspect in Natural Language Database Interfaces

Natural Language Processing

Volume 6

Exploring Time, Tense and Aspect in Natural Language Database Interfaces
by Ion Androutsopoulos

Exploring Time, Tense and Aspect in Natural Language Database Interfaces

Ion Androutsopoulos
Athens University of Economics and Business

John Benjamins Publishing Company
Amsterdam / Philadelphia

∞™ The paper used in this publication meets the minimum requirements of American National Standard for Information Sciences – Permanence of Paper for Printed Library Materials, ANSI Z39.48-1984.

Library of Congress Cataloging-in-Publication Data

Androutsopoulos, Ion

Exploring Time, Tense and Aspect in Natural Language Database Interfaces / Ion Androutsopoulos.

p. cm. (Natural Language Processing, ISSN 1567–8202 ; v. 6)

Includes bibliographical references and index.

1. Grammar, Comparative and general--Temporal constructions--Data processing. 2. Grammar, Comparative and general--Verb--Data processing. 3. Computational linguistics. I. Title. II. Natural language processing (Amsterdam, Netherlands) ; v. 6.

P294.5 A53 2002
415-dc21 2002074690
ISBN 90 272 4990 3 (Eur.) / 1 58811 269 1 (US) (Hb; alk. paper)

John Benjamins Publishing Co. · P.O. Box 36224 · 1020 ME Amsterdam · The Netherlands
John Benjamins North America · P.O. Box 27519 · Philadelphia PA 19118-0519 · USA

Table of contents

Chapter 1

Introduction

"No time like the present."

1.1 What this book is about

For at least four decades, a very significant amount of work in artificial intelligence and computational linguistics has been devoted to *natural language interaction*, i.e., creating computer systems that allow their users to formulate requests in natural language, and systems that generate automatically appropriate natural language responses (Androutsopoulos & Aretoulaki 2002; Reiter & Dale 2000). One form of natural language interaction that has been studied extensively, and which is also the focus of this book, is database querying, where the term *natural language interface* is often used (Perrault & Grosz 1988; Copestake & Sparck Jones 1990; Androutsopoulos, Ritchie, & Thanisch 1995b; Androutsopoulos & Ritchie 2000).

Natural language interfaces to databases (NLIDBS) allow their users to retrieve information from an underlying database by submitting natural language queries, as illustrated in the following dialogue, where 'U:' and 'S:' mark user requests and system responses, respectively.

U: *Which engineers work in the sales department?*
S: `J.Adams, T.Smith.`
U: *What are their salaries?*
S: `J.Adams 2400`
`T.Smith 1800`
U: *What is the average salary in the sales department?*
S: `2250.`

The interaction may, in general, be in either spoken or written form, although this book considers only the latter; i.e., it will be assumed that the user types on a keyboard. This sidesteps speech recognition and synthesis (Jelinek 1997;

Dutoit 1997; Gibbon, Moore, & Winski 1997; Hirschberg, Kamm, & Walker 1997; Bernsen, Dybkjaer, & Dybkjaer 1998).

One of the limitations of existing NLIDBS is that they were designed mainly to handle questions that refer to the present, as in the dialogue above or (1.1)–(1.3), and they do not support adequately the mechanisms that natural language employs to express time. For example, very few, if any, temporal adverbials (e.g., *in 1991*, *after 5:00 pm*) and verb forms (simple past, past continuous, past perfect, etc.) are typically supported, and their semantics are usually over-simplified or ignored.

(1.1) What is the salary of each engineer?
(1.2) Who is at site 4?
(1.3) Which generators are in operation?

Database researchers have been exploring *temporal database* systems. These are intended to store and manipulate in a principled manner information not only about the present, but also about the past and future (Tansel et al. 1993; Jensen et al. 1998; Wu, Jajodia, & Wang 1998; Snodgrass 2000). When interfacing to temporal databases, it becomes crucial for NLIDBS to interpret correctly the temporal mechanisms of natural language, which in questions like (1.4)–(1.6) include verb tenses, temporal adverbials, and temporal subordinate clauses.

(1.4) What was the salary of each engineer while ScotCorp was building bridge 5?
(1.5) Did anybody leave site 4 before the chief engineer had inspected the control room?
(1.6) Which systems did the chief engineer inspect on Monday after the auxiliary generator was in operation?

Supporting the notion of time in NLIDBS is a complex issue, as it requires ideas from three different time-related disciplines to be combined: linguistic theories of time, often referred to as *tense and aspect* theories (Comrie 1976; Comrie 1985; Smith 1997), *temporal logics* (van Benthem 1991; Gabbay, Hodkinson, & Reynolds 1994; Gabbay, Reynolds, & Finger 2000), and temporal databases. This point is easier to understand by considering Figure 1.1, which shows a simplified form of the architecture that many modern NLIDBS adopt.

As shown in Figure 1.1, the natural language question is first processed by a *linguistic front-end*. This analyses syntactically and semantically the question, and maps it to an expression of an intermediate meaning representation language, typically some kind of logic. The meaning representation expression captures formally what the system understands to be the meaning of the nat-

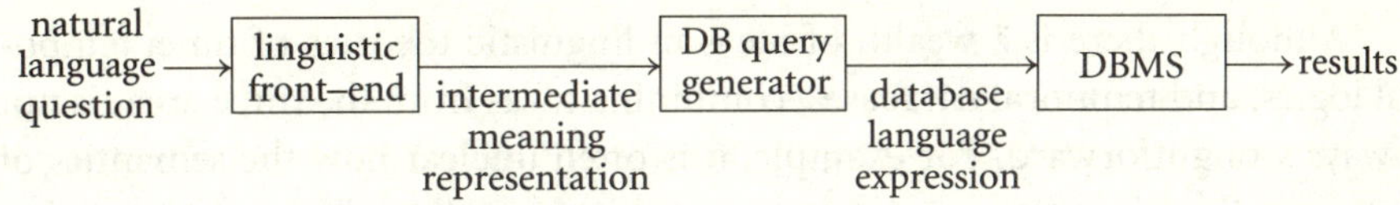

Figure 1.1 Simplified NLIDB architecture

ural language question. The expression is then translated into a database language, usually SQL (Melton & Simon 1993; Melton, Simon, & Gray 2001), that is supported by the underlying *database management system* (DBMS); the latter is the part of the database system that manipulates the information in the database. Unlike the intermediate meaning representation, the database language expression specifies what information needs to be retrieved in terms of particular database constructs (e.g., rows and columns of tables in the database). The DBMS retrieves this information by evaluating the database language expression, and the obtained information is reported back to the user. A response generator may also be involved, to convert the information to a form that is easier for the user to read; for simplicity, however, we will ignore response generation in the largest part of this book. The architecture of Figure 1.1 has proven to have several advantages (Androutsopoulos, Ritchie, & Thanisch 1995b; Androutsopoulos & Ritchie 2000); for example, the linguistic front-end is shielded from database-level issues, and it can be reused with DBMSs that support different database languages.

To support the notion of time in NLIDBs, then, one first needs a concrete understanding of the variety, syntax, and semantics of the temporal mechanisms in natural language. The discussion in this book is limited to English. Ideas from linguistic theories of time can be drawn at this point, though one has to focus on ideas that are relevant to NLIDB questions, as opposed, for example, to temporal phenomena that occur in longer event-reporting texts. A formally defined intermediate meaning representation language is also needed to represent the time-sensitive semantics of the questions; this is where ideas from temporal logics can be exploited. Furthermore, the meaning representation language must facilitate the mapping from natural language to formal representation; for example, by providing facilities that allow the semantic contribution of each temporal mechanism of natural language to be captured easily. Finally, an algorithm is needed to translate automatically from the meaning representation language to a temporal database language. The algorithm must be provably correct, in the sense that the database language expressions must preserve the semantics of the original meaning representations.

Although there is a wealth of ideas in linguistic theories of time, temporal logics, and temporal databases, combining ideas from the three areas is not always straightforward. For example, it is often unclear how the semantics of linguistic theories of time can be expressed in formal meaning representation languages; and although numerous forms of temporal logic have been proposed, very few systematic mappings from natural language to expressions of those logics exist. Furthermore, there may be components in the temporal ontologies of linguistic theories or meaning representation languages that have no counterparts in temporal database models. The goal of this book is to explore how ideas from the three areas can be combined and refined, for the purposes of database querying, in order to produce a theoretical framework that will serve both as a starting point for developers of natural language interfaces to temporal databases (NLITDBS) and as a basis for further research.

More specifically, Chapter 2 explores temporal linguistic phenomena that are likely to appear in English questions to NLITDBS. Drawing on existing tense and aspect theories, it formulates an account for many of these phenomena that is simple enough to be embodied in practical NLITDBS. Exploiting ideas from temporal logics, Chapter 3 then defines a temporal meaning representation language, called TOP, which is used to represent the semantics of the English questions. Chapter 4 shows how HPSG grammars (Pollard & Sag 1994) can be enhanced to incorporate the tense and aspect account of this book, and to map a wide range of English questions involving time to appropriate TOP expressions. Chapter 5 then presents a provably correct mapping that translates TOP expressions to appropriate TSQL2 queries (Snodgrass 1995), TSQL2 being a temporal extension of SQL. This way a theoretical framework that establishes a sound route from English questions involving time to a temporal database language is constructed. To demonstrate that the framework is workable, it was used to implement a prototype NLITDB using ALE (Carpenter 1992; Carpenter & Penn 2001) and Prolog. The prototype is freely available, and Chapter 6 provides more information about it. Finally, Chapter 7 compares the approach of this book to other attempts to build NLITDBS, and proposes directions for further research.

This book is a revised version of the author's PhD thesis (Androutsopoulos 1996). The reader will be pointed to the thesis for some mundane details, mostly parts of large proofs, that have not been included in the book. A summary of the thesis has also been published (Androutsopoulos, Ritchie, & Thanisch 1998).

Like any natural language, English possesses a very large variety of temporal mechanisms, and it would be impossible for a book to consider how all of them can be supported in NLITDBS. Hence, this book focuses on a rich sample of English temporal mechanisms, paying particular attention to the description of the sample's boundaries, and providing additional information to help the reader form a clear picture of what lies beyond them. Despite this limitation, the book should prove valuable to both people wishing to develop NLITDBS for practical applications, and those who plan further research, as it is essentially the first in-depth exploration of the time-related issues that arise in NLITDBS, from the linguistic level down to the database.

The remainder of this chapter provides additional information on natural language interfaces, tense and aspect theories, temporal logics, and temporal databases, to help the reader obtain a clearer view of the book's subject before moving on to the main discussion in following chapters. The book assumes that the reader has a solid background in symbolic approaches to natural language processing and computational linguistics, including unification-based grammars and formal semantics. Readers who do not have this background are advised to consult other introductory texts first (Shieber 1986; Gazdar & Mellish 1989; Allen 1995; Cole et al. 1997; Dale, Moisl, & Somers 2000; Jurafsky & Martin 2000; Mitkov 2002b).

1.2 Natural language interfaces to databases

Let us now examine in more detail the typical architecture of NLIDBS, as shown in Figure 1.2; the top three modules correspond to the linguistic front-end of Figure 1.1. The user's request first undergoes a *preprocessing* stage, which decomposes the input into tokens, i.e., words, punctuation marks, and other special symbols. The preprocessor also identifies and normalises expressions such as dates, times, and proper names. This is usually achieved by employing pattern-matching rules, and by consulting parts of the database or parts of the NLIDB's lexicon that contain proper names. For example, both *October 12, 2001* and *12/10/2001* would be mapped to a common format; we will use *dd/mm/yyyy* as the common date format in this book.

The preprocessed input is then parsed using a grammar, which in many systems includes rules that specify not only the possible syntactic structures, but also how these structures can be mapped to expressions of the meaning representation language. With a meaning representation language similar to first-order predicate logic, question (1.1) could be mapped to an expression like (1.7). The question marks are *interrogative quantifiers*; they mark the vari-

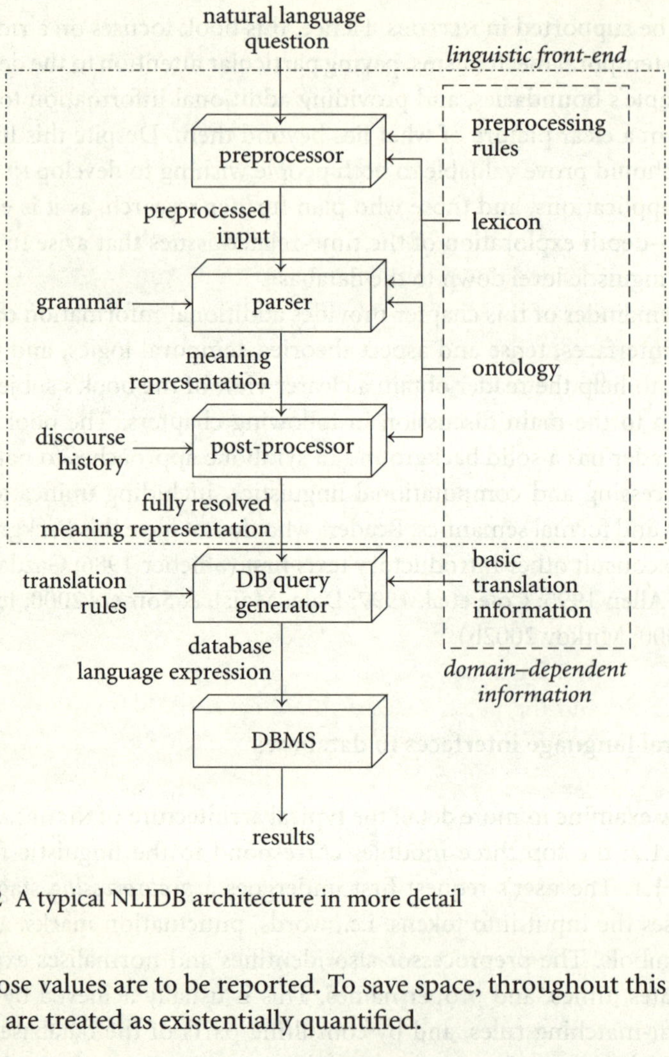

Figure 1.2 A typical NLIDB architecture in more detail

ables whose values are to be reported. To save space, throughout this book free variables are treated as existentially quantified.

(1.7) $?x_2\ ?x_3\ engineer\_name(x_1, x_2) \wedge salary\_of(x_1, x_3)$

Expression (1.7) requires all the x_2 and x_3 to be reported, such that x_2 is the name of an engineer x_1, and x_3 is the salary of x_1. In questions like (1.4)–(1.6), the meaning representation language must provide appropriate facilities to capture the semantics of the temporal mechanisms of natural language; we will turn to this issue in later sections.

The meaning representations that are generated at the end of the parsing are often *underspecified*; for example, they may not specify the exact entities that pronouns or other anaphoric expressions refer to. The underspecified parts of the meaning representations are resolved in a separate *post-processing* stage (Figure 1.2), which usually has access to broader information about the discourse; for example, in the form of a discourse history that records entities and facts that have been mentioned. In *dialogue systems*, where the emphasis is on engaging the users in dialogues until all the necessary information has been specified and interpretation problems have been solved, the post-processing is often one of the responsibilities of the *dialogue manager* (LuperFoy, Nijholt, & Veldhuijzen van Zanten 1996; Alexandersson 1999; Androutsopoulos & Aretoulaki 2002). This is a central coordinating module, which is also responsible for deciding when enough information is available to execute a user's request, or when additional information must be requested from the user by generating an appropriate response. This book focuses on stand-alone questions, rather than questions that are parts of larger dialogues. Consequently, dialogue management issues will not be discussed, and the simple pipeline architecture of Figure 1.2 will suffice. We will also not consider techniques to resolve anaphoric expressions (Hirst 1981; Hobbs 1986; Barros & De Roeck 1994; Lappin & Leass 1994; Mitkov 2002a), although several temporal anaphora phenomena will be identified throughout the book, and preliminary ideas on how to handle some of them will be discussed.

The parser and the post-processor often consult *ontologies*, mostly in the form of hierarchies that reflect the entity types of each application domain; for example, the hierarchy may show that a salesman is a type of employee, which is in turn a type of person. Additional restrictions on the possible relationships between entities of the various types are usually also present; for example, the manager of each employee must also be an employee, rather than, say, a product. Ontologies can be employed, among other things, to disambiguate user questions, as illustrated in (1.8). The intended meaning is (1.9); i.e., the holder of the licence is the employee. An NLIDB, however, would also have to consider (1.10), where the licence is held by the branch.

(1.8) List all the employees of Paris branches with driving licences.

(1.9) $?x_2\ employee\_name(x_1, x_2) \land branch\_name(x_3, x_4) \land$
$city\_name(x5, \text{"Paris"}) \land works\_at(x_1, x_3) \land located\_in(x_3, x_5) \land$
$licence(x_6) \land for\_driving(x_6) \land has(x_1, x_6)$

(1.10) $?x_2\ employee\_name(x_1, x_2) \land branch\_name(x_3, x_4) \land$
$city\_name(x5, \text{"Paris"}) \land works\_at(x_1, x_3) \land located\_in(x_3, x_5) \land$
$licence(x_6) \land for\_driving(x_6) \land has(x_3, x_6)$

In order to reject (1.10), the ontology would need to contain a restriction stating that when the second argument of $has(x, y)$ is a driving licence, the first one must be a person. The ontology's hierarchy, then, would show that employees are persons, while branches are not, which would rule out (1.10). There will be opportunities to consider ontologies of this kind in greater detail in Chapter 4.

The fully resolved meaning representation expressions that are generated at the end of the post-processing are subsequently translated into database language. This is often achieved using a recursive process. A ground mapping shows how basic meaning representation expressions relate to database constructs; for example, how predicates relate to database tables. Additional rules then specify how more complex meaning representation expressions can be translated, invoking recursively other rules to translate simpler subexpressions. This approach will be considered in more detail in Chapter 5.

As already mentioned, a *response generator* may also be present. In most NLIDBS, this is a rather simplistic module that formats the retrieved information to make it easier for the user to comprehend. More difficult is the generation of appropriate responses when the user's requests carry false presuppositions or do not express literally what the user wants to do. In the first question below, the system detects the false presupposition that a flight named *BA737* exists, and generates an appropriate warning. In the second question, it does not generate a simple affirmative response; it provides additional information, attempting to be more helpful.

U: *Does flight BA737 depart at 5:00 pm?*
S: `Flight BA737 does not exist.`
U: *Does any flight depart at 5:00 pm?*
S: `Yes, UK160 and BA534.`

Responses of this kind are known as *cooperative*, and in the general case require a *user model* to represent the user's goals and beliefs (Kobsa & Wahlster 1989). In many cases, however, relatively simple techniques suffice (Kaplan 1982). Although this book does not examine techniques to generate cooperative responses, several time-related phenomena that require responses of this kind will be identified. This implies that future work to add cooperative response capabilities to the theory of this book would be particularly useful; we will return to this point in Chapter 7.

A different kind of responses that some NLIDBS generate are *paraphrases* of the user's requests that reflect the system's understanding (De Roeck & Lowden 1986; Alshawi 1992; Alshawi et al. 1992). The paraphrases help the users detect cases where their requests have been misinterpreted. Paraphrases are also useful when ambiguities arise: unambiguous paraphrases of the original request can be generated, asking the user to select the paraphrase that corresponds to the intended reading.

A significant amount of work on NLIDBs has been devoted to *portability*, i.e., the ability to reuse NLIDBs in different application domains; for example, with a database that holds information about train tickets, rather than the employees of a company. As shown in Figure 1.2, the core components of NLIDBs are to a large extent domain-independent. Many of the resources that those components use, however, like the preprocessing rules, the lexicon, the ontology, and the mapping from basic meaning representation expressions to database constructs, are often domain-specific, and need to be configured whenever the NLIDB is ported to a new application.

The grammar of most NLIDBs is designed to be reusable in a range of application domains, and, hence, it can be considered, to some extent, domain-independent. It should be noted, however, that every NLIDB has a limited coverage of linguistic phenomena. Although Wizard of Oz experiments (Dahlbäck, Jönsson, & Ahrenberg 1993), where users interact with people pretending to be NLIDBs, can be performed to study the questions of representative users and adjust the grammar accordingly, mismatches between the coverage of the grammar and the questions that actual users will submit are inevitable. Clarification dialogues and *robust parsing* techniques (Stallard & Bobrow 1993; Bates et al. 1994; Briscoe 1997) can be employed to recover from such mismatches; these issues, however, are beyond the scope of this book. An alternative approach, which will also not be discussed further, is to make the linguistic capabilities of the NLIDB explicit to its users, in the form of a *controlled language* (Epstein 1985; CLAW 2000), possibly asking them to formulate their requests by selecting words from menus that reflect the available language constructs (Tennant et al. 1983).

1.3 Tense and aspect theories

In English, temporal information is conveyed by verb forms (e.g., simple past, past continuous, present perfect), nouns (e.g., *beginning*, *predecessor*, *day*), adjectives (*earliest*, *next*, *annual*), adverbs (*yesterday*, *twice*), prepositional phrases (*at 5:00 pm*, *for two hours*), and subordinate clauses (*while tank 4 was empty*), to mention just some of the available temporal mechanisms. A linguistic theory of time must account for the uses of these mechanisms; for example, it must specify the temporal semantic content of each verb form, and how temporal adverbials or temporal subordinate clauses affect the meanings of the overall sentences. The term *tense and aspect theory* is often used to refer to theories of this kind, although the precise meaning of 'tense' and 'aspect' varies from one theory to the other.

Roughly speaking, in linguistics 'tense' usually refers to the ability of some language expressions to change form in order to convey information about the location of a situation in time (Comrie 1985); verbs are a typical example of such expressions in many languages. In contrast, 'aspect' does not refer to the location of a situation in time, but to how the situation is viewed by the speaker; e.g., whether or not it is conceived as being in progress, or as being an action or a state (Comrie 1985; Smith 1997). The sentences *John sang* and *John was singing*, then, are identical in terms of location in time (they both locate the situation in the past), but they differ in terms of aspect. Although in English tense is a property of verbs, which possibly extends to the syntactic constituents that contain them, this book is also concerned with other English mechanisms that specify location in time; for example, temporal adverbials. Following common practice, we will use the term 'tense and aspect theory' with a broad, and strictly speaking imprecise, sense to refer to a theoretical treatment of all the temporal mechanisms of a natural language.

It is common in tense and aspect theories to classify natural language expressions or situations described by natural language expressions into *aspectual classes*; the German term *Aktionsarten*, kinds of action, is often used to refer to these classes. Many aspectual classifications are similar to Vendler's taxonomy (1967), which distinguishes between *state* verbs, *activity* verbs, *accomplishment* verbs, and *achievement* verbs.[1] For example, *to run*, as in *John ran*, is said to be an activity verb; *to know*, as in *John knows the answer*, is a state verb; *to build*, as in *John built a house*, is an accomplishment verb; and *to find*, as in *Mary found the treasure*, is an achievement verb.

Vendler's intuition seems to be that activity verbs, as in *John ran*, describe actions or changes in the world. In contrast, state verbs, as in *John knows the answer*, do not refer to any actions or changes. Accomplishment verbs are similar to activity verbs, in that they denote changes or actions. In the case of accomplishments, however, there is an inherent *climax*, a point that has to be reached for the action or change to be considered complete. In *build a house*, the climax is the point where the whole of the house has been built. If the building stops before this point has been reached, the building action is incomplete. In contrast, the action of the activity verb *to run*, as in *John ran*, with no object, does not seem to have any climax; the runner can stop at any time without the running being any more or less complete. If, however, *to run* is used with an object denoting a precise distance, as in *to run a mile*, then the action *does* have a climax: the point where the runner completes the distance. In this case, *to run* is an accomplishment verb. Finally, achievement verbs, like *to find*, describe instantaneous events. In *Mary found the treasure*, the actual finding is instantaneous; according to Vendler, the time when Mary was searching for the treasure is not part of the actual finding. In contrast, in *John built a house*, where the verb is an accomplishment, the actual building action may have lasted many years.

The so-called *imperfective paradox* (Dowty 1977; Lascarides 1988; Kent 1993) is a well-known example of semantic differences related to aspectual classes. The paradox is that if the answer to a question like (1.11) is affirmative, then the answer to the non-progressive (1.12) must also be affirmative. In contrast, an affirmative answer to (1.13) does not necessarily imply an affirmative answer to (1.14), because John may have abandoned the repair before completing it. Hence, if an NLITDB generates an affirmative response to (1.11), there must be some mechanism to guarantee that the NLITDB's answer to (1.12) will also be affirmative, unlike (1.13) and (1.14).

(1.11) Was IBI ever advertising a new computer?
(1.12) Did IBI ever advertise a new computer?
(1.13) Was J. Adams ever repairing engine 2?
(1.14) Did J. Adams ever repair engine 2?

The difference between (1.11)–(1.12) and (1.13)–(1.14) can be accounted for by classifying *to advertise* and *to repair* as activity and accomplishment verbs, respectively, and by stipulating that the simple past of an accomplishment verb requires the climax to have been reached, while the simple past of an activity, as well as the past continuous of any verb, impose no such requirement. It will become clear in Chapter 2 that aspectual taxonomies pertain to the semantics of almost all of the English temporal mechanisms.

1.4 Temporal logics

Time is an important research topic in logic, and many formal languages have been proposed to express temporal information (van Benthem 1991; Gabbay, Hodkinson, & Reynolds 1994; Gabbay, Reynolds, & Finger 2000). One of the simplest approaches is to use the traditional first-order predicate logic, introducing time as an extra argument of each predicate. Question (1.15) could be represented as (1.16), where t is a time-denoting variable, $\prec$ stands for temporal precedence, $\sqsubseteq$ for temporal inclusion, and *now* is a special term denoting the present moment.

(1.15) Did tank 2 contain water (some time) on 1/10/1999?

(1.16) $\exists t \; contain(tank2, water, t) \wedge t \prec now \wedge t \sqsubseteq 1/10/1999$

The answer to (1.15), then, is affirmative iff (1.16) evaluates to true, i.e., iff there is a time t, such that t precedes the present moment, t falls within 1/10/1999, and tank 2 contained water at t. (Throughout this book, 'iff' will be used as a shorthand for 'if and only if'.)

An alternative approach is to use *temporal operators*, like Prior's P (past) and F (future) operators (Prior 1967). In that case, formulae are evaluated with respect to particular times. Assuming that φ is a formula, $P\varphi$ is true at a time t iff there is a time t', such that t' precedes t, and φ is true at t'. Similarly, $F\varphi$ is true at t iff there is a t', such that t' follows t, and φ is true at t'. Then, (1.17), (1.19), (1.21), and (1.23) could be represented as (1.18), (1.20), (1.22), and (1.24), respectively.

(1.17) Tank 2 contains water.

(1.18) $contain(tank2, water)$

(1.19) Tank 2 contained water.

(1.20) $P \, contain(tank2, water)$

(1.21) Tank 2 will contain water.

(1.22) $F \, contain(tank2, water)$

(1.23) Tank 2 will have contained water.

(1.24) $F \, P \, contain(tank2, water)$

Additional operators can be introduced to capture the semantics of temporal adverbials, temporal subordinate clauses, etc. For example, an *On* operator could be introduced: if φ is a formula and κ specifies a day, then $On[\kappa, \varphi]$ is true at a time t iff t falls within the day specified by κ, and φ is true at t. Then, (1.15) could be represented as (1.25).

(1.25) $P \; On[1/10/1999, contains(tank2, water)]$

The intermediate meaning representation language of this book, TOP, uses temporal operators, mostly because they lead to more compact formulae, and make the semantic contribution of each linguistic mechanism easier to see. In fact, TOP stands for 'language with Temporal OPerators'. Temporal operators have also been used by several other researchers (Dowty 1982; Lascarides 1988; Richards et al. 1989; Kent 1993; Crouch & Pulman 1993; Pratt & Bree 1995). Unlike logics designed to be used in systems that reason about what changes or remains the same over time, what can or will happen, what could or would have happened, or how newly acquired information fits within already known facts or assumptions (McCarthy & Hayes 1969; McDermott 1982; Kowalski & Sergot 1986; Allen 1983; Allen 1984; Vila 1994), TOP is not intended to be used in reasoning. No inference rules for TOP will be provided, and this is why this book avoids calling TOP a logic. It is only a formal language, designed to facilitate the systematic mapping of English questions involving time to formal expressions, a mapping most of the above mentioned logics are not concerned with. In the theory of this book, the answers to the English questions are not generated by performing inferencing in TOP, but by translating the TOP expressions to database language expressions, which are then evaluated by the underlying DBMS. TOP will be defined in Chapter 3, where other ideas from temporal logics will also be discussed.

1.5 Temporal databases

In the *relational model*, currently the dominant database model, information is stored in *relations* (Ullman 1988). A relation can be thought of as a table, consisting of rows and columns. The *tuples* of the relation are, informally, the rows of the table, while the *attributes* of the relation are the table's columns. The *salaries* relation below shows the present salaries of the current employees of a company. It has two attributes, *employee* and *salary*, and one tuple per employee.

salaries	
employee	*salary*
J. Adams	21000
T. Smith	24000
...	...

Whenever the salary of an employee is changed, or whenever an employee leaves the company, the corresponding tuple is modified or deleted. Hence, the database 'forgets' past facts, and does not contain enough information to answer questions like '*What was the salary of T. Smith on 1/1/1992?*'.

It is certainly true that traditional database models and languages can, and have been, used to store temporal information. For example, two extra attributes, *from* and *to*, can be added to *salaries* to *time-stamp* its tuples, i.e., show when each employee had the corresponding salary, as in *salaries2* below. The lack of special temporal support in traditional database models and languages, however, complicates time-related data manipulations. We may want, for example, to compute from *salaries2* a new relation that shows the times when

J. Adams and T. Smith had the same salary, along with their common salary, as in *same_salaries* below. That is, for every tuple of J. Adams in *salaries2*, we need to check if the period specified by the *from* and *to* values of that tuple overlaps the period specified by the *from* and *to* values of a tuple for T. Smith with the same *salary* value. If they overlap, we need to compute the intersection of the two periods. This cannot be achieved easily in SQL-92 (Melton & Simon 1993), what was until very recently the latest standard for SQL, because SQL-92 does not have any special commands to compute the intersection of two periods; in fact, it does not even have a period datatype.

salaries2			
employee	*salary*	*from*	*to*
J. Adams	17000	1/1/1988	5/5/1990
J. Adams	18000	6/5/1990	9/8/1991
J. Adams	21000	10/8/1991	27/3/1993
...	...	...	...
T. Smith	17000	1/1/1989	1/10/1990
T. Smith	21000	2/10/1990	23/5/1992
T. Smith	24000	24/5/1992	28/10/1994
...	...	...	...

same_salaries		
salary	*from*	*to*
17000	1/1/1989	5/5/1990
21000	10/8/1991	23/5/1992
...	...	...

As a further example, adding *from* and *to* attributes to every relation allows relations like *rel1* and *rel2* below to be formed. Although *rel1* and *rel2* contain different tuples, they can be seen as representing the same information, if the *salary* attribute shows the monthly salary of each person during the corresponding period. Checking if the two relations represent the same information is not easy in SQL-92, because normalising them, i.e., turning them into *rel3*, an operation known as *coalescing* (Böhlen, Snodgrass, & Soo 1996), requires complex SQL-92 statements. Additional examples of cases where special temporal support is particularly desirable in databases can be found in Snodgrass (2000).

Numerous temporal versions of SQL and the relational model have been proposed, that simplify the handling of time-sensitive information (McKenzie 1986; Stam & Snodgrass 1988; McKenzie & Snodgrass 1991; Soo 1991; Kline 1993; Tsotras & Kumar 1996; Wu, Jajodia, & Wang 1998). This book adopts

TSQL2 (Snodgrass 1995), a temporal extension of SQL-92 that was designed by a committee of temporal database researchers and is a good representative of the various extensions that have been proposed. Chapter 5 presents a systematic and provably correct mapping from TOP to TSQL2.

rel1			
employee	*salary*	*from*	*to*
G. Foot	17000	1/1/1988	9/5/1988
G. Foot	17000	10/5/1988	9/5/1993
G. Foot	18000	10/5/1993	1/3/1994
G. Foot	18000	2/3/1994	11/2/1995

rel2			
employee	*salary*	*from*	*to*
G. Foot	17000	1/1/1988	31/5/1989
G. Foot	17000	1/6/1989	10/8/1992
G. Foot	17000	11/8/1992	9/5/1993
G. Foot	18000	10/5/1993	11/2/1995

rel3			
employee	*salary*	*from*	*to*
G. Foot	17000	1/1/1988	9/5/1993
G. Foot	18000	10/5/1993	11/2/1995

At the time this book was being written, ANSI recommendations on how to support time in the SQL/Temporal part of the new SQL:1999 standard (Melton, Simon, & Gray 2001), previously known as SQL3, had been forwarded to ISO (Snodgrass 2000). The recommendations are based on experience from TSQL2 (Snodgrass et al. 1998), but they differ from TSQL2 in many ways; the recommendations are closer to ATSQL (Böhlen, Jensen, & Snodgrass 2000), though again there are differences. Furthermore, to the best of the author's knowledge, the recommendations are currently on hold, i.e., they will be considered by ISO at a later point in time; hence, it is difficult to predict if they will be incorporated in SQL:1999, and in exactly what form.

Currently no major commercial DBMS provides direct support for TSQL2 or any of the other temporal extensions of SQL. However, at least two add-ons for commercial DBMSs exist, that support ATSQL or other closely related variants by translating their statements into equivalent, but often much more complex and hard to understand, statements of traditional SQL. The author is aware of two add-ons of this kind: TIGER and TIMEDB.[2] The prototype NLITDB of Chapter 6 is currently not linked to any of these add-ons, as this would require ironing the differences between the TSQL2 version of this book and the temporal SQL versions of the add-ons. Nevertheless, the TOP to TSQL2 mapping of this book should serve as a useful precedent for researchers and developers wishing to work on NLITDBS with forthcoming temporal versions of SQL. Similar mappings could be developed for other temporal flavours of SQL as they become more standard in commercial DBMSS.

Temporal database researchers distinguish between *valid time* and *transaction time.* A temporal database may contain information about the history of the world it models, including predictions about the future. Valid time is the time-axis that underlies this history. The contents of the database, however, can be updated, in effect allowing the history of the world to be rewritten. Some temporal database systems support queries that refer to previously stored versions of the history. This establishes a second time dimension, transaction time, which allows queries to refer to past 'beliefs' of the database. In (1.26), then, *on 2/1/1995* specifies the transaction time, while *1/1/1989* specifies the valid time.

(1.26) According to what the database believed on 2/1/1995, what was the salary of J. Adams on 1/1/1989?

This book focuses on valid time, assuming that the English questions always refer to the current history in the database; i.e., the transaction time will always be the present. Furthermore, we will focus on questions about the past and the present, ignoring any predictions about the future that may be present in the database; this narrows the range of linguistic phenomena to be considered. As a further simplification, we will examine only questions, as opposed to requests to update the contents of the database (Davidson & Kaplan 1983). Assertions like (1.27) will be treated as yes/no questions; i.e., (1.27) will be treated in the same way as (1.28).

(1.27) On 1/1/1999 the salary of T. Smith was 17000.
(1.28) Was the salary of T. Smith 17000 on 1/1/1999?

Finally, although the tuples of the relations in the database may be updated, it will be assumed that the structure of the database remains unchanged; for example, we will not consider cases where attributes or relations are added or removed over time (McKenzie & Snodgrass 1990).

1.6 Acknowledgements

The author wishes to thank Graeme Ritchie and Peter Thanisch, who supervised the work for his PhD thesis, on which this book is based, at the University of Edinburgh. The author is also grateful to the Greek State Scholarships Foundation (IKY) for funding that work. The writing of this book was partly made possible by a post-doctoral scholarship from the Greek National Centre for Scientific Research (NCSR) 'Demokritos', and extensive support from the Software and Knowledge Engineering Laboratory of the Institute of Informatics and Telecommunications of NCSR.

The ALE grammar of the prototype NLITDB (Chapter 6) is based on previous ALE encodings of HPSG fragments by Gerald Penn, Bob Carpenter, Suresh Manandhar, and Claire Grover; the author is indebted to all of them. Many thanks are also due to Chris Brew, who provided additional code for manipulating feature-structures in ALE, and Jo Calder for his help with ALE, PLEUK, and HPSG grammars.

The author is particularly indebted to Michael Böhlen, Rani Nelken, Maria Aretoulaki, and Stergos Afantenos, who provided comments on an earlier draft of this book.

Notes

1. According to Mourelatos (1978), a similar taxonomy was developed independently by Kenny (1963), who notes that his classification is similar to the distinction between *kineseis* and *energiai* introduced by Aristotle in *Metaphysics*, Θ.1048*b*, 18–36.

2. TIGER was developed by a team directed by Michael Böhlen; see `http://www.cs.auc.dk/tiger`. TIMEDB was developed by Andreas Steiner; see `http://www.timeconsult.com`.

CHAPTER 2

Linguistic data and an informal account

"There is a time for everything."

2.1 Introduction

This chapter explores how temporal information is conveyed in English, focusing on phenomena that are relevant to NLITDBS. Like any human language, English possesses a wealth of temporal mechanisms (Comrie 1976; Comrie 1985; Smith 1997). It would be impossible to consider all of them in this book. Hence, several English temporal mechanisms will be ignored, and simplifying assumptions will be introduced in some of the mechanisms that will be considered. One of the goals of this chapter is to help readers who are not familiar with tense and aspect phenomena appreciate their complexity. A second goal is to specify exactly which temporal phenomena this book will focus on. A wide range of English temporal mechanisms will be presented. From those, a subset containing mechanisms that seem both theoretically interesting and relevant to NLITDBS will be selected as the target *linguistic coverage* of this book. An informal account of the usage of the target mechanisms will also be provided; this will be formalised in subsequent chapters.

The linguistic coverage of this book is intended to serve only as a starting point towards supporting the notion of time in NLITDBS. No attempt is made here to cover *all* the temporal linguistic mechanisms that an NLITDB might be confronted with. In a real-life NLITDB, the linguistic coverage of this book would have to be tailored to the range of applications that the NLITDB targets; for example, using Wizard of Oz experiments (Section 1.2). Unsupported mechanisms that are common in the target range of applications would have to be added, and the semantics of existing mechanisms might have to be adjusted to avoid, for example, readings that are uncommon in the targeted applications.

Although the informal account of this chapter draws on existing analyses of tense and aspect, this book does not attempt to formulate a new or complete tense and aspect theory. The aim is more practical: to explore how ideas from existing tense and aspect treatments can be integrated into NLITDBS, in a way that leads to provably implementable systems.

2.2 Aspectual classes

Let us first examine more closely the notion of *aspectual classes*. As mentioned in Section 1.3, many tense and aspect treatments build upon Vendler's taxonomy (Vendler 1967), that distinguishes between *state* verbs (*John knows the answer*), *activity* verbs (*John ran*), *accomplishment* verbs (*John built a house*), and *achievement* verbs (*Mary found the treasure*).

Vendler proposes a number of linguistic tests to determine the aspectual classes of verbs. According to Vendler, activity and accomplishment verbs can appear in the progressive, as in (2.1) and (2.2), while state and achievement verbs cannot, as demonstrated in (2.3) and (2.4). (Throughout the book, asterisks will be used to mark ungrammatical sentences.)

(2.1) John is running.
(2.2) John is building a house.
(2.3) *John is knowing the answer.
(2.4) *Mary is finding the treasure.

Activity verbs are said to combine felicitously with *for* adverbials specifying duration, as in (2.5), but sound odd with *in* duration adverbials, as in (2.6). (Question marks indicate sentences that sound odd, though not ungrammatical.) Accomplishment verbs, in contrast, combine felicitously with *in* adverbials, as in (2.7), and sound odd with *for* adverbials, as in (2.8).

(2.5) John ran for two minutes.
(2.6) ?John ran in two minutes.
(2.7) John built a house in two weeks.
(2.8) ?John built a house for two weeks.

Finally, according to Vendler, state verbs combine felicitously with *for* adverbials, as in (2.9), while achievement verbs sound odd, as demonstrated in (2.10).

(2.9) John knew the answer for ten minutes (but then forgot it).
(2.10) ?Mary found the treasure for two hours.

The exact nature of the entities classified by Vendler is unclear. In most cases, Vendler's wording suggests that his taxonomy classifies verbs. Some of his examples, however, like the fact that *to run* with no object is said to be an activity, while *to run a mile* is said to be an accomplishment, suggest that the natural language expressions being classified are not always verbs, but sometimes larger syntactic constituents, perhaps verb phrases. In other cases, Vendler's arguments suggest that the entities being classified are not natural language expressions, but world situations denoted by natural language expressions. According to Vendler, '*Are you smoking?*' asks about an activity, while '*Do you smoke?*' asks about a state. In this case, the terms 'activity' and 'state' seem to refer to types of situations in the world, rather than types of natural language expressions. The first question probably asks if somebody is actually smoking at the present moment. The second one has a *habitual* meaning: it asks if somebody has the habit of smoking. Vendler concludes that habits "are also states in our sense".

Numerous variants of Vendler's taxonomy have been proposed. These differ in the number of aspectual classes they assume, the names of the classes, the nature of the entities being classified, and the properties assigned to each class. For example, Vlach (1993) distinguishes four aspectual classes of sentences, and assumes that there is a parallel fourfold taxonomy of world situations. Moens (1987) distinguishes between 'states', 'processes', 'culminated processes', 'culminations', and 'points', commenting that his taxonomy does not classify real world situations, but ways people use to describe world situations. Parsons (1989) distinguishes three kinds of 'eventualities' ('states', 'activities', and 'events'), treating eventualities as entities in the world. Lascarides (1988) classifies propositions, i.e., functions from time-periods to truth values, and distinguishes between 'state', 'process', and 'event' propositions.

2.3 The aspectual classes of this book

Four aspectual classes are employed in this book: *states*, *activities*, *culminating activities*, and *points*. Culminating activities and points correspond to Vendler's 'accomplishments' and 'achievements', respectively. Similar terms have been used elsewhere (Moens 1987; Blackburn, Gardent, & de Rijke 1994).

The four aspectual classes of this book correspond to *ways of viewing world situations* that people seem to use: a situation can be viewed as involving no change or action (state view), as an instantaneous change or action (point view), as a change or action with duration but no inherent climax (activity view), or as a change or action with both duration and inherent climax (culminating activity view). The *climax* is a point that has to be reached for the action or change to be considered complete, as in Section 1.3. Although there is evidence that people may distinguish between two subcases of point view, depending on whether or not the situation is seen as involving a change of state (Smith 1997), this distinction will be ignored in this book for the sake of simplicity.

Determining which view the speaker has in mind is important to understand what the speaker means. For example, '*Which tanks contained oil?*' is typically uttered with a state view. When an *at* temporal adverbial, like *at 5:00 pm*, is attached to a clause uttered with a state view, the speaker typically means that the situation of the clause simply holds at the time of the adverbial. There is normally no implication that the situation starts or stops at the time of the adverbial. For example, in '*Which tanks contained oil at 5:00 pm?*' there is normally no implication that the tanks must have started or stopped containing oil at 5:00 pm. In contrast, '*Who ran to the station?*' is typically uttered with a culminating activity view. In this case, an *at* adverbial usually specifies the time when the situation starts or is completed. For example, '*Who ran to the station at 5:00 pm?*' probably asks who started to run to the station or reached it at 5:00 pm.

Some linguistic markers seem to signal which view the speaker has in mind. For example, the progressive usually signals a state view. Unlike '*Who ran to the station at 5:00 pm?*', '*Who was running to the station at 5:00 pm?*' is typically uttered with a state view. In the progressive form, the running is simply ongoing at 5:00 pm; it does not start or finish at 5:00 pm. Often, however, there are no such explicit markers. The processes employed in those cases by hearers to determine the speaker's view are not yet fully understood. In an NLITDB, however, where questions refer to a restricted application domain, reasonable guesses can be made by observing that in each domain, each verb tends to be associated mainly with one particular view. Certain agreements about how situations are to be viewed will also have been made during the design of the database. For example, the designers of the database may have decided that some situations will be modelled as instantaneous, a decision that users should be made aware of. Such agreements provide additional information about how the situations of the various verbs are viewed in each domain.

More precisely, the following approach is adopted in this book. Whenever the NLITDB is configured for a new application domain, the base form of each verb is assigned to one of the four aspectual classes, using criteria to be discussed below. The criteria are intended to detect the view that is mainly associated with each verb in the particular domain. Following Dowty (1986), Moens (1987), Vlach (1993), Smith (1997) and others, aspectual class is treated as a property of not only verbs, but also verb phrases, clauses, and sentences. Normally, all verb forms inherit the aspectual classes of the corresponding base forms. Verb phrases, clauses, or sentences normally inherit the aspectual classes of their main verb forms. Some linguistic mechanisms, however, like the progressive or some temporal adverbials, may cause the aspectual class of a verb form to differ from that of the base form, or the aspectual class of a verb phrase, clause, or sentence to differ from that of its main verb form. The aspectual class of each verb phrase, clause, or sentence is intended to reflect the view that the users of the NLITDB typically have in mind when using that expression in the particular domain.

With verbs like *to run*, that typically involves a culminating activity view when used with an expression that specifies a particular destination or distance, as in *to run to the station* or *to run five miles*, but an activity view when used on its own, it will be assumed that there are two different homonymous verbs. One has a culminating activity base form, and requires a complement that specifies a particular destination or distance. The other has an activity base form, and does not accept such a complement. A similar distinction would be introduced in the case of verbs whose aspectual class depends on whether or not the verb's object denotes a countable or mass entity, as in *to drink a bottle of wine* vs. *to drink wine* (Mourelatos 1978).

Similarly, when a verb can be used in a domain with both habitual and non-habitual meanings, like *to depart* in (2.11) and (2.12), a distinction will be made between a homonym with a habitual meaning, and a homonym with a non-habitual meaning. The aspectual criteria that will be discussed below always classify the base forms of habitual homonyms as states. This agrees with Vendler, Vlach (1993), Moens and Steedman (1988), and Smith (1997), who all classify habituals as states. The aspectual classes of non-habitual homonyms will depend on the verbs and the application domain.

(2.11) BA737 (habitually) departs from Gatwick.

(2.12) BA737 (actually) departed from Gatwick five minutes ago.

Approaches that do not postulate homonyms are also possible. For example, one could treat *to run* as an activity, that is transformed into a culminating activity by a destination-denoting object, like *to the station*. Although perhaps less satisfactory from a theoretical point of view, the homonyms method leads to a more straightforward treatment in the HPSG grammar of Chapter 4, where the base form of each homonym will be mapped to a different lexical entry.

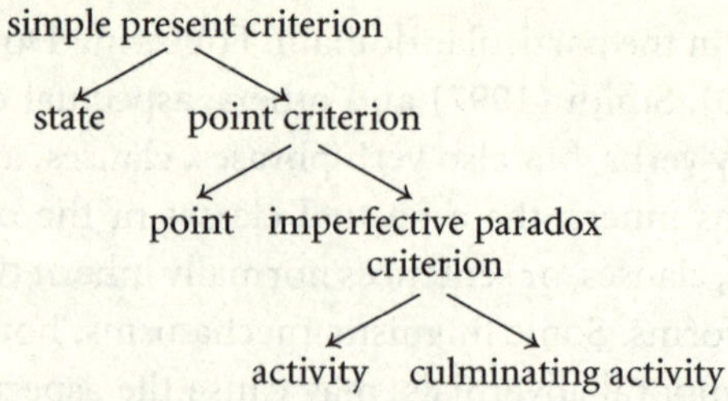

Figure 2.1 Determining the aspectual class of a verb's base form

In the rest of this book, the terms *state verb*, *activity verb*, *culminating activity verb*, and *point verb* refer to verbs whose base forms are classified as states, activities, culminating activities, or points, respectively.

2.4 Criteria for classifying base verb forms

Let us now turn to the criteria that determine the aspectual class of a verb's base form in a particular application domain. Three criteria are employed, and they are applied in the order of Figure 2.1.

2.4.1 The simple present criterion

The first criterion, the *simple present criterion*, distinguishes state verbs from point, activity, and culminating activity verbs. The criterion states that if the simple present of a verb can be used in the particular domain in single-clause questions with non-future meanings, the verb is a state one; otherwise it is a point, activity, or culminating activity verb. For example, in domains where (2.13) and (2.14) are possible, *to contain* and *to own* are state verbs.

(2.13) Does any tank contain oil?

(2.14) Which employees own a car?

Some clarifications are needed at this point. First, the simple present sometimes refers to something that is scheduled to happen. For example, (2.15) could refer to a scheduled assembling; in that case, (2.15) is similar to (2.16). We will count readings of this kind as future ones. Hence, this use of (2.15) does not constitute evidence that *to assemble* is a state verb.

(2.15) When does J. Adams assemble engine 5?

(2.16) When will J. Adams assemble engine 5?

Furthermore, in reporting contexts the simple present of verbs that we would not want to be classified as states can be used with non-future meanings. For example, in a context where the speaker reports events as they happen, (2.17) is possible.

(2.17) J. Adams arrives. He moves the container. He fixes the engine.

This use of the simple present, however, is unlikely in NLITDB questions. Hence, (2.17) does not constitute evidence that *to arrive*, *to move*, and *to fix* are state verbs.

The reader is reminded that when verbs have both habitual and non-habitual meanings, a distinction is made between a habitual and a non-habitual homonym (Section 2.3). Ignoring future meanings, that do not count for the simple present criterion, (2.18) and (2.19) can only have habitual meanings; i.e., they can only be understood as involving the habitual homonyms of *to land* and *to smoke*.

(2.18) Which flight lands on runway 2?
(2.19) Does any doctor smoke?

Therefore, in domains where (2.18) and (2.19) are possible, the habitual homonyms of *to land* and *to smoke* are state verbs. (2.18) and (2.19) do not constitute evidence that the non-habitual homonyms of *to land* and *to smoke* are state verbs.

2.4.2 The point criterion

The second criterion, the *point criterion*, distinguishes point verbs from activity and culminating activity ones; state verbs will have already been separated by the simple present criterion (Figure 2.1). Some verbs denote situations that are modelled in the database as being always instantaneous. The point criterion states that if a verb denotes situations of this kind, its base form should be classified as point; otherwise, it should be classified as activity or culminating activity.

Later on in this book, a hypothetical airport database will be considered. That database does not distinguish between the times at which a flight starts or stops entering an airspace sector. Entering a sector is modelled as instantaneous. Furthermore, *to enter* is only used to refer to flights entering sectors. Consequently, in that domain *to enter* is a point verb. If *to enter* were also used to refer to, for example, groups of passengers entering planes, and if situations of that kind were modelled in the database as non-instantaneous, we would distinguish between two homonyms of *to enter*: one used with flights entering sectors and one with passengers entering planes. The former would be classified as a point verb, while the latter would be classified as an activity or culminating activity verb.

In applying the point criterion, one will often have to decide exactly what is or is not part of the situations that the verbs denote. For example, before classifying the non-habitual homonym of *to depart*, one has to decide exactly what is or is not part of departing. Is boarding part of departing, i.e., is a flight departing when it is boarding? Is taxiing to a runway part of departing? Or does departing include only the time at which the flight actually leaves the ground? The database that will be considered in later sections distinguishes between the time at which the boarding starts and the time when the flight leaves the ground. Hence, if a flight starts to depart when it starts to board and finishes departing when it leaves the ground, then the base form of *to depart* should not be classified as point, because the database does not model departures as instantaneous. If, however, departing starts when the front wheels of the aircraft leave the ground and finishes when the rear wheels leave the ground, the base form of *to depart should* be classified as point, because the particular database does not distinguish between the two times. In any case, the user should be made aware of what *to depart* is taken to mean.

The point criterion is similar to observations made by Vendler (1967), Singh and Singh (1992), Vlach (1993), and others, that 'achievement' (point) verbs are understood as denoting instantaneous situations.

2.4.3 The imperfective paradox criterion

The third criterion, the *imperfective paradox criterion*, distinguishes activity from culminating activity verbs; state and point verbs will have been identified by the simple present and point criteria (Figure 2.1). This criterion is based on the imperfective paradox (Section 1.3). Assertions containing the past continuous and simple past of the verbs, like (2.20)–(2.23), are considered. The reader is reminded that assertions are treated as yes/no questions. If an affirmative answer to the past continuous assertion implies an affirmative answer to the simple past assertion, as in (2.20)–(2.21), the verb is an activity one; otherwise, as in (2.22)–(2.23), it is a culminating activity verb.

(2.20) John was running.
(2.21) John ran.
(2.22) John was building a house.

(2.23) John built a house.

As will be discussed in later sections, the past continuous sometimes has a future meaning. With this reading, (2.20) means that John was going to run, and an affirmative answer to (2.20) does not necessarily imply an affirmative answer to (2.21). When applying the imperfective paradox criterion, the past continuous must not have a future meaning.

In various forms, the imperfective paradox criterion has been used by Vendler (1967), Vlach (1993), Kent (1993), and others.

2.4.4 Other criteria

The three criteria above are not the only ones that could be used. The behaviour of verbs when appearing in various forms or when combining with some temporal adverbials varies depending on their aspectual classes. Alternative criteria can be formulated by observing this behaviour. For example, some authors classify verbs, or situations denoted by verbs, by observing how easily they appear in progressive forms, or how easily they combine with *for* and *in* duration adverbials; these phenomena will be examined in later sections. In some cases, the person classifying the base forms may be confronted with verbs for which the three criteria of Sections 2.4.1–2.4.3 do not yield clear verdicts. In such cases, additional evidence for or against classifying a base verb form into a particular class can be found by referring to following sections, where the typical behaviour of each class is examined.

2.4.5 Classifying base verb forms in the airport domain

To illustrate the use of the three criteria, let us now consider in more detail the hypothetical airport database, borrowing some terminology from Sripada et al. (1994). The airport domain will be used in examples throughout this book.

The airport database shows the times when flights arrived at, or departed from the airport, the times flights spent circling around the airport while waiting for permission to land, the runways they landed on or took off from, the gates where the flights boarded, etc. The database is occasionally queried using an NLITDB to determine the causes of accidents, and to collect data that are used to optimise the airport's traffic-handling strategies.

The airport's airspace is divided into sectors. Flights approaching or leaving the airport cross the boundaries of sectors, each time *leaving* a sector and *entering* another one. The airport is very busy, and some of its runways may also *be closed* for maintenance. Hence, approaching flights are often instructed to *circle* around the airport until a runway *becomes* free. When a runway is freed, flights *start* to *land*. Landing involves following a specific procedure. In some cases, the pilot may abort the landing procedure before completing it. Otherwise, the flight lands on a runway, and it then *taxies* to a gate that *is free*. The moment at which the flight *reaches* the gate is considered to be the time when the flight *arrived*; reaching a location and arriving are modelled as instantaneous. Normally (habitually) each flight arrives at the same gate and time every day. Due to traffic congestion, however, a flight may arrive at a gate or time other than its normal ones.

Before *taking off*, each flight is *serviced* by a service company. This involves carrying out a specific set of tasks. Unless all tasks have been carried out, the service is incomplete. Each service company normally (habitually) services particular flights. Sometimes, however, a company may be asked to service a flight that it does not normally service. After being serviced, a flight may be *inspected*. Apart from flights, inspectors also inspect gates and runways. In all cases, there are particular tasks to be carried out for the inspections to be considered complete.

Shortly before taking off, flights start to *board*. Unless all the passengers that have checked in enter the aircraft, the boarding is not complete, and the flight cannot depart. There are special arrangements for cases where passengers are too late. The flight then *leaves* the gate, and that moment is considered to be the time at which the flight *departed*; leaving a location and departing are modelled as instantaneous. Normally (habitually) each flight departs from the same gate at the same time every day. Sometimes, however, flights depart from gates or at times other than their normal ones. After leaving its gate, a flight may be told to *queue* for a particular runway, until that runway is freed. When the runway is free, the flight starts to *take off*, which involves following a specific procedure. As with landings, the pilot may abort the taking off procedure before completing it.

The database also records the status of parts of the airport's emergency system. There are, for example, emergency tanks used by the fire-brigade. Some of those may *contain* water, others may contain foam, and others may *be empty* for maintenance.

Table 2.1 shows some of the verbs that are used in the airport domain. The verbs *to depart*, *to arrive*, and *to service* are used with both habitual and non-habitual meanings. Ignoring future meanings, questions (2.24) and (2.26) have habitual meanings, while in (2.25) and (2.27) the verbs are probably used with

Table 2.1 Verbs in the airport domain

state verbs	activity verbs	culm. activity verbs	point verbs
service (habitually)	circle	land	cross, enter
arrive (habitually)	taxi (no destination)	take off	become
depart (habitually)	queue	service (actually)	reach, leave
contain		inspect	start, begin
be (non-auxiliary)		board	stop, finish
		taxi (to destination)	arrive (actually)
			depart (actually)

their non-habitual meanings. Following Section 2.3, we distinguish between habitual and non-habitual homonyms of *to depart*, *to arrive*, and *to service*.

(2.24) Which flights depart/arrive at 8:00 am?
(2.25) Which flight departed/arrived at 8:00 am yesterday?
(2.26) Which company services BA737?
(2.27) Which company serviced BA737 yesterday?

Similarly, two homonyms of *to taxi* are assumed, one that requires a complement denoting a destination, as in *BA737 was taxiing to gate 2*, and one that admits no such complement, as in *BA737 was taxiing*.

The simple present criterion and sentences like (2.28), (2.29), (2.24), and (2.26) imply that the non-auxiliary *to be*, *to contain*, and the habitual *to depart*, *to arrive*, and *to service* are state verbs.

(2.28) Which gates are free?
(2.29) Does any tank contain foam?

All the other verbs of Table 2.1 are not state verbs. For example, excluding habitual and future meanings, (2.30)–(2.32) sound unlikely or odd in the airport domain. (2.33)–(2.35) would be used instead.

(2.30) ?Which flights circle?
(2.31) ?Which flight taxies to gate 2?
(2.32) ?Which flight departs?
(2.33) Which flights are circling?
(2.34) Which flight is taxiing to gate 2?
(2.35) Which flight is departing?

The verbs in the rightmost column of Table 2.1 denote situations that are modelled as instantaneous in the airport's database. Consequently, by the point criterion, they are all point verbs. In contrast, the situations of the verbs in the two middle columns are not modelled as instantaneous. Therefore, those are activity or culminating activity verbs.

In the airport domain, a sentence like (2.37) means that BA737 spent some time circling around the airport. It does not imply that BA737 completed any circle around the airport. Hence, an affirmative answer to (2.36) implies an affirmative answer to (2.37). By the imperfective paradox criterion, then, *to circle* is an activity verb.

(2.36) BA737 was circling.
(2.37) BA737 circled.

Similar assertions and the imperfective paradox criterion imply that *to taxi* without a destination and *to queue* are also activity verbs. In contrast, the verbs in the third column of Table 2.1 are culminating activity verbs. For example, in the airport domain an affirmative answer to (2.38) does not imply an affirmative answer to (2.39). J. Adams may have aborted the inspection before completing all the inspection tasks, in which case the inspection is incomplete.

(2.38) J. Adams was inspecting runway 5.
(2.39) J. Adams inspected runway 5.

2.5 Verb forms

Let us now explore the temporal role of the English verb forms. As already mentioned in Section 1.5, questions referring to the future are not examined in this book. Hence, future verb forms, like the simple future and future perfect, as well as future meanings of other forms, like the scheduled-to-happen meaning of the simple present (Section 2.4.1), will not be considered. To simplify the linguistic data further, the present perfect continuous and the past perfect continuous, as in *J. Adams has/had been inspecting BA737*, will also not be considered; these forms combine complexities from both progressive and perfect forms. This leaves six finite verb forms to be discussed: simple present, simple past, present continuous, past continuous, present perfect, and past perfect.

2.5.1 Simple present

In the linguistic coverage of this book, the simple present can be used only with state verbs to refer to a situation that holds at the present, as in (2.40) and (2.41). We will examine below the rationale behind this statement.

(2.40) Which runways are closed?
(2.41) Does any tank contain water?

Excluding future readings, (2.42) and (2.43) can be understood only with habitual meanings, i.e., as involving the habitual homonyms of *to service* and *to depart*. These are state verbs, unlike the non-habitual homonyms, which are culminating activity and point verbs, respectively (Table 2.1). This is consistent with the statement that the simple present can only be used with state verbs.

(2.42) Which company services BA737?
(2.43) Which flights depart from gate 2?

In the airport domain, *to circle* is an activity verb; there is no state habitual homonym. Hence, not allowing the simple present to be used with non-state verbs rejects (2.44). This is reasonable, because (2.44) can be understood only with a habitual meaning, which is not available in the airport domain.

(2.44) ?Does BA737 circle?

Instead of simply rejecting (2.44), a cooperative NLITDB would inform the user that no habitual meaning of *to circle* is available, suggesting the rephrase of (2.45). As already mentioned in Section 1.2, however, mechanisms to generate cooperative responses are not considered in this book.

(2.45) Is BA737 circling?

One could point out that the simple present can be used with non-state verbs to describe events as they happen (Section 2.4.1), or with a historic meaning ('*In 1673 a fire destroys the palace.*'). These uses, however, are extremely unlikely in NLITDB questions. Hence, the statement that the simple present can be used only with state verbs remains valid for the purposes of this book.

2.5.2 Simple past

Unlike the simple present, the simple past can be used with verbs from all four classes, as in (2.46)–(2.51).

(2.46) Which tanks contained water on 1/1/1999?
(2.47) Did BA737 circle on 1/1/1999?
(2.48) Which flights (actually) departed from gate 2 on 1/1/1999?
(2.49) Which flights (habitually) departed from gate 2 in 1999?
(2.50) Which company (actually) serviced BA737 yesterday?
(2.51) Which company (habitually) serviced BA737 last year?

Questions (2.48)–(2.51) show that both the habitual and non-habitual homonyms of verbs like *to depart* or *to service* are generally possible in the simple past. (2.52) is ambiguous. It may refer either to flights that actually departed, perhaps only once, from gate 2 in 1999, or to flights that normally, habitually, departed from gate 2 in 1999.

(2.52) Which flights departed from gate 2 in 1999?

The simple past of culminating activity verbs normally implies that the situation of the verb reached its climax. For example, in (2.53) the service must have been completed, and in (2.54) BA737 must have reached gate 2 for the answer to be affirmative.

(2.53) Did Airserve service BA737?
(2.54) Did BA737 taxi to gate 2?

Although strictly speaking correct, a simple negative answer to a question like (2.54) may in practice be unsatisfactory, if, for example, BA737 was taxiing to gate 2, but never reached it. (2.55) would be a much more appropriate answer. Again, a mechanism for cooperative responses is needed to generate answers like (2.55), but this book does not consider such mechanisms.

(2.55) BA737 was taxiing to gate 2, but never reached it.

Finally, it should be noted that the simple past often has an *anaphoric* nature. For example, (2.53) is probably not asking if Airserve serviced BA737 at *any* time in the past. (2.53) would typically be used with a particular time in mind, perhaps the present day, to ask if Airserve serviced BA737 during that time. A temporal anaphora resolution mechanism is needed to determine the time that the speaker has in mind. Such mechanisms, however, are not considered in this book (Section 1.2), and (2.53) will be taken to refer to any past time. The same approach is adopted with all other verb forms that refer to past situations. Issues related to temporal anaphora will be considered further in Section 2.12.

2.5.3 Progressive forms

Let us now turn to the progressive verb forms that will be considered in this book: the present continuous and past continuous. The reader is reminded that future meanings are not considered. This means that, for example, the case where (2.56) has a reading similar to that of (2.57) will be ignored.

(2.56) Who is/was inspecting BA737?

(2.57) Who will/would inspect BA737?

In the following paragraphs, we will examine in turn the progressive forms of activity and culminating activity verbs, point verbs, and state verbs.

Activity and culminating activity verbs in progressive forms. The present and past continuous can be used with activity and culminating activity verbs to refer to a situation that is or was in progress, as in (2.58)–(2.59) in the airport domain.

(2.58) Are/Were any flights circling?
(2.59) Is/Was BA737 taxiing to gate 2?

In the case of culminating activity verbs, there is no requirement for the climax to be reached at any time. The past continuous version of (2.59), for example, does not require BA737 to have reached gate 2 (cf. (2.54)).

Point verbs in progressive forms. With point verbs, the use of progressive forms is often an indication that the user is unaware that the situation of the verb is modelled in the database as instantaneous. In the airport domain, for example, the non-habitual *to depart* is a point verb, and departing is taken to include only the time-point where the flight leaves its gate. In contrast, (2.60) seems to be referring to a situation with duration; a user who is aware that departures are modelled as instantaneous would normally use (2.61) instead. Similarly, (2.62) seems to be carrying the assumption that departures are not instantaneous, so that the speaker can talk while BA737 is departing.

(2.60) BA737 was departing.
(2.61) BA737 departed.
(2.62) BA737 is departing.

In sentences like (2.60)–(2.62), a cooperative NLITDB would warn the user that departures are modelled as instantaneous. In the absence of mechanisms to generate cooperative responses, the framework of this book silently accepts the progressive forms of point verbs as referring to the instantaneous situations of the verbs. The past continuous simply places the instantaneous situation of the verb in the past, as when the simple past is used; for example, (2.60) is taken to have the same meaning as (2.61). The present continuous asserts that the instantaneous situation of the verb occurs at the present time-point. As will be discussed in Chapter 5, in practice the database may model time-points as corresponding to minutes or even whole days. Hence, obtaining an affirmative answer to a yes/no question like (2.62) is less unlikely than the reader might think.

It is worth noting that people often seem to employ conceptual mechanisms that allow them to add duration to situations that would normally be thought of as instantaneous (Moens 1987). When confronted, for example, with a past continuous sentence like (2.63), which seems to require the normally instantaneous reaching to be seen as having duration, people often attach a preparatory process to the instantaneous situation of the verb; in (2.63), this could be the covering of a short remaining distance up to the gate. The progressive is then taken to assert that the preparatory process was in progress.

(2.63) At 5:00 pm BA737 was reaching gate 2.

In other cases, an *iterative* reading may be employed in order to add duration to the situation of the verb. In (2.64), for example, the most natural reading is that John is banging his hand repeatedly.

(2.64) John is banging his hand on the table.

Figuring out, however, exactly which preparatory process should be attached to an instantaneous situation, or exactly when an iterative reading is licensed is a difficult task for an NLITDB. Hence, the theoretical framework of this book provides no mechanisms for adding preparatory processes or for generating iterative readings.

State verbs in progressive forms. It has often been observed that state verbs are not normally used in progressive forms (cf. Vendler's tests in Section 2.2). For example, (2.65) and (2.67) are easily rejected by most native English speakers. It is assumed here that *to own* and *to consist* would be classified as state verbs, on the basis that simple present questions like (2.66) and (2.68) are possible.

(2.65) *Who is owning five cars?
(2.66) Who owns five cars?
(2.67) *Which engine is consisting of 34 parts?
(2.68) Which engine consists of 34 parts?

The claim that state verbs do not appear in the progressive is challenged by sentences like (2.69), from Smith (1986); Kent (1993) and Vlach (1993) provide similar examples. (2.69) shows that the non-auxiliary *to be*, which is typically classified as a state verb, can be used in the progressive.

(2.69) My daughter is being very naughty.

Furthermore, some native English speakers find (2.70) and (2.71) acceptable, though they would use the non-progressive forms instead. It is assumed here that *to border* would be classified as state verb, on the basis that (2.72) is possible.

(2.70) Tank 4 was containing water when the bomb exploded.
(2.71) Which countries were bordering France in 1937?
(2.72) Which countries border France?

Not allowing progressive forms of state verbs also seems problematic in questions like (2.73), that has a reading very similar to the habitual reading of (2.74).

(2.73) Which company was servicing BA737 in 1999?
(2.74) Which company serviced (habitually) BA737 in 1999?

The reader is reminded that in the airport domain a distinction is made between the habitual and non-habitual homonym of *to service*. The habitual homonym is a state verb, while the non-habitual one is a culminating activity verb. If progressive forms of state verbs are not allowed, then only the non-habitual homonym (actually servicing) is possible in (2.73). This does not account for the apparently habitual meaning of (2.73). One could argue that the reading of (2.73) is not really habitual, but iterative: servicing many times, as opposed to having a servicing habit. In sentences like (2.73)–(2.74), however, the difference between habitual and iterative meaning is hard to define.

Given that it seems harmless to accept sentences like (2.65) and (2.67) in an NLITDB, the theoretical framework of this book allows state verbs to be used in progressive forms, with the same meanings as the corresponding non-progressive forms. This causes (2.73) to receive two readings: one involving the habitual *to service* (servicing habitually in 1999), and one involving the non-habitual *to service* (actually servicing at some time in 1999); the latter reading is more likely without the adverbial. (2.65) and (2.67) are treated as equivalent to (2.66) and (2.68), respectively.

Aspectual shift of progressives. The progressive will be taken to cause an aspectual shift from activities and culminating activities to states; no shift is necessary in the case of points. In the airport domain, for example, although the base form of *to inspect* is a culminating activity, *was inspecting* will be a state. The shift will allow us to account for the meaning of progressives when they combine with temporal adverbials; this will be discussed further in Section 2.9.

In various forms, similar shifts have been employed by Dowty (1986), Moens (1987), Vlach (1993), Kent (1993), and others.

2.5.4 Present perfect

Like the simple past, the present perfect can be used with verbs of all four aspectual classes to refer to past situations, as in (2.75)–(2.79). With culminating activity verbs, the situation must have reached its climax; in (2.79), for example, the service must have been completed.

(2.75) Has BA737 (ever) been at gate 2?
(2.76) Which flights have circled today?
(2.77) Has BA737 reached gate 2?
(2.78) Which company has (habitually) serviced BA737 this year?
(2.79) Has Airserve (actually) serviced BA737?

Present perfect and present consequences. It has often been claimed that the English present perfect asserts that some consequence of the past situation holds at the present (Moens 1987; Vlach 1993; Blackburn, Gardent, & de Rijke 1994). For example, (2.80) seems to imply that there is a consequence of the fact that engine 5 caught fire that still holds. The consequence could be, for example, that engine 5 is still on fire, or that it was damaged by the fire and has not been repaired. In contrast, (2.81) does not seem to imply, at least not as strongly, that some consequence still holds.

(2.80) Engine 5 has caught fire.
(2.81) Engine 5 caught fire.

Although these claims are intuitively appealing, it is difficult to see how they could be used in an NLITDB. Perhaps in (2.82) the NLITDB should check not only that the landing was completed, but also that some consequence of the landing still holds.

(2.82) Has BA737 landed?

It is unclear, however, what this consequence should be. Should the NLITDB check that the plane is still at the airport? Should it check that the passengers of BA737 are still at the airport? Furthermore, in the first case, should the answer be negative if the plane has departed since the landing? Given this uncertainty, the framework of this book does not require the past situation to have present consequences.

A second, related point is that when the present perfect combines with *for* duration adverbials, there is often an implication that the past situation still holds at the present. This seems related to the claims that the past situation must have present consequences. For example, one reading of (2.83) is that J. Adams is still a manager. (An alternative reading is that J. Adams was simply a manager for two years, without the two years ending at the present moment.) In contrast, (2.84) carries no implication that J. Adams is still a manager; in fact, it seems to imply that he is no longer a manager.

(2.83) J. Adams has been a manager for two years.
(2.84) J. Adams was a manager for two years.

For simplicity, in the framework of this book the still-holding reading of sentences like (2.83) will be ignored, and (2.83) will be treated as having the same meaning as (2.84).

Present perfect and temporal adverbials. The present perfect does not combine felicitously with some temporal adverbials. For example, (2.85) and (2.88) sound unacceptable to most native English speakers; they would use (2.86) and (2.89) instead. In contrast, (2.87) and (2.90) are acceptable.

(2.85) *Which flights have landed yesterday?
(2.86) Which flights landed yesterday?
(2.87) Which flights have landed today?
(2.88) *Which flights has J. Adams inspected last week?
(2.89) Which flights did J. Adams inspect last week?
(2.90) Which flights has J. Adams inspected this week?

Questions (2.85)–(2.90) suggest that the present perfect can be used only if the time of the adverbial contains not only the time where the past situation occurred, but also the speech time, the time when the sentence was uttered. Thomson and Martinet (1986:167) provide a similar account. (2.87) is felicitous, because *today* contains the speech time. In contrast, (2.85) is unacceptable, because *yesterday* cannot contain the speech time. The hypothesis, however, that the time of the adverbial must include the speech time does not account for the fact that (2.91) is acceptable by most native English speakers, especially if the *ever* is added, even if the question is not uttered on a Sunday.

(2.91) Has J. Adams (ever) inspected BA737 on a Sunday?

Moens and Steedman (1988) also point out that a superstitious person could utter (2.92) on a day other than Friday the 13th.

(2.92) They have married on Friday 13th!

One could attempt to formulate more elaborate restrictions, to predict exactly when temporal adverbials can be used with the present perfect. In the case of an NLITDB, however, it is difficult to see why this would be worth the effort, as opposed to simply accepting questions like (2.85) as equivalent to (2.86). The framework of this book adopts the latter approach.

Given that the framework of this book does not associate present consequences with the present perfect, that the still-holding reading of sentences like (2.83) is not supported, and that questions like (2.85) are allowed, there is not much left to distinguish the present perfect from the simple past. Hence, for simplicity, in this book the present perfect will be treated as having the same meaning as the simple past.

2.5.5 Past perfect

The past perfect is often used to refer to a situation that occurred at some past time before some other past time. Following Reichenbach (1947), let us call the latter time the *reference time*. (2.93) and (2.94) have readings where *at 5:00 pm* specifies the reference time. In that case, (2.93) asks for flights that Airserve serviced before 5:00 pm, and (2.94) asks if BA737 was at gate 2 some time before 5:00 pm.

(2.93) Which flights had Airserve serviced at 5:00 pm?
(2.94) Had BA737 been at gate 2 at 5:00 pm?

With culminating activity verbs, the climax must have been reached before, or possibly at, the reference time. For example, in (2.93) the services must have been completed up to 5:00 pm. Perhaps some consequence of the past situation must still hold at the reference time. As with the present perfect, however, such consequential links will be ignored in this book.

When the past perfect combines with temporal adverbials, it is often unclear if the adverbial is intended to specify the reference time or directly the time of the past situation. For example, (2.95) could mean that BA737 had already reached gate 2 at 5:00 pm, or that it reached it at 5:00 pm. In the latter case, (2.95) is similar to the simple past (2.96), except that (2.95) creates the impression of a longer distance between the time of the reaching and the speech time.

(2.95) BA737 had reached gate 2 at 5:00 pm.
(2.96) BA737 reached gate 2 at 5:00 pm.
(2.97) BA737 had reached gate 2 by 5:00 pm.

By adverbials are often used in practice to clarify that the adverbial specifies the reference time, as in (2.97) (cf. (2.95)). *By* adverbials, however, are not considered in this book.

When the past perfect combines with *for* duration adverbials and a reference time is specified, there is often an implication that the past situation still held at the reference time. For example, (2.98) seems to imply that J. Adams was still a manager on 1/1/1999. As in the case of the present perfect, this implication will not be captured by the framework of this book.

(2.98) J. Adams had been a manager for two years on 1/1/1999.

Aspectual shift of past perfect. The past perfect will be taken to trigger an aspectual shift from activities, culminating activities, and points to states. For example, the base form of *to inspect* is a culminating activity in the airport domain, but *had inspected* will be treated as a state. This shift will allow us to account for the behaviour of the past perfect when combining with temporal adverbials, and it seems to be a property of all perfect forms. However, since the present perfect is treated as having the same meaning as the simple past (Section 2.5.4), no such shift will be postulated in the case of the present perfect. Similar shifts have been employed by Moens (1987), Vlach (1993), and others.

2.6 Temporal verbs

Through their various forms, all verbs can convey temporal information. Some verbs, however, like *to begin* or *to precede*, are of a more inherently temporal nature. They differ from ordinary ones, like *to build* or *to contain*, in that they do not describe directly situations, but rather refer to situations introduced by other verbs or nouns; Passonneau (1988) makes a similar observation. In (2.99), for example, *to begin* refers to the situation of *to build*. The verbs *to start, to end, to finish, to follow, to continue*, and *to happen* all belong to this category of special temporal verbs.

(2.99) They began to build terminal 9 in 1985.

Only four of these special verbs will be considered in this book: *to start, to begin, to stop*, and *to finish*. For simplicity, all four of them will be allowed to combine with state and activity verbs. It should be noted, however, that with state verbs *to begin* and *to finish* usually sound unnatural, as demonstrated in (2.100) and (2.101); and with activity verbs, as in (2.102), it could be argued that the use of *to begin* or *to finish* indicates that the speaker has a culminating activity view in mind, rather than an activity one.

(2.100) ?Which tank began to contain water on 27/7/1999?
(2.101) ?Which tank finished containing water on 27/7/1999?
(2.102) Which flight began/finished circling at 5:00 pm?

When combining with culminating activity verbs, *to start* and *to begin* have the same meanings. The verbs *to stop* and *to finish*, however, differ: *to finish* requires the climax to be reached, while *to stop* requires the action or change to simply stop, possibly without being completed. For example, in (2.103) the service must have simply stopped, while in (2.104) it must have been completed. Non-habitual readings are assumed here.

(2.103) Which company stopped servicing BA737 at 5:00 pm?
(2.104) Which company finished servicing BA737 at 5:00 pm?

With point verbs, like *to enter* and *to leave* in the airport domain, the use of *to start*, *to begin*, *to stop*, and *to finish*, as in (2.105) and (2.106), typically signals that the person submitting the question is unaware that the situation of the point verb is taken to be instantaneous. In such cases, the temporal verbs will be ignored, i.e., (2.105) and (2.106) will be treated as (2.107).

(2.105) Which flight started to enter sector 2 at 5:00 pm?
(2.106) Which flight finished leaving gate 2 at 5:00 pm?
(2.107) Which flight entered sector 2 at 5:00 pm?

Ideally, an NLITDB would also warn the user that the temporal verb is ignored, and that the situation is modelled as instantaneous. This is another case where cooperative responses are necessary.

2.7 Temporal nouns

In a similar manner, some nouns have a special temporal nature. Nouns like *development* or *inspection*, for example, are similar to verbs, in that they introduce world situations that occur in time. The role of *development* in (2.108) is very similar to that of *to develop* in (2.109).

(2.108) When did the development of MASQUE start?
(2.109) When did they start to develop MASQUE?

Other nouns, like *predecessor* and *successor*, indicate temporal order, or refer to start or end-points, like *beginning* or *end*. Finally, many nouns, as well as proper names, refer to time periods, points, or generally entities of the temporal ontology; e.g., *minute*, *July*, *event*.

This book will consider only nouns like *year*, *month*, *week*, *day*, *minute*, and proper names like *1999*, *July*, *1/1/1999*, *Monday*, *3:05 pm*. Temporal nouns of a more abstract nature, like *period*, *point*, *interval*, *event*, *time*, *duration*, nouns referring to start or end-points, nouns introducing situations, and nouns of temporal precedence will not be considered.

2.8 Temporal adjectives

There are also adjectives of a special temporal nature. Some refer to temporal order, like *current*, *previous*, *earlier*. Some refer to durations; e.g., *brief*, *long*. Others, like *annual* or *daily*, specify frequencies. Adjectives of this kind are not examined in this book, with the exception of *current*, which is supported to illustrate some issues related to temporal anaphora.

2.9 Temporal adverbials

We now turn to adverbials that convey temporal information. This book considers four types of temporal adverbials: *punctual adverbials*, *period adverbials*, and *duration adverbials* introduced by *for* and *in*. For each type, we will consider in turn the cases where the adverbials modify, i.e., attach to, expressions of the four aspectual classes: states, points, activities, and culminating activities.

2.9.1 Punctual adverbials

Some adverbials are understood as specifying time-points. Following Vlach (1993), the term *punctual adverbials* will be used to refer to them. In English, punctual adverbials are usually prepositional phrases introduced by *at*, as in *at 5:00 pm* or *at the end of the inspection*. In this book, only punctual adverbials consisting of *at* and clock-time expressions, like *at 5:00 pm*, will be considered.

Punctual adverbials with states. When combining with state expressions, punctual adverbials specify a time where the situation of the state expression holds. There is usually no implication that the situation of the state starts or stops at the time of the adverbial. (2.110), for example, asks if tank 5 was empty at 5:00 pm. There is no requirement that the tank must have started or stopped being empty at 5:00 pm. Similar comments apply to (2.111).

(2.110) Was tank 5 empty at 5:00 pm?
(2.111) Which flight was at gate 2 at 5:00 pm?

In other words, punctual adverbials normally have an *interjacent* meaning with states, not an *inchoative* (start time of situation) or a *terminal* one (end time of situation). These terms are borrowed from Kent (1993), who explores the behaviour of *at*, *for*, and *in* adverbials, arriving at conclusions similar to the ones presented here.

In narrative contexts, punctual adverbials combining with states sometimes have inchoative meanings. For example, the *at 8:10 am* in (2.112) most probably specifies the time when J. Adams arrived (started being) in Glasgow. In NLITDB questions, however, this inchoative meaning seems unlikely. For example, it seems unlikely that (2.113) would be used to enquire about persons that *arrived* in Glasgow at 8:10 am. Hence, for the purposes of this book, it seems reasonable to assume that punctual adverbials combining with states always have interjacent meanings.

(2.112) J. Adams left Edinburgh early in the morning, and
at 8:10 am he was in Glasgow.
(2.113) Who was in Glasgow at 8:10 am?

Punctual adverbials with points. With point expressions, punctual adverbials specify the time where the instantaneous situation of the point expression takes place, as in (2.114) and (2.115). The reader is reminded that *to enter* and *to reach* are point verbs in the airport domain (Section 2.4.5).

(2.114) Which flight entered sector 2 at 23:02?
(2.115) Which flight reached gate 5 at 23:02?

Question (2.116) is ambiguous. It may involve the non-habitual homonym of *to depart*, which is a point verb in the airport domain; in that case, 5:00 pm is the time of the actual departure. Alternatively, it may involve the state habitual homonym, in which case 5:00 pm is the habitual departure time. In the latter case, *at 5:00 pm* will be treated as a prepositional phrase complement of the habitual *to depart*, not as a temporal adverbial. This reflects the fact that the *at 5:00 pm* does not specify a time when the habit holds, but it forms part of the description of the habit, i.e., it is used in a way very similar to how *from gate 2* is used in (2.117).

(2.116) Which flight departed at 5:00 pm?
(2.117) Which flight departed (habitually) from gate 2 (last year)?

Punctual adverbials with activities. With activities, punctual adverbials usually have an inchoative meaning, but an interjacent one is also possible in some cases. (2.118), for example, could refer to a flight that either joined the queue of runway 2 at 5:00 pm or was simply in the queue at 5:00 pm. The reader is reminded that in the airport domain, *to queue* and *to taxi* without a destination are activity verbs. The inchoative meaning seems the preferred one in (2.118). It also seems the preferred one in (2.119), though an interjacent meaning is arguably also possible. The interjacent meaning is easier to accept in (2.120).

(2.118) Which flight queued for runway 2 at 5:00 pm?
(2.119) BA737 taxied at 5:00 pm.
(2.120) Which flights circled at 5:00 pm?

With past progressive forms of activity verbs, punctual adverbials normally have only interjacent meanings. Compare, for example, (2.118) and (2.119) to (2.121) and (2.122). One would not normally use punctual adverbials with present continuous forms, since in that case the situation is known to take place at the present.

(2.121) Which flight was queueing for runway 2 at 5:00 pm?
(2.122) BA737 was taxiing at 5:00 pm.

Following the arrangements of Section 2.5.3, it will be assumed that the progressive triggers an aspectual shift from activities and culminating activities to states. Hence, although *to queue* is an activity verb in the airport domain, *was queueing* is a state expression. Along with the assumption that punctual adverbials have only interjacent meanings when combining with states, this accounts for the fact that (2.121) can only be understood with an interjacent meaning. Similar comments apply to (2.122).

Punctual adverbials with culminating activities. With culminating activities, punctual adverbials usually have inchoative or terminal meanings; when they have terminal meanings, they specify the time at which the climax was reached. In the airport domain, for example, *to land*, *to taxi* to a destination, and *to inspect* are culminating activity verbs. The terminal reading is the preferred one in (2.123). In (2.124) both readings seem possible, while in (2.125) the inchoative meaning seems the preferred one.

(2.123) Which flight landed at 5:00 pm?
(2.124) Which flight taxied to gate 4 at 5:00 pm?
(2.125) Who inspected BA737 at 5:00 pm?

One could argue that in (2.123) the speaker does not have a culminating activity view in mind, but a point view, whereby the landing situation is seen as consisting of only the time-point at which the aircraft touches the ground. Indeed, as will be explained in following paragraphs, it will be assumed that punctual adverbials change the aspectual class of the expressions they modify to point. With culminating activities, this is achieved by forcing the modified expressions to refer to either the beginnings or the completions of the situations they would normally denote. In (2.123), the completion of the landing is conceptually more salient than its beginning, which is why the terminal reading is the preferred one. In (2.124) and (2.125), however, neither the beginning nor the completion is more salient, which is why the questions sound much more unclear than (2.123); in practice, a speaker would use temporal verbs like *to start* or *to finish* (Section 2.6) to specify the intended reading.

It could also be argued that, as with activities, an interjacent meaning is sometimes also possible when punctual adverbials combine with culminating activities. In that case, (2.124) would refer to a flight that was on its way to gate 4 at 5:00 pm. The inchoative or terminal reading, however, is usually much more dominant with culminating activities, and, for simplicity, the interjacent meaning will be ignored.

With progressive forms of culminating activity verbs, punctual adverbials normally have only interjacent meanings. Compare, for example, (2.123)–(2.125) to (2.126)–(2.128). This is in accordance with the assumption that the progressive triggers an aspectual shift to state (Section 2.5.3).

(2.126) Which flight was landing at 5:00 pm?
(2.127) Which flight was taxiing to gate 4 at 5:00 pm?
(2.128) Who was inspecting BA737 at 5:00 pm?

Punctual adverbials and past perfect. As already mentioned in Section 2.5.5, in sentences like (2.129) the adverbial can refer either directly to the situation, meaning that the taxiing started or ended at 5:00 pm, or to the reference time, in which case the taxiing had already finished at 5:00 pm.

(2.129) BA737 had taxied to gate 2 at 5:00 pm.

(2.130) BA737 had [taxied to gate 2 at 5:00 pm].
(2.131) BA737 [had taxied to gate 2] at 5:00 pm.

The treatment of sentences like (2.129) in this book will become clearer in Chapter 3. A rough description, however, can be given here. (2.129) is treated as syntactically ambiguous between (2.130), where the adverbial applies to the past participle *taxied*, and (2.131), where the adverbial applies to the past perfect *had taxied*. The past participle (*taxied*) inherits the aspectual class of the base form (culminating activity), and refers directly to the situation of the verb (the taxiing). In contrast, the past perfect (*had taxied*) is a state, because the past perfect causes an aspectual shift to state (Section 2.5.5). The past perfect refers to a time-period that starts immediately after the end of the situation of the verb (the end of the taxiing) and extends indefinitely. Let us call it the *consequent period*.

In (2.130), then, a punctual adverbial combines with the culminating activity past participle. According to the discussion above, two readings arise: an inchoative reading, whereby the taxiing started at 5:00 pm, and a terminal one, where the taxiing finishes at 5:00 pm. In contrast, in (2.131) the punctual adverbial combines with the past perfect *had taxied*, which is a state expression that refers to the consequent period. Hence, only an interjacent reading arises: the time of the adverbial must simply be within the consequent period, which implies that the taxiing must have been completed at the time of the adverbial. A similar arrangement is used when the past perfect combines with period adverbials, duration *for* and *in* adverbials, or temporal subordinate clauses.

Lexical, consequent, and progressive states. There is sometimes a need to distinguish between expressions that are states because they have inherited the state aspectual class of a base verb form, and expressions that are states because of an aspectual shift introduced by a past perfect or a progressive form. Following Moens (1987), the terms *lexical state*, *consequent state*, and *progressive state* will be used to distinguish the three genres, respectively. In the airport domain, for example, the base form of *to contain* is a lexical state, while the base form of *to queue* is an activity. The simple past *queued* and the past participle *queued* are also activities. The past perfect *had queued* is a consequent state, while the present continuous *is queueing* is a progressive state.

Aspectual shift of punctual adverbials. As already briefly mentioned, it is assumed that punctual adverbials cause the aspectual class of the syntactic constituent they modify to become point. This will allow us to account for sen-

Table 2.2 Punctual adverbials in this book

meanings of punctual adverbials	
with state	interjacent
with activity	inchoative or interjacent
with culm. activity	inchoative or terminal
with point	time of instantaneous situation
The resulting aspectual class is point.	

tences with multiple temporal adverbials in Chapter 4. In (2.131), for example, the *taxied to gate 2* inherits the culminating activity aspectual class of the base form. The past perfect causes the aspectual class of *had taxied to gate 2* to become consequent state. Finally, the *at 5:00 pm* causes the aspectual class of *had departed at 5:00 pm* to become point. Table 2.2 summarises the main observations of this section.

2.9.2 Period adverbials

Unlike punctual adverbials, that are understood as specifying points in time, adverbials like *in 1999*, *on Monday*, *yesterday*, as in (2.132)–(2.134), are usually understood as specifying longer, non-instantaneous periods of time. The term *period adverbial* will be used to refer to them.

(2.132) Who was the sales manager in 1999?

(2.133) Did BA737 circle on Monday?

(2.134) Which flights did J. Adams inspect yesterday?

Before and *after* adverbials, as in (2.135), can also be considered period adverbials, except that in this case one of the boundaries of the period is left unspecified. In (2.135), for example, the end of the period is the beginning of 2/5/1999; the beginning of the period is left unspecified. *Before* and *after* can also introduce temporal subordinate clauses; this will be discussed in Section 2.10.2.

(2.135) Which company serviced BA737 before 2/5/1999?

This book examines only period adverbials introduced by *in*, *on*, *before*, and *after*, as well as *today* and *yesterday*. *In* can also introduce duration adverbials, like *in two hours*; this will be discussed in Section 2.9.4. Other period adverbials, like *from 1996 to 1999*, *since 1996*, *last week*, or *two days ago*, will not be considered.

Period adverbials with states. When period adverbials combine with state expressions, the situation of the state expression must hold for at least some time during the period of the adverbial. In (2.136), for example, the person must have been a manager for at least some time in 1999. Similarly, in (2.137), the person must have been at gate 2 for at least some time on the previous day.

(2.136) Who was a manager in 1999?
(2.137) Who was at gate 2 yesterday?

There is often, however, an implication that the situation holds *throughout* the period of the adverbial. (2.138), for example, could mean that the tank was empty throughout January, not at simply some part of January. Similarly, in (2.139) the user could be referring to tanks that were empty throughout January. In that case, if a tank was empty only some days in January and the NLITDB included that tank in the answer, the user would be misled to believe that the tank was empty throughout January. Similar comments can be made for (2.140) and (2.141).

(2.138) Tank 4 was empty in January.
(2.139) Which tanks were empty in January?
(2.140) Was runway 2 open on 6/7/1999?
(2.141) Which flights departed (habitually) from gate 2 in 1999?

The same implication is possible in sentences with *before* or *after* adverbials. (2.142), for example, could mean that the runway was open all the time from some unspecified time up to 5:00 pm, and possibly longer.

(2.142) Runway 2 was open before 5:00 pm.

One way to deal with such implications is to treat sentences where period adverbials combine with states as ambiguous. That is, to distinguish between a reading where the situation holds throughout the adverbial's period, and a reading where the situation holds at simply some part of the adverbial's period. Vlach (1993: 256) uses the terms *durative* and *inclusive* to refer to the two readings. An NLITDB could paraphrase both readings and ask the user to select one, or it could provide answers to both readings, indicating which answer corresponds to which reading. This approach has the disadvantage that it always generates two readings, even when the durative reading is clearly impossible. For example, when the state expression combines not only with a period adverbial but also with a *for* duration adverbial, the meaning can never be that the situation must necessarily hold throughout the period of the period adverbial; (2.143) can never mean that the tank must have been empty throughout January (cf. (2.139)). Similarly, in time-asking questions like (2.144), the durative reading is impossible.

(2.143) Which tank was empty for two days in January?
(2.144) When on 6/7/1999 was runway 2 open?

Formulating an account of exactly when the durative reading is possible is difficult. Although Chapter 3 discusses how the distinction between durative and inclusive reading could be captured in TOP, for simplicity the rest of this book considers only the inclusive reading, ignoring the durative one.

Period adverbials with points. When period adverbials combine with point expressions, as in (2.145), the period of the adverbial must contain the time where the instantaneous situation of the point expression occurs.

(2.145) Did BA737 enter sector 5 on Monday?

Period adverbials with culminating activities. Two readings will be allowed when period adverbials combine with culminating activity expressions: (a) that the situation of the culminating activity expression both starts and reaches its completion within the adverbial's period, and (b) that the situation simply reaches its completion within the adverbial's period. In the second reading, the culminating activity expression will be treated as referring only to the completion of the situation it would normally denote, and the aspectual class of the overall expression will be shifted to point.

The first reading is the preferred one in (2.146), which is most naturally understood as referring to a runner who both started and finished running the forty miles on Wednesday. The verb *to run* with an object denoting a specific distance is typically classified as culminating activity.

(2.146) Who ran 40 miles on Wednesday?

In the airport domain, the first reading is also the preferred one in (2.147), i.e., the inspection both started and was completed on Monday.

(2.147) J. Adams inspected BA737 on Monday.

The second reading, that the situation simply reaches its completion within the adverbial's period, is needed in questions like (2.148) and (2.149). In the airport domain, *to land* and *to take off* are culminating activity verbs. If only the first reading were available, in (2.148) the NLITDB would report only flights that both started and finished landing on Monday. If a flight started the landing procedure at 23:55 on Sunday and finished it at 00:05 on Monday, that flight would not be reported. This seems over-restrictive; in (2.148), the most natural reading is that the flights must have simply touched down on Monday, and similar comments apply to (2.149) and (2.150) in domains where *to fix* is a culminating activity verb.

(2.148) Which flights landed on Monday?
(2.149) Which flights took off after 5:00 pm?
(2.150) Did J. Adams fix any faults yesterday?

The problem in these cases is that *to land*, *to take off*, and *to fix* need to be treated as point verbs referring only to the time-points where the corresponding situations were completed, even though they have been classified as culminating activity verbs. The second reading allows exactly this. The culminating activity expression is taken to refer only to the completion point of the situation, its aspectual class is changed to point, and the completion point is required to fall within the adverbial's period.

This arrangement may not always be entirely satisfactory. Let us assume, for example, that J. Adams started inspecting a flight late on Monday, and finished the inspection early on Tuesday. None of the two readings would include that flight in the answer to (2.151), because both require the completion point to fall on Monday. While strictly speaking this seems correct, it would be better if the NLITDB included in the answer inspections that *partially* overlap the adverbial's period, warning the user about the fact that these inspections are not completely contained in the adverbial's period. This is another case where cooperative responses are needed.

(2.151) Which flights did J. Adams inspect on Monday?

It should also be noted that with *before* adverbials, as in (2.152), the two readings are equivalent: requiring the situation to simply reach its completion before some time is equivalent to requiring the situation to both start and reach its completion before that time. To avoid generating equivalent readings, only the reading where the situation both starts and reaches its completion within the adverbial's period will be admitted in this case.

(2.152) Which flights took off before 5:00 pm?

Period adverbials with activities. When period adverbials combine with activities, the situation of the verb must hold for at least some time within the adverbial's period; this is the same as with states. In (2.153), for example, the

Table 2.3 Period adverbials in this book

meanings of period adverbials	
with state, activity	The situation holds for at least part of the adverbial's period.
with culm. activity	The situation starts and is completed within the adverbial's period, or the situation is simply completed within the adverbial's period.*†
with point	The situation occurs within the adverbial's period.

*The second reading is not available with *before* adverbials.
†In the second reading, the resulting aspectual class is point.
In all other cases, the aspectual class remains the same.

flight must have circled for at least some time on Monday, and in (2.154) the flights must have taxied for at least some time after 5:00 pm.

(2.153) Did BA737 circle on Monday?
(2.154) Which flights taxied after 5:00 pm?

Another stricter reading is sometimes possible, especially with *before* and *after*: that the situation does not extend past the boundaries of the adverbial's period. For example, (2.154) would refer to flights that *started* to taxi after 5:00 pm; a flight that started to taxi at 4:55 pm and continued to taxi until 5:05 pm would not be reported. This reading may also be possible with states (cf. (2.142)), though with activities it seems easier to accept. As a simplification, readings of this kind will be ignored.

Elliptical forms of period adverbials. Before and *after* are sometimes followed by noun phrases that do not denote entities of the temporal ontology, as in (2.155).

(2.155) Did J. Adams inspect BA737 before UK160?
(2.156) Did J. Adams inspect BA737 before he inspected UK160?

Questions like (2.155) can be considered elliptical forms of (2.156), i.e., in these cases *before* and *after* could be treated as when they introduce subordinate clauses (see Section 2.10.2 below). Elliptical forms are not examined in this book, and questions like (2.155) will not be discussed further. Table 2.3 summarises the main points of this section.

2.9.3 Duration adverbials introduced by 'for'

We now move on to temporal adverbials that specify durations, starting with duration adverbials introduced by *for*.

'For' adverbials with states and activities. When *for* adverbials combine with states or activities, one reading is that there must be a period with the duration of the *for* adverbial, such that the situation of the state or activity holds throughout that period. According to this reading, in (2.157) there must be a five-year period throughout which the person was a manager, and in (2.158) a twenty-minute period throughout which BA737 was circling. If J. Adams was a manager for six consecutive years, for example from 1981 to 1986, he would be reported in (2.157), because there is a five-year period, for example 1981 to 1985, throughout which he was a manager.

(2.157) Who was a manager for five years?
(2.158) Did BA737 circle for twenty minutes?

In some cases, however, *for* adverbials are used with a stricter meaning: they specify the duration of a *maximal* period where a situation held. In that case, if J. Adams started to be a manager at the beginning of 1981 and stopped being a manager at the end of 1986 (six consecutive years), he would *not* be included in the answer to (2.157). For simplicity, this stricter reading is ignored in this book.

In other cases, a *for* adverbial does not necessarily specify the duration of a *single* period, but a *total duration.* According to this reading, if J. Adams was a manager during several non-overlapping periods, and the total duration of these periods is five years, he would be included in the answer to (2.157), even if he was never a manager for a continuous five-year period. This reading of *for* adverbials is also not considered in this book.

It should also be noted that in sentences like (2.159), the duration adverbial can never be understood as specifying the duration of the consequent period (Section 2.9.1).

(2.159) BA737 had circled for two hours.

This will be discussed further in Chapter 4 (Section 4.11.3), once some formal apparatus has been established. For the moment, it suffices to say that *for* adverbials will not be allowed to combine with consequent states.

'For' adverbials with points. Adverbials introduced by *for* sometimes specify the duration of a situation that *follows* the situation of the verb. This is particularly common with point expressions. For instance, (2.160), which is based on an example by Hwang and Schubert (1994), does not mean that J. Adams was actually leaving his office for fifteen minutes. It means that he stayed, or intended to stay, out of his office for fifteen minutes. It is assumed here that *to*

leave is a point verb, as in the airport domain. This use of *for* adverbials is not considered in this book.

(2.160) J. Adams left his office for fifteen minutes.

For adverbials also give rise to iterative readings (Section 2.5.3). This is again particularly common with point expressions, as illustrated by Hwang and Schubert's example in (2.161); the verb *to win* is typically classified as point. The sentence has an iterative meaning, whereby Mary won several times. The reader is reminded that iterative readings are not considered in this book.

(2.161) Mary won the competition for four years.

Excluding iterative readings and readings where *for* adverbials refer to consequent situations, sentences in which *for* adverbials combine with point expressions either sound odd or signal that the user is unaware that the situation of the point expression is modelled as instantaneous. (Ideally, an explanatory message would be produced; yet another case where cooperative responses are needed.) Hence, for the purposes of this book it seems reasonable not to allow *for* adverbials to combine with point expressions.

'For' adverbials with culminating activities. When *for* adverbials combine with culminating activities, the sentences sometimes sound odd or even unacceptable. For example, *to build* is typically classified as culminating activity verb. (2.162) sounds odd or unacceptable to most native English speakers. In contrast, (2.163), where the adverbial combines with a progressive state, is easily acceptable.

(2.162) $^{?}$Housecorp built a shopping centre for two years.
(2.163) Housecorp was building a shopping centre for two years.

Based on similar examples, Vendler concludes that 'accomplishments' (culminating activities) do not combine with *for* adverbials (Section 2.2). This, however, seems over-restrictive. For example, (2.164) and (2.165) are acceptable.

(2.164) BA737 taxied to gate 2 for two minutes.
(2.165) Did J. Adams inspect BA737 for ten minutes?

Unlike (2.166), in (2.164) there is no requirement that the taxiing must have been completed, i.e., that BA737 must have reached the gate. Similar comments can be made for (2.165) and (2.167). *For* adverbials seem to cancel any requirement that the climax must have been reached. Similar observations are made by Dowty (1986), Moens and Steedman (1988), and Kent (1993).

Table 2.4 Duration adverbials introduced by 'for' in this book

meanings of duration adverbials introduced by *for*	
with lexical state, progressive state, activity, culminating activity	The situation holds continuously for at least that long.*
with consequent state, point	(Not allowed in the framework of this book.)

*With culminating activities, there is no need for the climax to be reached.

(2.166) BA737 taxied to gate 2.

(2.167) Did J. Adams inspect BA737?

The framework of this book allows *for* adverbials to combine with culminating activities, with the same meaning as in the case of states and activities, but with the proviso that any requirement that the climax must have been reached should be cancelled. That is, in (2.165) there must be a ten-minute period throughout which J. Adams was inspecting BA737; there is no requirement that the inspection must have been completed. Table 2.4 summarises the main points of this section.

2.9.4 Duration adverbials introduced by 'in'

This section discusses duration adverbials introduced by *in*, as in (2.168) and (2.169). Period *in* adverbials were discussed in Section 2.9.2.

(2.168) Airserve serviced BA737 in two hours.

(2.169) Which flight did J. Adams inspect in one hour?

'In' adverbials with culminating activities. With culminating activity expressions, *in* adverbials usually specify the length of a period that ends at the time-point where the situation of the culminating activity is completed. In (2.168), for example, two hours is probably the length of a period that ends at the time-point where the service was completed. (2.169) is similar. The period whose length is specified by the *in* adverbial usually starts at the time-point where the situation of the culminating activity begins. In (2.168), for example, the two hours probably start at the time-point where the service began. Sometimes, however, the period of the adverbial may not start at the beginning of the situation of the culminating activity, but at some other earlier time. In (2.168), the start of the two hours could be the time-point where Airserve was asked to service BA737, not the beginning of the actual service. In this book, we will

consider only the case where the period of the adverbial starts at the beginning of the situation of the culminating activity.

'In' adverbials with points. With point expressions, the period of the *in* adverbial starts before the instantaneous situation of the point expression, and ends at the time-point where the situation of the point expression occurs. In (2.170), the ten minutes end at the point where BA737 arrived at gate 2, and start at some earlier time-point; for example, when BA737 started to taxi to gate 2. (2.171) is similar.

(2.170) BA737 reached gate 2 in ten minutes.

(2.171) BA737 entered sector 2 in five minutes.

Determining exactly when the period of the adverbial starts, however, is often difficult. It is not clear, for example, when the five minutes of (2.171) start. As a simplification, the framework of this book does not allow duration *in* adverbials to combine with point expressions.

'In' adverbials with states and activities. When *in* adverbials are used with activity expressions, the speaker sometimes has a culminating activity view in mind. For example, in (2.172) the speaker may have a particular destination, say gate 2, in mind. In that case, (2.172) can be considered an elliptical form of (2.173). Elliptical forms are not examined in this book, and sentences like (2.172) will not be discussed further.

(2.172) BA737 taxied in ten minutes.

(2.173) BA737 taxied to gate 2 in ten minutes.

With state and activity expressions, *in* adverbials can also specify the duration of a period that ends at the *beginning* of the situation of the state or activity expression. In (2.174), for example, the two hours probably end at the time-point where tank 5 *started* to be empty. The beginning of the two hours could be, for example, a time-point where a pump started to empty the tank, or a time-point where a decision to empty the tank was taken. A similar reading is available in (2.172).

(2.174) Tank 5 was empty in two hours.

As with point expressions, determining exactly when the period of the adverbial starts is often difficult. Again, as a simplification, the framework of this book does not allow duration *in* adverbials to combine with states and activities. Table 2.5 summarises the main points of this section.

Table 2.5 Duration adverbials introduced by 'in' in this book

meanings of duration adverbials introduced by *in*	
with state, activity, point	(Not allowed in the framework of this book.)
with culminating activity	Distance from the start to the completion of the situation.

2.9.5 Other temporal adverbials

The linguistic coverage of this book does not include other kinds of temporal adverbials. Among the temporal adverbials that are not covered are several adverbials that specify boundaries, like *until 1/5/1999*, *since 1997*, *by Monday*, frequency adverbials, like *always*, *twice*, *every Monday*, and adverbials of temporal order, like *for the second time* and *earlier*.

2.10 Temporal subordinate clauses

Three types of temporal subordinate clauses will be examined in this book: clauses introduced by *while*, *before*, and *after*.

2.10.1 Clauses introduced by 'while'

Each *while* clause can be thought of as contributing a time period. The analysis below examines first how this period is established, and then how it relates to the situation of the main clause.

The period of the 'while' clause. The period contributed by the *while* clause must be a maximal period throughout which the situation of the clause holds. If there are several periods of this kind, then the contributed period can generally be any of them. Let us assume, for example, that J. Adams was a manager only from 1/1/1980 to 31/12/1983 and from 1/1/1987 to 31/12/1990. Then, in (2.175) the period of the *while* clause can be any of the two periods. In practice, the user may have in mind a particular period period among the two, in which case a temporal anaphora resolution mechanism is needed to determine that period. The framework of this book, however, provides no such mechanism, and the answer to (2.175) will include anybody who was fired during any of the two periods. Temporal anaphora is discussed further in Section 2.12 below.

(2.175) Who was fired while J. Adams was a manager?

Sentences where the aspectual class of the *while* clause is point, like (2.176) in the airport domain, typically signal that the user is unaware that the situation of the *while* clause is modelled as instantaneous. In the framework of this book, the answer to (2.176) will include any flight that was circling at the time-point where BA737 entered sector 2. Ideally, a message would also be generated to warn the user that entering a sector is modelled as instantaneous, but no mechanism to generate such cooperative messages is currently in place.

(2.176) Which flights were circling while BA737 entered sector 2?

Sentences containing *while* clauses whose aspectual class is consequent state usually sound unnatural or unacceptable. For example, (2.177)–(2.179) sound at least unnatural, and their intended meanings are unclear. Instead of (2.177), for example, one would normally use (2.180) or (2.181). Hence, *while* clauses whose aspectual class is consequent state will not be allowed in the framework of this book.

(2.177) ?Did any flight depart while BA737 had landed?
(2.178) ?Did ABM fire anybody while Adams had been the manager?
(2.179) ?Had any flight departed while Adams had inspected BA737?
(2.180) Did any flight depart while BA737 was landing?
(2.181) Did any flight depart after BA737 had landed?

When the aspectual class of the *while* clause is culminating activity, there is no requirement that the climax of the situation of the *while* clause must have been reached, even if the verb form of that clause normally requires this. In (2.183) and (2.186), for example, there does not seem to be any requirement that the service or the boarding must have been completed (cf. (2.182) and (2.185)). (2.183) and (2.186) appear to have the same meanings as (2.184) and (2.187). Table 2.6 summarises the main points about *while* clauses so far.

Table 2.6 Periods of 'while' clauses in this book

while clause	period specified by the *while* clause
consequent state	(not allowed in the framework of this book)
lexical state, progressive state, activity, culminating activity	maximal period where the situation of the *while* clause holds*
point	instantaneous period where the situation of the *while* clause occurs

*When the *while* clause is culminating activity, there is no need for the climax of its situation to be reached.

(2.182) Did Airserve service BA737?
(2.183) Which flights departed while Airserve serviced BA737?
(2.184) Which flights departed while Airserve was servicing BA737?
(2.185) Did BA737 board?
(2.186) Which flights departed while BA737 boarded?
(2.187) Which flights departed while BA737 was boarding?

Main clause modified by 'while' clause. Once the periods of the *while* clauses have been established following Table 2.6, the behaviour of *while* clauses appears to be the same as that of period adverbials, i.e., it follows Table 2.3 on page 50. With main clauses whose aspectual class is point, the instantaneous situation of the main clause must occur within the period of the *while* clause. For example, *to depart* is a point verb in the airport domain. In (2.188), the departures must have occurred during a maximal period where runway 5 was closed.

(2.188) Did any flight depart from gate 2 while runway 5 was closed?

With activity main clauses, the situation of the main clause must be ongoing some time during the period of the *while* clause. In (2.189), for example, the flights must have taxied some time during a maximal period where BA737 was circling (cf. Table 2.3). Stricter readings are sometimes possible with activity main clauses, as in the case of period adverbials (Section 2.9.2). For example, (2.189) could refer to flights that both started and stopped taxiing during a maximal period where BA737 was circling. As with period adverbials, these stricter readings will be ignored.

(2.189) Which flights taxied while BA737 circled?

As in the case of period adverbials, with culminating activity main clauses two readings are allowed: (a) that the situation of the main clause both starts and reaches its completion within the period of the *while* clause, or (b) that the situation of the main clause simply reaches its completion within the period of the *while* clause. In the second reading, the main clause is taken to refer only to the completion point of the situation it would normally denote, and its aspectual class is changed to point (cf. Table 2.3). In the airport domain, the first reading is the preferred one in (2.190). The second reading allows the answer to (2.191) to contain flights that simply touched down during the service, even if their landing procedures did not start during the service.

(2.190) Adams inspected BA737 while Airserve was servicing UK52.
(2.191) Which flights landed while Airserve was servicing UK52?

With state main clauses, the situation of the main clause is required to hold some time during the period of the *while* clause; this corresponds to the *inclusive reading* of Section 2.9.2. For example, the non-auxiliary *to be* is typically classified as state verb. In (2.192), the answer must contain anybody who was a lecturer some time during a maximal period where Adams was a professor. As with period adverbials, there is often an implication that the situation of the main clause holds *throughout* the period of the *while* clause; this corresponds to the *durative reading* of Section 2.9.2. According to the durative reading, (2.192) refers to people who were lecturers throughout the, presumably unique, maximal period where Adams was a professor; and (2.193), where the main clause is a progressive state, refers to a flight that was circling *throughout* a maximal period where runway 2 was closed.

(2.192) Who was a lecturer while Adams was a professor?
(2.193) Which flight was circling while runway 2 was closed?

As with period adverbials, Chapter 3 will demonstrate how durative readings can be captured in TOP, but these readings will not be considered further in the rest of this book.

It should be noted that the treatment of temporal subordinate clauses of this book is in many ways similar to that of Ritchie (1979). Ritchie also views temporal subordinate clauses as establishing periods. The exact relations between these periods and the situations of the main clauses depend on the aspectual classes of the main clauses and the words introducing the subordinate clauses.

2.10.2 Clauses introduced by 'before' and 'after'

Like the *before* and *after* adverbials of Section 2.9.2, clauses introduced by *before* and *after* are treated as establishing periods. In *before* clauses, the period starts at some unspecified time-point; in the absence of other constraints, this is the beginning of time. The end-point of the period is provided by the *before* clause. In *after* clauses, the period starts at a time-point provided by the *after* clause, and ends at some unspecified time-point, or the end of time. The terms *before-point* and *after-point* will be used to refer to the time-points provided by *before* and *after* clauses, respectively. Once the periods of the *before* and *after* clauses have been established, the behaviour of the clauses appears to be the same as that of period adverbials, i.e., it follows Table 2.3 on page 50.

State 'before' or 'after' clause. Let us first examine sentences where the aspectual class of the *before* or *after* clause is state. With *before* clauses, the before-point is a time-point where the situation of the *before* clause starts (Table 2.7). In (2.194), for example, the before-point is a time-point where runway 2 started to be open. In the airport domain, the aspectual class of the main clause is point. According to Table 2.3 on page 50, the departures must have occurred within the period of the *before* clause, i.e., before the time-point where runway 2 started to be open. Similar comments apply to (2.195), (2.196), where the *before* clause is a progressive state, and (2.197), where the *before* clause is a consequent state. In (2.197), the before-point is the beginning of the consequent period of the inspection (Section 2.9.1), i.e., the beginning of the period that contains all the time after the completion of the inspection. Hence, the departures must have happened before the inspection was completed.

(2.194) Which flights departed before runway 2 was open?
(2.195) Which flights departed before the emergency system was in operation?

(2.196) Which flights departed before BA737 was circling?
(2.197) Which flights departed before Adams had inspected BA737?

According to Table 2.3 on page 50, in (2.198) where the main clause is a state, the flight must have been at gate 2 some time during the period of the *before* clause, i.e., for some time before runway 2 started to be open. In (2.199), where the main clause is an activity, the flight must have circled for some time before runway 2 started to be open. In (2.200), which involves a culminating activity main clause, the inspections must have both started and been completed before runway 2 started to be open.

(2.198) Was any flight at gate 2 before runway 2 was open?
(2.199) Did any flight circle before runway 2 was open?
(2.200) Which flights did J. Adams inspect before runway 2 was open?

Table 2.7 Clauses introduced by 'before' in this book

aspectual class of *before* clause	**before-point (end-point of period specified by *before* clause)**
state, activity	time-point where the situation of the *before* clause starts
culm. activity	time-point where the situation of the *before* clause starts or is completed
point	time-point where the situation of the *before* clause occurs

As with the *before* adverbials of Section 2.9.2, in (2.200) it would be better if the NLITDB could also report inspections that started but were not completed before runway 2 opened, warning the user that those inspections were not completed before runway 2 opened. Again, a mechanism for cooperative responses is needed to achieve this.

In the case of *after* clauses, if the aspectual class of the *after* clause is a lexical or progressive state, the after-point is a time-point where the situation of the *after* clause either starts or ends (Table 2.8). For example, (2.201) has two readings: that the flights must have departed after runway 2 *started* to be open, or that the flights must have departed after runway 2 *stopped* being open. Similar comments apply to (2.202) and (2.203). In practice, additional temporal verbs, like *to start* or *to stop* would typically be included to clarify the intended meanings. Knowing the readings that are possible without these verbs, however, is still useful, as it allows the NLITDB to detect the possible ambiguities when users omit them.

(2.201) Which flights departed after runway 2 was open?
(2.202) Which flights departed after the emergency system was in operation?
(2.203) Which flights departed after BA737 was circling?

In sentences like (2.204), where the aspectual class of the *after* clause is consequent state, the after-point can only be the beginning of the consequent period, i.e., the first time-point after the completion of the inspection. It cannot be the end of the consequent period, because the end of the consequent period is the end of time. This explains the distinction between consequent and lexical or progressive states in Table 2.8.

(2.204) Which flights departed after Adams had inspected BA737?

Table 2.8 Clauses introduced by 'after' in this book

aspectual class of *before* clause	after-point (start-point of period specified by *after* clause)
lexical or progressive state	time-point where the situation of the *after* clause starts or ends
consequent state	time-point where the consequent period of the *after* clause starts
activity	time-point where the situation of the *after* clause ends
culm. activity	time-point where the situation of the *after* clause is completed
point	time-point where the situation of the *before* clause occurs

Point 'before' or 'after' clause. If the aspectual class of the *before* or *after* clause is point, the before- or after-point is the time-point where the instantaneous situation of the subordinate clause occurs. In (2.205), for example, the before- or after-point is the point where BA737 reached gate 2.

(2.205) Which flights departed before/after BA737 reached gate 2?

Activity 'before' or 'after' clause. With activity *before* clauses, the before-point is a time-point where the situation of the *before* clause starts. In (2.206) and (2.207), for example, the departures must have occurred before BA737 *started* to taxi or circle.

(2.206) Which flights departed before BA737 taxied?
(2.207) Which flights departed before BA737 circled?

With activity *after* clauses, the after-point must be a point where the situation of the *after* clause ends. In (2.208) and (2.209), for example, the departures must have occurred after BA737 *stopped* taxiing or circling.

(2.208) Which flights departed after BA737 taxied?
(2.209) Which flights departed after BA737 circled?

Another reading may sometimes be possible with *after* clauses: that the after-point is a time-point where the situation of the *after* clause *starts*. In this case, (2.209) would refer to departures that occurred after BA737 *started* to circle. This reading, however, seems less likely, and for simplicity it will be ignored. Again, in practice people would probably use additional temporal verbs, like *to start* or *to stop*, to clarify the intended meaning.

Culminating activity 'before' or 'after' clause. With *after* clauses whose aspectual class is culminating activity, the after-point is most likely a time-point where the situation of the *after* clause reaches its completion. In (2.210), for example, the most probably reading is that the departures must have occurred after the completion of the inspection, and in (2.211) after the time-point where BA737 reached gate 2. These questions may sound slightly unnatural, probably because in practice additional temporal verbs would be used to clarify their meanings. As commented above, however, there is value in attempting to identify the most likely readings in the absence of such verbs.

(2.210) Which flights departed after J. Adams inspected BA737?
(2.211) Which flights departed after BA737 taxied to gate 2?

With culminating activity *before* clauses, the before-point will be allowed to be a time-point where the situation of the *before* clause either starts or reaches its completion. In the airport domain, the first reading seems the preferred one in (2.212). The flights must have departed before the *beginning* of the inspection. The second reading seems the preferred one in (2.213). The flights must have departed before the *completion* of the landing. Both readings seems possible in (2.214).

(2.212) Which flights departed before J. Adams inspected BA737?
(2.213) Which flights departed before BA737 landed?
(2.214) Which flights departed before BA737 taxied to gate 2?

The simple past of culminating activity verbs normally requires the climax to have been reached. However, if the first reading above is adopted, i.e., if the situation of the *before* clause *starts* at the before-point, and the clause is in the simple past, it is unclear if the situation of that clause must have necessarily reached its climax. For example, let us assume that the first reading is adopted in (2.212). Should the before-point be the beginning of an inspection that was necessarily completed, or can it also be the beginning of an inspection that was never completed? The framework of this book currently adopts the first approach, but this is probably over-restrictive. It would be better if the NLITDB allowed the before-point to be the beginning of both inspections that were and were not completed, warning the user about inspections that were not completed. This is another case for cooperative responses.

Other uses. Before and *after* can be preceded by expressions specifying durations, as in (2.215). This use of *before* and *after* is not considered in this book.

(2.215) BA737 reached gate 2 five minutes after UK160 departed.

Before clauses also have counter-factual uses. For example, in (2.216), which is borrowed from an earlier form of Crouch and Pulman (1993), the situation where the car runs into the tree never takes place. This use of *before* is not considered in this book.

(2.216) Smith stopped the car before it ran into the tree.

2.10.3 Other temporal subordinate clauses

Temporal subordinate clauses that are not examined in this book include, for example, clauses introduced by *since*, *until*, and *when*. From these, *when* clauses seem the most challenging, as they often require large amounts of common sense knowledge to interpret (Ritchie 1979; Yip 1985; Hinrichs 1986; Moens 1987; Moens & Steedman 1988; Lascarides & Oberlander 1993).

2.10.4 Tense coordination

Some combinations of tenses in the main and subordinate clauses are unacceptable, as demonstrated in (2.217) and (2.218). This book makes no attempt to account for the unacceptability of such combinations. The reader is referred to Harper and Charniak (1986), and Brent (1990) for methods that could be used to reject sentences of this kind.

(2.217) *BA737 left gate 2 before runway 2 is free.

(2.218) *Which runways are closed while runway 2 was circling?

2.11 Noun phrases and temporal reference

A question like (2.219) can refer either to the present sales manager or to the person who was the sales manager in 1999. Similarly, (2.220) may refer either to present students or last year's students. In (2.221), *which closed runway* probably refers to a runway that is *currently* closed, while in (2.222) *a closed runway* probably refers to a runway that was closed at the time of the landing.

(2.219) What was the salary of the sales manager in 1999?

(2.220) Which students failed in physics last year?

(2.221) Which closed runway was open yesterday?

(2.222) Did BA737 ever land on a closed runway in 1999?

It seems that noun phrases like *the sales manager*, *which students*, *a closed runway* refer either to the present or to the time of the verb tense, if this time is different than the present. In (2.219), the simple past refers to some time in 1999. Therefore, there are two options: *the sales manager* can refer either to the present sales manager or to somebody who was the sales manager in 1999. Similar comments apply to (2.220). In contrast, in (2.223) the verb tense refers to the present. Hence, there is only one possibility: *the sales manager* refers to the present sales manager.

(2.223) What is the salary of the sales manager?

In (2.221), the verb tense refers to a time within the previous day where the runway was open. There should be two readings: it should be possible for *which closed runway* to refer either to a currently closed runway, or to a runway that was closed at the time it was open. Since a runway cannot be closed and open at the same time, the second reading is ruled out. This clash, however, cannot be spotted easily by an NLITDB without some inferential capability.

Unfortunately, the hypothesis that noun phrases refer either to the present or the time of the verb tense is not always adequate. For example, a person submitting (2.224) to the NLITDB of a university most probably refers to *previous* students of the university. In contrast, the hypothesis predicts that the question can refer only to *current* students. Enc (1986) provides similar examples.

(2.224) How many of our students are now professors?

The hypothesis also predicts that (2.225) can refer only to current Prime Ministers or to persons that were Prime Ministers at the time they were born, an extremely unlikely reading. There is, however, a reading where the question refers to all past and present Prime Ministers. This reading is incorrectly ruled out by the hypothesis.

(2.225) Which Prime Ministers were born in Scotland?

Hinrichs (1988) argues that determining the times to which noun phrases refer is part of a more general problem of determining the entities to which noun phrases refer. According to Hinrichs, a noun phrase like *every admiral* generally refers to anybody who was, is, or will be an admiral of any fleet in the world at any time. If, however, (2.226) is uttered in a context where the current personnel of the U.S. fleet is being discussed, the temporal scope of *every admiral* is restricted to current admirals, in the same way that the scope of *every admiral* is restricted to admirals of the U.S. fleet.

(2.226) Every admiral graduated from Annapolis.

The fact that Hinrichs does not limit the times of the noun phrases to the present and the time of the verb tense is in accordance with the fact that *our students* in (2.224) is not limited to present students, and the fact that *which Prime Ministers* in (2.225) may refer to all past and present Prime Ministers. Hinrichs' approach, however, requires some mechanism to restrict the scope of noun phrases as the discourse evolves, and Hinrichs offers only a very limited sketch of how such a mechanism could be constructed. Also, in the absence of previous discourse, Hinrichs' treatment suggests that (2.219) refers to the sales managers of all times, an unlikely interpretation. The hypothesis that noun phrases refer either to the present or to the time of the verb tense performs better in this case. Given these problems with Hinrichs' approach, this book adopts the initial hypothesis that noun phrases refer to the present or the time of the verb tense. An alternative approach would be to attempt to merge this hypothesis with Hinrichs' method; Dalrymple (1988) goes towards that direction.

A further improvement, however, can be made to the initial hypothesis. When a noun phrase is the complement of the predicative *to be*, it seems that the noun phrase can refer only to the time of the verb tense. For example, (2.227) can only be a request to report the 1999 sales manager, not the current sales manager. Similarly, (2.228) cannot mean that J. Adams is the current sales manager. This also accounts for the fact that in (2.219) *the salary of the sales manager*, i.e., the complement of *was*, can refer only to a 1999 salary, not to a present salary, unlike *the sales manager* which can refer either to the present or 1999. The restriction that the complement of the predicative *to be* must refer to the time of the verb tense does not extend to noun phrases that are subconstituents of that complement, like *the sales manager* in (2.219).

(2.227) Who was the sales manager in 1999?
(2.228) J. Adams was the sales manager in 1999.

The same restriction applies to bare adjectives used as complements of the predicative *to be*. In (2.221), *open* can only refer to runways that were open on the previous day. It cannot refer to currently open runways.

The hypothesis that noun phrases refer to the present or the time of the verb tense does not apply when a temporal adjective, like *current*, specifies explicitly the time of the noun phrase, as in (2.229).

(2.229) Which current students failed in Physics last year?

In Chapter 4, an additional mechanism will be introduced, which allows the person configuring the NLITDB to force some noun phrases to be treated as referring always to the time of the verb tense, or always to the present.

2.12 Temporal anaphora

There are several English expressions, like *that time, the following day, then, later* that refer implicitly to contextually salient times, in a way that is similar to how pronouns, possessive determiners, etc. refer to contextually salient world entities. The terms *temporal* and *nominal anaphora* are used to refer to these two phenomena; Partee (1984) discusses the parallels between temporal and nominal anaphora further. For example, the user of an NLITDB may submit (2.230), followed by (2.231). In (2.231), *at that time* refers to the time when John became manager, an instance of temporal anaphora. In a similar manner, *he* refers to John, a case of nominal anaphora.

(2.230) When did John become manager?
(2.231) Was he married at that time?

Names of months, days, etc. often have a similar temporal anaphoric nature. For example, in a context where several questions about the 1996 status of a company have just been asked, (2.232) most probably refers to the January of 1996, not any other January. In the absence of previous questions, (2.232) most probably refers to the January of the current year. Kamp and Reyle (1993: 613–634) provide related discussion.

(2.232) Who was the sales manager in January?

Verb tenses also seem to have a temporal anaphoric nature. The term *tense anaphora* is often used in this case. For example, the user may ask (2.233). Let us assume that the response is negative, and that the user then asks (2.234). In that case, the simple past *was* of (2.234) does not refer to an arbitrary past time. It refers to the past time of the previous question, i.e., 1998.

(2.233) Was Mary the personnel manager in 1998?
(2.234) Who was the personnel manager?

The anaphoric nature of verb tenses is clearer in multi-sentence text (Hinrichs 1986; Webber 1988; Kamp & Reyle 1993; Kameyama, Passonneau, & Poesio 1993). In (2.235), for example, the simple past *landed* refers to a landing that happened immediately after the permission of the first sentence was given. It does not refer to an arbitrary past time where BA737 landed on runway 2. Similar comments apply to *taxied*. Text of this form will not be considered in this book.

(2.235) BA737 was given permission to land at 5:00 pm. It landed on runway 2, and taxied to gate 4.

In dialogues like those of (2.233) and (2.234), a simplistic treatment of tense anaphora is to store the time of the adverbial of (2.233), and require the simple past of (2.234) to refer to that time. A more elaborate version of this approach will be sketched in Chapter 3, but it will not be considered any further. The behaviour of noun phrases like *the sales manager* of Section 2.11 can also be seen as a case of temporal anaphora. This is the only type of temporal anaphora that will be supported by the theoretical framework of this book. Expressions like *at that time, the following day*, etc. will not be examined, and verb forms referring to the past will be taken to refer to *any* past time. For example, (2.234) will be taken to refer to anybody who was the personnel manager at any past time.

2.13 Phenomena that will not be considered

We will now touch upon some additional time-related linguistic phenomena that will not be examined further in this book.

Cardinality and duration questions. Questions about the cardinality of a set or the duration of a situation, as in (2.236) and (2.237), will not be examined. This simplifies the definition of TOP in Chapter 3.

(2.236) How many flights have landed today?
(2.237) For how long was tank 2 empty?

Cardinality expressions and plurals. Although duration expressions like *five hours* will be considered, expressions specifying cardinalities of sets, like *eight passengers* or *two airplanes*, will be ignored. Expressions of the latter type give rise to a distinction between *distributive* and *collective* readings (Stirling 1985; Crouch & Pulman 1993). For example, (2.238) has a collective reading where the eight passengers arrive at the same time, and a distributive one where there are eight separate arrivals. To simplify TOP, cardinality expressions of this kind will not be examined.

(2.238) Eight passengers arrived.

Furthermore, plural noun phrases introduced by *some* and *which*, like *some flights* and *which passengers*, will be treated semantically as singular. For example, (2.239) and (2.241) will be treated as having the same meanings as (2.240) and (2.242), respectively.

(2.239) Which flights landed?
(2.240) Which flight landed?
(2.241) Some flights entered sector 2.
(2.242) A flight entered sector 2.

Quantifiers. Expressions introducing universal quantifiers, like *every* and *all*, will not be considered. This leaves only existential quantifiers at the logical level, and an interrogative version of them, which will be discussed in Chapter 3, avoiding issues related to quantifier scoping. More information about the task of quantifier scoping will be provided in Chapter 6.

Conjunction, disjunction, and negation. Conjunctions of words or phrases will not be considered. Among other things, this avoids phenomena related to sequencing of events (Hinrichs 1986; Hinrichs 1988; Webber 1988; Kamp & Reyle 1993; ter Meulen 1994; Hwang & Schubert 1994). For example, (2.243) is understood as saying that the patient died *after*, and probably as a result of, being given Qdrug (cf. (2.244)). In contrast, in (2.245) the patient was given Qdrug *while* he had high fever.

(2.243) Which patient was given Qdrug and died?
(2.244) ?Which patient died and was given Qdrug?
(2.245) Which patient had high fever and was given Qdrug?

Expressions introducing disjunction or negation, like *or*, *either*, *not*, *never*, will also not be considered. This simplifies TOP and the mapping to database language. Not supporting negation also avoids various temporal phenomena related to negation (Kamp & Reyle 1993: 546–555), and observations that negation causes aspectual shifts (Dowty 1986; Moens 1987).

Relative clauses. Relative clauses require special temporal treatment. For example, (2.246) most probably does not refer to a runway that was closed at an *arbitrary* past time. It probably refers to a runway that was closed at the time of the landing. The relation between the time of the relative clause and that of the main clause can vary. Dowty (1986) provides the example of (2.247), where the woman may have seen John during, before, or even after the stealing.

(2.246) Which flight landed on a runway that was closed?
(2.247) The woman that stole the book saw John.

Relative clauses can also be used with nouns that refer to the temporal ontology, like *period* in (2.248).

(2.248) Who was fired during the period that J. Adams was personnel manager?

Kamp and Reyle (1993: 663–664) provide additonal examples of temporal phenomena that involve relative clauses. As a simplification, relative clauses will not be considered in this book.

Passives. To simplify the HPSG grammar of Chapter 4, this book concentrates on active voice verb forms. It should be easy to extend the mechanisms of this book to cover passive forms as well.

2.14 Summary

This book uses an aspectual taxonomy of four classes: states, points, activities, and culminating activities. The taxonomy classifies verb forms, verb phrases, clauses, and sentences. Whenever the NLITDB is configured for a new application, the base form of each verb is assigned to one of the four aspectual classes. All the other verb forms normally inherit the aspectual class of the base form. Verb phrases, clauses, and sentences normally inherit the aspectual classes of their main verb forms. However, some linguistic mechanisms, like the progressive or some temporal adverbials, may cause the aspectual class of a verb form to differ from that of its base form, or the aspectual class of a verb phrase, clause, or sentence to differ from that of its main verb form. The aspectual taxonomy plays an important role in most time-related linguistic phenomena.

Six verb forms are examined in this book: simple present, simple past, present continuous, past continuous, present perfect, and past perfect; various simplifications have been introduced in their meanings. Some special temporal verbs were also identified; from these, *to start*, *to begin*, *to stop*, and *to finish* will be considered. Among temporal nouns, this book considers nouns like *year*, *month*, *day*, etc., and proper names like *Monday*, *January*, and *1/5/1999*. Temporal adjectives, are not considered, with the exception of *current*, which will be used to demonstrate the anaphoric behaviour of some noun phrases.

Among temporal adverbials, this book focuses on punctual adverbials, like *at 5:00 pm*, period adverbials introduced by *on*, *in*, *before*, or *after*, *today* and *yesterday*, and duration adverbials introduced by *for* and *in*. Temporal subordinate clauses are similar to temporal adverbials; this book considers subordinate clauses introduced by *while*, *before*, and *after*. Temporal anaphora is not considered in any detail, with the exception of the temporal anaphoric nature of noun phrases. Table 2.9 summarises in more detail the time-related linguistic phenomena of this book.

Table 2.9 Coverage of time-related linguistic phenomena in this book

verb forms	√ simple present (excluding scheduled meaning) √ simple past √ present continuous (excluding future meaning) √ past continuous (excluding future meaning) √ present perfect (treated as simple past) √ past perfect × other forms
temporal verbs	√ *to start*, *to begin*, *to stop*, *to finish* × other temporal verbs (e.g., *to happen*, *to follow*)
temporal nouns	√ *year*, *month*, *day*, etc. × *period*, *event*, *time*, etc. × nouns introducing situations (e.g., *inspection*) × nouns of temporal order (e.g., *predecessor*)
temporal adjectives	× (only *current*)
temporal adverbials	√ punctual adverbials (e.g., *at 5:00 pm*) √ period adverbials (only those introduced by *on*, *in*, *before*, or *after*, and *today*, *yesterday*) √ *for* duration adverbials √ *in* duration adverbials (only with culm. act. verbs) × frequency adverbials (e.g., *twice*) × order adverbials (e.g., *for the second time*) × other boundary adverbials (e.g., *since 1997*)
subordinate clauses	√ *while* clauses √ *before* and *after* clauses × relative clauses × other subordinate clauses (e.g., introduced by *when*)
anaphora	√ noun phrases and temporal reference × *January*, *August*, etc. (taken to refer to any of them) × tense anaphora × *that time*, *the following day*, etc.
other phenomena	× iterative meanings × cardinality and duration queries (*how many/long*) × cardinality expressions (e.g., *five flights*) and plurals × conjunctions of words or phrases × expressions introducing universal quantifiers, disjunction, negation

Chapter 3

The TOP meaning representation language

"Time will tell."

3.1 Introduction

This chapter defines TOP, the intermediate meaning representation language that will be used to represent the semantics of the English questions before translating them into database language. As already mentioned in Chapter 1, TOP employs temporal operators. For example, (3.1) is represented in TOP as (3.2). Roughly speaking, the *Past* operator requires *contain*(*tank*2, *water*) to be true at some past time e^v, and the *At* operator requires that time to fall within 1/10/1999. The answer to (3.1) is affirmative iff (3.2) evaluates to true.

(3.1) Did tank 2 contain water (some time) on 1/10/1999?

(3.2) $At[1/10/1999, Past[e^v, contain(tank2, water)]]$

An alternative operator-less approach is to introduce time as an extra argument of each predicate (Section 1.4). Temporal operators, however, lead to more compact formulae, and make the semantic contribution of each linguistic mechanism easier to see. In (3.2), for example, the simple past contributes the *Past* operator, while the *on* adverbial contributes the *At* operator. It is, nevertheless, entirely possible to capture the semantics of temporal linguistic mechanisms using operator-less representations, or to devise additional mappings to translate from TOP to operator-less representations (Androutsopoulos 2000); the latter will be discussed further in Chapter 7.

TOP is period-based, in the sense that the truth of a TOP formula is evaluated with respect to a time-period, i.e., a segment of the time-axis, rather than an individual time-point. A TOP formula may be true at a time-period without being true at the subperiods of that period. More precisely, following the Reichenbachian tradition (Reichenbach 1947), TOP formulae are evaluated with respect to three times: *speech time* (*st*), which is the time when the question is submitted, *event time* (*et*), which is a time when the situation described by the formula holds, and *localisation time* (*lt*), a temporal window within which *et* must be placed. TOP's localisation time is different from Reichenbach's 'reference time' (Section 2.5.5), but similar to the 'location time' of Kamp and Reyle (1993). While *st* is always a time-point, *et* and *lt* are generally periods, which is why TOP can be considered period-based, and in that sense similar to formal languages employed by Dowty (1982), Allen (1984), Lascarides (1988), Richards et al. (1989), Pratt and Bree (1995), and others. TOP was influenced by the representation language of Crouch and Pulman (1993), which was used in a natural language interface to a planner; see also Pirie et al. (1990). Comparisons between the two languages will be made at several points in this chapter, to demonstrate alternatives.

Although the aspectual classes of linguistic expressions affect how these expressions are represented in TOP, it is not always possible to tell the aspectual class of a linguistic expression by examining the corresponding TOP formula. The approach here is different from those of Dowty (1977; 1986), Lacarides (1988), and Kent (1993), where aspectual class is a property of formulae or denotations of formulae.

3.2 The syntax of TOP

Let us first define TOP's syntax. Informal comments about the semantics of TOP will also be given, to make the syntax definition easier to follow. The semantics of TOP, however, will be defined formally in later sections.

Terms. Two disjoint sets of strings, *CONS* and *VARS*, are assumed. *CONS* contains all the TOP constants, and *VARS* all the TOP variables. The suffix "*v*" distinguishes variables from constants. For example, *runway*^{v}, *gate*^{v} $\in$ *VARS*, while *ba737*, *1/5/1999* $\in$ *CONS*. *TERMS* is the set *CONS* $\cup$ *VARS*; it contains TOP's *terms*.

Predicate functors. *PFUNS* is a set containing all the strings that can be used as predicate functors in TOP's atomic formulae; this will be discussed further below.

Complete partitioning names. *CPARTS* is a set containing all the strings that can be used as names of *complete partitionings* of the time-axis. A complete partitioning of the time-axis is a set of consecutive non-overlapping periods, such that the union of all the periods covers the whole time-axis. A formal definition will be given in later sections. For example, the word *day* corresponds to the complete partitioning that contains the period which covers exactly the day 13/10/1999, the period which covers exactly 14/10/1999, etc. No two day-periods overlap, and together all the day-periods cover the whole time-axis. Similarly, *month* corresponds to the partitioning that contains the period for October 1999, the period for November 1999, etc. The suffix '^{c}' is used with elements of *CPARTS*; for example, day^c, $month^c$.

Gappy partitioning names. *GPARTS* is a set containing all the strings that can be used as names of *gappy partitionings* of the time-axis. A gappy partitioning of the time-axis is a set of non-overlapping periods, such that the union of all the periods does *not* cover the whole time-axis. For example, the word *Monday* corresponds to the gappy partitioning that contains the period which covers exactly the Monday 19/3/2001, the period which covers exactly the Monday 26/3/2001, etc. No Monday-period overlaps another Monday-period, and all the Monday-periods together do not cover the whole time-axis. Similarly, the English expression *5:00 pm* can be taken to denote the gappy partitioning that contains the period which covers exactly the 5:00 pm minute of 24/10/1999, the period which covers the 5:00 pm minute of 25/10/1999, etc. The suffix '^{g}' is used with elements of *GPARTS*; for example, $monday^g$, $5{:}00pm^g$.

Partitioning names. *PARTS* is the set *CPARTS* ∪ *GPARTS*.

Atomic formulae. *AFORMS* contains all the atomic formulae of TOP. It is the smallest possible set, such that:

- If $\pi \in PFUNS$, and $\tau_1, \tau_2, \ldots, \tau_n \in TERMS$, then $\pi(\tau_1, \tau_2, \ldots, \tau_n) \in AFORMS$. $\pi(\tau_1, \tau_2, \ldots, \tau_n)$ is called a *predicate*. $\tau_1, \tau_2, \ldots, \tau_n$ are the *arguments* of the predicate.
- If $\sigma \in PARTS$, $\beta \in VARS$, and $\nu_{ord} \in \{\ldots, -3, -2, -1, 0\}$, then $Part[\sigma, \beta, \nu_{ord}] \in AFORMS$ and $Part[\sigma, \beta] \in AFORMS$.

Greek letters are used as meta-variables, i.e., they stand for expressions of TOP. Predicates, like $be\_at(ba737, gate^v)$, describe situations in the world. $Part[\sigma, \beta, \nu_{ord}]$ means that β is a period in the partitioning σ. The ν_{ord} is used to select a particular period from the partitioning. If $\nu_{ord} = 0$, then β is the current period of the partitioning, i.e., the period that contains *st*. If $\nu_{ord} < 0$, then β is the $-\nu_{ord}$-th period of the partitioning before the current one. When there is no need to select a particular period from a partitioning, the $Part[\sigma, \beta]$ form is used.

Yes/no formulae. Yes/no formulae represent questions that are to be answered with a *yes* or *no* (e.g., '*Is BA737 circling?*'). *YNFORMS* is the set of all these formulae. It is the smallest possible set, such that if $\pi \in PFUNS$, $\tau, \tau_1, \ldots, \tau_n \in TERMS$, $\varphi, \varphi_1, \varphi_2 \in YNFORMS$, $\sigma_c \in CPARTS$, $\nu_{qty} \in \{1, 2, 3, \ldots\}$, and $\beta \in VARS$, then all the following hold:

- $AFORMS \subseteq YNFORMS$
- $\varphi_1 \wedge \varphi_2 \in YNFORMS$
- $Pres[\varphi], Past[\beta, \varphi], Perf[\beta, \varphi] \in YNFORMS$
- $At[\tau, \varphi], At[\varphi_1, \varphi_2] \in YNFORMS$
- $Before[\tau, \varphi], Before[\varphi_1, \varphi_2], After[\tau, \varphi], After[\varphi_1, \varphi_2] \in YNFORMS$
- $Ntense[\beta, \varphi], Ntense[now^*, \varphi] \in YNFORMS$
- $For[\sigma_c, \nu_{qty}, \varphi], Fills[\varphi] \in YNFORMS$
- $Begin[\varphi], End[\varphi] \in YNFORMS$
- $Culm[\pi(\tau_1, \ldots, \tau_n)] \in YNFORMS$

In the expressions above, β must not occur in φ. This restriction simplifies the translation to database language of Chapter 5, without imposing any additional restrictions to the linguistic coverage. No negation and disjunction connectives are defined, because English expressions introducing these connectives are not considered (Section 2.13). For the same reason, no universal quantifiers are defined. All variables can be thought of as existentially quantified; hence, no explicit existential quantifier is needed. An informal explanation of the operators above follows; their semantics will be defined formally, using *st*, *et*, and *lt* in subsequent sections.

$Pres[\varphi]$ means that φ is true at the present. For example, (3.3) is represented as (3.4). $Past[\beta, \varphi]$ means that φ is true at some past time β. The *Perf* operator is used along with the *Past* operator to express the past perfect. For example, (3.5) and (3.7) are represented as (3.6) and (3.8), respectively. Roughly speaking, e^v and $e2^v$ act as pointers to the times where the runway was open, while $e1^v$ points to the reference time of the past perfect (Section 2.5.5); the role of these variables will become clearer in later sections.

(3.3) Runway 2 is open.
(3.4) $Pres[open(runway2)]$
(3.5) Runway 2 was open.
(3.6) $Past[e^v, open(runway2)]$
(3.7) Runway 2 had been open.
(3.8) $Past[e1^v, Perf[e2^v, open(runway2)]]$

$At[\tau, \varphi]$ means that φ holds some time within a period τ, and $At[\varphi_1, \varphi_2]$ means that φ_2 holds at some time where φ_1 holds. For example, (3.9) and (3.11) are represented as (3.10) and (3.12), respectively.

(3.9) Runway 2 was open (some time) on 1/1/1999.
(3.10) $At[1/1/1999, Past[e^v, open(runway2)]]$
(3.11) Runway 2 was open (some time) while BA737 was circling.
(3.12) $At[Past[e1^v, circling(ba737)], Past[e2^v, open(runway2)]]$

$Before[\tau, \varphi]$ means that φ is true at some time before a period τ, and $Before[\varphi_1, \varphi_2]$ means that φ_2 is true at some time before a time where φ_1 is true. $After[\tau, \varphi]$ and $After[\varphi_1, \varphi_2]$ have similar meanings. For example, (3.13) and (3.15) are represented as (3.14) and (3.16), respectively.

(3.13) Tank 2 was empty (some time) after 1/1/1999.
(3.14) $After[1/1/1999, Past[e^v, empty(tank2)]]$
(3.15) Tank 2 was empty (some time) before the bomb exploded.
(3.16) $Before[Past[e1^v, explode(bomb)], Past[e2^v, empty(tank2)]]$

Ntense is used to capture the anaphoric nature of noun phrases (Section 2.11). $Ntense[\beta, \varphi]$ means that φ holds at a time β, and $Ntense[now^*, \varphi]$ means that φ holds at the present. The reading of (3.17) that refers to the person who was the president during the visit is represented as (3.18); the reading that refers to the current president is represented as (3.19).

(3.17) The president was visiting Edinburgh.
(3.18) $Ntense[e1^v, president(p^v)] \wedge Past[e1^v, visiting(p^v, edinburgh)]$
(3.19) $Ntense[now^*, president(p^v)] \wedge Past[e1^v, visiting(p^v, edinburgh)]$

$For[\sigma_c, \nu_{qty}, \varphi]$ means that φ holds throughout a period that is ν_{qty} σ_c-periods long. For example, (3.20) is represented as (3.21).

(3.20) Runway 2 was open for two days.
(3.21) $For[day^c, 2, Past[e^v, open(runway2)]]$

The *Fills* operator can be used to capture durative readings (Section 2.9.2). The reading of (3.22) whereby the tank was empty *throughout* 1998 is captured by (3.23). In contrast, (3.24) means that the tank was empty some time in 1998, but not necessarily throughout that year.

(3.22) Tank 2 was empty in 1998.
(3.23) $At[1998, Past[e^v, Fills[empty(tank2)]]]$
(3.24) $At[1998, Past[e^v, empty(tank2)]]$

$Begin[\varphi]$ refers to a time-point where the situation denoted by φ starts, and $End[\varphi]$ to a point where it stops. For example, (3.25) and (3.27) can be represented as (3.26) and (3.28), respectively.

(3.25) BA737 started to land.
(3.26) $Past[e^v, Begin[landing(ba737)]]$
(3.27) Tank 2 stopped being empty.
(3.28) $Past[e^v, End[empty(tank2)]]$

Finally, *Culm* is used to represent sentences where culminating activity verbs appear in forms that require the climax to have been reached. The *Culm* operator will be discussed further in subsequent sections.

Wh-formulae. Wh-formulae are used to represent questions that contain interrogatives (e.g., '*Which/Who/When* ... ?'). *WHFORMS* is the set of all wh-formulae. $WHFORMS \stackrel{def}{=} WHFORMS_1 \cup WHFORMS_2$, where:

– $WHFORMS_1$ is the set of the expressions $?\beta_1\ ?\beta_2\ \dots\ ?\beta_n\ \varphi$, where $\beta_1, \beta_2, \dots, \beta_n \in VARS$, $\varphi \in YNFORMS$, and each one of $\beta_1, \beta_2, \dots, \beta_n$ occurs at least once within φ.
– $WHFORMS_2$ is the set of all the expressions $?_{mxl}\beta_1\ ?\beta_2\ ?\beta_3\ \dots\ ?\beta_n\ \varphi$, where $\beta_1, \beta_2, \beta_3, \dots, \beta_n \in VARS$, $\varphi \in YNFORMS$, each one of $\beta_2, \dots, \beta_n$ occurs at least once within φ, and β_1 occurs at least once within φ as the first argument of a *Past*, *Perf*, *At*, *Before*, *After*, or *Ntense* operator, or as the second argument of a *Part* operator.

The '?' is the *interrogative quantifier*, and '$?_{mxl}$' is the *interrogative-maximal quantifier*. The interrogative quantifier is similar to an explicit existential quantifier, but it has the additional effect of reporting the values of its variables that satisfy its scope. Intuitively, $?\beta_1\ ?\beta_2\ \dots\ ?\beta_n\ \varphi$ means "report all $\beta_1, \beta_2, \dots, \beta_n$, such that φ". For example, (3.29) is represented as (3.30).

(3.29) Which runways are open?
(3.30) $?r^v\ Ntense[now^*, runway(r^v)] \wedge Pres[open(r^v)]$

The constraint that each one of $\beta_1, \dots, \beta_n$ must occur at least once within φ rules out meaningless formulae like $?o^v\ Past[manager(john)]$, where the o^v does not have any relation to the rest of the formula. This constraint is similar to the notion of *safety* in DATALOG (Ullman 1988), and is needed in the translation from TOP to database language; see also van Gelder and Topor (1991).

The interrogative-maximal quantifier is similar, except that it reports only *maximal* periods. $?_{mxl}$ is intended to be used only with variables that denote periods, and this is why in the case of $?_{mxl}$ the syntax of TOP requires β_1 to occur at certain positions that guarantee it will denote a period. Intuitively, $?_{mxl}\beta_1\ ?\beta_2\ \ldots ?\beta_n\ \varphi$ means "report all the maximal periods β_1, and all $\beta_2, \ldots, \beta_n$, such that φ". The interrogative-maximal quantifier is used in '*When … ?*' questions, where we want the answer to contain only the *maximal* periods during which a situation held, not all of these periods. If, for example, gate 2 was open from 9:00 am to 11:00 am and from 3:00 pm to 5:00 pm, we want the answer to (3.31) to contain only the two maximal periods 9:00 am to 11:00 am and 3:00 pm to 5:00 pm, not any of their subperiods, like 9:30 am to 10:30 am. To achieve this, the question is represented as (3.32).

(3.31) When was gate 2 open?
(3.32) $?_{mxl}e^v\ Past[e^v, open(gate2)]$

Formulae. *FORMS*, the set of all TOP formulae, is the union *YNFORMS* ∪ *WHFORMS*.

3.3 TOP's temporal ontology

Before proceeding to the semantics of TOP, we will examine more closely the temporal ontology on which TOP is based.

TOP assumes that time is discrete, linear, bounded, and consisting of time-points. *PTS* is the set of all time-points. More formally, a binary precedence relation $\prec$ over $PTS \times PTS$ is assumed, and time is taken to have the following properties:

– If $t_1, t_2, t_3 \in PTS$, $t_1 \prec t_2$, and $t_2 \prec t_3$, then $t_1 \prec t_3$ (*transitivity*).
– If $t \in PTS$, then $t \prec t$ does not hold (*irreflexivity*).
– If $t_1, t_2 \in PTS$ and $t_1 \neq t_2$, then exactly one of the following holds: $t_1 \prec t_2$ or $t_2 \prec t_1$ (*linearity*).
– There is a $t_{first} \in PTS$, such that for all $t \in PTS$, $t_{first} \preceq t$ (*left boundedness*). Similarly, there is a $t_{last} \in PTS$, such that for all $t \in PTS$, $t \preceq t_{last}$ (*right boundedness*).
– For every $t_1, t_2 \in PTS$, with $t_1 \neq t_2$, there is at most a finite number of $t_3 \in PTS$, such that $t_1 \prec t_3 \prec t_2$ (*discreteness*).

Hereafter, $next(t_1)$ denotes the time-point immediately after t_1. More formally, if $t_1 \in PTS - \{t_{last}\}$, then $next(t_1) = t_2$ iff $t_2 \in PTS$, $t_1 \prec t_2$, and for no $t_3 \in PTS$ is it true that $t_1 \prec t_3 \prec t_2$. In a similar manner, if $t_1 \in PTS - \{t_{first}\}$, then $prev(t_1)$ denotes the time-point immediately before t_1. Below, whenever $next(t)$ is used, it is assumed that $t \neq t_{last}$. Similarly, when $prev(t)$ is used, $t \neq t_{first}$.

A *period* p is a non-empty subset of *PTS* with the following property:

– If $t_1, t_2 \in p$, $t_3 \in PTS$, and $t_1 \prec t_3 \prec t_2$, then $t_3 \in p$ (*convexity*).

PERIODS is the set of all periods. *PERIODS** is the set $PERIODS \cup \{\emptyset\}$, i.e., *PERIODS** contains also the empty set, which is not a period. A period that contains only one time-point is called an *instantaneous period*. *INSTANTS* is the set of all instantaneous periods. Note that the term 'interval' is often used in the literature instead of 'period'. Unfortunately, the database language of Chapter 5 assigns a different meaning to 'interval'. Hence, this book uses 'period' instead of 'interval'.

Iff $p_1, p_2 \in PERIODS$ and $p_1 \subseteq p_2$, then p_1 is a *subperiod* of p_2. The notation $p_1 \sqsubseteq p_2$ is used in this case; $p_1 \subseteq p_2$ is weaker than $p_1 \sqsubseteq p_2$, because it does not guarantee that $p_1, p_2 \in PERIODS$. Iff $p_1, p_2 \in PERIODS$ and $p_1 \subset p_2$, then p_1 is a *proper subperiod* of p_2, written $p_1 \sqsubset p_2$. The definitions of *superperiod* and *proper superperiod* are similar.

If S is a set of periods, then $mxlpers(S)$ is the set of *maximal periods* of S. A period of S is maximal iff it is not a proper subperiod of another period in S. If $S \subseteq PTS$, $minpt(S)$ and $maxpt(S)$ denote the earliest and latest time-points in S, respectively. Following standard conventions, $[t_1, t_2]$ denotes the set $\{t \in PTS \mid t_1 \preceq t \preceq t_2\}$, and $(t_1, t_2]$ denotes the set $\{t \in PTS \mid t_1 \prec t \preceq t_2\}$. $[t_1, t_2)$ and (t_1, t_2) are defined similarly.

3.4 TOP model

We now turn to the semantics of TOP, defining first TOP's *models*. A TOP model is a tuple $M = \langle OBJS, f_{cons}, f_{pfuns}, f_{culms}, f_{gparts}, f_{cparts}\rangle$, such that $PERIODS \subseteq OBJS$, and f_{cons}, f_{pfuns}, f_{culms}, f_{gparts}, and f_{cparts} are as below.

OBJS is a set containing all the objects in the modelled world that can be denoted by TOP terms. In the airport domain, for example, *OBJS* contains all the gates and runways of the airport, the inspectors, the flights, etc. The constraint $PERIODS \subseteq OBJS$ ensures that all the periods are treated as world objects; this simplifies the semantics of TOP.

f_{cons} is a function $CONS \mapsto OBJS$. The notation $D \mapsto R$ denotes a function with domain D and range R. f_{cons} specifies which world object each constant denotes. In the airport domain, f_{cons} would map the constant *gate*2 to a gate object, and *ba*737 to a flight object.

f_{pfuns} is a function that maps each pair $\langle \pi, n \rangle$, where $\pi \in PFUNS$ and $n \in \{1, 2, 3, \dots\}$, to another function $(OBJS)^n \mapsto pow(PERIODS)$. $pow(S)$ denotes the *powerset* of S, i.e., the set of all subsets of S. $(OBJS)^n$ is the n-ary cartesian product $OBJS \times OBJS \times \cdots \times OBJS$. That is, for every $\pi \in PFUNS$ and each $n \in \{1, 2, 3, \dots\}$, $f_{pfuns}(\pi, n)$ is a function that maps each n-tuple of elements of $OBJS$ to a set of periods (an element of $pow(PERIODS)$). Intuitively, if $\tau_1, \tau_2, \dots, \tau_n$ are TOP terms denoting the world objects $o_1, o_2, \dots, o_n$, then $f_{pfuns}(\pi, n)(o_1, o_2, \dots, o_n)$ is the set of the maximal periods where the situation represented by $\pi(\tau_1, \tau_2, \dots, \tau_n)$ is true. For example, if the constant *ba*737 denotes a flight-object o_1, *gate*2 denotes a gate object o_2, and *be_at*(*ba*737, *gate*2) represents the situation whereby flight o_1 is located at gate o_2, then $f_{pfuns}(be\_at, 2)(o_1, o_2)$ will be the set that contains all the maximal periods where flight o_1 is located at gate o_2.

For every $\pi \in PFUNS$, $n \in \{1, 2, 3, \dots\}$, and $\langle o_1, \dots, o_n \rangle \in (OBJS)^n$, it must be the case that:

$$\text{if } p_1, p_2 \in f_{pfuns}(\pi, n)(o_1, \dots, o_n) \text{ and } p_1 \cup p_2 \in PERIODS, \text{ then } p_1 = p_2.$$

This ensures that no two different periods p_1, p_2 in $f_{pfuns}(\pi, n)(o_1, \dots, o_n)$ overlap or are adjacent, because if they overlap or they are adjacent, then their union is also a period, and then it must be true that $p_1 = p_2$. Intuitively, if p_1 and p_2 overlap or are adjacent, we want $f_{pfuns}(\pi, n)(o_1, \dots, o_n)$ to contain their union $p_1 \cup p_2$ instead of p_1 and p_2.

f_{culms} is a function that maps each pair $\langle \pi, n \rangle$, where $\pi \in PFUNS$ and $n \in \{1, 2, 3, \dots\}$, to another function $(OBJS)^n \mapsto \{T, F\}$. T and F are the two truth values. That is, for every $\pi \in PFUNS$ and $n \in \{1, 2, 3, \dots\}$, $f_{culms}(\pi, n)$ is a function that maps each n-tuple of $OBJS^n$ to T or F. f_{culms} is consulted only for predicates that represent actions or changes that have inherent climaxes. If $\pi(\tau_1, \dots, \tau_n)$ represents such an action or change, and $\tau_1, \dots, \tau_n$ denote the world objects $o_1, \dots, o_n$, then $f_{pfuns}(\pi, n)(o_1, \dots, o_n)$ is the set of maximal periods where the action or change is ongoing. $f_{culms}(\pi, n)(o_1, \dots, o_n)$ shows whether or not the climax is reached at the end of the latest maximal period. For example, if the constant *j_adams* denotes a person o_1, *bridge*2 denotes an object o_2, and *building*(*j_adams*, *ba*737) represents the situation whereby o_1 is building o_2, then $f_{pfuns}(building, 2)(o_1, o_2)$ is the set of all maximal periods where o_1 is building o_2. $f_{culms}(building, 2)(o_1, o_2)$ will be T if the building is completed at the end-point of the latest maximal period, and F otherwise. The role of f_{culms} will become clearer in subsequent sections.

f_{gparts} is a function that maps each element of *GPARTS* to a gappy partitioning (Section 3.2). More formally, a gappy partitioning is a subset S of *PERIODS*, such that for every $p_1, p_2 \in S$, $p_1 \cap p_2 = \emptyset$ and $\bigcup_{p \in S} p \neq PTS$. Similarly, f_{cparts} is a function that maps each element of *CPARTS* to a complete partitioning. A complete partitioning is a subset S of *PERIODS*, such that for every $p_1, p_2 \in S$, $p_1 \cap p_2 = \emptyset$ and $\bigcup_{p \in S} p = PTS$. For example, $f_{gparts}(monday^g)$ could be the gappy partitioning of all Monday-periods, and $f_{cparts}(day^c)$ the complete partitioning of all day-periods.

3.5 Variable assignment

A variable assignment with respect to (w.r.t.) a TOP model M is a function $g : VARS \mapsto OBJS$. That is, g assigns a world object to each variable. G_M, or simply G, is the set of all possible variable assignments w.r.t. M, i.e., the set of all functions $VARS \mapsto OBJS$.

If $g \in G$, $\beta \in VARS$, and $o \in OBJS$, then g_o^β is the variable assignment defined as follows: $g_o^\beta(\beta) = o$, and for every $\beta' \in VARS$ with $\beta' \neq \beta$, $g_o^\beta(\beta') = g(\beta')$.

3.6 Denotation of a TOP expression

As already mentioned, TOP formulae, and generally TOP expressions, are evaluated with respect to three times: speech time (*st*), event time (*et*), and localisation time (*lt*). More formally, $st \in PTS$, $et \in PERIODS$, and $lt \in PERIODS^*$. Intuitively, *st* is the time-point where the English question is submitted to the NLITDB; *et* is a period, not necessarily maximal, where the situation represented by the TOP expression takes place; and *lt* can be thought of as a temporal window, within which *et* must be located. When computing the denotation of a TOP expression, *lt* is initially set to *PTS*. That is, the temporal window covers the whole time-axis, and *et* is allowed to be located anywhere. Various operators, however, may narrow down *lt*, imposing constraints on where *et* can be placed.

The denotation of a TOP expression ξ w.r.t. a model M, *st*, *et*, *lt*, and a variable assignment g is written $\|\xi\|^{M,st,et,lt,g}$ or simply $\|\xi\|^{st,et,lt,g}$. When the denotation does not depend on *st*, *et*, and *lt*, the notation $\|\xi\|^{M,g}$, or simply $\|\xi\|^{g}$, will be used.

Denotation of terms and atomic formulae w.r.t. M, st, et, lt, g. The denotations of TOP expressions w.r.t. *M*, *st*, *et*, *lt*, and *g* are defined recursively, starting with the denotations of terms and atomic formulae, which are defined below.

- If $\kappa \in CONS$, then $\|\kappa\|^{g} = f_{cons}(\kappa)$.
- If $\beta \in VARS$, then $\|\beta\|^{g} = g(\beta)$.
- If $\varphi \in YNFORMS$, then $\|\varphi\|^{st,et,lt,g} \in \{T, F\}$.

The general rule above means that with yes/no formulae, we only need to define when the denotation is *T*; in all other cases the denotation is *F*.

- If $\varphi_1, \varphi_2 \in YNFORMS$, then $\|\varphi_1 \wedge \varphi_2\|^{st,et,lt,g} = T$ iff $\|\varphi_1\|^{st,et,lt,g} = T$ and $\|\varphi_2\|^{st,et,lt,g} = T$.
- If $\sigma \in PARTS$, $\beta \in VARS$, and $\nu_{ord} \in \{\ldots,-3,-2,-1,0\}$, then $\|Part[\sigma,\beta,\nu_{ord}]\|^{g}$ is *T* iff all the following hold. Below $f = f_{cparts}$ if $\sigma \in CPARTS$, and $f = f_{gparts}$ if $\sigma \in GPARTS$:
  - $g(\beta) \in f(\sigma)$.
  - If $\nu_{ord} = 0$, then $st \in g(\beta)$.
  - If $\nu_{ord} \leq -1$, then there are exactly $-\nu_{ord} - 1$ elements in the set: $\{p \in f(\sigma) \mid maxpt(g(\beta)) \prec minpt(p) \text{ and } maxpt(p) \prec st\}$

That is, if $\nu_{ord} = 0$, then β must denote the current period of the partitioning. If $\nu_{ord} \leq -1$, β must denote the $-\nu_{ord}$-th period of the partitioning that is completely situated before the speech time. For example, if $\nu_{ord} = -4$, then β must denote the 4th period which is completely situated before *st*; that is, there must be $-\nu_{ord} - 1 = 3$ periods in the partitioning that fall completely between the end of the period of β and *st*. If $f_{cparts}(day^c)$ is the partitioning of all day-periods, then $\|Part[day^c,\beta,0]\|^{g}$ is *T* iff $g(\beta)$ covers exactly the whole current day; this captures the meaning of *today*. Similarly, $\|Part[day^c,\beta,-1]\|^{g}$ is *T* iff $g(\beta)$ covers exactly the whole previous day; the meaning of *yesterday*. The definition of *Part* could be extended to allow positive values as its third argument, to express *tomorrow*, *next January*, etc.

- If $\sigma \in PARTS$ and $\beta \in VARS$, then $\|Part[\sigma,\beta]\|^{g} = T$ iff $g(\beta) \in f(\sigma)$, where f as above.
- If $\pi \in PFUNS$ and $\tau_1, \ldots, \tau_n \in TERMS$, then $\|\pi(\tau_1, \ldots, \tau_n)\|^{st,et,lt,g}$ is *T* iff $et \sqsubseteq lt$ and for some $p_{mxl} \in f_{pfuns}(\pi, n)(\|\tau_1\|^{g}, \|\tau_2\|^{g}, \ldots, \|\tau_n\|^{g})$, $et \sqsubseteq p_{mxl}$.

That is, for the denotation of a predicate to be T, et must fall within lt, and et must be a subperiod of a maximal period where the situation described by the predicate holds.

It is easy to prove that the definition above causes all TOP predicates to be *homogeneous*. A TOP formula is *homogeneous* iff for every $st \in PTS$, $et \in PERIODS$, $lt \in PERIODS^*$, and $g \in G$, the following implication holds:

$$\text{if } et' \sqsubseteq et \text{ and } \|\varphi\|^{st,et,lt,g} = T, \text{ then } \|\varphi\|^{st,et',lt,g} = T.$$

Intuitively, if a predicate is true at some et, then it is also true at any subperiod et' of et. Although TOP predicates are homogeneous, more complex formulae are not always homogeneous. Various versions of homogeneity have been used by Allen (1984), Lascarides (1988), Richards et al. (1989), Kent (1993), Pratt and Bree (1995), and others. The term 'homogeneity' is also used in the temporal databases literature, but with a completely different meaning (Jensen et al. 1998).

Denotation of wh-formula w.r.t. M, st, et, lt, g. The denotation of a wh-formula w.r.t. M, st, et, lt, and g is defined below, where it is assumed that $\beta_1, \ldots, \beta_n \in VARS$ and $\varphi \in YNFORMS$.

– $\|?\beta_1 \ldots ?\beta_n\ \varphi\|^{st,et,lt,g} = \{\langle g(\beta_1), \ldots, g(\beta_n)\rangle \mid \|\varphi\|^{st,et,lt,g} = T\}$

That is, if $\|\varphi\|^{st,et,lt,g} = T$, then $\|?\beta_1 \ldots ?\beta_n\ \varphi\|^{st,et,lt,g}$ is a one-element set: it contains one tuple that holds the world-objects assigned to $\beta_1, \ldots, \beta_n$ by g. Otherwise, $\|?\beta_1 \ldots ?\beta_n\ \varphi\|^{st,et,lt,g}$ is the empty set.

– $\|?_{mxl}\beta_1\ ?\beta_2 \ldots ?\beta_n\ \varphi\|^{st,et,lt,g} =$
$\{\langle g(\beta_1), g(\beta_2), \ldots, g(\beta_n)\rangle \mid \|\varphi\|^{st,et,lt,g} = T$ and
for no $et' \in PERIODS$ and $g' \in G$ is it true that
$\|\varphi\|^{st,et',lt,g'} = T,\ g(\beta_1) \sqsubset g'(\beta_1),\ g(\beta_2) = g'(\beta_2),\ \ldots,\ g(\beta_n) = g'(\beta_n)\}$

The denotation $\|?_{mxl}\beta_1\ ?\beta_2 \ldots ?\beta_n\ \varphi\|^{st,et,lt,g}$ is either a one-element set, that contains a tuple holding the world-objects $g(\beta_1), g(\beta_2), \ldots, g(\beta_n)$, or the empty set. The tuple contains the values assigned to $\beta_1, \beta_2, \ldots, \beta_n$ by g, if these values satisfy φ, and there is no other et' and variable assignment g' that assigns the same values to $\beta_2, \ldots, \beta_n$ and a superperiod of $g(\beta_1)$ to β_1, while still satisfying φ. That is, it must not be possible to extend any further the period assigned to β_1 by g, preserving at the same time the values assigned to $\beta_2, \ldots, \beta_n$, and satisfying φ. Otherwise, the denotation of $?_{mxl}\beta_1\ ?\beta_2 \ldots ?\beta_n\ \varphi$ is the empty set.

The syntax of TOP (Section 3.2) requires β_1 to appear at least once within φ as the first argument of a *Past*, *Perf*, *At*, *Before*, *After*, or *Ntense* operator, or as the second argument of a *Part* operator. The semantics of these operators require variables occurring at these positions to denote periods. Hence, variable assignments g that do not assign a period to β_1 will never satisfy φ, and no tuples for these variable assignments will be included in $\|?_{mxl}\beta_1\ ?\beta_2 \ldots ?\beta_n\ \varphi\|^{st,et,lt,g}$.

The denotations w.r.t. M, st, et, lt, and g of other TOP expressions will be defined in later sections.

Denotation w.r.t. M, st. We have so far considered the denotations of TOP expressions with respect to M, st, et, lt, and g. We will now define the denotations of TOP expressions with respect to only M and st. The denotation w.r.t. M and st is similar to the denotation w.r.t. M, st, et, lt, g, except that there is an implicit existential quantification over all $g \in G$ and $et \in PERIODS$, and lt is set to PTS, i.e., the whole time-axis. The denotation of φ w.r.t. M, st, written $\|\varphi\|^{M,st}$ or simply $\|\varphi\|^{st}$, is defined only for TOP formulae:

– If $\varphi \in YNFORMS$, then $\|\varphi\|^{st} =$

  – T, if for some $g \in G$ and $et \in PERIODS$, $\|\varphi\|^{st,et,PTS,g} = T$,
  – F, otherwise

– If $\varphi \in WHFORMS$, then $\|\varphi\|^{st} = \bigcup_{g \in G,\ et \in PERIODS} \|\varphi\|^{st,et,PTS,g}$.

Each question will be mapped to a TOP formula φ. (If the question is ambiguous, multiple formulae will be generated, one for each reading.) $\|\varphi\|^{st}$ specifies what the NLITDB's answer should report. When $\varphi \in YNFORMS$, $\|\varphi\|^{st} = T$, i.e., the answer should be affirmative, if for some assignment to the variables of φ and for some event time, φ is satisfied; otherwise $\|\varphi\|^{st} = F$, and the answer should be negative. The localisation time is set to PTS, the whole time-axis, to reflect the fact that initially there is no restriction on where et may be located. As already mentioned, however, when computing the denotations of the subformulae of φ, temporal operators may narrow down lt, placing restrictions on et.

In the case where $\varphi \in WHFORMS$, i.e., when $\varphi = ?\beta_1 \ldots ?\beta_n\ \varphi'$ or $\varphi = ?_{mxl}\beta_1 \ldots ?\beta_n\ \varphi'$ with $\varphi' \in YNFORMS$, $\|\varphi\|^{st}$ is the union of all $\|\varphi\|^{st,et,PTS,g}$, for every $g \in G$ and $et \in PERIODS$. For each g and et, $\|\varphi\|^{st,et,PTS,g}$ is either an empty set or a one-element set containing a tuple that holds values of $\beta_1, \ldots, \beta_n$ that satisfy φ'; β_1 must also be maximal if $\varphi \in WHFORMS_2$. Hence, $\|\varphi\|^{st}$, the union of all $\|\varphi\|^{st,et,PTS,g}$, is the set of all the tuples that hold values of

$\beta_1, \ldots, \beta_n$ that satisfy φ'. The answer should report these tuples to the user, or be a message like "No answer found" if $\|\varphi\|^{st} = \emptyset$.

3.7 The *Pres* operator

The *Pres* operator is used to express the simple present and present continuous. For $\varphi \in YNFORMS$:

– $\|Pres[\varphi]\|^{st,et,lt,g} = T$, iff $st \in et$ and $\|\varphi\|^{st,et,lt,g} = T$.

For example, (3.33) is represented as (3.34). Let us assume that the only maximal periods where BA737 is at gate 2 are p_{mxl_1} and p_{mxl_2}, i.e., (3.35) holds (Section 3.4). Let us also assume that (3.33) is submitted at a time-point st_1, such that (3.36) holds (Figure 3.1).

(3.33) Is BA737 at gate 2?
(3.34) $Pres[be\_at(ba737, gate2)]$
(3.35) $f_{pfuns}(be\_at, 2)(f_{cons}(ba737), f_{cons}(gate2)) = \{p_{mxl_1}, p_{mxl_2}\}$
(3.36) $st_1 \in p_{mxl_2}$

The answer to (3.33) will be affirmative iff (3.37) is T; and (3.37) is T iff for some $g \in G$ and $et \in PERIODS$, (3.38) holds (Section 3.6).

(3.37) $\|Pres[be\_at(ba737, gate2)]\|^{st_1}$
(3.38) $\|Pres[be\_at(ba737, gate2)]\|^{st_1,et,PTS,g} = T$

By the definition of *Pres*, (3.38) holds iff both (3.39) and (3.40) hold.

(3.39) $st_1 \in et$
(3.40) $\|be\_at(ba737, gate2)\|^{st_1,et,PTS,g} = T$

By the definitions of $\|\pi(\tau_1, \ldots, \tau_n)\|^{st,et,lt,g}$ and $\|\kappa\|^g$ (Section 3.6), (3.40) holds iff for some p_{mxl}, (3.41)–(3.43) hold.

(3.41) $et \sqsubseteq PTS$

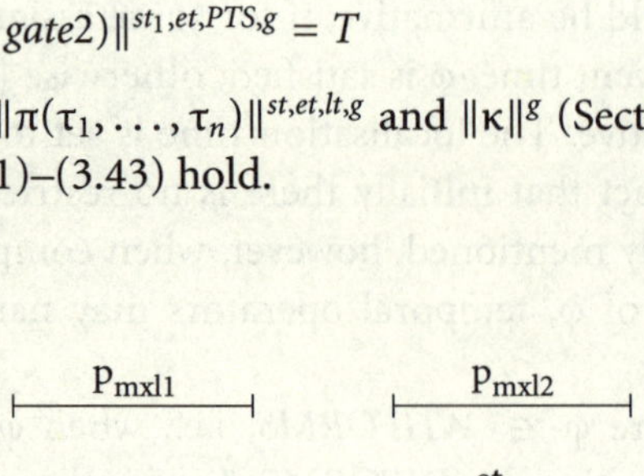

Figure 3.1 The semantics of the *Pres* operator

(3.42) $p_{mxl} \in f_{pfuns}(be\_at, 2)(f_{cons}(ba737), f_{cons}(gate2))$
(3.43) $et \sqsubseteq p_{mxl}$

By (3.35), (3.42) is equivalent to (3.44).

(3.44) $p_{mxl} \in \{p_{mxl_1}, p_{mxl_2}\}$

The answer to (3.33), then, will be affirmative iff for some $et \in PERIODS$ and some p_{mxl}, (3.39), (3.41), (3.43), and (3.44) hold. They all hold for $p_{mxl} = p_{mxl_2}$ and et any subperiod of p_{mxl_2} that contains st_1 (Figure 3.1). Hence, the answer to (3.33) will be affirmative, as one would expect. In contrast, if the question is submitted at an st_2 that falls outside p_{mxl_1} and p_{mxl_2} (Figure 3.1), then the answer will be negative, because in that case there is no subperiod et of p_{mxl_1} or p_{mxl_2} that contains st_2.

The present continuous is expressed similarly. For example, the reading of (3.45) where Airserve is actually servicing BA737 at the present moment is expressed as (3.46). Unlike proposals by Dowty (1977), Lascarides (1988), Crouch and Pulman (1993), and others, progressive forms do not introduce any progressive operator in TOP expressions. This will be discussed further when defining the semantics of the *Culm* operator.

(3.45) Airserve is (actually) servicing BA737.
(3.46) *Pres*[*servicing*(*airserve*, *ba*737)]

The habitual (3.47) is represented using a different predicate functor from that of (3.46), as in (3.48). (3.45) is taken to involve the non-habitual homonym of *to service*, while (3.47) is taken to involve the habitual one (Section 2.3). As will be explained in Chapter 4, the two homonyms introduce different predicate functors.

(3.47) Airserve (habitually) services BA737.
(3.48) *Pres*[*hab_server_of*(*airserve*, *ba*737)]

TOP's *Pres* operator is similar to that of Pirie et al. (1990). The main difference is that the *Pres* operator of Pirie et al. does not require *st* to fall within *et*. Instead, it narrows *lt* to start at or after *st*. This, in combination with the requirement $et \sqsubseteq lt$, requires *et* to start at or after *st*. Using this version of *Pres* in (3.34) causes the answer to be affirmative if (3.33) is submitted at st_2 (Figure 3.1), i.e., at a point where BA737 is not at gate 2, because there is an *et* at which BA737 is at gate 2 (e.g., the *et* of Figure 3.1), and this *et* starts after st_2. This version of *Pres* was adopted by Pirie et al. to cope with sentences like '*Who in-*

spects BA737 tomorrow?, where the simple present refers to a future inspection (Section 2.5.1), and *et* must be allowed to start after *st*.

To restrict the semantics of their *Pres* operator when it is over-permissive, Pirie et al. employ a post-processing mechanism, which is invoked after the English sentence is translated into meaning representation language. If the *Pres* is introduced by a state verb, excluding progressive states, and the verb is not modified by a temporal adverbial, then *et* is set to {*st*}. For example, in *J. Adams is at site 2* where the verb is a lexical state, the mechanism causes *et* to be set to {*st*}, which correctly requires J. Adams to be at site 2 at *st*. In *J. Adams is at site 2 tomorrow*, where the state verb is modified by a temporal adverbial, the post-processing has no effect, and *et* is allowed to start at or after *st*. In *J. Adams is inspecting site 2*, where the verb is a progressive state, the post-processing has again no effect, and *et* can start at or after *st*. The rationale in this case is that *et* cannot be set to {*st*}, because there is a reading where the present continuous refers to a future inspection (Section 2.5.3). For the purposes of this book, where future readings are ignored, TOP's *Pres* operator is adequate. If, however, future readings were to be supported, a more permissive *Pres* operator, like that of Pirie et al., might have to be adopted.

3.8 The *Past* operator

The *Past* operator is used when expressing the simple past, the past continuous, the past perfect, and the present perfect. TOP's *Past* operator is essentially the same as that of Pirie et al. (1990). For $\varphi \in YNFORMS$ and $\beta \in VARS$:

– $\|Past[\beta, \varphi]\|^{st,et,lt,g} = T$, iff $g(\beta) = et$ and $\|\varphi\|^{st,et,lt \cap [t_{first}, st),g} = T$.

The *Past* operator narrows the localisation time, forcing it to end before *st*. When computing the denotation of φ, *et* will be required to be a subperiod of the localisation time. Hence, *et* will be required to end before *st*. β is used as a pointer to *et*: its value is required to be *et*. β is useful in formulae that contain *Ntense* operators, to be discussed in subsequent sections. It is also useful in time-asking questions, where *et* has to be reported. For example, (3.49) is represented as (3.50). The latter reports the maximal *et*s that end before *st*, such that gate 2 is open throughout *et*.

(3.49) When was gate 2 open?

(3.50) $?_{mxl}e^v\ Past[e^v, open(gate2)]$

3.9 Progressives, non-progressives and the *Culm* operator

We now examine in more detail how TOP represents the simple past and the past continuous. We start from verbs whose base forms are culminating activities, like *to inspect* in the airport domain. The past continuous (3.51) is represented as (3.52).

(3.51) Was J. Adams inspecting BA737?
(3.52) $Past[e^v, inspecting(ja, ba737)]$

Let us assume that the inspection of BA737 by J. Adams started at the beginning of p_{mxl_1} (Figure 3.2), that it stopped temporarily at the end of p_{mxl_1}, that it was resumed at the beginning of p_{mxl_2}, and that it was completed at the end of p_{mxl_2}. Let us also assume that there is no other time where J. Adams is inspecting BA737. Then, (3.53) and (3.54) hold.

(3.53) $f_{pfuns}(inspecting, 2)(f_{cons}(ja), f_{cons}(ba737)) = \{p_{mxl_1}, p_{mxl_2}\}$
(3.54) $f_{culms}(inspecting, 2)(f_{cons}(ja), f_{cons}(ba737)) = T$

From the TOP definitions so far, it follows that (3.55) is T iff there is an *et* that is a subperiod of p_{mxl_1} or p_{mxl_2} and that ends before *st*.

(3.55) $\|Past[e^v, inspecting(ja, ba737)]\|^{st}$

If (3.51) is submitted at the st_1 or st_2 of Figure 3.2, then (3.55) is T, because in both cases there is an *et*, for example the et_1 of Figure 3.2, that ends before st_1 and st_2, and that is a subperiod of p_{mxl_1}. In contrast, if the question is submitted at st_3, (3.55) is F, because in this case there is no subperiod of p_{mxl_1} or p_{mxl_2} that ends before st_3. This is correct: at st_1 or st_2 the answer to (3.51) is affirmative, because J. Adams has already spent some time inspecting BA737; in contrast, at st_3 J. Adams has not yet spent any time inspecting BA737, and the answer is negative.

Let us now consider the simple past (3.56). We want the answer to be affirmative if (3.56) is submitted at st_1 or any other time-point after the end of p_{mxl_2},

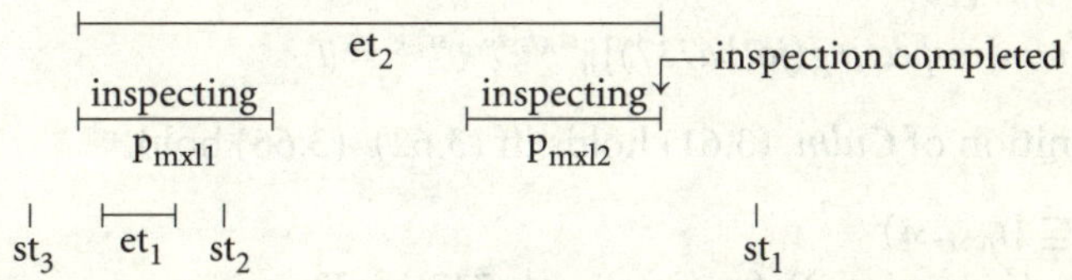

Figure 3.2 The semantics of the *Past* operator

but not if it is submitted at st_2 or any other time-point before the end of p_{mxl_2}, because at st_2 J. Adams has not yet completed the inspection. (3.56) cannot be represented as (3.52), because this would cause the answer to be affirmative if the question is submitted at st_2. Instead, (3.56) is represented as (3.57). The same predicate *inspecting(ja, ba737)* of (3.52) is used, but an additional *Culm* operator is inserted.

(3.56) Did J. Adams inspect BA737?
(3.57) $Past[e^v, Culm[inspecting(ja, ba737)]]$

Intuitively, the *Culm* operator requires the event time to be the et_2 of Figure 3.2, i.e., to cover the whole time from the point where the inspection starts to the point where the inspection is completed. If the inspection is never completed, the *Culm* operator causes the denotation of (3.57) to be *F*. Combined with the *Past* operator, the *Culm* operator causes the answer to be affirmative if (3.56) is submitted at st_1, because et_2 ends before st_1, and negative if the question is submitted at st_2, because et_2 does not end before st_2. More formally, for $\pi \in PFUNS$ and $\tau_1, \ldots, \tau_n \in TERMS$:

– $\|Culm[\pi(\tau_1, \ldots, \tau_n)]\|^{st,et,lt,g} = T$, iff
$et \sqsubseteq lt$, $f_{culms}(\pi, n)(\|\tau_1\|^g, \ldots, \|\tau_n\|^g) = T$, $S \neq \emptyset$, and
$et = [minpt(S), maxpt(S)]$, where $S = \bigcup_{p \in f_{pfuns}(\pi,n)(\|\tau_1\|^g,\ldots,\|\tau_n\|^g)} p$.

The $f_{culms}(\pi)(\|\tau_1\|^g, \ldots, \|\tau_n\|^g) = T$ means that the change or action of $\pi(\tau_1, \ldots, \tau_n)$ must reach its climax at the latest time-point where it is ongoing. The $et = [minpt(S), maxpt(S)]$ requires *et* to start at the first time-point where the change or action is ongoing, and to end at the latest point.

Let us now check formally that the denotation (3.58) of (3.57) is in order. (3.58) is *T* iff for some $g \in G$ and $et \in PERIODS$, (3.59) holds.

(3.58) $\|Past[e^v, Culm[inspecting(ja, ba737)]]\|^{st}$
(3.59) $\|Past[e^v, Culm[inspecting(ja, ba737)]]\|^{st,et,PTS,g} = T$

By the definition of *Past*, (3.59) holds iff (3.60) and (3.61) hold.

(3.60) $g(e^v) = et$
(3.61) $\|Culm[inspecting(ja, ba737)]\|^{st,et,[t_{first},st),g} = T$

By the definition of *Culm*, (3.61) holds iff (3.62)–(3.66) hold.

(3.62) $et \sqsubseteq [t_{first}, st)$
(3.63) $f_{culms}(inspecting, 2)(f_{cons}(ja), f_{cons}(ba737)) = T$
(3.64) $S \neq \emptyset$

(3.65) $et = [minpt(S), maxpt(S)]$
(3.66) $S = \bigcup_{p \in f_{pfuns}(inspecting,2)(f_{cons}(ja), f_{cons}(ba737))} p$

By (3.53), and assuming that $maxpt(p_{mxl_1}) \prec minpt(p_{mxl_2})$ as in Figure 3.2, (3.64)–(3.66) are equivalent to (3.67)–(3.68). (3.67) holds, because the union of two periods is never the empty set.

(3.67) $p_{mxl_1} \cup p_{mxl_2} \neq \emptyset$
(3.68) $et = [minpt(p_{mxl_1}), maxpt(p_{mxl_2})]$

(3.63) is the same as (3.54), which was assumed to hold. Hence, (3.58) is *T* iff for some $g \in G$ and $et \in PTS$, (3.60), (3.62), and (3.68) hold.

Let $et_2 = [minpt(p_{mxl_1}), maxpt(p_{mxl_2})]$, as in Figure 3.2, and let us assume that (3.56) is submitted at an *st* that follows the end of et_2; for example, st_1 in Figure 3.2. For $et = et_2$, (3.62) and (3.68) are satisfied. (3.60) is also satisfied by choosing $g = g_1$, where g_1 as below. Hence, the answer to (3.56) will be affirmative, as required.

$$g_1(\beta) = \begin{cases} et_2 & \text{if } \beta = e^v \\ o & \text{otherwise, where } o \text{ is an arbitrary element of } OBJS \end{cases}$$

In contrast, if (3.56) is submitted before the end of et_2, for example at st_2 or st_3 in Figure 3.2, then the answer will be negative, because there is no *et* that satisfies both (3.62) and (3.68).

In the case of verbs whose base forms are processes, states, or points, the simple past does not introduce a *Culm* operator. In this case, when both the simple past and the past continuous are possible, they are represented using the same TOP formula. For example, in the airport domain where *to circle* is a process, both (3.69) and (3.70) are represented as (3.71).

(3.69) Was BA737 circling?
(3.70) Did BA737 circle?
(3.71) $Past[e^v, circling(ba737)]$

The TOP definitions above imply that the denotation of (3.71) w.r.t. *st* is *T*, i.e., the answer to (3.69) and (3.70) is affirmative, iff there is an *et* which is a subperiod of a maximal period where BA737 was circling, and *et* ends before *st*. That is, the answer is affirmative iff BA737 was circling at some time before *st*. There is no requirement for the climax to have been reached.

The reader will have noticed that in the case of verbs whose base forms are culminating activities, the non-progressive form, in this case the simple past, is represented by adding a *Culm* operator to the TOP expression that represents the corresponding progressive form, here the past continuous. For example, assuming that *to build* is a culminating activity, (3.72) is represented as (3.73), and (3.74) as (3.75).

(3.72) Housecorp was building bridge 2.
(3.73) $Past[e^v, building(housecorp, bridge2)]$
(3.74) Housecorp built bridge 2.
(3.75) $Past[e^v, Culm[building(housecorp, bridge2)]]$

A similar approach is adopted by Parsons (1989). In contrast, Dotwy (1977), Lascarides (1988), Pirie et al. (1990), Kamp and Reyle (1993), and others represent progressive forms by adding a 'progressive' operator to the expressions that represent the non-progressive forms. For example, ignoring some details, Pirie et al. represent (3.72) and (3.74) as (3.76) and (3.77), respectively.

(3.76) $Past[e^v, Prog[build(housecorp, bridge2)]]$
(3.77) $Past[e^v, build(housecorp, bridge2)]$

In (3.77), the semantics that Pirie et al. assign to *build*(*housecorp*, *bridge*2) require *et* to cover the *whole* building of the bridge, from its beginning to the point where the building is complete. (In contrast, the semantics of TOP require *et* to be simply a period throughout which Housecorp was building bridge 2.) The *Past* operator of (3.77) requires *et* to end before *st*. Hence, the answer to (3.74) is affirmative iff the building was completed before *st*.

In (3.76), the semantics that Pirie et al. assign to *Prog* require *et* to be a subperiod of another period *et′* that covers the entire building, from start to completion, as in Figure 3.3. The *Past* operator of (3.76) requires *et* to end before *st*. If, for example, (3.72) is submitted at an *st* that falls between the end of *et* and the end of *et′* (Figure 3.3), the answer will be affirmative. This is correct, because at that *st* Housecorp has already been building the bridge for some time, although the bridge is not yet complete.

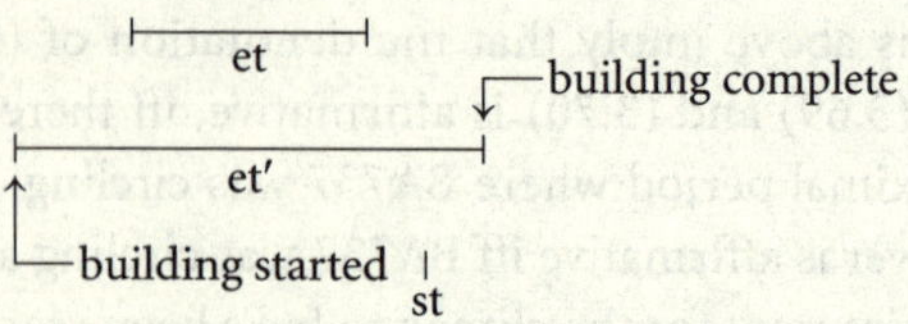

Figure 3.3 A flawed *Prog* operator

The *Prog* of Pirie et al., however, has a flaw (Crouch & Pulman 1993): (3.76) implies that there is a period *et′*, such that the building is completed at the end of *et′*; i.e., according to (3.76) the building was or will be necessarily completed at some time-point. This does not capture correctly the semantics of (3.72), which carries no implication that the building was or will ever be completed. TOP's representation of (3.72), i.e., (3.73), does not suffer from this problem, because it does not assume that the building is ever completed.

To overcome similar problems with *Prog* operators, 'branching' models of time or 'possible worlds' have been employed (Dowty 1977; McDermott 1982; Mays 1986; Kent 1993); see also Lascarides (1988) for criticism of possible-worlds approaches. Branching time and possible worlds, however, seem unnecessarily complex for the purposes of this book.

3.10 The *At*, *Before* and *After* operators

The *At*, *Before*, and *After* operators are used to express punctual adverbials, period adverbials, and subordinate clauses introduced by *while*, *before*, and *after* (Sections 2.9 and 2.10). For $\varphi, \varphi_1, \varphi_2 \in \mathit{YNFORMS}$ and $\tau \in \mathit{TERMS}$:

- $\|At[\tau, \varphi]\|^{st,et,lt,g} = T$, iff $\|\tau\|^g \in \mathit{PERIODS}$ and $\|\varphi\|^{st,et,lt \cap \|\tau\|^g,g} = T$.
- $\|At[\varphi_1, \varphi_2]\|^{st,et,lt,g} = T$, iff for some et' $et' \in mxlpers(\{e \in \mathit{PERIODS} \mid \|\varphi_1\|^{st,e,PTS,g} = T\})$ and $\|\varphi_2\|^{st,et,lt \cap et',g} = T$.

In the first form of the *At* operator, τ must denote a period. The localisation time is narrowed to the intersection of the original *lt* with the period of τ. In the second form of the *At* operator, the localisation time of φ_2 is narrowed to the intersection of the original *lt* with a maximal event time period *et′* where φ_1 holds.

For example, (3.78) is represented as (3.79). In (3.79), *lt* initially covers the whole time-axis. Assuming that the constant *25/9/1999* denotes the obvious period, the *At* operator causes *lt* to become the period that covers exactly 25/9/1999. The *Past* operator then forces *lt* to end before *st*. If 25/9/1999 is entirely in the past, the *Past* operator has no effect. The answer to (3.78) is affirmative iff it is possible to find an *et* that is a subperiod of the resulting *lt*, such that tank 2 was empty during *et*.

(3.78) Was tank 2 empty (some time) on 25/9/1999?

(3.79) $At[\mathit{25/9/1999}, Past[e^v, empty(tank2)]]$

If (3.78) is submitted *before* 25/9/1999, the NLITDB's answer will be negative, because the *At* and *Past* operators cause *lt* to become the empty set, and hence it is impossible to find a subperiod *et* of *lt* where tank 2 is empty. This is not entirely satisfactory. (3.78) is unacceptable, if uttered before 25/9/95, and the system should warn the user about this. The unacceptability of (3.78) in this case seems related to the unacceptability of (3.80), which would be represented as (3.81). (The definition of *Part* would have to be extended to allow positive values of its third argument.)

(3.80) *Was tank 2 empty tomorrow?
(3.81) $Part[day^c, tom^v, 1] \land At[tom^v, Past[e^v, empty(tank2)]]$

In both cases, the combination of the simple past and the adverbial causes *lt* to become the empty set. In (3.81), for example, tom^v denotes the period that covers exactly the day after *st*. The *At* and *Past* operators set *lt* to the intersection of that period with $[t_{first}, st)$. The two periods do not overlap, i.e., $lt = \emptyset$; hence, it is impossible to find a subperiod *et* of *lt*. This causes the answer to be always negative, regardless of what happens in the world, i.e., regardless of when tank 2 is empty. It may be the case that the questions sound unacceptable, because people, using a concept similar to TOP's *lt*, realise that the answers can never be affirmative. This suggests that the NLITDB should generate a cooperative response when $lt = \emptyset$, explaining that the question is problematic. This would be similar to the 'overlap rule' of Harper (1986) and the 'non-triviality constraint' of Kamp and Reyle (1993:653). As this book does not consider cooperative responses (Section 1.2), mechanisms of this type will not be explored further.

Moving to further examples, (3.82) and (3.84) are represented as (3.83) and (3.85), respectively. Unlike the *on 25/9/1999* of (3.78), which is represented using a constant (*25/9/1999*), the *on Monday* of (3.82) is represented using a variable (mon^v) that ranges over the periods of the partitioning of Monday-periods. Similarly, the *at 5:00 pm* of (3.84) is represented using a variable (fv^v) that ranges over the 5:00 pm minute-periods.

(3.82) Was tank 2 empty on Monday?
(3.83) $Part[monday^g, mon^v] \land At[mon^v, Past[e^v, empty(tank2)]]$
(3.84) Was tank 2 empty on Monday at 5:00 pm?
(3.85) $Part[monday^g, mon^v] \land Part[5{:}00pm^g, fv^v] \land At[mon^v, At[fv^v, Past[e^v, empty(tank2)]]]$

(3.83) requires tank 2 to have been empty at some past *et* that falls within some Monday. No attempt is made to determine exactly which Monday the user has in mind (Section 2.12). Similarly, (3.85) requires tank 2 to have been empty at some past *et* that falls within the intersection of some 5:00 pm minute-period with some Monday-period.

Assuming that *to inspect* is a culminating activity, as in the airport domain, the reading of (3.86) that requires the inspection to have both started and been completed within the previous day (Section 2.9.2) is represented as (3.87). The *Culm* requires *et* to cover exactly the whole inspection, from its beginning to its completion. The *Past* requires *et* to end before *st*, and the *At* requires *et* to fall within the day before *st*.

(3.86) Did J. Adams inspect BA737 yesterday?
(3.87) $Part[day^c, y^v, -1] \land At[y^v, Past[e^v, Culm[inspecting(ja, ba737)]]]$

In contrast, (3.88) is represented as (3.89). In this case, *et* must be simply a subperiod of a maximal period where J. Adams was inspecting BA737, and it must be located within the previous day.

(3.88) Was J. Adams inspecting BA737 yesterday?
(3.89) $Part[day^c, y^v, -1] \land At[y^v, Past[e^v, inspecting(ja, ba737)]]$

Finally, (3.90) is represented as (3.91), which requires BA737 to have been circling at some past period $e2^v$, that falls within some past maximal period $e1^v$ where gate 2 was open.

(3.90) Did BA737 circle while gate 2 was open?
(3.91) $At[Past[e1^v, open(gate2)], Past[e2^v, circling(ba737)]]$

The *Before* and *After* operators are similar. They are used to express adverbials and subordinate clauses introduced by *before* and *after*. For $\varphi, \varphi_1, \varphi_2 \in$ *YNFORMS* and $\tau \in$ *TERMS*:

- $\|Before[\tau, \varphi]\|^{st,et,lt,g} = T$, iff $\|\tau\|^g \in PERIODS$ and $\|\varphi\|^{st,et,lt \cap [t_{first}, minpt(\|\tau\|^g)), g} = T$.
- $\|Before[\varphi_1, \varphi_2]\|^{st,et,lt,g} = T$, iff for some et' $et' \in mxlpers(\{e \in PERIODS \mid \|\varphi_1\|^{st,e,PTS,g} = T\})$ and $\|\varphi_2\|^{st,et,lt \cap [t_{first}, minpt(et')), g} = T$.
- $\|After[\tau, \varphi]\|^{st,et,lt,g} = T$, iff $\|\tau\|^g \in PERIODS$ and $\|\varphi\|^{st,et,lt \cap (maxpt(\|\tau\|^g), t_{last}], g} = T$.
- $\|After[\varphi_1, \varphi_2]\|^{st,et,lt,g} = T$, iff for some et' $et' \in mxlpers(\{e \in PERIODS \mid \|\varphi_1\|^{st,e,PTS,g} = T\})$ and $\|\varphi_2\|^{st,et,lt \cap (maxpt(et'), t_{last}], g} = T$.

In the first form of the *Before* operator, τ must denote a period, and the localisation time is required to end before the beginning of τ's period. In the second form of the *Before* operator, the localisation time of φ_2 is required to end before the beginning of a maximal event time period et' where φ_1 holds. The *After* operator is similar.

For example, (3.92) is expressed as (3.93). The reading of (3.94) that requires BA737 to have departed after the *end* of a maximal period where the emergency system was in operation is expressed as (3.95). It is assumed here that *to depart* is a point, as in the airport domain.

(3.92) Was tank 2 empty before 25/9/1999?

(3.93) $Before[25/9/1999, Past[e^v, empty(tank2)]]$

(3.94) BA737 departed after the emergency system was in operation.

(3.95) $After[Past[e1^v, in\_oper(emerg\_sys)], Past[e2^v, depart(ba737)]]$

(3.94) also has a reading where BA737 must have departed after the emergency system *started* to be in operation (Section 2.10.2). To express this reading, an additional *Begin* operator is needed. We will return to this reading when defining the semantics of the *Begin* operator.

TOP's *At*, *Before*, and *After* operators are similar to those of Pirie et al. (1990). The operators of Pirie et al., however, do not narrow *lt* as in TOP. Instead, they place directly restrictions on *et*. For example, ignoring some details, the $After[\varphi_1, \varphi_2]$ operator of Pirie et al. requires φ_2 to hold at an event time et_2 that follows an et_1 where φ_1 holds; both et_1 and et_2 must fall within *lt*. Instead, TOP's $After[\varphi_1, \varphi_2]$ requires et_1 to be a maximal period where φ_1 holds, not necessarily within the original *lt*, and evaluates φ_2 with respect to a narrowed *lt*, which is the intersection of the original *lt* with et_1. In most cases, both approaches lead to similar results. However, TOP's approach, i.e., narrowing *lt*, is advantageous in sentences like (3.96) when expressing the durative reading, whereby the tank was empty *throughout* 26/9/1999 (Section 2.9.2).

(3.96) Tank 2 was empty on 26/9/1999.

In these cases *et* must cover all the available time, i.e., all the time where the tense and the adverbial allow *et* to be placed. TOP's *lt* captures this notion of available time. Hence, in TOP the durative reading can be expressed easily using an additional *Fills* operator that forces *et* to cover the whole *lt*; this will be discussed further in Section 3.11 below. This method cannot be used in the language of Pirie et al. Their *Past* operator narrows *lt* to the time-axis up to *st*, but their *At* operator does not narrow *lt* any further. Instead, it imposes a direct restriction on *et*. Hence, *lt* is left to be the time-axis up to *st*, and the durative reading cannot be captured by requiring *et* to be equal to *lt*.

3.11 The *Fills* operator

Let us now define the *Fills* operator, that allows the durative reading of (3.96) to be captured. For $\varphi \in YNFORMS$:

– $\|Fills[\varphi]\|^{st,et,lt,g} = T$, iff $et = lt$ and $\|\varphi\|^{st,et,lt,g} = T$.

The *Fills* operator requires *et* to cover the entire *lt*, i.e., all the time where *et* is allowed to be placed. The durative reading of (3.96) can now be expressed as (3.97). In contrast, (3.98) captures the inclusive reading; the tank must have been empty simply at some part of 26/9/1999.

(3.97) $At[26/9/1999, Past[e^v, Fills[empty(tank2)]]]$

(3.98) $At[26/9/1999, Past[e^v, empty(tank2)]]$

Similarly, the reading of (3.99) whereby BA737 was at gate 2 throughout the entire inspection is captured by (3.100). In (3.101), the durative reading is that tank 2 was empty throughout the previous August; this is captured by (3.102).

(3.99) BA737 was at gate 2 while J. Adams was inspecting UK160.

(3.100) $At[Past[e1^v, inspecting(ja, uk160)],$
$Past[e2^v, Fills[be\_at(ba737, gate2)]]]$

(3.101) Tank 2 was empty in August last summer.

(3.102) $Part[august^g, aug^v] \land Part[summer^g, sum^v, -1] \land$
$At[aug^v, At[sum^v, Past[e^v, Fills[empty(tank2)]]]]$

When both the durative and the inclusive readings are possible, an NLITDB could paraphrase both and ask the user to select one of them, or it could provide answers to both readings, indicating which answer corresponds to which reading. As discussed in Section 2.9.2, however, determining exactly when the durative readings are possible is a difficult task. For simplicity, only inclusive readings will be considered in the rest of this book.

3.12 The *Begin* and *End* operators

The *Begin* and *End* operators are used to refer to the time-points where a situation starts or ends. For $\varphi \in YNFORMS$:

– $\|Begin[\varphi]\|^{st,et,lt,g} = T$, iff
$et' \in mxlpers(\{e \in PERIODS \mid \|\varphi\|^{st,e,PTS,g} = T\})$,
$et = \{minpt(et')\}$, and $et \sqsubseteq lt$.

– $\|End[\varphi]\|^{st,et,lt,g} = T$, iff
$et' \in mxlpers(\{e \in PERIODS \mid \|\varphi\|^{st,e,PTS,g} = T\})$,
$et = \{maxpt(et')\}$, and $et \sqsubseteq lt$.

Begin[φ] is true only at instantaneous event times *et* that are beginnings of maximal event times *et′* where φ holds. The *End* operator is similar.

The *Begin* and *End* operators can express *to start*, *to stop*, *to begin*, and *to finish* (Section 2.6). For example, (3.103) is expressed as (3.104).

(3.103) Did T. Smith start to inspect BA737 before J. Adams finished inspecting UK160?

(3.104) $Before[Past[e1^v, End[Culm[inspecting(ja, uk160)]]],$
$Past[e2^v, Begin[inspecting(ts, ba737)]]]$

Intuitively, *Culm*[*inspecting*(*ja*, *uk*160)] refers to an event-time period that covers exactly an entire inspection of UK160 by J. Adams, from start to completion. *End*[*Culm*[*inspecting*(*ja*, *uk*160)]] refers to the completion point of the inspection. *Begin*[*inspecting*(*ts*, *ba*737)] refers to the beginning of an inspection of BA737 by T. Smith. (3.104) requires the beginning of T. Smith's inspection to precede the completion point of J. Adams' inspection, and both points to fall in the past.

The reading of (3.94) (Section 3.10) that requires BA737 to have departed after the emergency system *started* to be in operation can now be expressed as (3.105).

(3.105) $After[Past[e1^v, Begin[in\_operation(emerg\_sys)]],$
$Past[e2^v, depart(ba737)]]$

3.13 The *Ntense* operator

The framework of this book allows noun phrases to refer either to the present or to the time of the verb tense (Section 2.11). In (3.106), for example, *the sales manager* can refer either to the current sales manager or to the 1991 sales manager. The two readings are represented using the *Ntense* operator, as in (3.107) and (3.108), respectively.

(3.106) What was the salary of the sales manager in 1991?

(3.107) $?slr^v\ Ntense[now^*, manager\_of(mgr^v, sales)] \land$
$At[1991, Past[e^v, salary\_of(mgr^v, slr^v)]]$

(3.108) $?slr^v$ $Ntense[e^v, manager\_of(mgr^v, sales)] \wedge$
$At[1991, Past[e^v, salary\_of(mgr^v, slr^v)]]$

Intuitively, (3.107) reports any slr^v, such that slr^v was the salary of mgr^v at some past time e^v that falls within 1991, and mgr^v is the *current* manager of the sales department. In contrast, in (3.108) mgr^v must be the manager of the sales department at e^v. Notice that in (3.108) the first argument of the *Ntense* is the same as the first argument of the *Past*, which is a pointer to the past event time where $salary\_of(mgr^v, slr^v)$ is true (Section 3.8).

TOP's *Ntense* operator is borrowed from Crouch and Pulman (1993). For $\varphi \in YNFORMS$ and $\beta \in VARS$:

- $\|Ntense[\beta, \varphi]\|^{st,et,lt,g} = T$, iff for some $et' \in PERIODS$, it is true that $g(\beta) = et'$ and $\|\varphi\|^{st,et',PTS,g} = T$.
- $\|Ntense[now^*, \varphi]\|^{st,et,lt,g} = T$, iff $\|\varphi\|^{st,\{st\},PTS,g} = T$.

Ntense evaluates φ with respect to a new event time et', which may be different from the original event time et that is used to evaluate the part of the formula outside the *Ntense*. Within the *Ntense*, the localisation time is reset to *PTS*, i.e., the whole time-axis, freeing et' from restrictions imposed on the original et. If the first argument of *Ntense* is now^*, the new event time is the instantaneous period that contains only st, i.e., the object to which the noun phrase refers must have at st the property described by φ. If the first argument of *Ntense* is a variable β, the new event time et' can generally be any period, and β denotes et'. In (3.108), however, β is the same as the first argument of the *Past* operator, which denotes the original et that the *Past* operator requires to be placed before st. This means that $manager\_of(mgr^v, sales)$ must hold at the same event time where $salary\_of(mgr^v, slr^v)$ holds, i.e., the person mgr^v must be the sales manager at the same time where the salary of mgr^v is slr^v.

If the first argument of the *Ntense* in (3.108) and the first argument of the *Past* were different variables, the answer would contain any 1991 salary of anybody who was, is, or will be the sales manager at any time. Using different variables in the two arguments would be useful in (3.109), where the preferred reading is that *Prime Minister* refers to the Prime Ministers of all times, a reading captured by (3.110).

(3.109) Which Prime Ministers were born in Scotland?

(3.110) $?pm^v$ $Ntense[e1^v, pminister(pm^v)] \wedge Past[e2^v, birth\_in(pm^v, scotland)]$

The framework of this book, however, does not currently generate (3.110). (3.109) receives only two formulae, one for current Prime Ministers, and one for persons that were Prime Ministers at the time they were born. The latter reading is unlikely in this case.

Questions like (3.111) and (3.113), where temporal adjectives specify explicitly the times of the noun phrases, can be represented as (3.112) and (3.114), respectively. In the rest of this book, however, we will not consider temporal adjectives other than *current* (Section 2.8).

(3.111) What was the salary of the current sales manager in 1991?

(3.112) $?slr^v\ Ntense[now^*, manager\_of(mgr^v, sales)] \land$
$At[1991, Past[e^v, salary\_of(mgr^v, slr^v)]]$

(3.113) What was the salary of the 1988 sales manager in 1991?

(3.114) $?slr^v\ Ntense[e1^v, At[1988, manager\_of(mgr^v, sales)]] \land$
$At[1991, Past[e2^v, salary\_of(mgr^v, slr^v)]]$

3.14 The *For* operator

The *For* operator will be used to express duration adverbials introduced by *for* and *in* (Sections 2.9.3 and 2.9.4). For $\sigma_c \in CPARTS$, $\nu_{qty} \in \{1, 2, 3, \ldots\}$, and $\varphi \in YNFORMS$:

– $\|For[\sigma_c, \nu_{qty}, \varphi]\|^{st,et,lt,g} = T$, iff $\|\varphi\|^{st,et,lt,g} = T$ and for some $p_1, p_2, \ldots, p_{\nu_{qty}} \in f_{cparts}(\sigma_c)$, $minpt(p_1) = minpt(et)$, $next(maxpt(p_1)) = minpt(p_2)$, $next(maxpt(p_2)) = minpt(p_3), \ldots,$ $next(maxpt(p_{\nu_{qty}-1})) = minpt(p_{\nu_{qty}})$, and $maxpt(p_{\nu_{qty}}) = maxpt(et)$.

$For[\sigma_c, \nu_{qty}, \varphi]$ requires φ to be true at an event time period that is ν_{qty} σ_c-periods long. For example, assuming that $month^c$ denotes the partitioning of month-periods, i.e., the period that covers exactly the August of 1995, the period for September of 1995, etc., (3.115) can be expressed as (3.116).

(3.115) Was tank 2 empty for three months?

(3.116) $For[month^c, 3, Past[e^v, empty(tank2)]]$

(3.116) requires an event time *et* to exist, such that *et* covers exactly three consecutive months, and tank 2 was empty throughout *et*. As noted in Section 2.9.3, *for* adverbials are sometimes used to specify the duration of a *maximal* period where a situation holds, or to refer to the *total duration* of possibly non-overlapping periods where some situation holds. These readings are not considered in this book, and hence we will not define TOP mechanisms to capture them.

Expressions like *one week*, *three months*, *two years*, *two hours*, etc., are often used to specify durations of seven days, 3 × 30 days, 2 × 365 days, 2 × 60 minutes, etc., respectively. (3.116) expresses (3.115) if *three months* refers to *calendar* months; for example, from the beginning of a June to the end of the following August. If *three months* means 3 × 30 days, (3.117) has to be used instead. It is assumed here that day^c denotes the partitioning of day-periods, i.e., the period that covers exactly 26/9/1999, the period for 27/9/1999, etc.

(3.117) $For[day^c, 90, Past[e^v, empty(tank2)]]$

Assuming that *to inspect* is a culminating activity, as in the airport domain, (3.119) represents the reading of (3.118) where 42 minutes is the duration from the beginning of the inspection to the inspection's completion (Section 2.9.4).

(3.118) J. Adams inspected BA737 in 42 minutes.
(3.119) $For[minute^c, 42, Past[e^v, Culm[inspecting(ja, ba737)]]]$

Unlike (3.118), (3.120) does not require the inspection to have been completed (Section 2.9.3). (3.120) is represented as (3.121), i.e., without the *Culm* operator.

(3.120) J. Adams inspected BA737 for 42 minutes.
(3.121) $For[minute^c, 42, Past[e^v, inspecting(ja, ba737)]]$

3.15 The *Perf* operator

The *Perf* operator is used when expressing the past perfect. For example, (3.122) is expressed as (3.123). The *Perf* operator could also be used in present perfect sentences; e.g., (3.124) would be represented as (3.125). In this book, however, the present perfect is taken to have the same meaning as the simple past (Section 2.5.4). Hence, (3.124) will be mapped to (3.127), the same formula that expresses (3.126).

(3.122) BA737 had departed.
(3.123) $Past[e1^v, Perf[e2^v, depart(ba737)]]$
(3.124) BA737 has departed.
(3.125) $Pres[Perf[e^v, depart(ba737)]]$
(3.126) BA737 departed.
(3.127) $Past[e^v, depart(ba737)]$

TOP's *Perf* operator has been influenced by similar operators proposed by Dowty (1982), Richards et al. (1989), Pirie et al. (1990), and Crouch et al. (1993). For $\varphi \in YNFORMS$ and $\beta \in VARS$:

– $\|Perf[\beta, \varphi]\|^{st,et,lt,g} = T$, iff $et \sqsubseteq lt$ and for some $et' \in PERIODS$, it is true that $g(\beta) = et'$, $maxpt(et') \prec minpt(et)$, and $\|\varphi\|^{st,et',PTS,g} = T$.

$Perf[\beta, \varphi]$ holds at the event time *et*, only if *et* is preceded by a new event time *et′* where φ holds (Figure 3.4). The original *et* must be a subperiod of *lt*. In contrast, *et′* does not need to be a subperiod of *lt*, because the localisation time in $\|\varphi\|^{st,et',PTS,g}$ above is reset to *PTS*, the whole time-axis. The β argument is a pointer to *et′*, as in $Past[\beta, \varphi]$ (Section 3.8). Ignoring constraints imposed by *lt*, the *et* where $Perf[\beta, \varphi]$ is true can be placed anywhere within the period that starts immediately after the end of *et′* and extends up to t_{last}. The term *consequent period* was used in Section 2.9.1 to refer to this period.

Using the *Perf* operator, the reading of (3.128) where the inspection happens at some time before, or possibly on, 27/9/1995 is expressed as (3.129). In this case, *on 27/9/1995* provides a reference time; see Section 2.5.5. In contrast, the reading of (3.128) where the inspection happens on 27/9/1995 is expressed as (3.130).

(3.128) J. Adams had inspected gate 2 on 27/9/1995.
(3.129) $At[27/9/1995, Past[e1^v, Perf[e2^v, Culm[inspecting(ja, g2)]]]]$
(3.130) $Past[e1^v, Perf[e2^v, At[27/9/1995, Culm[inspecting(ja, g2)]]]]$

Let us explore formally the denotations of (3.129) and (3.130). The denotation of (3.129) w.r.t. *st* is *T* iff for some $et \in PERIODS$ and $g \in G$, (3.131) holds.

(3.131) $$\|At[27/9/1995, Past[e1^v, Perf[e2^v, Culm[inspecting(ja, g2)]]]]\|^{st,et,PTS,g} = T$$

Assuming that *27/9/1995* denotes the obvious period, by the definition of *At*, (3.131) holds iff (3.132) is true.

(3.132) $$\|Past[e1^v, Perf[e2^v, Culm[inspecting(ja, g2)]]]\|^{st,et,f_{cons}(27/9/1995),g} = T$$

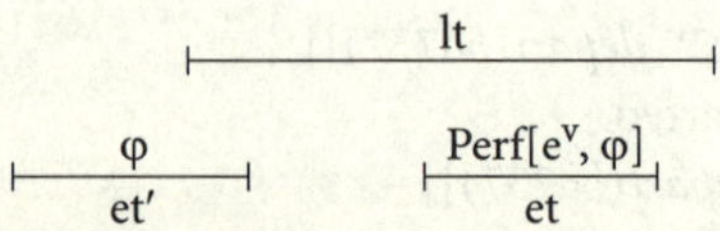

Figure 3.4 The semantics of the *Perf* operator

By the definition of *Past*, ignoring $e1^v$ which does not play any interesting role here, and assuming that *st* follows 27/9/1995, (3.132) becomes (3.133).

(3.133) $\|Perf[e2^v, Culm[inspecting(ja, g2)]]\|^{st,et,f_{cons}(27/9/1995),g} = T$

By the definition of *Perf*, ignoring $e2^v$, (3.133) holds iff for some $et' \in PERIODS$, (3.134)–(3.136) hold.

(3.134) $et \sqsubseteq f_{cons}(27/9/1995)$
(3.135) $maxpt(et') \prec minpt(et)$
(3.136) $\|Culm[inspecting(ja, g2)]\|^{st,et',PTS,g} = T$

By the definition of *Culm*, (3.136) holds iff (3.137)–(3.141) hold.

(3.137) $et' \sqsubseteq PTS$
(3.138) $f_{culms}(inspecting, 2)(f_{cons}(ja), f_{cons}(g2)) = T$
(3.139) $S = \bigcup_{p \in f_{pfuns}(inspecting,2)(f_{cons}(ja), f_{cons}(g2))} p$
(3.140) $S \neq \emptyset$
(3.141) $et' = [minpt(S), maxpt(S)]$

Let us assume that there is only one maximal period where J. Adams is inspecting BA737, and that the inspection is completed at the end of that period. Then, the *S* of (3.139) is that maximal period, and (3.138) and (3.140) hold. (3.141) requires *et'* to be the same period as *S*, and (3.137) is satisfied. The denotation of (3.129) w.r.t. *st*, then, is *T* iff for some *et*, (3.134) and (3.135) hold, i.e., iff there is an *et* within 27/9/1995, such that *et* follows the period $S = et'$ that covers the entire inspection. The situation is depicted in Figure 3.5. In other words, 27/9/1995 must contain an *et* where the inspection has already been completed.

Let us now consider (3.130). Its denotation w.r.t. *st* will be true iff for some $et \in PERIODS$ and $g \in G$, (3.142) holds.

(3.142) $\|Past[e1^v, Perf[e2^v, At[27/9/1995, Culm[inspecting(ja, g2)]]]]\|^{st,et,PTS,g} = T$

By the definition of *Past*, ignoring again $e1^v$ and $e2^v$ which do not play any interesting role here, (3.142) holds iff (3.143) is *T*.

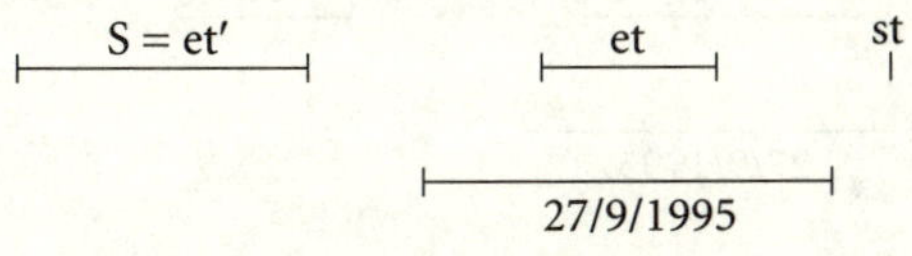

Figure 3.5 First reading of "J. Adams had inspected gate 2 on 27/9/1995"

(3.143) $\|Perf[e2^v, At[27/9/1995, Culm[inspecting(ja, g2)]]]\|^{st,et,[t_{first},st),g} = T$

By the definition of *Perf*, (3.143) is true iff for some $et' \in PERIODS$, (3.144)–(3.146) hold.

(3.144) $et \sqsubseteq [t_{first}, st)$
(3.145) $maxpt(et') \prec minpt(et)$
(3.146) $\|At[27/9/1995, Culm[inspecting(ja, g2)]]\|^{st,et',PTS,g} = T$

By the definition of the *At* operator, (3.146) holds iff (3.147) holds.

(3.147) $\|Culm[inspecting(ja, g2)]\|^{st,et',f_{cons}(27/9/1995),g} = T$

By the definition of *Culm*, (3.147) holds iff (3.148)–(3.152) are true.

(3.148) $et' \sqsubseteq f_{cons}(27/9/1995)$
(3.149) $f_{culms}(inspecting, 2)(f_{cons}(ja), f_{cons}(g2)) = T$
(3.150) $S = \bigcup_{p \in f_{pfuns}(inspecting,2)(f_{cons}(ja), f_{cons}(g2))} p$
(3.151) $S \neq \emptyset$
(3.152) $et' = [minpt(S), maxpt(S)]$

Assuming again that there is only one maximal period where J. Adams is inspecting BA737, and that the inspection is completed at the end of the period, the *S* of (3.150) is that maximal period, and (3.149) and (3.151) hold. (3.152) sets *et'* to *S*. The denotation of (3.130) w.r.t. *st*, then, is *T* iff for some *et*, (3.144), (3.145), and (3.148) hold. That is, there must be some past *et* that follows the period $S = et'$ of the entire inspection, and $S = et'$ must be located within 27/9/1995 (Figure 3.6). In other words, in this case the inspection must have been completed within 27/9/1995.

In (3.153), where there are no temporal adverbials, the corresponding formula (3.154) requires some past *et* (pointed to by $e1^v$) to exist, such that *et* follows an *et'* (pointed to by $e2^v$) that covers exactly the whole inspection of gate 2 by J. Adams, from start to completion. The net effect is that the inspection must have been completed in the past.

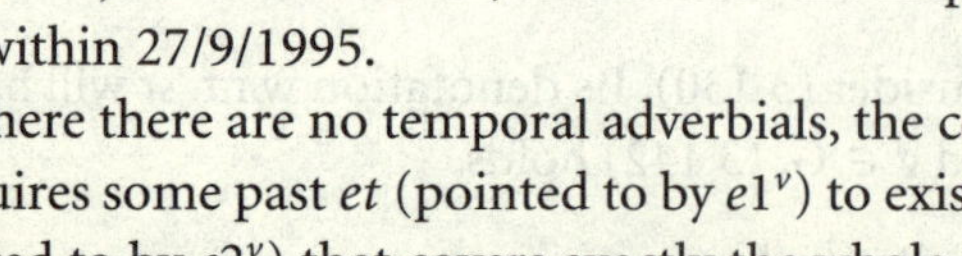

Figure 3.6 Second reading of "J. Adams had inspected gate 2 on 27/9/1995"

(3.153) J. Adams had inspected gate 2

(3.154) *Past*[*e1*^{v}, *Perf*[*e2*^{v}, *Culm*[*inspecting*(*ja*, *g2*)]]]

3.16 Occurrence identifiers

In this book, predicates introduced by culminating activity verbs will often have an extra argument that acts as an *occurrence identifier*. Let us consider, for example, a scenario involving an engineer, John, who worked on engine 2 repairing faults of the engine at several past times. John started to repair a fault of engine 2 on 1/6/1998 at 9:00 am (Figure 3.7). He continued to work on that fault up to 1:00 pm, at which point he temporarily abandoned the repair without completing it. He resumed the repair at 3:00 pm on 25/6/1998, and completed it at 5:00 pm on the same day.

In 1999, John was asked to repair another fault of engine 2. He started the repair on 1/7/1999 at 9:00 am, and continued to work on that fault up to 1:00 pm on the same day without completing the repair. He then abandoned the repair for ever, because he was not qualified to fix that fault, and the repair was assigned to another engineer. Finally, in 2000 John was asked to repair a third fault of engine 2. He started to repair the fault on 1/6/2000 at 9:00 am, and continued to work on that fault up to 1:00 pm, without completing the repair. He resumed the repair at 3:00 pm, and completed it at 5:00 pm on the same day.

Representing (3.155) as (3.156) is problematic. (Here *j* denotes John, and *e2* denotes engine 2.) Let us assume that the question is submitted after 1/6/2000. One would expect the answer to be affirmative, since a complete past repair of engine 2 by John falls within 1/6/2000. In contrast, (3.156) causes the answer to be negative. The semantics of the *Culm* operator (Section 3.9)

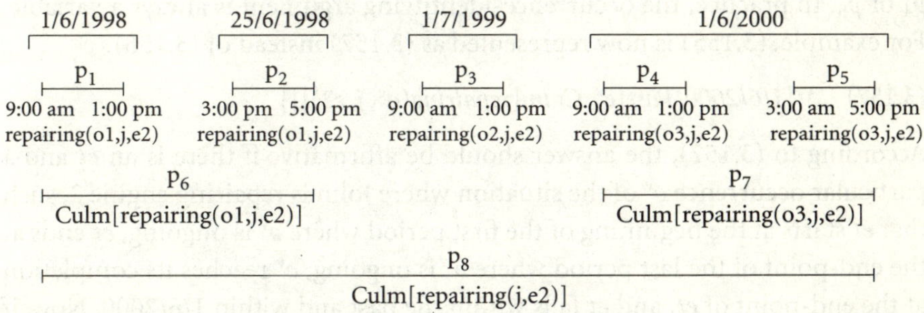

Figure 3.7 Occurrence identifiers

requires *et* to start at the beginning of the earliest maximal period where *repairing*(*j*, *e*2) holds, i.e., at the beginning of p_1 in Figure 3.7, and to end at the end-point of the latest maximal period where *repairing*(*j*, *e*2) holds, i.e., at the end of p_5 in Figure 3.7. In other words, *et* must be p_8 of Figure 3.7. The *At* operator requires *et*, i.e., p_8, to be also a subperiod of 1/6/2000. This is not the case, and the answer is negative.

(3.155) Did John repair engine 2 on 1/6/2000?
(3.156) $At[1/6/2000, Past[e^v, Culm[repairing(j, e2)]]]$

The problem is that although John was repairing engine 2 during all five periods (p_1, p_2, p_3, p_4, p_5), the five periods intuitively belong to different occurrences of the situation where John is repairing engine 2. The first two periods have to do with the repair of the first fault (occurrence 1), the third period has to do with the repair of the second fault (occurrence 2), and the last two periods relate to the repair of the third fault (occurrence 3). The *Culm*[*repairing*(*j*, *e*2)] of (3.156), however, does not distinguish between the three occurrences, and forces *et* to start at the beginning of p_1 and end at the end-point of p_5. Instead, we would like *Culm*[*repairing*(*j*, *e*2)] to distinguish between the three occurrences: to require *et* to start at the beginning of p_1 (beginning of the first repair) and to end at the end-point of p_2 (completion of the first repair), or to require *et* to start at the beginning of p_4 (beginning of the third repair) and to end at the end-point of p_5 (completion of the third repair). *Culm*[*repairing*(*j*, *e*2)] should not allow *et* to be p_3, because the second repair does not reach its completion at the end-point of p_3.

To achieve this, an occurrence-identifying argument is employed. Assuming that *o*1, *o*2, and *o*3 denote the three occurrences, *repairing*(*o*1, *j*, *e*2) is true only at *ets* that are subperiods of p_1 or p_2, *repairing*(*o*2, *j*, *e*2) only at *ets* that are subperiods of p_3, and *repairing*(*o*3, *j*, *e*2) only at *ets* that are subperiods of p_4 or p_5. In practice, the occurrence-identifying argument is always a variable. For example, (3.155) is now represented as (3.157) instead of (3.156).

(3.157) $At[1/6/2000, Past[e^v, Culm[repairing(o^v, j, e2)]]]$

According to (3.157), the answer should be affirmative if there is an *et* and a particular occurrence o^v of the situation where John is repairing engine 2, such that *et* starts at the beginning of the first period where o^v is ongoing, *et* ends at the end-point of the last period where o^v is ongoing, o^v reaches its completion at the end-point of *et*, and *et* falls within the past and within 1/6/2000. Now, if (3.155) is submitted after 1/6/2000, the answer is affirmative.

Occurrence identifiers are a step towards formalisms that treat occurrences of situations, sometimes called 'events', as objects in the modelled world (Parsons 1990; Kamp & Reyle 1993; Blackburn, Gardent, & de Rijke 1994; Hwang & Schubert 1994). In TOP all terms, i.e., all constants and variables, denote objects of the modelled world. Thus, allowing occurrence-identifying terms, like o^v in (3.157), implies that occurrences of situations are also world objects. Unlike other formalisms, however, TOP does not treat these occurrence-identifying terms in any special way, and there is nothing in the definition of TOP to distinguish objects denoted by occurrence-identifiers from objects denoted by other terms.

3.17 Tense anaphora and localisation time

Although tense anaphora is not examined in any detail in this book (Section 2.12), it should be pointed out that TOP's localisation time could be used to handle some cases of tense anaphora. In some cases, the anaphoric nature of tenses can be handled by storing the temporal window established by adverbials and verb forms of previous questions, and by requiring the situations of follow-up questions to fall within that window. TOP's localisation time can capture this notion of previous window. Assuming, for example, that (3.158) is submitted after 1999, the *At* and *Past* operators of the corresponding formula (3.159) narrow *lt* to the period that covers exactly 1999. This period could be stored and used as the initial value of *lt* in (3.161), that expresses the follow-up question (3.160). In effect, (3.160) would be taken to mean (3.162).

(3.158) Was Mary the personnel manager in 1999?
(3.159) $At[1999, Past[e^v, manager\_of(mary, personnel)]]$
(3.160) Who was the personnel manager?
(3.161) $?wh^v\ Past[e^v, manager\_of(wh^v, personnel)]$
(3.162) Who was the personnel manager in 1999?

This is only a rough sketch of the necessary mechanisms; improvements would be needed. For example, if (3.158) and (3.160) are followed by (3.163), which is represented as (3.164), *lt* must be reset to the whole time axis.

(3.163) Who is (now) the personnel manager?
(3.164) $?wh^v\ Pres[manager\_of(wh^v, personnel)]$

3.18 Generic representatives of partitionings

As noted in Section 3.7, habitual readings are taken to involve habitual homonyms of verbs, which introduce different predicates than the corresponding non-habitual homonyms. A remaining issue is how to represent habitual readings that involve times, as in (3.165). (3.165) cannot be represented as (3.166), because (3.166) says that at 5:00 pm on some day during the previous month BA737 had the habit of departing. In contrast, the reading that we wish to capture is that during the previous month BA737 had the habit of departing at 5:00 pm.

(3.165) Last month BA737 (habitually) departed at 5:00 pm.

(3.166) $Part[month^c, mon^v, -1] \wedge Part[5{:}00pm^g, fv^v] \wedge$
$At[mon^v, At[fv^v, Past[e^v, hab\_depart(ba737)]]]$

To capture such habitual readings one would have to allow gappy partitioning names, like $5{:}00pm^g$, to appear as predicate arguments, or add universal quantification to TOP, to allow statements to be made about all the elements of a gappy partitioning. To avoid complicating the definition of TOP, we will instead assume that for each gappy partitioning, there is a pseudo-entity in the world that can be used as a *generic representative* of all the elements of the partitioning. (3.165) will, then, be represented as (3.167), where *5:00pm* denotes the generic representative of the gappy partitioning $5{:}00pm^g$. Constants denoting generic representatives will be the same as the corresponding partitioning names, but without the '^{g}' suffix.

(3.167) $Part[month^c, mon^v, -1] \wedge$
$At[mon^v, Past[e^v, hab\_depart\_time(ba737, 5{:}00pm)]]$

3.19 Summary

TOP is a formal language, used to represent the meanings of the English questions that are submitted to the NLITDB. The denotation of a TOP formula with respect to *st*, the time point where the question is submitted, specifies what the answer to the corresponding English question should report. The denotations of formulae with respect to *st* are defined in terms of their denotations with respect to *st*, *et*, and *lt*. The event time *et* is a time period where the situation described by the formula holds, and *lt*, the localisation time, is a temporal window within which *et* must be placed.

Temporal linguistic mechanisms are expressed in TOP using temporal operators that manipulate *st*, *et*, and *lt*. Several operators were defined. The *Part* operator picks a period from a partitioning of the time-axis. *Pres* and *Past* are used when expressing present and past verb forms. *Perf* is used in combination with *Past* to express the past perfect. *Culm* is used to represent non-progressive forms of culminating activity verbs. *At*, *Before*, and *After* are employed when expressing punctual and period adverbials, and when expressing subordinate clauses introduced by *while*, *before*, and *after*. Duration adverbials introduced by *in* and *for* are expressed using *For*. *Fills* can be used to represent durative readings, where the situation of the verb covers the whole localisation time. *Begin* and *End* are used to refer to time-points where situations start or stop. Finally, *Ntense* is employed to allow noun phrases to refer either to *st* or to the time of the verb's tense.

The next chapter shows how English questions can be mapped systematically to appropriate TOP formulae.

Chapter 4

From English to TOP

"One step at a time."

4.1 Introduction

This chapter shows how English questions submitted to an NLITDB can be mapped systematically to appropriate TOP formulae. The mapping is based on a slightly modified version of HPSG, which remains close to the theory of Pollard and Sag (1994). The HPSG version of this book contains additional mechanisms to handle temporal phenomena, and replaces Pollard and Sag's semantic constructs by feature structures that represent TOP expressions. For the sake of brevity, HPSG mechanisms for phenomena not considered in this book will be ignored or presented in a simplified manner.

Readers familiar with the main concepts of unification-based grammars (Shieber 1986) should be able to follow most of the discussion in this chapter. To grasp the full details, however, readers not acquainted with HPSG may wish to consult Pollard and Sag (1994) first. The HPSG version of this book was implemented as a grammar of the ALE system (Carpenter 1992; Carpenter & Penn 2001); this will be discussed further in Chapter 6.

4.2 HPSG basics

In HPSG, each word and syntactic constituent is mapped to a *sign*, a feature structure of a particular form that provides information about the word or syntactic constituent. An HPSG grammar consists of signs for words, hereafter called *lexical signs*, as well as *lexical rules*, *schemata*, *principles*, and a *sort hierarchy*, all discussed below.

4.2.1 Lexical signs, lexical rules and sort hierarchy

Lexical signs provide information about individual words. For example, the lexical sign of (4.1) provides information about the base form of *to land* in the airport domain (Section 2.4.5).

(4.1)
$$\left[\begin{array}{ll} \text{PHON} & \langle \textit{land} \rangle \\ \text{SYNSEM} & \left[\begin{array}{ll} \text{LOC} & \left[\begin{array}{ll} \text{CAT} & {}_{\textit{cat}}\left[\begin{array}{ll} \text{HEAD} & {}_{\textit{verb}}\left[\begin{array}{ll}\text{VFORM} & \textit{bse}\\ \text{AUX} & -\end{array}\right] \\ \text{ASPECT} & \textit{culmact} \\ \text{SPR} & \langle\rangle \\ \text{SUBJ} & \langle \text{NP}[\text{-PRD}]_{\boxed{1}} \rangle \\ \text{COMPS} & \langle \text{PP}[\text{-PRD, PFORM } \textit{on}]_{\boxed{2}} \rangle \end{array}\right] \\ \text{CONT} & {}_{\textit{landing\_on}}\left[\begin{array}{ll} \text{ARG1} & \textit{occr\_var} \\ \text{ARG2} & \boxed{1} \\ \text{ARG3} & \boxed{2}\end{array}\right] \end{array}\right] \end{array}\right] \end{array}\right]$$

The '<' and '>' delimiters denote lists. Roughly speaking, the PHON feature shows the sequence of words the sign corresponds to. (4.1) corresponds to the single word *land*. Apart from PHON, every sign has a SYNSEM feature, as well as other features that are not shown in (4.1). (Features not relevant to the discussion will often be omitted.) The value of SYNSEM in (4.1) is itself a feature structure that has a feature LOC. The value of LOC is in turn a feature structure that has the features CAT and CONT; these correspond roughly to the syntactic category and the semantic content, respectively.

Each HPSG feature structure belongs to a particular *sort*. The *sort hierarchy* of HPSG shows the available sorts, and the subsorts of each sort. It also specifies which features the members of each sort have, and the sorts the values of these features must belong to. In (4.1), for example, the value of HEAD is a feature structure of sort *verb*; the sort name appears near the bottom left corner of the feature structure. The value of HEAD signals that the word is the base form (VFORM *bse*) of a non-auxiliary (AUX –) verb. The sort hierarchy of Pollard and Sag (1994) specifies that the value of HEAD must be of sort *head*, and that *verb* is a subsort of *head*. This allows feature structures of sort *verb* to be used as values of HEAD. The value of VFORM in (4.1) is an *atomic feature structure*, i.e., a feature structure with no features, of sort *bse*. For simplicity, when showing feature structures, uninteresting sort names are ommitted; for example, (4.1) does not show the sort of LOC's value.

ASPECT is the only new HPSG feature of this book. This feature will be present in feature structures of sort *cat*, which comprises all feature structures that can be used as values of the feature CAT. The values of ASPECT are feature structures of sort *aspect*. The *aspect* sort, which is an addition of this book, contains only atomic feature structures, and has the subsorts: *state*, *activity*, *culmact* (culminating activity), and *point*. The *state* sort is in turn partitioned into: *lex_state* (lexical state), *progressive* (progressive state), and *cnsq_state* (consequent state). These sorts reflect the aspectual taxonomy of Chapter 2. Following Table 2.1 on page 29, (4.1) classifies the base form of *to land* as culminating activity.

The SPR, SUBJ, and COMPS features of (4.1) provide information about the specifier, subject, and complements, respectively, that the verb has to combine with. Specifiers are determiners, like *the*, or words like *much* in *much more* and *too* in *too late*. Verbs do not admit specifiers, and hence the value of SPR in (4.1) is the empty list.

The SUBJ value of (4.1) means that the verb requires a noun phrase as its subject. The $\text{NP}[\text{-PRD}]_{\boxed{1}}$ in (4.1) has the same meaning as in Pollard and Sag's book (1994). Roughly speaking, it is an abbreviation for a sign that corresponds to a noun phrase. The -PRD means that the noun phrase must be non-predicative; this will be discussed further in later sections. The $\boxed{1}$ is intuitively a pointer to the world entity that the noun phrase denotes. Similarly, the COMPS value of (4.1) means that the verb requires as its complement a non-predicative prepositional phrase introduced by *on*. The $\boxed{2}$ is intuitively a pointer to the world entity of the prepositional phrase; for example, if the prepositional phrase is *on a runway*, the $\boxed{2}$ is a pointer to the runway.

The value of CONT in (4.1) stands for the TOP predicate *landing_on*(β, τ_1, τ_2), where τ_1 and τ_2 are TOP terms corresponding to $\boxed{1}$ and $\boxed{2}$, and β is a TOP variable acting as an occurrence identifier (Section 3.16).[1] The exact relation between HPSG feature structures and TOP expressions will be discussed in later sections.

To reduce the number of lexical signs that need to be provided manually, *lexical rules* can be used. These generate new lexical signs from existing ones. For example, lexical rules can be used to generate automatically the lexical signs of non-base verb forms from the corresponding base-form lexical signs. There will be several opportunities in this chapter to introduce and discuss lexical rules.

4.2.2 Schemata and principles

HPSG *schemata* specify basic combination patterns that are used when words or syntactic constituents combine to form larger constituents. For example, the *head-complement schema* is the pattern that is used, among other cases, when a verb combines with its complements. This is the schema that is used when *landed* combines with a complement like *on runway 2*; the verb is said to be the *head daughter* of the constituent *landed on runway 2*. The *head-subject schema* is used, among other cases, when a verb phrase combines with its subject. It is used, for example, when *landed on runway 2* combines with its subject *BA737*; in this case, the verb phrase is the head daughter of *BA737 landed on runway 2*. No modifications to the schemata of Pollard and Sag (1994) will be introduced in the HPSG version of this book, and hence schemata will not be discussed further.

HPSG *principles* control the propagation of feature values from the signs of words or syntactic constituents to the signs of their super-constituents. The *head-feature principle*, for example, specifies that the sign of the super-constituent inherits the HEAD value of the head daughter's sign. This causes the sign of *landed on runway 2* to inherit the HEAD value of the sign of *landed*, and the same value to be inherited by the sign of *BA737 landed on runway 2*. This book uses simplified versions of Pollard and Sag's *semantics principle* and *constituent ordering principle*, and introduces one new principle, the *aspect principle*; all three principles will be discussed in later sections. All other principles follow Pollard and Sag (1994).

4.3 Representing TOP yes/no formulae in HPSG

According to Pollard and Sag (1994), the CONT value of (4.1) would actually be (4.2).

(4.2)
$$\left[\begin{array}{ll} \textsc{quants} & \langle\rangle \\ \textsc{nucleus} & \left[\begin{array}{ll} \textsc{arg1} & \textit{occr\_var} \\ \textsc{arg2} & \boxed{1} \\ \textsc{arg3} & \boxed{2} \end{array}\right]_{\textit{landing\_on}} \end{array}\right]_{\textit{psoa}}$$

The sort name '*psoa*' stands for 'parameterised state of affairs', a term from situation theory (Cooper, Mukai, & Perry 1990). The semantic analysis of this book is not situation-theoretic, but the term 'psoa' is still used for compatibility

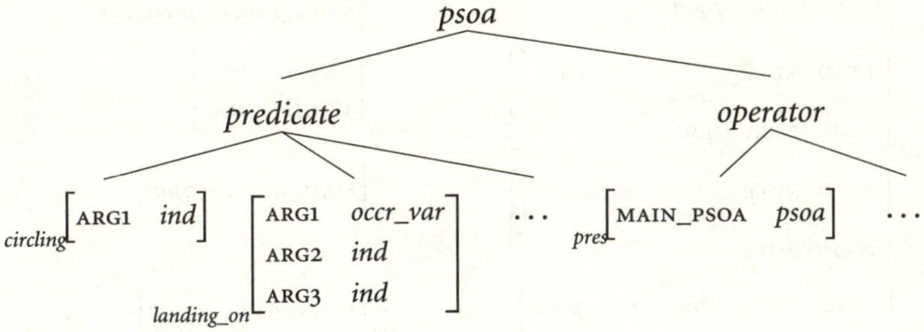

Figure 4.1 Subsorts of *psoa* in this book

with Pollard and Sag. In Pollard and Sag's treatment, feature structures of sort *psoa* have two features: QUANTS and NUCLEUS. The QUANTS feature, which is part of HPSG's quantifier scoping mechanisms, is not used in this book. This leaves only one feature, NUCLEUS, in *psoa*s. For simplicity, NUCLEUS will also be ignored, and the *psoa* sort will be taken to contain the feature structures that would be values of NUCLEUS in Pollard and Sag's treatment.

More precisely, in this book *psoa* has two subsorts: *predicate* and *operator* (Figure 4.1). Feature structures of sort *psoa* are used to represent TOP yes/no formulae. The *predicate* sort contains feature structures that represent TOP predicates, while *operator* contains feature structures that represent all other yes/no formulae. The *predicate* sort has domain-specific subsorts, corresponding to domain-specific predicate functors. In the airport domain, for example, *landing_on* is a subsort of *predicate*. The feature structures in the subsorts of *predicate* carry features named ARG1, ARG2, ARG3, etc., which represent the arguments of the predicates. The values of ARG1, ARG2, etc. are of sort *ind*. In (4.1) and (4.2), *occr_var* is a subsort of *ind* that is used to represent occurrence identifiers (Section 3.16). The *ind* sort and its subsorts will be discussed further below.

The *operator* sort has the subsorts shown in Figure 4.2, which correspond to the TOP operators of Chapter 3. There is no subsort for *Fills*, as this operator is ignored in the remainder of this book. There is also no subsort for the $Part[\sigma, \beta, \nu_{ord}]$ version of the *Part* operator; to save space, this operator is not used in the rest of this book, and the periods of words like *yesterday* are represented using TOP constants, rather than expressions of the form $Part[day^c, \beta, -1]$. An additional subsort, *and*, is present in Figure 4.2; this stands for TOP's conjunction. The order of the features in Figure 4.2 corresponds to the order of the arguments of the TOP operators. For example, the

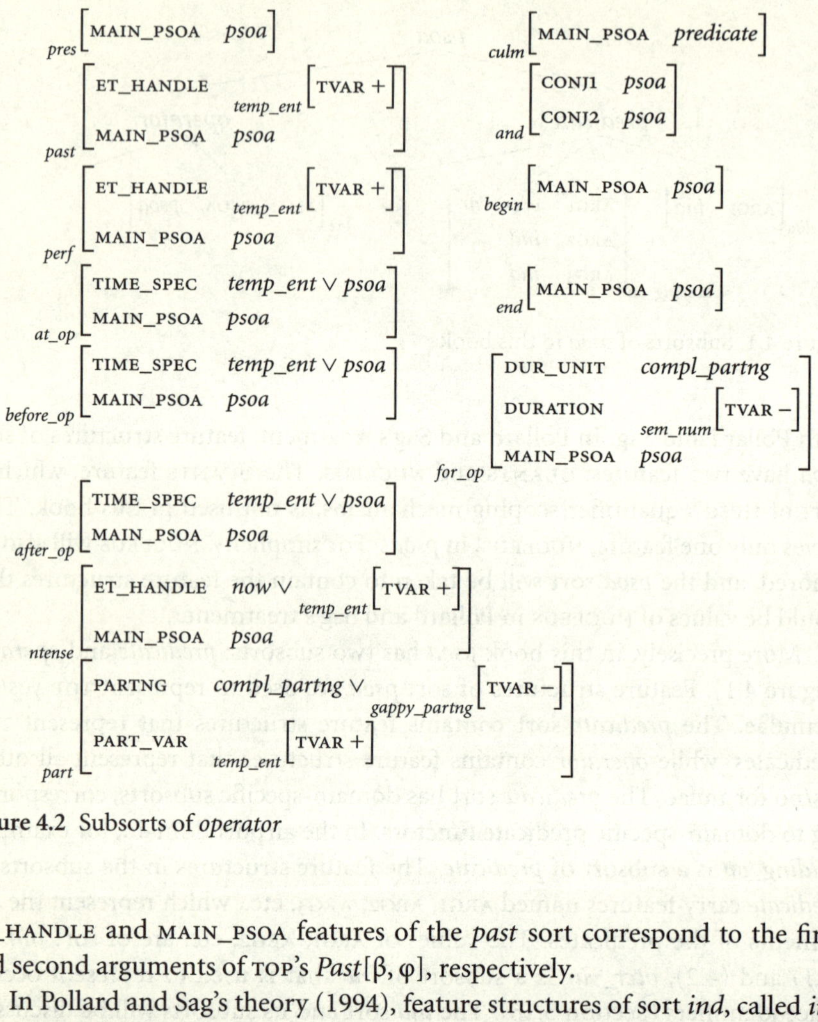

Figure 4.2 Subsorts of *operator*

ET_HANDLE and MAIN_PSOA features of the *past* sort correspond to the first and second arguments of TOP's *Past*[β, φ], respectively.

In Pollard and Sag's theory (1994), feature structures of sort *ind*, called *indices*, have the features *person*, *number*, and *gender*, which are used to enforce person, number, and gender agreement, respectively. For simplicity, these features are ignored in the HPSG version of this book, and no agreement checks are made. Pollard and Sag's subsorts of *ind* (*ref*, *there*, *it*), which are used in HPSG's binding theory, are also ignored. In this book, indices stand for TOP terms, i.e, constants or variables. The situation is roughly speaking as in Figure 4.3. For each TOP constant, for example, *ba737* or *gate2*, there is a subsort of *ind* that represents that constant. There is also a subsort *var* of *ind*, whose indices represent TOP variables. A TVAR feature is used to distinguish indices that represent constants from indices that represent variables. All indices of

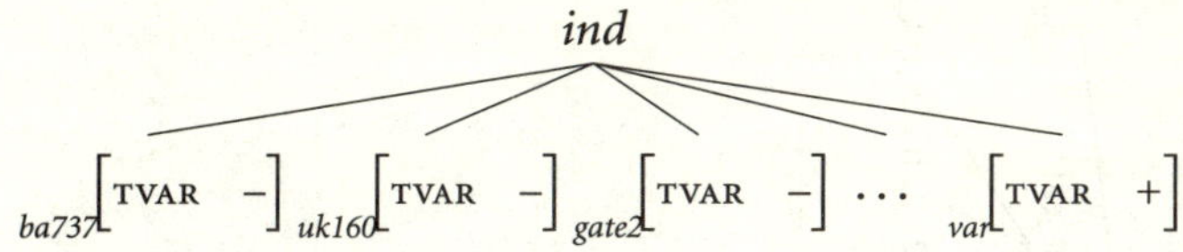

Figure 4.3 Subsorts of *ind* in this book – simplified version

constant-representing sorts have their TVAR set to –. Indices of *var* have their TVAR set to +.

The fact that there is only one subsort for TOP variables in Figure 4.3, *var*, does not mean that only one TOP variable can be represented: *var* is a *sort* of feature structures, containing infinitely many feature-structure members. Unless unified, any two of these members are taken to represent different TOP variables. Each subsort of *ind* that represents a TOP constant also contains infinitely many different feature-structure members. In this case, however, all members of the subsort are taken to represent the same constant. For example, any feature structure of sort *gate2* represents the TOP constant *gate*2.

4.4 More on the subsorts of *ind*

The subsorts of *ind* are actually more complicated than in Figure 4.3. As discussed in Section 1.2, natural language interfaces often employ a domain-dependent hierarchy of entity types, as part of their ontology. Here, a hierarchy of this kind is mounted under the *ind* sort (Androutsopoulos & Dale 2000), as explained below.

In the airport domain, there are temporal entities, like the year 2000, the Monday 27/8/2001, etc., and non-temporal entities, such as flight BA737 and gate 2. Indices representing temporal entities are classified into a subsort of *ind* called *temp_ent*, while indices representing non-temporal entities are classified into *non_temp_ent*; see Figure 4.4, ignoring *partng* and its subsorts for the moment. The *non_temp_ent* sort has in turn subsorts like *mass*, which comprises indices representing mass entities, such as foam or water, and *flight_ent*, which includes indices representing flights. The *flight_ent* sort has one subsort for each TOP constant that denotes a flight (e.g., *ba737*, *uk160*), plus one sort, called *flight_ent_var*, whose indices represent TOP variables that denote flights; this is similar to the *var* sort in the simplified version of Figure 4.3. The other subsorts of *non_temp_ent* are organised in a similar manner.

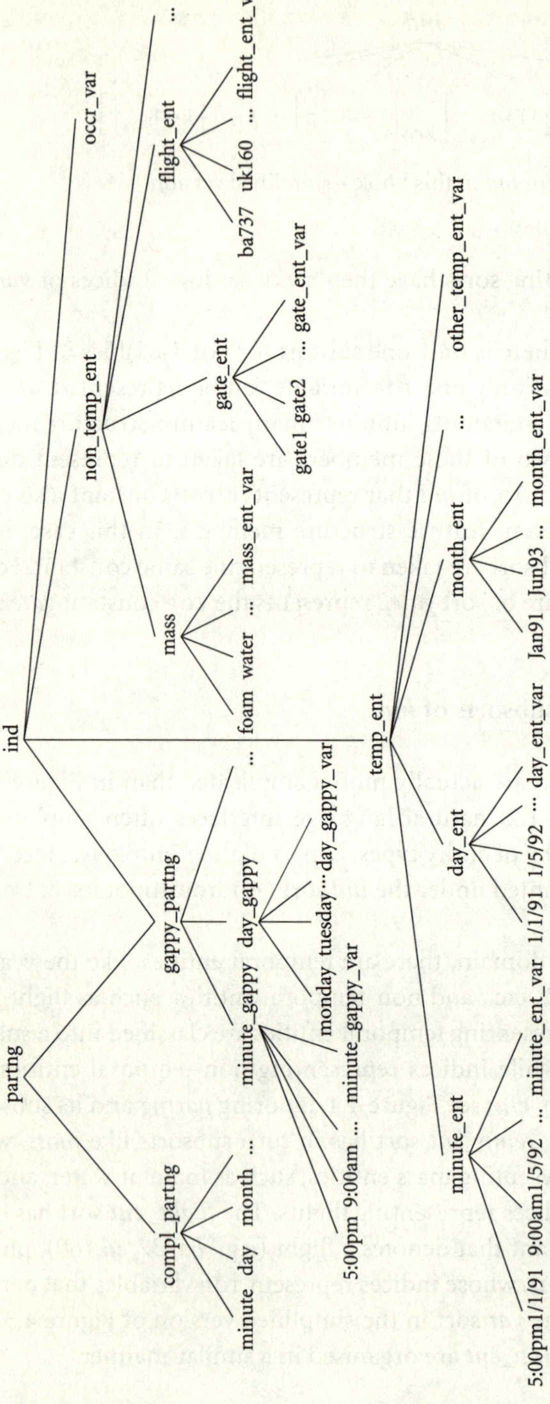

Figure 4.4 The sorts *partng* and *ind* with their subsorts

The *temp_ent* sort has subsorts like *minute_ent*, which comprises indices representing particular minutes, such as the 5:00 pm minute of 1/1/2001, *day_ent*, which comprises indices representing particular days, etc. The *minute_ent* sort has one subsort for each TOP constant that denotes a particular minute, plus the sort *minute_ent_var*, whose indices represent TOP *variables* that denote particular minutes; this is again similar to the *var* sort of Figure 4.3. The other subsorts of *temp_ent* are similar.

As in Section 4.3, indices of sorts that represent TOP constants have their TVAR set to –, while indices of sorts that represent TOP variables have their TVAR set to +. The *occr_var* sort of Figure 4.4 contains indices that represent TOP variables used as occurrence identifiers (Section 3.16). There is also a special sort *now*, not shown in Figure 4.4, which is used to represent the TOP expression now^* (Section 3.13). Going back to Figure 4.2, it should now be easy to see that its sorts mirror the definitions of TOP's operators. For example, the *ntense* sort reflects the fact that the first argument of an *Ntense* operator must be now^* or a variable (TVAR +) denoting a period (*temp_ent*), while the second argument must be a yes/no formula (*psoa*). The *sem_num* sort in *for_op* is a child of *non_temp_ent*, not shown in Figure 4.4, with subsorts that represent the numbers 1, 2, 3, etc.

Let us now examine the *partng* sort of Figure 4.4 and its subsorts *compl_partng* and *gappy_partng*, which do not exist in Pollard and Sag's (1994) treatment. For each TOP complete or gappy partitioning name, such as $minute^c$, day^c, $5{:}00pm^g$, or $monday^g$, there is a leaf-subsort of *compl_partng* or *gappy_partng*, respectively, which represents that name. In Figure 4.4, the sorts *5:00pm*, *9:00am*, etc. are grouped under *minute_gappy* to reflect the fact that the corresponding partitionings contain minute-periods. Similarly, *monday*, *tuesday*, etc. are grouped under *day_gappy* as the partitionings contain day-periods. Section 4.12 below provides examples where sorts like *minute_gappy* and *day_gappy* prove useful.

Apart from gappy partitioning names, the subsorts of *gappy_partng* are also used to represent TOP terms that denote generic representatives of gappy partitionings (Section 3.18). This is why *gappy_partng* is a subsort of both *partng* and *ind* in Figure 4.4. For example, (4.4), which expresses the habitual reading of (4.3), is represented as (4.5). In this case, the subsort *5:00pm* of *gappy_partng* represents the TOP constant *5:00pm*, which in turn denotes the generic representative of the gappy partitioning $5{:}00pm^g$.

(4.3) BA737 departs (habitually) at 5:00 pm

(4.4) $Pres[hab\_departs\_at(ba737, 5{:}00pm)]$

(4.5)
$$
{}_{\textit{pres}}\begin{bmatrix} \text{MAIN\_PSOA} & {}_{\textit{hab\_departs\_at}}\begin{bmatrix} \text{ARG1} & {}_{\textit{ba737}}\begin{bmatrix} \text{TVAR} - \end{bmatrix} \\ \text{ARG2} & {}_{\textit{5:00pm}}\begin{bmatrix} \text{TVAR} - \end{bmatrix} \end{bmatrix} \end{bmatrix}
$$

In contrast, (4.7), which expresses the non-habitual reading of (4.6), is represented as (4.8). In this case, the subsort *5:00pm* of *gappy_partng* stands for TOP's partitioning name $5{:}00pm^g$. (It cannot represent a TOP term, because TOP terms cannot be used as first arguments of *Part* operators.) The two $\boxed{1}$s in (4.8) force the values of PART_VAR and TIME_SPEC to be unified, i.e., they must represent the same TOP variable.

(4.6) BA737 departed (actually) at 5:00 pm.

(4.7) $Part[5{:}00pm^g, fv^v] \land At[fv^v, Past[e^v, depart(ba737)]]$

(4.8)
$$
{}_{\textit{and}}\begin{bmatrix} \text{CONJ1} & {}_{\textit{part}}\begin{bmatrix} \text{PARTNG} & {}_{\textit{5:00pm}}\begin{bmatrix} \text{TVAR} - \end{bmatrix} \\ \text{PART\_VAR} & {}_{\textit{temp\_ent}}\begin{bmatrix} \text{TVAR} + \end{bmatrix}\boxed{1} \end{bmatrix} \\ \text{CONJ2} & {}_{\textit{at\_op}}\begin{bmatrix} \text{TIME\_SPEC} & \boxed{1} \\ \text{MAIN\_PSOA} & {}_{\textit{past}}\begin{bmatrix} \text{ET\_HANDLE} & {}_{\textit{temp\_ent}}\begin{bmatrix} \text{TVAR} + \end{bmatrix} \\ \text{MAIN\_PSOA} & {}_{\textit{depart}}\begin{bmatrix} \text{ARG1} & {}_{\textit{ba737}}\begin{bmatrix} \text{TVAR} - \end{bmatrix} \end{bmatrix} \end{bmatrix} \end{bmatrix} \end{bmatrix}
$$

Sorts like *minute_gappy_var* and *day_gappy_var* in Figure 4.4 are used to represent TOP variables that denote generic representatives of gappy partitionings. The indices of these sorts have their TVAR set to +, while the indices of all other leaf-subsorts of *gappy_partng* have their TVAR set to –.

The hierarchy under *ind* is domain-dependent. For example, in an application where the database contains information about a company, the subsorts of *non_temp_ent* would correspond to departments, managers, etc. It is assumed, however, that in all application domains, *ind* would have at least the immediate subsorts *temp_ent*, *non_temp_ent*, *occr_var*, and *gappy_partng*. It is also assumed that the subsorts of *partng* and *temp_ent* would have the general form of Figure 4.4, though they would have to be adjusted to reflect the partitionings and temporal entities used in the particular application.

4.5 Representing TOP quantifiers in HPSG

We have so far examined how TOP yes/no formulae are represented in the HPSG version of this book using feature-structures of sort *psoa* (Figure 4.1). To represent TOP wh-formulae, i.e., formulae with interrogative or interrogative-maximal quantifiers, additional feature-structure sorts are needed, as discussed below.

In HPSG (Pollard & Sag 1994), feature structures of sort *quant* represent unresolved quantifiers, i.e., quantifiers whose scope is not known. They have two features: DET and RESTIND (restricted index), as shown in (4.9). The DET feature shows the type of the quantifier; in this book, DET can have the values *exists* (existential quantifier), *interrog* (interrogative quantifier), and *interrog_mxl* (interrogative-maximal quantifier).

(4.9)
$$ {}_{quant}\left[\begin{array}{ll} \text{DET} & exists \vee interrog \vee interrog\_mxl \\ \text{RESTIND} & {}_{nom\_obj}\left[\begin{array}{ll} \text{INDEX} & {}_{ind}\left[\text{TVAR} \quad +\right] \\ \text{RESTR} & set(psoa) \end{array}\right] \end{array}\right] $$

The values of RESTIND are feature structures of sort *nom_obj* (nominal object).[2] These have the features INDEX, whose values are of sort *ind*, and RESTR, whose values are sets of *psoas*. When a *nom_obj* feature structure is the value of RESTIND, the INDEX corresponds to the TOP variable being quantified, and the RESTR corresponds to the range of the quantifier. If the RESTR set contains more than one *psoas*, the *psoa*-elements of the set are treated as forming a conjunction. For example, (4.10) represents (4.11).

(4.10)
$$ {}_{quant}\left[\begin{array}{ll} \text{DET} & interrog \\ \text{RESTIND} & {}_{nom\_obj}\left[\begin{array}{ll} \text{INDEX} & {}_{ind}\left[\text{TVAR} \quad +\right]\boxed{1} \\ \text{RESTR} & \left\{ {}_{flight}\left[\text{ARG1} \quad \boxed{1}\right] \right\} \end{array}\right] \end{array}\right] $$

(4.11) $?f^v \; flight(f^v)$

Although TOP does not use explicit existential quantifiers, the HPSG version of this book represents existential quantifiers explicitly, using *quants* whose DET is *exists*, for compatibility with Pollard and Sag (1994). As will be explained in Section 4.6 below, these explicit existential quantifiers are removed when extracting TOP formulae from HPSG signs.

4.6 Extracting TOP formulae from HPSG signs

During the parsing, each question is mapped to one or more signs, with each sign corresponding to a possible reading of the question. An example of a resulting sign is shown in (4.12). We ignore in this section *Ntense* operators, which will be discussed further in Section 4.9. It is also assumed that multi-token names, like *gate 2*, have been concatenated during the preprocessing stage; we will return to this point in later sections.

(4.12)
$$\begin{bmatrix} \text{PHON} & \langle \textit{which, inspector, was, at, gate2} \rangle \\ \text{SYNSEM} \mid \text{LOC} & \begin{bmatrix} \text{CAT} & \begin{bmatrix} \text{HEAD} & {}_{\textit{verb}}\begin{bmatrix} \text{VFORM} & \textit{fin} \\ \text{AUX} & + \end{bmatrix} \\ \text{ASPECT} & \textit{lex\_state} \\ \text{SPR} & \langle\rangle \\ \text{SUBJ} & \langle\rangle \\ \text{COMPS} & \langle\rangle \end{bmatrix} \\ \text{CONT} & {}_{\textit{past}}\begin{bmatrix} \text{ET\_HANDLE} & {}_{\textit{temp\_ent}}\begin{bmatrix} \text{TVAR} & + \end{bmatrix} \\ \text{MAIN\_PSOA} & {}_{\textit{located\_at}}\begin{bmatrix} \text{ARG1} & \boxed{1} \\ \text{ARG2} & \textit{gate2} \end{bmatrix} \end{bmatrix} \end{bmatrix} \\ \text{QSTORE} & \left\{ {}_{\textit{quant}}\begin{bmatrix} \text{DET} & \textit{interrog} \\ \text{RESTIND} & {}_{\textit{nom\_obj}}\begin{bmatrix} \text{INDEX} & {}_{\textit{person\_ent}}\begin{bmatrix} \text{TVAR} & + \end{bmatrix}\boxed{1} \\ \text{RESTR} & \left\{ {}_{\textit{inspector}}\begin{bmatrix} \text{ARG1} & \boxed{1} \end{bmatrix} \right\} \end{bmatrix} \end{bmatrix} \right\} \end{bmatrix}$$

Apart from the features that were discussed in Section 4.2, signs also have the feature QSTORE (quantifier store), whose values are sets of *quant*s (Section 4.5). In the HPSG version of this book, the CONT value of signs that correspond to questions is of sort *psoa*, i.e., it represents a TOP yes/no formula. The QSTORE value represents quantifiers that must be inserted in front of the formula of CONT. In the prototype NLITDB that will be presented in Chapter 6, there is an *extractor* of TOP formulae that examines the CONT and QSTORE features of the question's sign, and generates the corresponding TOP formula. The extractor first examines recursively the features of CONT, rewriting them in term notation; in (4.12), this generates (4.13). For each element of QSTORE, the extractor then adds a suitable quantifier in front of the formula of CONT; in (4.12), this transforms (4.13) into (4.14).

(4.13) $Past[e^v, located\_at(p^v, gate2)]$
(4.14) $?p^v\ inspector(p^v) \wedge Past[e^v, located\_at(p^v, gate2)]$

Since free TOP variables are implicitly existentially quantified, with elements of QSTORE that correspond to existential quantifiers, no explicit existential quantifier is added to the formula of CONT; only the expression that corresponds to the RESTR of the *quant*-element is added. For example, if the DET of (4.12) were *exists*, (4.14) would be (4.15).

(4.15) $inspector(p^v) \wedge Past[e^v, located\_at(p^v, gate2)]$

4.7 Verb forms

Let us now examine in more detail how the various linguistic constructs are treated in the HPSG grammar of this book, focusing on the temporal mechanisms of Chapter 2; these are not addressed by Pollar and Sag (1994).

4.7.1 Single-word verb forms

Single-word non-base verb forms are generated automatically from the signs of the corresponding base forms using lexical rules. The signs for simple present forms are generated by (4.16).

(4.16) SIMPLE PRESENT LEXICAL RULE:

$$\begin{bmatrix} \text{PHON} & \langle\lambda\rangle \\ \text{SYNSEM}\mid\text{LOC} & \begin{bmatrix} \text{CAT} & \begin{bmatrix} \text{HEAD} & {}_{verb}\begin{bmatrix}\text{VFORM} & bse \\ \text{AUX} & - \end{bmatrix} \\ \text{ASPECT} & lex\_state \end{bmatrix} \\ \text{CONT} & \boxed{1} \end{bmatrix}\end{bmatrix}$$

$$\Downarrow$$

$$\begin{bmatrix} \text{PHON} & \langle morph(\lambda, simple\_present)\rangle \\ \text{SYNSEM}\mid\text{LOC} & \begin{bmatrix} \text{CAT} & \begin{bmatrix} \text{HEAD} & {}_{verb}\begin{bmatrix}\text{VFORM} & fin \\ \text{AUX} & - \end{bmatrix} \\ \text{ASPECT} & lex\_state \end{bmatrix} \\ \text{CONT} & {}_{pres}\begin{bmatrix}\text{MAIN\_PSOA} & \boxed{1}\end{bmatrix} \end{bmatrix}\end{bmatrix}$$

For each lexical sign that matches the first feature structure, the *left-hand side* of the rule, a new lexical sign is generated as shown in the second feature structure, the *right hand side* of the rule. Following standard HPSG notation, SYNSEM|LOC refers to the LOC feature of the value of SYNSEM. The HEAD value of the left-hand side requires the original sign to correspond to the base form of a non-auxiliary verb; auxiliary verbs are treated separately. The HEAD value of the right-hand side signals that the resulting sign corresponds to a finite verb form, i.e., a form that does not need to combine with an auxiliary verb. The CONT of the new sign is the same as the CONT of the original one, except that it contains an additional *Pres* operator. Features of the original sign not shown in the left-hand side, for example SUBJ and COMPS, have the same values in the generated sign. The original sign is required to correspond to a lexical state base form. No simple present signs are generated for verbs whose base forms are not states, in accordance with the assumption of Section 2.5.1 that the simple present can be used only with state verbs.

The notation *morph*(λ, *simple_present*) in the rule denotes a morphological transformation that generates the simple present form (e.g., *contains*) from the base form (e.g., *contain*). The prototype NLITDB of Chapter 6 actually employs two different simple present lexical rules. These generate signs for singular and plural simple present forms, respectively. As mentioned in Sections 2.13 and 4.3, plurals are treated semantically as singulars, and no number agreement checks are made. Hence, the two lexical rules differ only in the PHON values of the generated signs.

(4.17) shows the base form sign of *to contain* in the airport domain. From (4.17), (4.16) generates (4.18). The *tank_ent* and *mass_ent* in (4.17) and (4.18) require the indices introduced by the subject and object to be of sort *tank_ent* and *mass_ent*, respectively; *tank_ent* is a sister of *flight_ent* in Figure 4.4. Hence, the semantically anomalous *gate 2 contains water*, where the subject introduces an index of sort *gate2*, which is not a subsort of *tank_ent*, would be rejected. All lexical signs of verb forms have their QSTORE set to {}. To save space, the QSTORE features are not shown here.

(4.17)
$$\begin{bmatrix} \textsc{phon} & \langle \textit{contain} \rangle \\ \textsc{synsem} \mid \textsc{loc} & \begin{bmatrix} \textsc{cat} & \begin{bmatrix} \textsc{head} & {}_{\textit{verb}}\begin{bmatrix} \textsc{vform} & \textit{bse} \\ \textsc{aux} & - \end{bmatrix} \\ \textsc{aspect} & \textit{lex\_state} \\ \textsc{spr} & \langle\rangle \\ \textsc{subj} & \langle \textsc{np}\begin{bmatrix} \textsc{-prd} \end{bmatrix}_{\textit{tank\_ent}} \boxed{1} \rangle \\ \textsc{comps} & \langle \textsc{np}\begin{bmatrix} \textsc{-prd} \end{bmatrix}_{\textit{mass\_ent}} \boxed{2} \rangle \end{bmatrix} \\ \textsc{cont} & {}_{\textit{contains}}\begin{bmatrix} \textsc{arg1} & \boxed{1} \\ \textsc{arg2} & \boxed{2} \end{bmatrix} \end{bmatrix} \end{bmatrix}$$

(4.18)
$$\begin{bmatrix} \textsc{phon} & \langle \textit{contains} \rangle \\ \textsc{synsem} \mid \textsc{loc} & \begin{bmatrix} \textsc{cat} & \begin{bmatrix} \textsc{head} & {}_{\textit{verb}}\begin{bmatrix} \textsc{vform} & \textit{fin} \\ \textsc{aux} & - \end{bmatrix} \\ \textsc{aspect} & \textit{lex\_state} \\ \textsc{spr} & \langle\rangle \\ \textsc{subj} & \langle \textsc{np}\begin{bmatrix} \textsc{-prd} \end{bmatrix}_{\textit{tank\_ent}} \boxed{1} \rangle \\ \textsc{comps} & \langle \textsc{np}\begin{bmatrix} \textsc{-prd} \end{bmatrix}_{\textit{mass\_ent}} \boxed{2} \rangle \end{bmatrix} \\ \textsc{cont} & {}_{\textit{pres}}\begin{bmatrix} \textsc{main\_psoa} & {}_{\textit{contains}}\begin{bmatrix} \textsc{arg1} & \boxed{1} \\ \textsc{arg2} & \boxed{2} \end{bmatrix} \end{bmatrix} \end{bmatrix} \end{bmatrix}$$

The simple past signs of culminating activity verbs are generated by the lexical rule of (4.19). The simple past signs of non-culminating activity verbs are generated by a lexical rule that is similar to (4.19), except that it does not introduce a *Culm* operator in the resulting sign.

(4.19) Simple Past Lexical Rule (Culm. Activity Base Form):

$$\begin{bmatrix} \textsc{phon} & \langle \lambda \rangle \\ \textsc{synsem} \mid \textsc{loc} & \begin{bmatrix} \textsc{cat} & \begin{bmatrix} \textsc{head} & {}_{\textit{verb}}\begin{bmatrix} \textsc{vform} & \textit{bse} \\ \textsc{aux} & - \end{bmatrix} \\ \textsc{aspect} & \textit{culmact} \end{bmatrix} \\ \textsc{cont} & \boxed{1} \end{bmatrix} \end{bmatrix}$$

$$\Downarrow$$

$$\left[\begin{array}{ll} \text{PHON} & \langle \textit{morph}(\lambda, \textit{simple\_past})\rangle \\ \text{SYNSEM} \mid \text{LOC} & \left[\begin{array}{ll} \text{CAT} & \left[\begin{array}{ll} \text{HEAD} & {}_{\textit{verb}}\left[\begin{array}{ll} \text{VFORM} & \textit{fin} \\ \text{AUX} & - \end{array}\right] \\ \text{ASPECT} & \textit{culmact} \end{array}\right] \\ \text{CONT} & {}_{\textit{past}}\left[\begin{array}{ll} \text{ET\_HANDLE} & {}_{\textit{temp\_ent}}\left[\text{TVAR} \; +\right] \\ \text{MAIN\_PSOA} & {}_{\textit{culm}}\left[\text{MAIN\_PSOA} \; \boxed{1}\right] \end{array}\right] \end{array}\right] \end{array}\right]$$

The signs of past participles (e.g., *inspected* in '*Who had inspected BA737?*') are generated by two lexical rules that are similar to the simple past ones. There is a rule for culminating activity verbs, which introduces a *Culm* operator in the past participle sign, and a rule for non-culminating activity verbs, which does not introduce a *Culm* operator. The generated signs have their VFORM set to *psp* (past participle), and the same ASPECT as the base signs, i.e., their ASPECT is not changed to *cnsq_state* (consequent state). The shift to consequent state takes place when the auxiliary *had* combines with the past participle; this will be discussed in Section 4.7.2.

The signs for present participles (e.g., *servicing* in '*Which company is servicing BA737?*') are generated by (4.20). The present participle signs are the same as the base ones, except that their VFORM is *prp* (present participle), and their ASPECT is *progressive* (progressive state).

In English, there is no morphological distinction between *gerunds* and present participles. HPSG and most traditional grammars, however, distinguish between the two (Thomson & Martinet 1986). In (4.21), the *inspecting* is the gerund of *to inspect*, while in (4.22), it is the present participle. Gerund signs are generated by a lexical rule that is similar to (4.20), except that the generated signs retain the ASPECT of the original ones, and have their VFORM set to *ger*.

(4.20) PRESENT PARTICIPLE LEXICAL RULE:

$$\left[\begin{array}{ll} \text{PHON} & \langle \lambda \rangle \\ \text{SYNSEM} \mid \text{LOC} & \left[\begin{array}{ll} \text{CAT} & \left[\begin{array}{ll} \text{HEAD} & {}_{\textit{verb}}\left[\begin{array}{ll} \text{VFORM} & \textit{bse} \\ \text{AUX} & - \end{array}\right] \\ \text{ASPECT} & \textit{aspect} \end{array}\right] \\ \text{CONT} & \boxed{1} \end{array}\right] \end{array}\right]$$

$$\Downarrow$$

$$\begin{bmatrix} \text{PHON} & \langle \mathit{morph}(\lambda, \mathit{present\_participle})\rangle \\ \text{SYNSEM} \mid \text{LOC} & \begin{bmatrix} \text{CAT} & \begin{bmatrix} \text{HEAD} & {}_{\mathit{verb}}\begin{bmatrix}\text{VFORM} & \mathit{prp} \\ \text{AUX} & - \end{bmatrix} \\ \text{ASPECT} & \mathit{progressive} \end{bmatrix} \\ \text{CONT} & \boxed{1} \end{bmatrix} \end{bmatrix}$$

(4.21) J. Adams finished inspecting BA737.

(4.22) J. Adams was inspecting BA737.

The fact that gerund signs retain the ASPECT of the base signs is used in the treatment of verbs like *to finish* (Section 2.6). The simple past *finished* receives multiple signs, which are generated from corresponding base form signs by the simple past lexical rules. (4.23) is used when *finished* combines with a culminating activity verb phrase, and (4.24) when it combines with a state or activity verb phrase ('SS|L' is an abbreviation of 'SYNSEM|LOC').

(4.23)
$$\begin{bmatrix} \text{PHON} & \langle \mathit{finished}\rangle \\ \text{SS} \mid \text{L} & \begin{bmatrix} \text{CAT} & \begin{bmatrix} \text{HEAD} & {}_{\mathit{verb}}\begin{bmatrix}\text{VFORM} & \mathit{fin} \\ \text{AUX} & - \end{bmatrix} \\ \text{ASPECT} & \mathit{point} \\ \text{SPR} & \langle\rangle \\ \text{SUBJ} & \langle \boxed{1} \rangle \\ \text{COMPS} & \left\langle \text{VP}\begin{bmatrix} \text{SUBJ}\ \langle\boxed{1}\rangle,\ \text{VFORM}\ \mathit{ger}, \\ \text{ASPECT}\ \mathit{culmact} \end{bmatrix} : \boxed{2} \right\rangle \end{bmatrix} \\ \text{CONT} & {}_{\mathit{past}}\begin{bmatrix} \text{ET\_HANDLE} & {}_{\mathit{temp\_ent}}\begin{bmatrix}\text{TVAR} + \end{bmatrix} \\ \text{MAIN\_PSOA} & {}_{\mathit{end}}\begin{bmatrix} \text{MAIN\_PSOA} & {}_{\mathit{culm}}\begin{bmatrix} \text{MAIN\_PSOA} & \boxed{2} \end{bmatrix} \end{bmatrix} \end{bmatrix} \end{bmatrix} \end{bmatrix}$$

$$
(4.24)\quad \begin{bmatrix}
\text{PHON} & \langle \textit{finished} \rangle \\
\text{SS}\,|\,\text{L} & \begin{bmatrix} \text{CAT} & \begin{bmatrix} \text{HEAD} & {}_{\textit{verb}}\begin{bmatrix}\text{VFORM} & \textit{fin}\\ \text{AUX} & -\end{bmatrix} \\ \text{ASPECT} & \textit{point} \\ \text{SPR} & \langle\rangle \\ \text{SUBJ} & \langle \boxed{1} \rangle \\ \text{COMPS} & \langle \text{VP}\begin{bmatrix}\text{SUBJ}\ \langle\boxed{1}\rangle,\ \text{VFORM}\ \textit{ger},\\ \text{ASPECT}\ \textit{state} \lor \textit{activity}\end{bmatrix}:\boxed{2}\,\rangle \end{bmatrix} \\ \text{CONT} & {}_{\textit{past}}\begin{bmatrix} \text{ET\_HANDLE} & {}_{\textit{temp\_ent}}\begin{bmatrix}\text{TVAR}\ +\end{bmatrix} \\ \text{MAIN\_PSOA} & {}_{\textit{end}}\begin{bmatrix}\text{MAIN\_PSOA} & \boxed{2}\end{bmatrix}\end{bmatrix}\end{bmatrix}
\end{bmatrix}
$$

In (4.23), the COMPS value means that *finished* requires as its complement a gerund verb phrase, i.e., a gerund that has combined with its complements but not its subject, whose aspect must be culminating activity. The $\boxed{1}$ of COMPS points to a description of the required subject of the gerund verb phrase, and the $\boxed{2}$ is a pointer to the CONT value of the sign of the gerund verb phrase. The two $\boxed{1}$s in (4.23) have the effect that *finished* requires as its subject whatever the gerund verb phrase requires as its subject. The two $\boxed{2}$s cause the sign of *finished* to inherit the CONT value of the sign of the gerund verb phrase, but with additional *Past*, *End*, and *Culm* operators. (4.24) is similar, but it introduces no *Culm* operator.

In (4.21), the sign of the gerund *inspecting* retains the ASPECT of the base sign, which in the airport domain is *culmact*. The sign of the gerund verb phrase *inspecting BA737* inherits the *culmact* ASPECT of the gerund sign; this follows from the aspect principle, which will be discussed in Section 4.11.1. Hence, (4.23) is used, causing (4.21) to receive a sign whose CONT represents (4.25), i.e., the inspection must have been completed.

(4.25) $Past[e^v, End[Culm[inspecting(occr^v, ja, ba737)]]]$

In contrast, in (4.26) the sign of *circling* inherits the *activity* ASPECT of the base sign, causing (4.24) to be used. This leads to (4.27), which does not require any completion point to have been reached.

(4.26) BA737 finished circling.

(4.27) $Past[e^v, End[circling(ba737)]]$

There is also a sign of the simple past *finished* for the case where the gerund verb phrase is a point. In that case, the CONT of the sign of *finished* is identical to the the CONT of the sign of the gerund verb phrase, i.e., *finished* has no semantic contribution, in accordance with Section 2.6. The signs of *started*, *stopped*, and *began* are similar, except that they introduce *Begin* operators instead of *End* ones. Unlike *finished*, the signs of *stopped* do not introduce *Culm* operators when *stopped* combines with culminating activities, reflecting the fact that there is no need for a completion point to have been reached.

4.7.2 Auxiliary verbs and multi-word verb forms

We now move on to auxiliary verbs and multi-word verb forms, such as *had departed* and *is inspecting*. The sign of the simple past auxiliary *had* is shown in (4.28). The sign requires a past participle verb phrase to be used as a complement of *had*. The effect of the $\boxed{1}$s is that *had* requires as its subject whatever the past participle verb phrase requires as its subject. The $\boxed{2}$s cause the MAIN_PSOA value of the *perf* to be the same as the CONT value of the sign of the past participle verb phrase.

$$
(4.28)\quad \begin{bmatrix}
\text{PHON} & \langle \textit{had} \rangle \\
\text{SS}\,|\,\text{L} & \begin{bmatrix}
\text{CAT} & \begin{bmatrix}
\text{HEAD} & {}_{\textit{verb}}\begin{bmatrix}\text{VFORM} & \textit{fin}\\ \text{AUX} & + \end{bmatrix}\\
\text{ASPECT} & \textit{cnsq\_state}\\
\text{SPR} & \langle\rangle\\
\text{SUBJ} & \langle \boxed{1} \rangle\\
\text{COMPS} & \langle \text{VP}\begin{bmatrix}\text{SUBJ}\ \langle\boxed{1}\rangle,\ \text{VFORM}\ \textit{psp}\end{bmatrix}:\boxed{2}\rangle
\end{bmatrix}\\
\text{CONT} & {}_{\textit{past}}\begin{bmatrix}
\text{ET\_HANDLE} & {}_{\textit{temp\_ent}}\begin{bmatrix}\text{TVAR} & +\end{bmatrix}\\
\text{MAIN\_PSOA} & {}_{\textit{perf}}\begin{bmatrix}\text{ET\_HANDLE} & {}_{\textit{temp\_ent}}\begin{bmatrix}\text{TVAR} & +\end{bmatrix}\\ \text{MAIN\_PSOA} & \boxed{2}\end{bmatrix}
\end{bmatrix}
\end{bmatrix}
\end{bmatrix}
$$

In the airport domain, the past participle *departed* receives multiple signs, corresponding to various habitual and non-habitual uses of the verb; these are generated from the corresponding base form signs by the lexical rules of Section 4.7.1. In (4.29), the sign of (4.30) is used. According to (4.30), *departed* requires no complements, i.e., it counts as a verb phrase and can be used as the complement of *had*. When *had* combines with *departed*, the SUBJ of (4.28) becomes the same as the SUBJ of (4.30), and the MAIN_PSOA of the *perf* in (4.28) becomes the same as the CONT of (4.30), because of the $\boxed{1}$s and $\boxed{2}$s in (4.28), respectively. The resulting constituent *had departed* receives (4.31).

(4.29) BA737 had departed.

(4.30)
$$\begin{bmatrix} \text{PHON} & \langle \textit{departed} \rangle \\ \text{SS}\,|\,\text{L} & \begin{bmatrix} \text{CAT} & \begin{bmatrix} \text{HEAD} & {}_{\textit{verb}}\begin{bmatrix} \text{VFORM} & \textit{psp} \\ \text{AUX} & - \end{bmatrix} \\ \text{ASPECT} & \textit{point} \\ \text{SPR} & \langle\rangle \\ \text{SUBJ} & \langle \text{NP}\begin{bmatrix}\text{-PRD}\end{bmatrix}_{\textit{flight\_ent}\boxed{3}} \rangle \\ \text{COMPS} & \langle\rangle \end{bmatrix} \\ \text{CONT} & {}_{\textit{actl\_depart}}\begin{bmatrix} \text{ARG1} & \boxed{3} \end{bmatrix} \end{bmatrix} \end{bmatrix}$$

(4.31)
$$\begin{bmatrix} \text{PHON} & \langle \textit{had, departed} \rangle \\ \text{SS}\,|\,\text{L} & \begin{bmatrix} \text{CAT} & \begin{bmatrix} \text{HEAD} & {}_{\textit{verb}}\begin{bmatrix} \text{VFORM} & \textit{fin} \\ \text{AUX} & + \end{bmatrix} \\ \text{ASPECT} & \textit{cnsq\_state} \\ \text{SPR} & \langle\rangle \\ \text{SUBJ} & \langle \text{NP}\begin{bmatrix}\text{-PRD}\end{bmatrix}_{\textit{flight\_ent}\boxed{3}} \rangle \\ \text{COMPS} & \langle\rangle \end{bmatrix} \\ \text{CONT} & {}_{\textit{past}}\begin{bmatrix} \text{ET\_HANDLE} & {}_{\textit{temp\_ent}}\begin{bmatrix} \text{TVAR} + \end{bmatrix} \\ \text{MAIN\_PSOA} & {}_{\textit{perf}}\begin{bmatrix} \text{ET\_HANDLE} & {}_{\textit{temp\_ent}}\begin{bmatrix} \text{TVAR} + \end{bmatrix} \\ \text{MAIN\_PSOA} & {}_{\textit{actl\_depart}}\begin{bmatrix} \text{ARG1} & \boxed{3} \end{bmatrix} \end{bmatrix} \end{bmatrix} \end{bmatrix} \end{bmatrix}$$

The HPSG principles, including the semantics and aspect principles that will be discussed in later sections, cause (4.31) to inherit the HEAD, ASPECT, SPR, SUBJ, and CONT values of (4.28). Consequently, the aspect of *had departed* becomes consequent state, whereas *departed* was a point; this is in accordance with the aspectual shift of Section 2.5.5.

As will be explained further in Section 4.9, the proper name *BA737* contributes an index that represents the flight BA737. When *had departed* combines with its subject *BA737*, the index of *BA737* becomes the ARG1 value of (4.31), because of the $\boxed{3}$s of (4.31). This causes (4.29) to receive a sign whose CONT corresponds to (4.32).

(4.32) $Past[e1^v, Perf[e2^v, actl\_depart(ba737)]]$

As discussed in Sections 2.5.4 and 3.15, present perfect forms are treated semantically as simple past forms. This is why the sign of *has*, shown in (4.33), does not introduce a *Perf* operator, and preserves the aspect of the past participle, unlike the sign of *had*. This causes *BA737 has departed* to receive the same TOP formula as *BA737 departed*.

(4.33)
$$
\left[\begin{array}{ll}
\text{PHON} & \langle \textit{has} \rangle \\
\text{SS}\,|\,\text{L} & \left[\begin{array}{ll}
\text{CAT} & \left[\begin{array}{ll}
\text{HEAD} & {}_{\textit{verb}}\left[\begin{array}{ll} \text{VFORM} & \textit{fin} \\ \text{AUX} & + \end{array}\right] \\
\text{ASPECT} & \boxed{1} \\
\text{SPR} & \langle\rangle \\
\text{SUBJ} & \langle \boxed{2} \rangle \\
\text{COMPS} & \langle \text{VP}\left[\text{SUBJ}\ \langle\boxed{2}\rangle,\ \text{VFORM}\ \textit{psp},\ \text{ASPECT}\ \boxed{1}\right]{:}\boxed{3} \rangle
\end{array}\right] \\
\text{CONT} & {}_{\textit{past}}\left[\begin{array}{ll}
\text{ET\_HANDLE} & {}_{\textit{temp\_ent}}\left[\text{TVAR}\ +\right] \\
\text{MAIN\_PSOA} & \boxed{3}
\end{array}\right]
\end{array}\right]
\end{array}\right]
$$

The auxiliary *does* is given the sign of (4.34), which indicates that a base verb phrase is required as a complement. In accordance with the assumption of Section 2.5.1 that the simple present can be used only with state verbs, the verb phrase complement of *does* is required to be a lexical state. (4.34) and the habitual base sign of (4.35) cause (4.36) to receive (4.37); in this case, *Airserve* is the subject of both *does* and *service*.

(4.34)
$$\begin{bmatrix} \text{PHON} & \langle \textit{does} \rangle \\ \text{SS}\,|\,\text{L} & \begin{bmatrix} \text{CAT} & \begin{bmatrix} \text{HEAD} & {}_{\textit{verb}}\begin{bmatrix} \text{VFORM} & \textit{fin} \\ \text{AUX} & + \end{bmatrix} \\ \text{ASPECT} & \textit{lex\_state}\ \boxed{1} \\ \text{SPR} & \langle\rangle \\ \text{SUBJ} & \langle \boxed{2} \rangle \\ \text{COMPS} & \langle \text{VP}\begin{bmatrix} \text{SUBJ}\ \langle \boxed{2} \rangle, \text{VFORM}\ \textit{bse}, \text{ASPECT}\ \boxed{1} \end{bmatrix}{:}\boxed{3} \rangle \end{bmatrix} \\ \text{CONT} & {}_{\textit{pres}}\begin{bmatrix} \text{MAIN\_PSOA} & \boxed{3} \end{bmatrix} \end{bmatrix} \end{bmatrix}$$

(4.35)
$$\begin{bmatrix} \text{PHON} & \langle \textit{service} \rangle \\ \text{SS}\,|\,\text{L} & \begin{bmatrix} \text{CAT} & \begin{bmatrix} \text{HEAD} & {}_{\textit{verb}}\begin{bmatrix} \text{VFORM} & \textit{bse} \\ \text{AUX} & - \end{bmatrix} \\ \text{ASPECT} & \textit{lex\_state} \\ \text{SPR} & \langle\rangle \\ \text{SUBJ} & \langle \text{NP}\begin{bmatrix} \text{-PRD} \end{bmatrix}_{\textit{company\_ent}\boxed{4}} \rangle \\ \text{COMPS} & \langle \text{NP}\begin{bmatrix} \text{-PRD} \end{bmatrix}_{\textit{flight\_ent}\boxed{5}} \rangle \end{bmatrix} \\ \text{CONT} & {}_{\textit{hab\_servicer\_of}}\begin{bmatrix} \text{ARG1} & \boxed{4} \\ \text{ARG2} & \boxed{5} \end{bmatrix} \end{bmatrix} \end{bmatrix}$$

(4.36) Does Airserve service BA737?

(4.37)
$$\begin{bmatrix} \text{PHON} & \langle \textit{does, Airserve, service, BA737} \rangle \\ \text{SS}\,|\,\text{L} & \begin{bmatrix} \text{CAT} & \begin{bmatrix} \text{HEAD} & {}_{\textit{verb}}\begin{bmatrix} \text{VFORM} & \textit{bse} \\ \text{AUX} & + \end{bmatrix} \\ \text{ASPECT} & \textit{lex\_state} \\ \text{SPR} & \langle\rangle \\ \text{SUBJ} & \langle\rangle \\ \text{COMPS} & \langle\rangle \end{bmatrix} \\ \text{CONT} & {}_{\textit{pres}}\begin{bmatrix} \text{MAIN\_PSOA} & {}_{\textit{hab\_servicer\_of}}\begin{bmatrix} \text{ARG1} & \textit{airserve} \\ \text{ARG2} & \textit{ba737} \end{bmatrix} \end{bmatrix} \end{bmatrix} \end{bmatrix}$$

In the airport domain, there is an additional sign for the base form of *to service*, which corresponds to the non-habitual homonym. This is similar to (4.35), but it introduces the predicate functor *actl_servicing* and its ASPECT is *culmact*. This sign cannot be used in (4.36), because (4.34) requires the verb phrase complement to be a state, not a culminating activity. This correctly predicts that (4.36) cannot be asking if Airserve is actually servicing BA737 at the present moment.

The auxiliary *did* receives two signs. The first one, shown in (4.38), is for culminating activity verb phrase complements. The second one is used with state, activity, and point verb phrase complements; it is similar to (4.38), but does not introduce a *Culm*. In both cases, a *Past* is added.

(4.38)
$$\begin{bmatrix} \text{PHON} & \langle \textit{did} \rangle \\ \text{SS} \mid \text{L} & \begin{bmatrix} \text{CAT} & \begin{bmatrix} \text{HEAD} & {}_{\textit{verb}}\begin{bmatrix} \text{VFORM} & \textit{fin} \\ \text{AUX} & + \end{bmatrix} \\ \text{ASPECT} & \textit{culmact}\ \boxed{1} \\ \text{SPR} & \langle\rangle \\ \text{SUBJ} & \langle \boxed{2} \rangle \\ \text{COMPS} & \langle \text{VP}\begin{bmatrix} \text{SUBJ}\ \langle \boxed{2} \rangle,\ \text{VFORM}\ \textit{bse},\ \text{ASPECT}\ \boxed{1} \end{bmatrix} : \boxed{3} \rangle \end{bmatrix} \\ \text{CONT} & {}_{\textit{past}}\begin{bmatrix} \text{ET\_HANDLE} & {}_{\textit{temp\_ent}}\begin{bmatrix} \text{TVAR} + \end{bmatrix} \\ \text{MAIN\_PSOA} & {}_{\textit{culm}}\begin{bmatrix} \text{MAIN\_PSOA} & \boxed{3} \end{bmatrix} \end{bmatrix} \end{bmatrix} \end{bmatrix}$$

The non-habitual sign of *service* and (4.38) cause (4.39) to be mapped to (4.40), which requires Airserve to have actually serviced BA737 in the past. The habitual sign of (4.35) and the *did* sign for non-culminating activity complements cause (4.39) to be mapped to (4.41), which requires Airserve to have been a past habitual servicer of BA737.

(4.39) Did Airserve service BA737?

(4.40) $Past[e^v, Culm[actl\_servicing(occr^v, airserve, ba737)]]$

(4.41) $Past[e^v, hab\_servicer\_of(airserve, ba737)]$

The sign for the *is* auxiliary is shown in (4.42). Its functionality can be illustrated by considering the present participle *servicing*, which receives two signs in the airport domain: a non-habitual one, shown in (4.43), and a habitual one. The latter is similar to (4.43), but it introduces the functor *hab_servicer_of*, and its ASPECT is *lex_state*.

(4.42)
$$\begin{bmatrix} \text{PHON} & \langle \textit{is} \rangle \\ \text{SS}\mid\text{L} & \begin{bmatrix} \text{CAT} & \begin{bmatrix} \text{HEAD} & {}_{\textit{verb}}\begin{bmatrix}\text{VFORM} & \textit{fin}\\ \text{AUX} & +\end{bmatrix} \\ \text{ASPECT} & \textit{progressive} \\ \text{SPR} & \langle\rangle \\ \text{SUBJ} & \langle \boxed{1} \rangle \\ \text{COMPS} & \langle \text{VP}\begin{bmatrix}\text{SUBJ } \langle\boxed{1}\rangle, \text{VFORM } \textit{prp}\end{bmatrix}{:}\boxed{2} \rangle \end{bmatrix} \\ \text{CONT} & {}_{\textit{pres}}\begin{bmatrix}\text{MAIN\_PSOA} & \boxed{2}\end{bmatrix}\end{bmatrix}\end{bmatrix}$$

(4.43)
$$\begin{bmatrix} \text{PHON} & \langle \textit{servicing} \rangle \\ \text{SS}\mid\text{L} & \begin{bmatrix} \text{CAT} & \begin{bmatrix} \text{HEAD} & {}_{\textit{verb}}\begin{bmatrix}\text{VFORM} & \textit{prp}\\ \text{AUX} & -\end{bmatrix} \\ \text{ASPECT} & \textit{culmact} \\ \text{SPR} & \langle\rangle \\ \text{SUBJ} & \langle \text{NP}\begin{bmatrix}\text{-PRD}\end{bmatrix}_{\textit{company\_ent}}\boxed{1} \rangle \\ \text{COMPS} & \langle \text{NP}\begin{bmatrix}\text{-PRD}\end{bmatrix}_{\textit{flight\_ent}}\boxed{2} \rangle \end{bmatrix} \\ \text{CONT} & {}_{\textit{actl\_servicing}}\begin{bmatrix}\text{ARG1} & \textit{occr\_var} \\ \text{ARG2} & \boxed{1} \\ \text{ARG3} & \boxed{2}\end{bmatrix}\end{bmatrix}\end{bmatrix}$$

(4.42) and (4.43) cause (4.44) to be mapped to (4.45), which requires Airserve to be actually servicing BA737 at the present. In contrast, (4.42) and the habitual present participle sign of *servicing* cause (4.44) to be mapped to (4.46), which requires Airserve to be the current habitual servicer of BA737. The latter reading follows from the arrangements of Section 2.5.3, which allow state verbs to be used in progressive forms with the same meanings as the corresponding non-progressive forms.

(4.44) Airserve is servicing BA737.

(4.45) $\mathit{Pres}[\mathit{actl\_servicing}(\mathit{occr}^v, \mathit{airserve}, \mathit{ba737})]$

(4.46) $\mathit{Pres}[\mathit{hab\_servicer\_of}(\mathit{airserve}, \mathit{ba737})]$

The sign for the auxiliary *was* is similar to (4.42), except that it introduces a *Past* operator instead of a *Pres* one.

4.8 Predicative and non-predicative prepositions

Following Pollard and Sag (1987:65), prepositions receive separate signs for their *predicative* and *non-predicative* uses. In sentences like (4.47) and (4.48), where the prepositions introduce complements of *to be*, the prepositions are said to be predicative. In (4.49) and (4.50), where they introduce complements of other verbs, the prepositions are non-predicative.

(4.47) BA737 is at gate 2.
(4.48) BA737 was on runway 3.
(4.49) BA737 (habitually) arrives at gate 2.
(4.50) BA737 landed on runway 3.

Predicative prepositions introduce their own TOP predicates, while non-predicative prepositions have no semantic contribution; this is discussed further in the following paragraphs.

4.8.1 Predicative prepositions

The predicative sign of *at* is shown in (4.51); the predicative signs of other prepositions are similar. The 'PRD +' shows that the sign is predicative. The PFORM feature reflects the preposition the sign corresponds to. Signs for prepositional phrases inherit the PFORM of the preposition's sign, which is useful with verbs that require prepositional phrases introduced by particular prepositions.

(4.51)
$$\left[\begin{array}{ll} \text{PHON} & \langle at \rangle \\ \text{SS}\,|\,\text{L} & \left[\begin{array}{ll} \text{CAT} & \left[\begin{array}{ll} \text{HEAD} & {}_{prep}\left[\begin{array}{ll}\text{PFORM} & at \\ \text{PRD} & + \end{array}\right] \\ \text{SPR} & \langle\rangle \\ \text{SUBJ} & \langle \text{NP}[-\text{PRD}]_{\boxed{1}} \rangle \\ \text{COMPS} & \langle \text{NP}[-\text{PRD}]_{\boxed{2}}\rangle \end{array}\right] \\ \text{CONT} & {}_{located\_at}\left[\begin{array}{ll}\text{ARG1} & \boxed{1} \\ \text{ARG2} & non\_temp\_ent\boxed{2}\end{array}\right] \end{array}\right] \end{array}\right]$$

The PRD feature is also used to distinguish predicative from non-predicative uses of adjectives and nouns; this will be discussed in Sections 4.9 and 4.10. According to (4.51), *at* requires a non-predicative noun phrase as its subject, and another one as its complement; in (4.47), the noun phrases are *BA737* and *gate 2*, respectively. The $\boxed{1}$ and $\boxed{2}$ of (4.51) correspond to the indices that denote the entities of *BA737* and *gate 2*, respectively. (4.52) shows the resulting sign for the prepositional phrase *at gate 2*.

(4.52)
$$\begin{bmatrix} \text{PHON} & \langle \textit{at, gate2}\rangle \\ \text{SS}\,|\,\text{L} & \begin{bmatrix} \text{CAT} & \begin{bmatrix} \text{HEAD} & {}_{\textit{prep}}\begin{bmatrix}\text{PFORM} & \textit{at}\\ \text{PRD} & +\end{bmatrix} \\ \text{SPR} & \langle\rangle \\ \text{SUBJ} & \langle \text{NP}\big[\text{-PRD}\big]_{\boxed{1}}\rangle \\ \text{COMPS} & \langle\rangle \end{bmatrix} \\ \text{CONT} & {}_{\textit{located\_at}}\begin{bmatrix}\text{ARG1} & \boxed{1}\\ \text{ARG2} & \textit{gate2}\end{bmatrix}\end{bmatrix}\end{bmatrix}$$

Apart from (4.42), which is used when *is* combines with a present-participle complement, the *is* auxiliary is also given the lexical sign of (4.53), which is used when *is* combines with predicative prepositional phrases.

(4.53)
$$\begin{bmatrix} \text{PHON} & \langle \textit{is}\rangle \\ \text{SS}\,|\,\text{L} & \begin{bmatrix} \text{CAT} & \begin{bmatrix} \text{HEAD} & {}_{\textit{verb}}\begin{bmatrix}\text{VFORM} & \textit{fin}\\ \text{AUX} & +\end{bmatrix} \\ \text{ASPECT} & \textit{lex\_state} \\ \text{SPR} & \langle\rangle \\ \text{SUBJ} & \langle\boxed{3}\rangle \\ \text{COMPS} & \langle \text{PP}\big[\text{SUBJ}\ \langle\boxed{3}\rangle,\ \text{PRD}\ +\big]\!:\!\boxed{4}\ \rangle \end{bmatrix} \\ \text{CONT} & {}_{\textit{pres}}\begin{bmatrix}\text{MAIN\_PSOA} & \boxed{4}\end{bmatrix}\end{bmatrix}\end{bmatrix}$$

According to (4.53), *is* requires as its complement a predicative prepositional phrase, i.e., a predicative preposition that has combined with its complements but not its subject, like the *at gate 2* of (4.52). (4.52) and (4.53) cause (4.47) to receive (4.54).

(4.54)
$$\begin{bmatrix} \text{PHON} & \langle \textit{BA737, is, at, gate2} \rangle \\ \text{SS} \mid \text{L} & \begin{bmatrix} \text{CAT} & \begin{bmatrix} \text{HEAD} & {}_{\textit{verb}}\begin{bmatrix} \text{VFORM} & \textit{fin} \\ \text{AUX} & + \end{bmatrix} \\ \text{ASPECT} & \textit{lex\_state} \\ \text{SPR} & \langle\rangle \\ \text{SUBJ} & \langle\rangle \\ \text{COMPS} & \langle\rangle \end{bmatrix} \\ \text{CONT} & {}_{\textit{pres}}\begin{bmatrix} \text{MAIN\_PSOA} & {}_{\textit{located\_at}}\begin{bmatrix} \text{ARG1} & \textit{ba737} \\ \text{ARG2} & \textit{gate2} \end{bmatrix} \end{bmatrix} \end{bmatrix} \end{bmatrix}$$

Like *is*, the *was* auxiliary receives two signs: one for present participle complements, as in *BA737 was circling*, and one for predicative prepositional phrase complements, as in (4.48). These are similar to the signs of *is*, but they introduce *Past* operators rather than *Pres* ones.

4.8.2 Non-predicative prepositions

The non-predicative sign of *at* is shown in (4.55); the non-predicative signs of other prepositions are similar. The effect of the $\boxed{1}$s is that the CONT value of the sign of *at* is the same as the CONT value of the sign of the noun phrase complement of *at*; i.e., the *at* has no additional semantic contribution.

(4.55)
$$\begin{bmatrix} \text{PHON} & \langle \textit{at} \rangle \\ \text{SS} \mid \text{L} & \begin{bmatrix} \text{CAT} & \begin{bmatrix} \text{HEAD} & {}_{\textit{prep}}\begin{bmatrix} \text{PFORM} & \textit{at} \\ \text{PRD} & - \end{bmatrix} \\ \text{SPR} & \langle\rangle \\ \text{SUBJ} & \langle\rangle \\ \text{COMPS} & \langle \text{NP}\begin{bmatrix}\text{-PRD}\end{bmatrix}\text{:}\boxed{1} \rangle \end{bmatrix} \\ \text{CONT} & \boxed{1} \end{bmatrix} \end{bmatrix}$$

(4.55) and the habitual sign of *arrives* of (4.56) cause (4.49) to receive (4.57).

(4.56)
$$\begin{bmatrix} \text{PHON} & \langle \textit{arrives} \rangle \\ \text{SS} \mid \text{L} & \begin{bmatrix} \text{CAT} & \begin{bmatrix} \text{HEAD} & {}_{\textit{verb}}\begin{bmatrix} \text{VFORM} & \textit{fin} \\ \text{AUX} & - \end{bmatrix} \\ \text{ASPECT} & \textit{lex\_state} \\ \text{SPR} & \langle\rangle \\ \text{SUBJ} & \langle \text{NP}\begin{bmatrix}\text{-PRD}\end{bmatrix}_{\textit{flight\_ent}}\boxed{1} \rangle \\ \text{COMPS} & \langle \text{PP}\begin{bmatrix}\text{-PRD, PFORM } \textit{at}\end{bmatrix}_{\textit{gate\_ent}}\boxed{2} \rangle \end{bmatrix} \\ \text{CONT} & {}_{\textit{pres}}\begin{bmatrix} \text{MAIN\_PSOA} & {}_{\textit{hab\_arrive\_at}}\begin{bmatrix} \text{ARG1} & \boxed{1} \\ \text{ARG2} & \boxed{2} \end{bmatrix} \end{bmatrix} \end{bmatrix} \end{bmatrix}$$

(4.57)
$$\begin{bmatrix} \text{PHON} & \langle \textit{BA737, arrives, at, gate2} \rangle \\ \text{SS} \mid \text{L} & \begin{bmatrix} \text{CAT} & \begin{bmatrix} \text{HEAD} & {}_{\textit{verb}}\begin{bmatrix} \text{VFORM} & \textit{fin} \\ \text{AUX} & - \end{bmatrix} \\ \text{ASPECT} & \textit{lex\_state} \\ \text{SPR} & \langle\rangle \\ \text{SUBJ} & \langle\rangle \\ \text{COMPS} & \langle\rangle \end{bmatrix} \\ \text{CONT} & {}_{\textit{pres}}\begin{bmatrix} \text{MAIN\_PSOA} & {}_{\textit{hab\_arrive\_at}}\begin{bmatrix} \text{ARG1} & \textit{ba737} \\ \text{ARG2} & \textit{gate2} \end{bmatrix} \end{bmatrix} \end{bmatrix} \end{bmatrix}$$

The predicative and non-predicative prepositional signs of this section are not used when prepositions introduce temporal adverbials, as in *BA737 departed (actually) at 5:00 pm.* There are additional prepositional signs for these cases, which will be discussed in Section 4.11.

4.9 Nouns

Like prepositions, nouns receive different signs for their predicative and non-predicative uses. Nouns used as heads (main nouns) in noun phrase complements of *to be*, like the *president* in (4.58), are *predicative.* The noun phrase complements are also said to be predicative. In all other cases, like *the president* in (4.59), the nouns and noun phrases are *non-predicative.*

(4.58) J. Adams is the president.

(4.59) The president was at gate 2.

4.9.1 Non-predicative nouns

Let us first examine non-predicative nouns. (4.60) shows the sign of *president* that would be used in (4.59). The PRD value signals that the sign corresponds to a non-predicative use of the noun. The SPR value declares that the noun requires as its specifier a determiner (e.g., *a*, *the*).

(4.60)

$$
\left[\begin{array}{ll}
\text{PHON} & \langle \textit{president} \rangle \\
\text{SS}\,|\,\text{L} & \left[\begin{array}{ll}
\text{CAT} & \left[\begin{array}{ll}
\text{HEAD} & {}_{\textit{noun}}\left[\text{PRD}\ -\right] \\
\text{SPR} & \left\langle \left[\text{LOC}\,|\,\text{CAT}\,|\,\text{HEAD}\ \ \textit{det}\right] \right\rangle \\
\text{SUBJ} & \langle\rangle \\
\text{COMPS} & \langle\rangle
\end{array}\right] \\
\text{CONT} & {}_{\textit{nom\_obj}}\left[\begin{array}{ll}
\text{INDEX} & \textit{person\_ent}\,\boxed{1} \\
\text{RESTR} & \left\{ {}_{\textit{ntense}}\left[\begin{array}{ll}
\text{ET\_HANDLE} & {}_{\textit{temp\_ent}}\left[\text{TVAR}\ +\right] \lor \textit{now} \\
\text{MAIN\_PSOA} & {}_{\textit{president}}\left[\text{ARG1}\ \ \boxed{1}\right]
\end{array}\right] \right\}
\end{array}\right]
\end{array}\right] \\
\text{QSTORE} & \{\}
\end{array}\right]
$$

The CONT values of signs that correspond to non-predicative nouns are of sort *nom_obj* (Section 4.5). The INDEX value stands for the world entity described by the noun, and the RESTR value represents TOP expressions that are introduced by the noun.

For simplicity, the determiner *the* will be treated as equivalent to the determiner *a*. The sign of *the* that is used in (4.59) is shown in (4.61), where 'SPEC|L' is an abbreviation of 'SPEC|LOC'.

(4.61)

$$\begin{bmatrix} \text{PHON} & \langle \textit{the} \rangle \\ \text{SS}\,|\,\text{L} & \begin{bmatrix} \text{CAT} & \begin{bmatrix} \text{HEAD} & {}_{det}\begin{bmatrix} \text{SPEC}\,|\,\text{L} & \begin{bmatrix} \text{CAT} & \begin{bmatrix} \text{HEAD} & {}_{noun}\begin{bmatrix} \text{PRD} & - \end{bmatrix} \\ \text{SPR} & \langle \_ \rangle \\ \text{SUBJ} & \langle\rangle \\ \text{COMPS} & \langle\rangle \end{bmatrix} \\ \text{CONT} & \boxed{2} \end{bmatrix} \end{bmatrix} \\ \text{SPR} & \langle\rangle \\ \text{SUBJ} & \langle\rangle \\ \text{COMPS} & \langle\rangle \end{bmatrix} \\ \text{CONT} & {}_{quant}\begin{bmatrix} \text{DET} & \textit{exists} \\ \text{RESTIND} & \begin{bmatrix} \text{INDEX} & \begin{bmatrix} \text{TVAR} & + \end{bmatrix} \end{bmatrix}\boxed{2} \end{bmatrix}\boxed{3} \end{bmatrix} \\ \text{QSTORE} & \left\{ \boxed{3} \right\} \end{bmatrix}$$

The SPEC feature of (4.61) declares that *the* must be used as the specifier of a non-predicative $\bar{N}$, i.e., as the specifier of a non-predicative noun that has combined with its complements and requires a specifier (SPR < _ >). The $\boxed{3}$s of (4.61) cause an existential quantifier to be inserted into the quantifier store (Section 4.6), and the $\boxed{2}$s cause the RESTIND of that quantifier to be unified with the CONT of the $\bar{N}$'s sign.

According to (4.60), *president* is non-predicative, it does not need to combine with any complements, and requires a specifier. Hence, it satisfies the SPEC restrictions of (4.61), and *the* can be used as the specifier of *president*. When *the* combines with *president*, the RESTIND of (4.61) is unified with the CONT of (4.60), and the QSTORE of (4.61) becomes a set containing (4.62). The resulting noun phrase receives (4.63), where $\boxed{2}$ and $\boxed{3}$ are as in (4.62).

(4.62)

$${}_{quant}\begin{bmatrix} \text{DET} & \textit{exists} \\ \text{RESTIND} & {}_{nom\_obj}\begin{bmatrix} \text{INDEX} & {}_{person\_ent}\begin{bmatrix} \text{TVAR} & + \end{bmatrix}\boxed{1} \\ \text{RESTR} & \left\{ {}_{ntense}\begin{bmatrix} \text{ET\_HANDLE} & {}_{temp\_ent}\begin{bmatrix} \text{TVAR} & + \end{bmatrix} \vee \textit{now} \\ \text{MAIN\_PSOA} & {}_{president}\begin{bmatrix} \text{ARG1} & \boxed{1} \end{bmatrix} \end{bmatrix} \right\} \end{bmatrix}\boxed{2} \end{bmatrix}\boxed{3}$$

$$(4.63)\quad \begin{bmatrix} \text{PHON} & \langle \textit{the, president} \rangle \\ \text{SS} \mid \text{L} & \begin{bmatrix} \text{CAT} & \begin{bmatrix} \text{HEAD} & {}_{\textit{noun}}\begin{bmatrix} \text{PRD} & - \end{bmatrix} \\ \text{SPR} & \langle\rangle \\ \text{SUBJ} & \langle\rangle \\ \text{COMPS} & \langle\rangle \end{bmatrix} \\ \text{CONT} & \boxed{2} \end{bmatrix} \\ \text{QSTORE} & \left\{ \boxed{3} \right\} \end{bmatrix}$$

By the head feature principle (Section 4.2.2), (4.63) inherits the HEAD of (4.60), which is the sign of the head daughter in this case. The propagation of CONT and QSTORE is controlled by the semantics principle, which in this book has the simplified form of (4.64). (4.64) uses the terminology of Pollard and Sag (1994); it is explained further directly below.

(4.64) SEMANTICS PRINCIPLE (SIMPLIFIED VERSION OF THIS BOOK):
In a headed phrase, (a) the QSTORE value is the union of the QSTORE values of the daughters, and (b) the SYNSEM|LOC|CONT value is token-identical with that of the semantic head. (In a headed phrase, the *semantic head* is the ADJUNCT-DAUGHTER if any, and the HEAD-DAUGHTER otherwise.)

Part (a) of the semantics principle means that the QSTORE of each syntactic constituent is the union of the QSTORES of its subconstituents. Part (b) means that each syntactic constituent inherits the CONT of its head daughter (this is the main noun in noun phrases, the main verb in verb phrases, and the preposition in prepositional phrases), except for cases where the head daughter combines with an adjunct daughter (a modifier), where the mother syntactic constituent inherits the CONT of the adjunct daughter (this case will be discussed further in Section 4.11). Readers familiar with Pollard and Sag's book (1994) will have noticed that the semantics principle of this book does not allow quantifiers to be unstored from QSTORE. Apart from this, the principle remains as in Pollard and Sag's book.

The semantics principle causes the QSTORE of (4.63) to become the union of the QSTORES of (4.60) and (4.61), i.e., the union of the empty set with a set that contains (4.62). Since *the president* involves no adjuncts, the 'semantic head' is the head daughter i.e., *president*, and (4.63) inherits the CONT of (4.60), which is now the RESTIND of (4.62).

The *gate 2* of (4.59) is treated as a one-word proper name. In the prototype NLITDB of Chapter 6, the user types multi-word names, like *gate 2* and *J. Adams*, as single words. In real-life applications, the words of such names would be concatenated during a preprocessing stage (Section 1.2). Proper names are mapped to signs whose CONT is a *nom_obj* with an empty RESTR.[3] For example, (4.65) shows the lexical sign of *gate 2*.

(4.65)

$$\begin{bmatrix} \text{PHON} & \langle \textit{gate2} \rangle \\ \text{SS}\,|\,\text{L} & \begin{bmatrix} \text{CAT} & \begin{bmatrix} \text{HEAD} & {}_{\textit{noun}}\begin{bmatrix} \text{PRD} & - \end{bmatrix} \\ \text{SPR} & \langle\rangle \\ \text{SUBJ} & \langle\rangle \\ \text{COMPS} & \langle\rangle \end{bmatrix} \\ \text{CONT} & {}_{\textit{nom\_obj}}\begin{bmatrix} \text{INDEX} & \textit{gate2} \\ \text{RESTR} & \{\} \end{bmatrix} \end{bmatrix} \\ \text{QSTORE} & \{\} \end{bmatrix}$$

The predicative sign of *at* of (4.51), (4.65), and the predicative sign of *was*, which is similar to (4.53), except that it introduces a *Past* operator, cause *was at gate 2* in (4.59) to receive (4.66). When *was at gate 2* combines with *the president*, (4.59) receives (4.67), where QSTORE contains the feature structure of (4.62). According to the semantics principle, the QSTORE of (4.67) is the union of the QSTOREs of (4.66) and (4.63), and the CONT of (4.67) is the same as the CONT of (4.66).

(4.66)

$$\begin{bmatrix} \text{PHON} & \langle \textit{was, at, gate2} \rangle \\ \text{SS}\,|\,\text{L} & \begin{bmatrix} \text{CAT} & \begin{bmatrix} \text{HEAD} & {}_{\textit{verb}}\begin{bmatrix} \text{VFORM} & \textit{fin} \\ \text{AUX} & + \end{bmatrix} \\ \text{ASPECT} & \textit{lex\_state} \\ \text{SPR} & \langle\rangle \\ \text{SUBJ} & \langle \text{NP}\begin{bmatrix}\text{-PRD}\end{bmatrix}_{\boxed{1}} \rangle \\ \text{COMPS} & \langle\rangle \end{bmatrix} \\ \text{CONT} & {}_{\textit{past}}\begin{bmatrix} \text{ET\_HANDLE} & {}_{\textit{temp\_ent}}\begin{bmatrix} \text{TVAR} & + \end{bmatrix} \\ \text{MAIN\_PSOA} & {}_{\textit{located\_at}}\begin{bmatrix} \text{ARG1} & \boxed{1} \\ \text{ARG2} & \textit{gate2} \end{bmatrix} \end{bmatrix} \end{bmatrix} \\ \text{QSTORE} & \{\} \end{bmatrix}$$

$$
(4.67)\quad \begin{bmatrix}
\mathrm{PHON} & \langle \textit{the, president, was, at, gate2} \rangle \\
\mathrm{SS}\,|\,\mathrm{L} & \begin{bmatrix}
\mathrm{CAT} & \begin{bmatrix}
\mathrm{HEAD} & {}_{verb}\begin{bmatrix} \mathrm{VFORM} & fin \\ \mathrm{AUX} & + \end{bmatrix} \\
\mathrm{ASPECT} & lex\_state \\
\mathrm{SPR} & \langle\rangle \\
\mathrm{SUBJ} & \langle\rangle \\
\mathrm{COMPS} & \langle\rangle
\end{bmatrix} \\
\mathrm{CONT} & {}_{past}\begin{bmatrix}
\mathrm{ET\_HANDLE} & {}_{temp\_ent}\begin{bmatrix} \mathrm{TVAR} & + \end{bmatrix} \\
\mathrm{MAIN\_PSOA} & {}_{located\_at}\begin{bmatrix} \mathrm{ARG1} & \boxed{1} \\ \mathrm{ARG2} & gate2 \end{bmatrix}
\end{bmatrix}
\end{bmatrix} \\
\mathrm{QSTORE} & \left\{\boxed{3}\right\}
\end{bmatrix}
$$

The TOP formula (4.68) is then extracted from (4.67), as discussed in Section 4.6. Whenever an *Ntense* operator is encountered during the extraction of the TOP formulae, if there is no definite information showing that the first argument of the *Ntense* should be *now**, the first argument is taken to be a variable. For example, the QSTORE value of (4.67), shown in (4.62), specifies that the first argument of the *Ntense* can be either a TOP variable or *now**. Hence, in (4.68) the first argument of the *Ntense* has become a variable (t^v). During a post-processing phase, to be discussed in Section 4.17, the *Ntense* of (4.68) would give rise to two separate formulae: one where the first argument of the *Ntense* is replaced by *now** (current president), and one where the first argument of the *Ntense* is replaced by the e^v of the *Past* operator (president when at gate 2). In contrast, if the sign shows that the first argument of the *Ntense* is definitely *now**, the first argument of the *Ntense* in the extracted formula is *now**, and the post-processing has no effect on this argument.

$$(4.68)\quad Ntense[t^v, president(p^v)] \land Past[e^v, located\_at(p^v, gate2)]$$

It is possible to force a (non-predicative) noun to be interpreted as referring always to the speech time, or always to the time of the verb tense. (The same mechanism applies to non-predicative adjectives, to be discussed in Section 4.10.) To force a noun to refer always to the speech time, one sets the ET_HANDLE of the *ntense* in the noun's sign to simply *now*, instead of allowing it to be either *now* or a variable-representing index as in (4.60). This way, the ET_HANDLE of the *ntense* in the QSTORE of (4.67), shown in (4.62), would be *now*. (4.68) would contain now^* instead of t^v, and the post-processing mechanism would have no effect.

To force a noun to refer always to the time of the verb tense, one simply omits the *Ntense* from the noun's sign. This would cause the formula extracted from the sign of (4.59) to be (4.69).

(4.69) $president(p^v) \land Past[e^v, located\_at(p^v, gate2)]$

The semantics of TOP's conjunction and *Past* operator (Sections 3.6 and 3.8, respectively) require $president(p^v)$ and $located\_at(p^v, gate2)$ to be true at the same (past) event time. Hence, (4.69) expresses the reading where the person at gate 2 was the president of that time.

There are however, two complications when (non-predicative) noun signs do not introduce *Ntense* operators. (These also apply to adjective signs.) First, a past perfect sentence like (4.70) receives only (4.71) in the case where the adverbial specifies the reference time. This requires $president(p^v)$ to be true at the time of $e1^v$, i.e., at the reference time, which is required to fall within 1/1/1995. That is, *the president* is taken to refer to somebody who was the president on 1/1/1995, and who may not have been the president during the visit.

(4.70) The president had visited Rome on 1/1/1995.

(4.71) $president(p^v) \land$
$At[1/1/1995, Past[e1^v, Perf[e2^v, visiting(p^v, rome)]]]$

In contrast, if the sign of *president* introduces an *Ntense*, the formula extracted from the sign of (4.70) is (4.72). The post-processing, then, generates three formulae, corresponding to readings where *president* refers to the time of the visit (t^v replaced by $e2^v$), the reference time (t^v replaced by $e1^v$, equivalent to (4.71)), or the speech time (t^v replaced by now^*).

(4.72) $Ntense[t^v, president(p^v)] \land$
$At[1/1/1995, Past[e1^v, Perf[e2^v, visiting(p^v, rome)]]]$

The second complication is that (non-predicative) nouns that do not introduce *Ntense* operators are taken to refer to the time of the *main clause's* tense, even if the nouns appear in subordinate clauses. For example, if *president* does not introduce an *Ntense*, (4.73) is mapped to (4.74). The semantics of (4.74) requires the visitor to have been president during the building of terminal 2.

(4.73) Housecorp built terminal 2 before the president visited terminal 3.

(4.74) $president(p^v) \land Before[Past[e1^v, visiting(p^v, term3)],$
$Past[e2^v, Culm[building(hcorp, term2)]]]$

In contrast, if *president* introduces an *Ntense*, the post-processing generates three readings, where *president* refers to the speech time, the time of the building, or the time of the visit. The treatment of subordinate clauses will be discussed in Section 4.14.

Before moving on to predicative nouns, let us also examine the non-predicative signs of nouns like *day* or *summer*, which refer to members of partitionings (Section 3.4). The signs of these nouns are similar to the non-predicative signs of ordinary nouns, like *president*, except that they introduce *Part* operators and do not introduce *Ntense* operators. (4.75), for example, shows the non-predicative sign of *day*. (The *day* and *day_ent_var* sorts are as in Figure 4.4 on page 116.)

(4.75)
$$\begin{bmatrix} \text{PHON} & \langle \textit{day} \rangle \\ \text{SS} \mid \text{L} & \begin{bmatrix} \text{CAT} & \begin{bmatrix} \text{HEAD} & {}_{\textit{noun}}\begin{bmatrix} \text{PRD} & - \end{bmatrix} \\ \text{SPR} & \left\langle \begin{bmatrix} \text{LOC} \mid \text{CAT} \mid \text{HEAD} & \textit{det} \end{bmatrix} \right\rangle \\ \text{SUBJ} & \langle\rangle \\ \text{COMPS} & \langle\rangle \end{bmatrix} \\ \text{CONT} & {}_{\textit{nom\_obj}}\begin{bmatrix} \text{INDEX} & \textit{day\_ent\_var}\boxed{1} \\ \text{RESTR} & \left\{ {}_{\textit{part}}\begin{bmatrix} \text{PARTNG} & \textit{day} \\ \text{PART\_VAR} & \boxed{1} \end{bmatrix} \right\} \end{bmatrix} \end{bmatrix} \\ \text{QSTORE} & \{\} \end{bmatrix}$$

Names of months and days (e.g., *Monday*, *January*) that can be used both with and without determiners (e.g., *on a Monday*, *on Monday*) receive two non-predicative signs each: one that requires a determiner, and one that does not. Finally, proper names that refer to particular time-periods (e.g., the year-name *1991* or the date *25/10/1995*) receive non-predicative signs that are similar to those of common proper names (e.g., *gate 2*), except that their INDEX values are subsorts of *temp_ent* rather than *non_temp_ent*. Later sections will demonstrate how the signs of temporal nouns and proper names are used to form the signs of temporal adverbials, like *for two days*, or *before 25/10/1995*.

4.9.2 Predicative nouns

Let us now examine predicative nouns, like the *president* of (4.58). (4.76) shows the predicative sign of *president*. Unlike the signs of non-predicative nouns, whose CONT values are of sort *nom_obj*, the CONT values of the signs of predicative nouns are of sort *psoa* (Section 4.3). The *president* in (4.76) is a subsort of *psoa*.

(4.76)
$$\begin{bmatrix} \text{PHON} & \langle \textit{president} \rangle \\ \text{SS}\,|\,\text{L} & \begin{bmatrix} \text{CAT} & \begin{bmatrix} \text{HEAD} & {}_{\textit{noun}}\begin{bmatrix}\text{PRD} & + \end{bmatrix} \\ \text{SPR} & \left\langle \begin{bmatrix}\text{LOC}\,|\,\text{CAT}\,|\,\text{HEAD} & \textit{det}\end{bmatrix} \right\rangle \\ \text{SUBJ} & \langle \text{NP}\begin{bmatrix}\text{-PRD}\end{bmatrix}_{\boxed{1}} \rangle \\ \text{COMPS} & \langle\rangle \end{bmatrix} \\ \text{CONT} & {}_{\textit{president}}\begin{bmatrix}\text{ARG1} & \textit{person\_ent}\boxed{1}\end{bmatrix} \end{bmatrix} \\ \text{QSTORE} & \{\} \end{bmatrix}$$

Also, unlike non-predicative nouns that do not require subjects (e.g., (4.60)), predicative nouns do require subjects. In (4.76), *president* requires a non-predicative noun phrase as its subject; the $\boxed{1}$ stands for the index of that noun phrase.

In the HPSG version of this book, the predicative signs of nouns are generated automatically from the non-predicative ones by (4.77); for example, (4.76) is generated from (4.60).[4] As with previous lexical rules, features not shown in (4.77) (e.g., SPR, COMPS) have the same values in both the original and the generated signs. The *remove_ntense*($\boxed{2}$) in (4.77) means that if $\boxed{2}$, i.e., the element of the RESTR set in the non-predicative sign is of sort *ntense*, then the CONT of the predicative sign should be the MAIN_PSOA of $\boxed{2}$ (cf. (4.60)); otherwise, the CONT of the predicative sign should be $\boxed{2}$. In other words, if the non-predicative sign introduces an *Ntense* operator, the operator is removed in the predicative sign. This is in accordance with the observation in Section 2.11 that noun phrases that are complements of *to be* always refer to the time of the verb tense. For example, (4.78) means that J. Adams was the president in 1992, not at the speech time. (4.78) is represented correctly by (4.79), which does not contain an *Ntense* operator.

(4.77) Predicative Nouns Lexical Rule:

$$\left[\text{SS}\,|\,\text{L}\ \begin{bmatrix} \text{CAT} & \begin{bmatrix}\text{HEAD} & {}_{noun}\begin{bmatrix}\text{PRD} & -\end{bmatrix} \\ \text{SUBJ} & \langle\rangle\end{bmatrix} \\ \text{CONT} & {}_{nom\_obj}\begin{bmatrix}\text{INDEX} & \boxed{1} \\ \text{RESTR} & \left\{\boxed{2}\right\}\end{bmatrix}\end{bmatrix}\right]$$

$$\Downarrow$$

$$\left[\text{SS}\,|\,\text{L}\ \begin{bmatrix} \text{CAT} & \begin{bmatrix}\text{HEAD} & {}_{noun}\begin{bmatrix}\text{PRD} & +\end{bmatrix} \\ \text{SUBJ} & \langle \text{NP}\begin{bmatrix}\text{-PRD}\end{bmatrix}_{\boxed{1}} \rangle\end{bmatrix} \\ \text{CONT} & remove\_ntense(\boxed{2})\end{bmatrix}\right]$$

(4.78) J. Adams was the president in 1992.

(4.79) $At[1992, Past[e^v, president(ja)]]$

TOP predicates introduced by predicative nouns end up within the operators of the tenses of *to be*; for example, the *president(ja)* in (4.79) ends up within the *Past*. This requires the predicates to hold at the times of the tenses.

In this book, determiners are also given different signs for their uses in predicative and non-predicative noun phrases.[5] For example, apart from (4.61), the determiner *the* is also given (4.80), where 'SPEC|L' is again an abbreviation of 'SPEC|LOC'. The SPEC of (4.80) shows that the sign can only be used with predicative nouns (cf. (4.61)). Unlike determiners of non-predicative noun phrases, determiners of predicative noun phrases have no additional semantic contribution. For example, the SS|L|CONT of (4.80) is simply a copy of the CONT of the noun, and no quantifier is introduced in QSTORE (cf. (4.61)).

$$
(4.80)\quad \begin{bmatrix}
\text{PHON} & \langle \textit{the} \rangle \\
\text{SS}\,|\,\text{L} & \begin{bmatrix}
\text{CAT} & \begin{bmatrix}
\text{HEAD} & {}_{det}\begin{bmatrix} \text{SPEC}\,|\,\text{L} & \begin{bmatrix} \text{CAT} & \begin{bmatrix} \text{HEAD} & {}_{noun}\begin{bmatrix}\text{PRD} & + \end{bmatrix} \\ \text{SPR} & \langle \_ \rangle \\ \text{SUBJ} & \langle \_ \rangle \\ \text{COMPS} & \langle\rangle \end{bmatrix} \\ \text{CONT} & \boxed{2} \end{bmatrix} \end{bmatrix} \\
\text{SPR} & \langle\rangle \\
\text{SUBJ} & \langle\rangle \\
\text{COMPS} & \langle\rangle
\end{bmatrix} \\
\text{CONT} & \boxed{2}
\end{bmatrix} \\
\text{QSTORE} & \{\}
\end{bmatrix}
$$

Going back to (4.58), when *the* combines with *president*, the resulting noun phrase receives (4.81). HPSG's principles, including the semantics principle of (4.64), cause (4.81) to inherit the HEAD, SUBJ, and CONT values of (4.76).

$$
(4.81)\quad \begin{bmatrix}
\text{PHON} & \langle \textit{the, president} \rangle \\
\text{SS}\,|\,\text{L} & \begin{bmatrix}
\text{CAT} & \begin{bmatrix}
\text{HEAD} & {}_{noun}\begin{bmatrix}\text{PRD} & + \end{bmatrix} \\
\text{SPR} & \langle\rangle \\
\text{SUBJ} & \langle \text{NP}\begin{bmatrix}\text{-PRD}\end{bmatrix}_{\boxed{1}} \rangle \\
\text{COMPS} & \langle\rangle
\end{bmatrix} \\
\text{CONT} & {}_{president}\begin{bmatrix} \text{ARG1} & \textit{person\_ent}\,\boxed{1} \end{bmatrix}
\end{bmatrix} \\
\text{QSTORE} & \{\}
\end{bmatrix}
$$

Apart from (4.42) and (4.53), the *is* auxiliary is also given (4.82), which allows the complement of *is* to be a predicative noun phrase. (There are similar signs for *was*.) The $\boxed{4}$s in (4.82) stand for the CONT value of the predicative noun phrase.

$$(4.82)\quad \begin{bmatrix} \text{PHON} & \langle \textit{is} \rangle \\ \text{SS}\mid\text{L} & \begin{bmatrix} \text{CAT} & \begin{bmatrix} \text{HEAD} & {}_{\textit{verb}}\begin{bmatrix} \text{VFORM} & \textit{fin} \\ \text{AUX} & + \end{bmatrix} \\ \text{ASPECT} & \textit{lex\_state} \\ \text{SPR} & \langle\rangle \\ \text{SUBJ} & \langle \boxed{3} \rangle \\ \text{COMPS} & \langle \text{NP}\begin{bmatrix} \text{SUBJ } \langle \boxed{3} \rangle, \text{ PRD } + \end{bmatrix}\!:\!\boxed{4} \rangle \end{bmatrix} \\ \text{CONT} & {}_{\textit{pres}}\begin{bmatrix} \text{MAIN\_PSOA} & \boxed{4} \end{bmatrix} \end{bmatrix} \\ \text{QSTORE} & \{\} \end{bmatrix}$$

(4.82) and (4.81) cause the *is the president* of (4.58) to receive (4.83). Finally, when *is the president* combines with *J. Adams*, (4.58) receives a sign with an empty QSTORE, whose CONT represents (4.84).

$$(4.83)\quad \begin{bmatrix} \text{PHON} & \langle \textit{is, the, president} \rangle \\ \text{SS}\mid\text{L} & \begin{bmatrix} \text{CAT} & \begin{bmatrix} \text{HEAD} & {}_{\textit{verb}}\begin{bmatrix} \text{VFORM} & \textit{fin} \\ \text{AUX} & + \end{bmatrix} \\ \text{ASPECT} & \textit{lex\_state} \\ \text{SPR} & \langle\rangle \\ \text{SUBJ} & \langle \text{NP}\begin{bmatrix} \text{-PRD} \end{bmatrix}_{\boxed{1}} \rangle \\ \text{COMPS} & \langle\rangle \end{bmatrix} \\ \text{CONT} & {}_{\textit{pres}}\begin{bmatrix} \text{MAIN\_PSOA} & {}_{\textit{president}}\begin{bmatrix} \text{ARG1} & \textit{person\_ent}\boxed{1} \end{bmatrix} \end{bmatrix} \end{bmatrix} \\ \text{QSTORE} & \{\} \end{bmatrix}$$

(4.84) *Pres*[*president*(*ja*)]

There are two additional complications with predicative noun phrases. The first one is that in the non-predicative signs of proper names (e.g., (4.65)), the value of RESTR is the empty set. Hence, (4.77) does not generate the corresponding predicative signs, because the non-predicative signs do not match the RESTR description of the left-hand side of (4.77), which requires the RESTR value to be a one-element set. This causes (4.85) to be rejected, because there is no predicative sign for *J. Adams*. To solve this problem, the additional lexical rule of (4.86) can be used.

(4.85) The inspector is J. Adams.

(4.86) Additional Predicative Nouns Lexical Rule:

$$\begin{bmatrix} \text{SS}\,|\,\text{L} & \begin{bmatrix} \text{CAT} & \begin{bmatrix} \text{HEAD} & {}_{noun}\begin{bmatrix}\text{PRD} & -\end{bmatrix} \\ \text{SUBJ} & \langle\rangle \end{bmatrix} \\ \text{CONT} & {}_{nom\_obj}\begin{bmatrix} \text{INDEX} & \boxed{1} \\ \text{RESTR} & \{\} \end{bmatrix} \end{bmatrix} \end{bmatrix}$$

$$\Downarrow$$

$$\begin{bmatrix} \text{SS}\,|\,\text{L} & \begin{bmatrix} \text{CAT} & \begin{bmatrix} \text{HEAD} & {}_{noun}\begin{bmatrix}\text{PRD} & +\end{bmatrix} \\ \text{SUBJ} & \langle \text{NP}\begin{bmatrix}\text{-PRD}\end{bmatrix}_{\boxed{2}} \rangle \end{bmatrix} \\ \text{CONT} & {}_{identity}\begin{bmatrix} \text{ARG1} & \boxed{1} \\ \text{ARG2} & \boxed{2} \end{bmatrix} \end{bmatrix} \end{bmatrix}$$

This would generate (4.87) from the non-predicative sign of *J. Adams*; the latter is similar to (4.65). (4.82) and (4.87) would then cause (4.85) to be mapped to (4.88). For simplicity, it is assumed here that the non-predicative *inspector* does not introduce an *Ntense* operator (Section 4.9.1).

(4.87)
$$\begin{bmatrix} \text{PHON} & \langle \textit{J.Adams} \rangle \\ \text{SS}\,|\,\text{L} & \begin{bmatrix} \text{CAT} & \begin{bmatrix} \text{HEAD} & {}_{noun}\begin{bmatrix}\text{PRD} & +\end{bmatrix} \\ \text{SPR} & \langle\rangle \\ \text{SUBJ} & \langle \text{NP}\begin{bmatrix}\text{-PRD}\end{bmatrix}_{\boxed{2}} \rangle \\ \text{COMPS} & \langle\rangle \end{bmatrix} \\ \text{CONT} & {}_{identity}\begin{bmatrix} \text{ARG1} & ja \\ \text{ARG2} & \boxed{2} \end{bmatrix} \end{bmatrix} \\ \text{QSTORE} & \{\} \end{bmatrix}$$

(4.88) $inspector(insp^v) \land Pres[identity(ja, insp^v)]$

The $identity(\tau_1, \tau_2)$ is intended to be true at event times where its two arguments denote the same entity. This calls for a special domain-independent semantics for $identity(\tau_1, \tau_2)$, an issue that will not be explored further.

The second complication is that the non-predicative sign of *Monday*, which is similar to (4.75), and the treatment of predicative noun phrases above lead to an attempt to map (4.89) to (4.90).

(4.89) 23/10/1995 was a Monday.

(4.90) $Past[e^v, Part[monday^g, 23/10/1995]]$

(4.90) is problematic for two reasons. First, the past tense of (4.89) is in effect ignored, because the denotation of $Part[\sigma, \beta]$ does not depend on *lt*, which is what the *Past* operator affects (Sections 3.6 and 3.8). Hence, the implication of (4.89) that 23/10/1995 is a past day is not captured. This problem could be solved by adding the constraint $g(\beta) \sqsubseteq lt$ in the semantics of $Part[\sigma, \beta]$. Second, (4.90) violates the syntax of TOP, which does not allow the second argument of a *Part* operator to be a constant; this could be solved by enhancing the definition of *Part* accordingly. Since, sentences like (4.89) are rare in database querying, however, these issues will not be investigated further.

4.10 Adjectives

Following Pollard and Sag (1987:64–65), adjectives are also given different signs for their predicative and non-predicative uses. When used as complements of *to be*, as with *closed* in (4.91), adjectives are said to be predicative. In all other cases, for example (4.92), adjectives are non-predicative.

(4.91) Runway 2 was closed.
(4.92) BA737 landed on a closed runway.

Sentence (4.91) is actually ambiguous. The *closed* may be a predicative adjective or the passive of *to close*. However, since passives are ignored in this book (Section 2.13), the passive reading of (4.91) will be ignored.

In the airport domain, the predicative adjectival sign of *closed* is (4.93).

(4.93)
$$\begin{bmatrix} \text{PHON} & \langle \textit{closed} \rangle \\ \text{SS}\,|\,\text{L} & \begin{bmatrix} \text{CAT} & \begin{bmatrix} \text{HEAD} & {}_{adj}\begin{bmatrix} \text{PRD} & + \end{bmatrix} \\ \text{SPR} & \langle\rangle \\ \text{SUBJ} & \langle \text{NP}\begin{bmatrix} \text{-PRD} \end{bmatrix}_{\boxed{1}} \rangle \\ \text{COMPS} & \langle\rangle \end{bmatrix} \\ \text{CONT} & {}_{closed}\begin{bmatrix} \text{ARG1} & (\textit{gate\_ent} \vee \textit{runway\_ent})\boxed{1} \end{bmatrix} \end{bmatrix} \\ \text{QSTORE} & \{\} \end{bmatrix}$$

The *is* and *was* auxiliaries receive four signs each. One for progressive forms (see (4.42)), one for prepositional phrase complements (see (4.53)), one for noun phrase complements (see (4.82)), and one for adjectival complements ((4.94) below). (4.94) and (4.93) cause (4.91) to be mapped to (4.95).

(4.94)
$$\begin{bmatrix} \textsc{phon} & \langle \textit{was} \rangle \\ \textsc{ss}\,|\,\textsc{l} & \begin{bmatrix} \textsc{cat} & \begin{bmatrix} \textsc{head} & {}_{\textit{verb}}\begin{bmatrix} \textsc{vform} & \textit{fin} \\ \textsc{aux} & + \end{bmatrix} \\ \textsc{aspect} & \textit{lex\_state} \\ \textsc{spr} & \langle\rangle \\ \textsc{subj} & \langle \boxed{3} \rangle \\ \textsc{comps} & \left\langle \begin{bmatrix} \textsc{loc} & \begin{bmatrix} \textsc{cat} & \begin{bmatrix} \textsc{head} & {}_{\textit{adj}}\begin{bmatrix} \textsc{prd} & + \end{bmatrix} \\ \textsc{subj} & \langle \boxed{3} \rangle \\ \textsc{comps} & \langle\rangle \end{bmatrix} \\ \textsc{cont} & \boxed{2} \end{bmatrix} \end{bmatrix} \right\rangle \end{bmatrix} \\ \textsc{cont} & {}_{\textit{past}}\begin{bmatrix} \textsc{et\_handle} & {}_{\textit{temp\_ent}}\begin{bmatrix} \textsc{tvar} & + \end{bmatrix} \\ \textsc{main\_psoa} & \boxed{2} \end{bmatrix} \end{bmatrix} \\ \textsc{qstore} & \{\} \end{bmatrix}$$

(4.95) $\mathit{Past}[e^v, \mathit{closed}(\mathit{runway2})]$

The non-predicative sign of *closed* in the airport domain is shown in (4.96). The *closed* in (4.92) is a modifier (adjunct) of *runway*. The MOD|L in (4.96) refers to the SYNSEM|LOC (abbreviated as SS|L) of the modified noun. The SS|L|CONT of (4.96) is the same as the one of the noun, except that an *Ntense* is added to the RESTR of the noun-sign, which requires the entity described by the noun to be closed at some unspecified time. The INDEX of the noun's sign is also required to represent a gate or runway.

(4.96)
$$
\left[\begin{array}{ll}
\textsc{phon} & \langle \textit{closed} \rangle \\
\textsc{ss} \mid \textsc{l} & \left[\begin{array}{ll}
\textsc{cat} & \left[\begin{array}{ll}
\textsc{head} & \left[\begin{array}{ll}
\textsc{prd} & - \\
\textsc{mod} \mid \textsc{l} & \left[\begin{array}{ll}
\textsc{cat} & \left[\begin{array}{ll}
\textsc{head} & \textit{noun} \\
\textsc{spr} & \langle \_ \rangle \\
\textsc{comps} & \langle \rangle
\end{array}\right] \\
\textsc{cont} & {}_{\textit{nom\_obj}}\left[\begin{array}{ll}
\textsc{index} & \boxed{1} \\
\textsc{restr} & \boxed{2}
\end{array}\right]
\end{array}\right]
\end{array}\right]_{\textit{adj}} \\
\textsc{spr} & \langle \rangle \\
\textsc{subj} & \langle \rangle \\
\textsc{comps} & \langle \rangle
\end{array}\right] \\
\textsc{cont} & \left[\begin{array}{ll}
\textsc{index} & (\textit{gate\_ent} \vee \textit{runway\_ent})\boxed{1} \\
\textsc{restr} & \boxed{2} \cup \left\{ {}_{\textit{ntense}}\left[\begin{array}{ll}
\textsc{et\_handle} & {}_{\textit{temp\_ent}}\left[\textsc{tvar}\ +\right] \vee \textit{now} \\
\textsc{main\_psoa} & {}_{\textit{closed}}\left[\textsc{arg1}\ \boxed{1}\right]
\end{array}\right] \right\}
\end{array}\right]_{\textit{nom\_obj}}
\end{array}\right] \\
\textsc{qstore} & \{\}
\end{array}\right]
$$

The non-predicative sign of *runway* in the airport domain is shown in (4.97). It is assumed here that *runway* does not introduce an *Ntense* operator (Section 4.9.1). In (4.92), *closed* combines with *runway* according to HPSG's head-adjunct schema (Pollard & Sag 1994), leading to (4.98), where $\boxed{3}$ is the set of (4.99). (Sets of *psoa*s correspond to conjunctions.) The principles of HPSG cause (4.98) to inherit the HEAD and SPR of (4.97). (4.98) also inherits the CONT of (4.96), according to the semantics principle of (4.64); in this case, the 'semantic head' is the adjunct *closed*. Then, (4.98), along with the sign of *landed*, which is the same as (4.1), except that it also introduces *Past* and *Culm* operators, and the non-predicative sign of *on*, which is similar to (4.55), cause (4.92) to be mapped to (4.100). During the post-processing, to be discussed in Section 4.17, (4.100) gives rise to two different formulae, one where t^v is replaced by now^* (currently closed runway), and one where t^v is replaced by e^v (closed during the landing).

(4.97)
$$\begin{bmatrix} \text{PHON} & \langle \textit{runway} \rangle \\ \text{SS}\,|\,\text{L} & \begin{bmatrix} \text{CAT} & \begin{bmatrix} \text{HEAD} & {}_{\textit{noun}}\begin{bmatrix}\text{PRD} & -\end{bmatrix} \\ \text{SPR} & \left\langle \begin{bmatrix}\text{LOC}\,|\,\text{CAT}\,|\,\text{HEAD} & \textit{det}\end{bmatrix} \right\rangle \\ \text{SUBJ} & \langle\rangle \\ \text{COMPS} & \langle\rangle \end{bmatrix} \\ \text{CONT} & {}_{\textit{nom\_obj}}\begin{bmatrix} \text{INDEX} & \textit{runway\_ent}\boxed{1} \\ \text{RESTR} & \left\{ {}_{\textit{runway}}\begin{bmatrix}\text{ARG1} & \boxed{1}\end{bmatrix} \right\} \end{bmatrix} \end{bmatrix} \\ \text{QSTORE} & \{\} \end{bmatrix}$$

(4.98)
$$\begin{bmatrix} \text{PHON} & \langle \textit{closed, runway} \rangle \\ \text{SS}\,|\,\text{L} & \begin{bmatrix} \text{CAT} & \begin{bmatrix} \text{HEAD} & {}_{\textit{noun}}\begin{bmatrix}\text{PRD} & -\end{bmatrix} \\ \text{SPR} & \left\langle \begin{bmatrix}\text{LOC}\,|\,\text{CAT}\,|\,\text{HEAD} & \textit{det}\end{bmatrix} \right\rangle \\ \text{SUBJ} & \langle\rangle \\ \text{COMPS} & \langle\rangle \end{bmatrix} \\ \text{CONT} & {}_{\textit{nom\_obj}}\begin{bmatrix} \text{INDEX} & \textit{runway\_ent}\boxed{1} \\ \text{RESTR} & \boxed{3} \end{bmatrix} \end{bmatrix} \\ \text{QSTORE} & \{\} \end{bmatrix}$$

(4.99)
$$\left\{ {}_{\textit{runway}}\begin{bmatrix}\text{ARG1} & \boxed{1}\end{bmatrix},\ {}_{\textit{ntense}}\begin{bmatrix} \text{ET\_HANDLE} & {}_{\textit{temp\_ent}}\begin{bmatrix}\text{TVAR} & +\end{bmatrix} \vee \textit{now} \\ \text{MAIN\_PSOA} & {}_{\textit{closed}}\begin{bmatrix}\text{ARG1} & \boxed{1}\end{bmatrix} \end{bmatrix} \right\}\boxed{3}$$

(4.100) $runway(r^v) \wedge Ntense[t^v, closed(r^v)] \wedge$
$Past[e^v, Culm[landing\_on(occr^v, ba737, r^v)]]$

An additional sign is needed for each non-predicative adjective to allow sentences like (4.101), where a non-predicative adjective (*closed*) combines with a predicative noun (*runway*).

(4.101) Runway 2 is a closed runway.

The sign of (4.96) cannot be used in (4.101), because here *runway* is predicative, and hence the CONT value of its sign is a *psoa* (the predicative sign of *runway* is similar to (4.76)); in contrast, (4.96) assumes that the CONT of the noun is a *nom_obj*. One has to use the additional sign of (4.102). Then, (4.101) is mapped to (4.103), which requires runway 2 to be closed at the speech time.

(4.102)

$$\begin{bmatrix} \mathrm{PHON} & \langle \textit{closed} \rangle \\ \mathrm{SS} \mid \mathrm{L} & \begin{bmatrix} \mathrm{CAT} & \begin{bmatrix} \mathrm{HEAD} & {\begin{bmatrix} \mathrm{PRD} & - \\ \mathrm{MOD} \mid \mathrm{L} & \begin{bmatrix} \mathrm{CAT} & \begin{bmatrix} \mathrm{HEAD} & {\begin{bmatrix} \mathrm{PRD} & + \end{bmatrix}}_{noun} \\ \mathrm{SPR} & \langle \_ \rangle \\ \mathrm{SUBJ} & \langle \mathrm{NP}[\mathrm{-PRD}]_{\boxed{1}} \rangle \\ \mathrm{COMPS} & \langle\rangle \end{bmatrix} \\ \mathrm{CONT} & \boxed{2} \end{bmatrix} \end{bmatrix}}_{adj} \\ \mathrm{SPR} & \langle\rangle \\ \mathrm{SUBJ} & \langle\rangle \\ \mathrm{COMPS} & \langle\rangle \end{bmatrix} \\ \mathrm{CONT} & {\begin{bmatrix} \mathrm{CONJ1} & \boxed{2} \\ \mathrm{CONJ2} & {\begin{bmatrix} \mathrm{ARG1} & \boxed{1} \end{bmatrix}}_{closed} \end{bmatrix}}_{and} \end{bmatrix} \\ \mathrm{QSTORE} & \{\} \end{bmatrix}$$

(4.103) $Pres[runway(runway2) \land closed(runway2)]$

As discussed in Section 2.8, temporal adjectives such as *former* or *annual* are not considered in this book. The prototype NLITDB of Chapter 6 allows only non-predicative uses of the temporal adjective *current*, as in (4.104), to allow its users to force noun phrases to refer to the present. The sign of *current* sets the first argument of the noun's *Ntense* to *now**.

(4.104) The current president was at terminal 2.

4.11 Temporal adverbials

We now turn to the treatment of temporal adverbials, starting from punctual adverbials (Section 2.9.1).

4.11.1 Punctual adverbials

Apart from (4.51) and (4.55), which are used in sentences like (4.47) and (4.49), *at* is also given signs that are used when it introduces punctual adverbials, as in (4.105). (4.106) shows one of these signs. The MOD feature refers to the SYNSEM (abbreviated as SS) of the constituent that is modified by *at*. The S[VFORM *fin*]:$\boxed{2}$ is an abbreviation for a finite sentence, i.e., a finite verb form that has combined with its subject and complements; the $\boxed{2}$ refers to the CONT of the finite sentence. Similarly, VP[VFORM *psp*]:$\boxed{2}$ stands for a past participle verb phrase, i.e., a past participle that has combined with its complements, but not its subject. (4.106) can be used when *at* modifies finite sentences or past participle verb phrases, whose aspect is state, activity, or point. Generally, in this book temporal adverbials and temporal subordinate clauses are allowed to modify only finite sentences and past participle verb phrases.

(4.105) Tank 2 was empty at 5:00 pm.

(4.106)

$$\begin{bmatrix} \textsc{phon} & \langle at \rangle \\ \textsc{ss}\,|\,\textsc{l} & \begin{bmatrix} \textsc{cat} & \begin{bmatrix} \textsc{head} & \begin{bmatrix} \textsc{prd} & - \\ \textsc{mod} & \textsc{s}\begin{bmatrix}\textsc{vform}\ fin\end{bmatrix}:\boxed{2} \vee \textsc{vp}\begin{bmatrix}\textsc{vform}\ psp\end{bmatrix}:\boxed{2} \\ \textsc{mod}\,|\,\textsc{l}\,|\,\textsc{cat}\,|\,\textsc{aspect} & state \vee activity \vee point \end{bmatrix}_{prep} \\ \textsc{spr} & \langle\rangle \\ \textsc{subj} & \langle\rangle \\ \textsc{comps} & \langle \textsc{np}\begin{bmatrix}\textsc{-prd}\end{bmatrix}_{minute\_ent}\boxed{1} \rangle \\ \textsc{aspect} & point \end{bmatrix} \\ \textsc{cont} & \begin{bmatrix} \textsc{time\_spec} & \boxed{1} \\ \textsc{main\_psoa} & \boxed{2} \end{bmatrix}_{at\_op} \end{bmatrix} \\ \textsc{qstore} & \{\} \end{bmatrix}$$

As with multi-word proper names (Section 4.9), time expressions like *5:00 pm* are treated as single words, assuming that in real-life applications their tokens would be concatenated during a preprocessing stage. The sign of *5:00 pm* is shown in (4.107). Along with (4.106), it causes *at 5:00 pm* to receive (4.108). The *5:00 pm* acts as the noun phrase complement of *at*.

(4.107)
$$\begin{bmatrix}
\text{PHON} & \langle \textit{5:00pm} \rangle \\
\text{SS}\,|\,\text{L} & \begin{bmatrix}
\text{CAT} & \begin{bmatrix} \text{HEAD} & {}_{noun}\begin{bmatrix}\text{PRD} & -\end{bmatrix} \\ \text{SPR} & \langle\rangle \\ \text{SUBJ} & \langle\rangle \\ \text{COMPS} & \langle\rangle \end{bmatrix} \\
\text{CONT} & {}_{nom_obj}\begin{bmatrix} \text{INDEX} & \textit{minute_ent_var}\,\boxed{1} \\ \text{RESTR} & \left\{ {}_{part}\begin{bmatrix} \text{PARTNG} & \textit{5:00pm} \\ \text{PART_VAR} & \boxed{1} \end{bmatrix} \right\} \boxed{3} \end{bmatrix}
\end{bmatrix} \\
\text{QSTORE} & \left\{ \begin{bmatrix} \text{DET} & \textit{exists} \\ \text{RESTIND} & \boxed{3} \end{bmatrix} \right\}
\end{bmatrix}$$

(4.108)
$$\begin{bmatrix}
\text{PHON} & \langle \textit{at, 5:00pm} \rangle \\
\text{SS}\,|\,\text{L} & \begin{bmatrix}
\text{CAT} & \begin{bmatrix} \text{HEAD} & {}_{prep}\begin{bmatrix}\text{PRD} & - \\ \text{MOD} & \text{S}\begin{bmatrix}\text{VFORM}\ \textit{fin}\end{bmatrix}{:}\boxed{2} \vee \\ & \text{VP}\begin{bmatrix}\text{VFORM}\ \textit{psp}\end{bmatrix}{:}\boxed{2} \\ \text{MOD}\,|\,\text{L}\,|\,\text{CAT}\,|\,\text{ASPECT} & \textit{state} \vee \textit{activity} \\ & \vee\, \textit{point} \end{bmatrix} \\ \text{SPR} & \langle\rangle \\ \text{SUBJ} & \langle\rangle \\ \text{COMPS} & \langle\rangle \\ \text{ASPECT} & \textit{point} \end{bmatrix} \\
\text{CONT} & {}_{at_op}\begin{bmatrix} \text{TIME_SPEC} & \boxed{1} \\ \text{MAIN_PSOA} & \boxed{2} \end{bmatrix}
\end{bmatrix} \\
\text{QSTORE} & \left\{ \begin{bmatrix} \text{DET} & \textit{exists} \\ \text{RESTIND} & \begin{bmatrix} \text{INDEX} & \textit{minute_ent_var}\,\boxed{1} \\ \text{RESTR} & \left\{ {}_{part}\begin{bmatrix} \text{PARTNG} & \textit{5:00pm} \\ \text{PART_VAR} & \boxed{1} \end{bmatrix} \right\} \end{bmatrix} \end{bmatrix} \right\}
\end{bmatrix}$$

According to HPSG's head feature principle (Section 4.2.2), (4.108) inherits the HEAD of (4.106); here *at* is the 'head daughter' of *at 5:00 pm*, and *5:00 pm* is the 'complement daughter'. Following the semantics principle of (4.64), the QSTORE of (4.108) is the union of the QSTOREs of (4.106) and (4.107), and the

CONT of (4.108) is the same as the CONT of (4.106); in this case, the 'semantic head' is the head daughter, i.e., *at*.

The propagation of ASPECT is controlled by (4.109), a new principle of this book. The principle is first stated in Pollard and Sag's (1994) terminology, and then explained in following paragraphs.

(4.109) ASPECT PRINCIPLE:

In a headed-phrase, the SYNSEM|LOC|CAT|ASPECT value is token-identical with that of the semantic head. (In a headed phrase, the *semantic head* is the ADJUNCT-DAUGHTER if any, and the HEAD-DAUGHTER otherwise.)

According to the principle, each syntactic constituent inherits the ASPECT of its head daughter (this is the main noun in noun phrases, the main verb in verb phrases, and the preposition in prepositional phrases), except for cases where the head daughter combines with an adjunct daughter (a modifier), where the mother syntactic constituent inherits the CONT of the adjunct daughter. (4.109) causes (4.108) to inherit the ASPECT value of the semantic head *at*.

In (4.105), the *tank 2 was empty* receives (4.110). Then, when *tank 2 was empty* combines with *at 5:00 pm*, (4.105) receives (4.111). In this case, *tank 2 was empty* is the head daughter, and *at 5:00 pm* is an adjunct daughter (a modifier). Hence, according to (4.109), (4.111) inherits the ASPECT of (4.108), i.e., *point*; in contrast, the ASPECT of (4.110) was *lex_state*. This is in accordance with the arrangements of Section 2.9.1, whereby punctual adverbials trigger an aspectual shift to point.

(4.110)
```
[ PHON    ⟨tank2, was, empty⟩
  SS | L  [ CAT   [ HEAD    verb[ VFORM  fin
                                  AUX    + ]
                    ASPECT  lex_state
                    SPR     ⟨⟩
                    SUBJ    ⟨⟩
                    COMPS   ⟨⟩ ]
            CONT  past[ ET_HANDLE   temp_ent[ TVAR  + ]
                        MAIN_PSOA   empty[ ARG1  tank2 ] ] ]
  QSTORE  {} ]
```

(4.111)

$$
\left[\begin{array}{ll}
\text{PHON} & \langle \textit{tank2, was, empty, at, 5:00pm} \rangle \\
\text{SS}\,|\,\text{L} & \left[\begin{array}{ll}
\text{CAT} & \left[\begin{array}{ll}
\text{HEAD} & {}_{\textit{verb}}\left[\begin{array}{ll}\text{VFORM} & \textit{fin}\\ \text{AUX} & +\end{array}\right]\\
\text{ASPECT} & \textit{point}\\
\text{SPR} & \langle\rangle\\
\text{SUBJ} & \langle\rangle\\
\text{COMPS} & \langle\rangle
\end{array}\right]\\
\text{CONT} & {}_{\textit{at\_op}}\left[\begin{array}{ll}
\text{TIME\_SPEC} & \boxed{1}\\
\text{MAIN\_PSOA} & {}_{\textit{past}}\left[\begin{array}{ll}
\text{ET\_HANDLE} & {}_{\textit{temp\_ent}}\left[\text{TVAR}\ \ +\right]\\
\text{MAIN\_PSOA} & {}_{\textit{empty}}\left[\text{ARG1}\ \ \textit{tank2}\right]
\end{array}\right]
\end{array}\right]
\end{array}\right]\\
\text{QSTORE} & \left\{\left[\begin{array}{ll}
\text{DET} & \textit{exists}\\
\text{RESTIND} & \left[\begin{array}{ll}
\text{INDEX} & \textit{minute\_ent\_var}\boxed{1}\\
\text{RESTR} & \left\{{}_{\textit{part}}\left[\begin{array}{ll}\text{PARTNG} & \textit{5:00pm}\\ \text{PART\_VAR} & \boxed{1}\end{array}\right]\right\}
\end{array}\right]
\end{array}\right]\right\}
\end{array}\right]
$$

According to the semantics principle, (4.111) also inherits the CONT of (4.108), which is the sign of the modifier, and the QSTORE of (4.111) is the union of the QSTORES of (4.108) and (4.110). Finally, according to the head feature principle (Section 4.2.2), (4.111) inherits the HEAD of (4.110), which is the sign of the head daughter. The QSTORE and CONT of (4.111) represent (4.112).

(4.112) $Part[5{:}00pm^{g}, fv^{v}] \land At[fv^{v}, Past[e^{v}, empty(tank2)]]$

The reader may wonder why temporal adverbials (e.g., *at 5:00 pm* in (4.105)) are taken to modify whole finite sentences (*tank 2 was empty*), rather than finite verb phrases (*was empty*). The latter approach leads to problems in questions like '*Was tank 2 empty at 5:00 pm?*', where *was* combines in one step with both its subject *tank 2* and its complement *empty*, following Pollard and Sag's (1994) head-subject-complement schema. Hence, there is no verb phrase constituent, i.e., no verb that has combined with its complements but not its subject, to be modified by *at 5:00 pm*.

Apart from finite sentences, temporal adverbials are also allowed to modify past participle verb phrases, as shown in the MOD of (4.106). This is needed in past perfect sentences like (4.113).

(4.113) BA737 had entered sector 2 at 5:00 pm.

As discussed in Section 2.5.5, (4.113) has two readings: one where the entrance occurs at 5:00 pm, and one where 5:00 pm is a reference time, a time where the entrance has already occurred. The two readings are expressed by (4.115) and (4.117), respectively (Section 3.15). These follow from the fact that (4.113) is taken to be syntactically ambiguous with two possible parses, sketched in (4.114) and (4.116), respectively.

(4.114) BA737 had [[entered sector 2] at 5:00 pm].

(4.115) $Part[5{:}00pm^g, fv^v] \land$
$Past[e1^v, Perf[e2^v, At[fv^v, enter(ba737, sector2)]]]$

(4.116) [BA737 had [entered sector 2]] at 5:00 pm.

(4.117) $Part[5{:}00pm^g, fv^v] \land$
$At[fv^v, Past[e1^v, Perf[e2^v, enter(ba737, sector2)]]]$

One complication of this approach is that it generates two equivalent formulae for the present perfect (4.118), shown in (4.120) and (4.122), which correspond to the parses of (4.119) and (4.121), respectively. The reader is reminded that *has* does not introduce a *Perf* operator, as shown in (4.33).

(4.118) BA737 has entered sector 2 at 5:00 pm.

(4.119) [BA737 has [entered sector 2]] at 5:00 pm.

(4.120) $Part[5{:}00pm^g, fv^v] \land At[fv^v, Past[e^v, enter(ba737, sector2)]]$

(4.121) BA737 has [[entered sector 2] at 5:00 pm].

(4.122) $Part[5{:}00pm^g, fv^v] \land Past[e^v, At[fv^v, enter(ba737, sector2)]]$

In the prototype NLITDB of Chapter 6, the sign of *has* is slightly more complex than (4.33). It requires the CONT of the verb phrase complement to be of sort *predicate*. This blocks (4.121) and (4.122), because in (4.121) the *at 5:00 pm* causes the CONT of *entered sector 2 at 5:00 pm* to become of sort *at_op* (it inserts an *At* operator), which is not a subsort of *predicate*.

The sign of (4.106) corresponds to the interjacent meaning of punctual adverbials, which according to Table 2.2 on page 46 is possible only with states and activities. (4.106) also covers cases where punctual adverbials combine with points. The inchoative and terminal meanings of punctual adverbials are covered by additional signs for *at*, which are similar to (4.106), but introduce additional *Begin* or *End* operators, and require the modified constituent to have the appropriate aspect.

4.11.2 Period adverbials

We now move on to period adverbials (Section 2.9.2). (4.123) shows one of the signs of *on* that are used when *on* introduces period adverbials.

(4.123)
$$\left[\begin{array}{ll} \text{PHON} & \langle \textit{on} \rangle \\ \text{SS}\,|\,\text{L} & \left[\begin{array}{ll} \text{CAT} & \left[\begin{array}{ll} \text{HEAD} & {}_{\textit{prep}}\left[\begin{array}{ll} \text{PRD} & - \\ \text{MOD} & \text{S}\left[\text{VFORM } \textit{fin}\right]{:}\boxed{2} \lor \\ & \text{VP}\left[\text{VFORM } \textit{psp}\right]{:}\boxed{2} \\ \text{MOD}\,|\,\text{L}\,|\,\text{CAT}\,|\,\text{ASPECT} & \textit{culmact} \end{array}\right] \\ \text{SPR} & \langle\rangle \\ \text{SUBJ} & \langle\rangle \\ \text{COMPS} & \langle \text{NP}\left[\text{-PRD}\right]_{\textit{day\_ent}}\boxed{1} \rangle \\ \text{ASPECT} & \textit{point} \end{array}\right] \\ \text{CONT} & {}_{\textit{at\_op}}\left[\begin{array}{ll} \text{TIME\_SPEC} & \boxed{1} \\ \text{MAIN\_PSOA} & {}_{\textit{end}}\left[\text{MAIN\_PSOA } \boxed{2}\right] \end{array}\right] \end{array}\right] \\ \text{QSTORE} & \{\} \end{array}\right]$$

According to its MOD feature, (4.123) can be used only when the *on* adverbial modifies a culminating activity. (4.123) corresponds to the reading where the situation of the culminating activity simply reaches its completion within the adverbial's period, and causes the aspectual class of the culminating activity to become point; see Table 2.3 on page 50. For example, (4.123) causes (4.124) to be mapped to (4.125). (It is assumed here that *to repair* is classified as culminating activity verb, as in the airport domain.) Intuitively, (4.125) requires a past period e^v to exist, such that e^v covers a whole repair of engine 2 by J. Adams, from start to completion, and the end-point of e^v falls within some Monday. That is, the repair must have been completed on Monday, but it may have started before Monday.

(4.124) J. Adams repaired engine 2 on Monday.

(4.125) $Part[monday^g, m^v] \land$
$At[m^v, End[Past[e^v, [Culm[repairing(occr^v, ja, eng2)]]]]]$

There is also an *on* sign that is similar to (4.123), but that does not introduce an *End* operator, preserves the ASPECT of the modified expression, and can be used when *on* adverbials modify expressions from all four aspectual classes.

This sign causes (4.124) to be mapped to (4.126). (The prototype NLITDB of Chapter 6 generates both (4.125) and (4.126).) (4.126) corresponds to the reading where the repair must have both started and been completed within the same Monday. The *on* sign that does not introduce an *End* operator also gives rise to appropriate formulae when *on* adverbials modify state, activity, or point expressions.

(4.126) $Part[monday^g, m^v] \land$
$At[m^v, Past[e^v, [Culm[repairing(occr^v, ja, eng2)]]]$

Both signs of *on* require the noun phrase complement of *on* to introduce an index of sort *day_ent*. The signs of *1/1/1991* and *Monday* introduce indices of sorts *1/1/1991* and *day_ent_var* respectively, which are subsorts of *day_ent* (Figure 4.4 on page 116). Hence, *1/1/1991* and *Monday* are legitimate complements of *on* in period adverbials. In contrast, *5:00 pm* introduces an index of sort *minute_ent_var*, as can be seen in (4.107), which is not a subsort of *day_ent*. Consequently, (4.127) is correctly rejected.

(4.127) *Tank 2 was empty on 5:00 pm.

The signs of other prepositions that introduce period adverbials (e.g., *in 1991*, *before 29/10/1995*, *after 5:00 pm*) and the signs of *yesterday* and *today* are similar to the signs of *on*, except that *before* and *after* introduce *Before* and *After* operators instead of *At* operators. Also, the *before* preposition is given only one sign, that does not introduce an *End* operator, i.e., there is no *before* sign for culminating activities analogous to (4.123), which introduces an *End*. This is in accordance with the observation made in Section 2.9.2 that in the case of *before* adverbials, requiring the situation of a culminating activity to simply reach its completion before some time (reading with *End*) is equivalent to requiring the situation to both start and reach its completion before that time (reading without *End*).

4.11.3 Duration adverbials

The treatment of duration adverbials is rather ad hoc from a syntactic point of view. In an adverbial like *for two days*, both *two* and *days* are taken to be complements of *for*, instead of treating *two* as the determiner of *days*, and *two days* as a noun phrase complement of *for*. Words like *one*, *two*, *three*, etc. are mapped to signs like (4.128). Their RESTRS are empty, and their indices represent the corresponding numbers. The *2* of (4.128) is a subsort of *sem_num*

(Section 4.4). The *none* value of the SPEC feature reflects the fact that these signs are not intended to be used when the corresponding words act as determiners.

(4.128)
$$\begin{bmatrix} \textsc{phon} & \langle \textit{two} \rangle \\ \textsc{ss}\,|\,\textsc{l} & \begin{bmatrix} \textsc{cat} & \begin{bmatrix} \textsc{head} & {}_{\textit{det}}\begin{bmatrix}\textsc{spec} & \textit{none}\end{bmatrix} \\ \textsc{spr} & \langle\rangle \\ \textsc{subj} & \langle\rangle \\ \textsc{comps} & \langle\rangle \end{bmatrix} \\ \textsc{cont} & {}_{\textit{nom\_obj}}\begin{bmatrix}\textsc{index} & \textit{2} \\ \textsc{restr} & \{\}\end{bmatrix} \end{bmatrix} \\ \textsc{qstore} & \{\} \end{bmatrix}$$

The sign of *for* that is used in duration adverbials is shown in (4.129). The feature structures that correspond to $\boxed{5}$ and $\boxed{6}$ are shown in (4.130) and (4.131). The COMPS of (4.129) means that *for* requires two complements: a determiner that introduces a number-denoting index (*sem_num*), such as the *two* of (4.128), and a noun that introduces a *Part* operator whose first argument is a complete partitioning name, like the *day* of (4.75). The adverbial *for two days* receives (4.135). No number agreement checks are made (Section 4.3), and plural nouns are treated semantically as singular ones. Hence, apart from PHON, the sign of *days* is the same as (4.75).

(4.129)
$$\left[\begin{array}{ll} \text{PHON} & \langle \textit{for} \rangle \\ \text{SS} \mid \text{L} & \left[\begin{array}{ll} \text{CAT} & \left[\begin{array}{ll} \text{HEAD} & {}_{prep}\left[\begin{array}{ll} \text{PRD} & - \\ \text{MOD} & \text{S}\left[\text{VFORM } \textit{fin}\right]\text{:}\boxed{4} \lor \\ & \text{VP}\left[\text{VFORM } \textit{psp}\right]\text{:}\boxed{4} \\ \text{MOD} \mid \text{L} \mid \text{CAT} \mid \text{ASPECT} & (\textit{lex\_state} \\ & \lor\ \textit{progressive} \\ & \lor\ \textit{activity})\boxed{1} \end{array}\right] \\ \text{SPR} & \langle\rangle \\ \text{SUBJ} & \langle\rangle \\ \text{COMPS} & \langle \boxed{5}, \boxed{6} \rangle \\ \text{ASPECT} & \boxed{1} \end{array}\right] \\ \text{CONT} & {}_{for\_op}\left[\begin{array}{ll} \text{DUR\_UNIT} & \boxed{2} \\ \text{DURATION} & \boxed{3} \\ \text{MAIN\_PSOA} & \boxed{4} \end{array}\right] \end{array}\right] \\ \text{QSTORE} & \{\} \end{array}\right]$$

(4.130)
$$\left[\text{LOC} \left[\begin{array}{ll} \text{CAT} \mid \text{HEAD} & \textit{det} \\ \text{CONT} \mid \text{INDEX} & \textit{sem\_num}\boxed{3} \end{array}\right]\right]\boxed{5}$$

(4.131)
$$\left[\text{LOC} \left[\begin{array}{ll} \text{CAT} & \left[\begin{array}{ll} \text{HEAD} & \textit{noun} \\ \text{SPR} & \langle \_ \rangle \\ \text{SUBJ} & \langle\rangle \\ \text{COMPS} & \langle\rangle \end{array}\right] \\ \text{CONT} \mid \text{RESTR} & \left\{ {}_{part}\left[\text{PARTNG } \textit{compl\_partng}\boxed{2}\right] \right\} \end{array}\right]\right]\boxed{6}$$

In (4.132), when *tank 2 was empty* combines with its modifier *for two days*, the $\boxed{4}$ of (4.135) becomes a feature structure that represents the TOP formula for *tank 2 was empty*, i.e., (4.133). According to the semantics principle of (4.64), the sign of (4.132) inherits the CONT of (4.135), where $\boxed{4}$ now represents (4.133). Hence, (4.132) is mapped to (4.134).

(4.132) Tank 2 was empty for two days.

(4.133) $Past[e^{v}, empty(tank2)]$

(4.134) $For[day^{c}, 2, Past[e^{v}, empty(tank2)]]$

$$
(4.135)\quad \begin{bmatrix}
\text{PHON} & \langle \textit{for, two, days}\rangle \\
\text{SS}\,|\,\text{L} & \begin{bmatrix}
\text{CAT} & \begin{bmatrix}
\text{HEAD} & {}_{\textit{prep}}\begin{bmatrix}
\text{PRD} & - \\
\text{MOD} & \text{S}\begin{bmatrix}\text{VFORM}\ \textit{fin}\end{bmatrix}:\boxed{4} \lor \\
 & \text{VP}\begin{bmatrix}\text{VFORM}\ \textit{psp}\end{bmatrix}:\boxed{4} \\
\text{MOD}\,|\,\text{L}\,|\,\text{CAT}\,|\,\text{ASPECT} & (\textit{lex\_state} \\
 & \lor\ \textit{progressive} \\
 & \lor\ \textit{activity})\boxed{1}
\end{bmatrix} \\
\text{SPR} & \langle\rangle \\
\text{SUBJ} & \langle\rangle \\
\text{COMPS} & \langle\rangle \\
\text{ASPECT} & \boxed{1}
\end{bmatrix} \\
\text{CONT} & {}_{\textit{for\_op}}\begin{bmatrix}
\text{DUR\_UNIT} & \textit{day} \\
\text{DURATION} & 2 \\
\text{MAIN\_PSOA} & \boxed{4}
\end{bmatrix}
\end{bmatrix} \\
\text{QSTORE} & \{\}
\end{bmatrix}
$$

Following Table 2.4 on page 53, (4.129) does not allow *for* adverbials to modify point expressions (the MOD|L|CAT|ASPECT of (4.129) cannot be *point*). It also does not allow *for* adverbials to modify consequent states; otherwise, apart from (4.137), (4.136) would also receive (4.138).

(4.136) BA737 had circled for two hours.

(4.137) $Past[e1^v, Perf[e2^v, For[hour^c, 2, circling(ba737)]]]$

(4.138) $For[hour^c, 2, Past[e1^v, Perf[e2^v, circling(ba737)]]]$

(4.137) corresponds to the parse of (4.136) where *for two hours* modifies the past participle *circled* before *circled* combines with *had*. In that case, the *for* adverbial modifies an activity, because past participles retain the aspectual class of the base form (*to circle* is an activity verb in the airport domain). (4.138) corresponds to the parse where *for two hours* modifies the whole sentence *BA737 had circled*. In that case, the *for* adverbial modifies a consequent state, because the *had* has caused the aspectual class of *BA737 had circled* to become consequent state. By not allowing *for* adverbials to modify consequent states, (4.138) is blocked. This is needed, because in (4.138) the two hours is the duration of a period (pointed to by $e1^v$) that follows a period (pointed to by $e2^v$) where BA737 was circling. This reading is never available when *for* adverbials are used in past perfect sentences. The *for* adverbial of (4.136) can only specify the duration of the circling, as in (4.137). Kamp and Reyle (1993: 587) make a similar observation.

The treatment of *for* duration adverbials causes (4.139) to receive (4.140), which does not capture correctly the meaning of (4.139), because it requires the taxiing to have been completed, i.e., BA737 to have reached gate 2. In contrast, as discussed in Section 2.9.3, the *for* adverbial cancels the normal implication of *BA737 taxied to gate 2* that the taxiing was completed. The post-processing stage that will be discussed in Section 4.17 removes the *Culm* operator of (4.140), generating a formula that does not require the taxiing to have been completed.

(4.139) BA737 taxied to gate 2 for five minutes.

(4.140) $For[minute^c, 5, Past[e^v, Culm[taxiing\_to(ba737, gate2)]]]$

Duration adverbials introduced by *in*, as in (4.141), are treated by mapping *in* to a sign that is the same as (4.129), except that it allows the adverbial to modify only culminating activities. As discussed in Section 2.9.4, the framework of this book does not allow *in* duration adverbials to modify states, activities, or points.

(4.141) BA737 taxied to gate 2 in five minutes.

This causes (4.141) to be mapped to (4.140), which correctly requires the taxiing to have been completed, and the duration of the taxiing, from start to completion, to be five minutes. In this case, the post-processing does not remove the *Culm* operator.

4.12 Temporal complements of habituals

Let us now examine more closely the status of temporal prepositional phrases, like *at 5:00 pm* and *on Monday* in (4.142)–(4.145).

(4.142) BA737 departed at 5:00 pm.

(4.143) BA737 departs at 5:00 pm.

(4.144) J. Adams inspected gate 2 on Monday.

(4.145) J. Adams inspects gate 2 on Monday.

(4.142) has both a habitual and a non-habitual reading. The non-habitual reading refers to an actual departure that took place at 5:00 pm. The habitual reading means that BA737 had the habit of departing at 5:00 pm; this reading is easier to accept if an adverbial like *in 1999* is added. In (4.143), only the habitual reading is possible, i.e., BA737 currently has the habit of departing at 5:00 pm. A scheduled-to-happen reading is also possible in (4.143), but as discussed in Section 2.5.1, this is ignored in this book. Similar comments apply to (4.144) and (4.145).

To account for the habitual and non-habitual readings of *to depart* in (4.142) and (4.143), the base form of the verb is given the signs of (4.146) and (4.147), which correspond to what Chapter 2 called informally the habitual and non-habitual homonyms of *to depart.* (4.146) classifies the habitual homonym as (lexical) state, while (4.147) classifies the non-habitual homonym as point; this agrees with Table 2.1 on page 29. According to (4.146), the habitual homonym requires a prepositional phrase introduced by *at* that specifies the habitual departure time. In contrast, the non-habitual homonym of (4.147) requires no complement.

(4.146)
$$\begin{bmatrix} \text{PHON} & \langle \textit{depart} \rangle \\ \text{SS}\,|\,\text{L} & \begin{bmatrix} \text{CAT} & \begin{bmatrix} \text{HEAD} & {}_{\textit{verb}}\begin{bmatrix} \text{VFORM} & \textit{bse} \\ \text{AUX} & - \end{bmatrix} \\ \text{ASPECT} & \textit{lex\_state} \\ \text{SPR} & \langle\rangle \\ \text{SUBJ} & \langle\, \text{NP}\begin{bmatrix}\text{-PRD}\end{bmatrix}_{\textit{flight\_ent}}\boxed{1}\, \rangle \\ \text{COMPS} & \langle\, \text{PP}\begin{bmatrix}\text{-PRD, PFORM } \textit{at}\end{bmatrix}_{\textit{minute\_gappy}}\boxed{2}\,\rangle \end{bmatrix} \\ \text{CONT} & {}_{\textit{hab\_departs\_at}}\begin{bmatrix}\text{ARG1} & \boxed{1} \\ \text{ARG2} & \boxed{2}\end{bmatrix} \end{bmatrix} \\ \text{QSTORE} & \{\} \end{bmatrix}$$

(4.147)
$$\begin{bmatrix} \text{PHON} & \langle \textit{depart} \rangle \\ \text{SS}\,|\,\text{L} & \begin{bmatrix} \text{CAT} & \begin{bmatrix} \text{HEAD} & {}_{\textit{verb}}\begin{bmatrix} \text{VFORM} & \textit{bse} \\ \text{AUX} & - \end{bmatrix} \\ \text{ASPECT} & \textit{point} \\ \text{SPR} & \langle\rangle \\ \text{SUBJ} & \langle\, \text{NP}\begin{bmatrix}\text{-PRD}\end{bmatrix}_{\textit{flight\_ent}}\boxed{1}\, \rangle \\ \text{COMPS} & \langle\rangle \end{bmatrix} \\ \text{CONT} & {}_{\textit{actl\_depart}}\begin{bmatrix}\text{ARG1} & \boxed{1}\end{bmatrix} \end{bmatrix} \\ \text{QSTORE} & \{\} \end{bmatrix}$$

In the airport domain, there are actually two habitual signs for *to depart*: one where *to depart* requires a prepositional phrase complement introduced by *at*, as in (4.146), and one where *to depart* requires a prepositional phrase complement introduced by *from*; the latter is needed in (4.148). There are also two non-habitual signs of *to depart*, one where *to depart* requires no complement, as in (4.147), and one where *to depart* requires a prepositional phrase complement introduced by *from*; the latter is needed in (4.149). For simplicity, these extra signs will be ignored here.

(4.148) BA737 (habitually) departs from gate 2.
(4.149) BA737 (actually) departed from gate 2.

The signs of (4.146) and (4.147), along with the simple past lexical rules of Section 4.7.1, lead to two signs for the simple past *departed*, a habitual and a non-habitual one. These are the same as (4.146) and (4.147), except that they contain additional *Past* operators. In contrast, the simple present lexical rule of Section 4.7.1 generates only one sign for *departs*. This is the same as (4.146), except that it contains an additional *Pres* operator. No simple present sign is generated from (4.147), because the simple present lexical rule requires the aspect of the base sign to be state.

The non-habitual simple past sign of *departed*, the *at* sign of (4.106), and the *5:00 pm* sign of (4.107), cause (4.142) to be mapped to (4.150), which expresses the non-habitual reading of (4.142). In this case, *at 5:00 pm* is treated as a temporal adverbial modifier of *BA737 departed*, as discussed in Section 4.11.1.

(4.150) $Part[5{:}00pm, fv^v] \land At[fv^v, Past[e^v, act\_depart(ba737)]]$

In the habitual reading of (4.142), the habitual sign of *departed* is used, which is derived from (4.146). In this case, *at 5:00 pm* is treated as a prepositional phrase complement of *departed*, and the sign of *at* that introduces non-predicative prepositional phrase complements, i.e., (4.55), is used. The intention is to map (4.142) to (4.151), where *5:00pm* is a constant acting as a generic representative of 5:00 pm minutes (Section 3.18).

(4.151) $Past[e^v, hab\_departs\_at(ba737, 5{:}00pm)]$

The problem is that in this case the *5:00 pm* sign of (4.107) cannot be used, because it inserts a *Part* operator in QSTORE. The semantics principle would cause this *Part* operator to be inherited by the sign of the overall (4.142), and thus the *Part* operator would appear in the resulting formula. To address this problem, an extra sign, shown in (4.152), is given to *5:00 pm*, which does not introduce a *Part* operator. Similarly, an extra sign for *Monday* is needed in (4.144). The *5:00 pm* sign of (4.152), the *at* sign of (4.55), and the habitual *departed* sign, which is derived from (4.146), cause (4.142) to be mapped to (4.151).

$$
(4.152)\quad \begin{bmatrix} \text{PHON} & \langle \textit{5:00pm} \rangle \\ \text{SS}\,|\,\text{L} & \begin{bmatrix} \text{CAT} & \begin{bmatrix} \text{HEAD} & {}_{\textit{noun}}\begin{bmatrix}\text{PRD} & - \end{bmatrix} \\ \text{SPR} & \langle\rangle \\ \text{SUBJ} & \langle\rangle \\ \text{COMPS} & \langle\rangle \end{bmatrix} \\ \text{CONT} & {}_{\textit{nom\_obj}}\begin{bmatrix} \text{INDEX} & \textit{5:00pm} \\ \text{RESTR} & \{\} \end{bmatrix} \end{bmatrix} \\ \text{QSTORE} & \{\} \end{bmatrix}
$$

The habitual *departed* sign, which derives from (4.146), requires the index of the prepositional phrase complement to be of sort *minute_gappy*. As desired, this does not allow the *5:00 pm* sign of (4.107), the one that introduces a *Part* operator, to be used in the prepositional phrase complement of the habitual *departed*, because the index of the prepositional phrase would then be of sort *minute_ent_var*, which is not a subsort of *minute_gappy* (Figure 4.4 on page 116). In contrast, (4.152) introduces an index of sort *5:00pm*, which is a subsort of *minute_gappy*, and hence that sign can be used in the complement of the habitual *departed*.

The treatment of the simple present (4.143) is similar. In this case, the habitual simple present sign, which is derived from (4.146), is used, and (4.143) is mapped to (4.153). As noted above, the simple present lexical rule does not generate a non-habitual sign for the simple present *departs*. Consequently, no TOP formula is generated for the impossible non-habitual reading of (4.143).

(4.153) *Pres*[*hab_departs_at*(*ba*737, *5:00pm*)]

4.13 Fronted temporal modifiers

As discussed in Section 4.11, temporal adverbial modifiers, like *at 5:00 pm* in (4.154) and (4.155) or *on Monday* in (4.156) and (4.157), are allowed to modify either whole finite sentences or past participle verb phrases.

(4.154) BA737 entered sector 2 at 5:00 pm.

(4.155) At 5:00 pm BA737 entered sector 2.
(4.156) Tank 2 was empty on Monday.
(4.157) On Monday tank 2 was empty.

In HPSG, the order in which a modifier and the modified constituent can appear in a sentence is controlled by the *constituent ordering principle*. This is a general principle that controls the order in which the various constituents can appear in a sentence (Pollard & Sag 1987). This book uses a simplified version of the principle, which places no restriction on the order between temporal modifiers and modified constituents when the modified constituents are sentences. This allows *at 5:00 pm* to either follow or precede *BA737 entered sector 2*, as in (4.154) and (4.155), respectively. Similarly, *on Monday* may either follow or precede *tank 2 was empty*, as in (4.156) and (4.157), respectively.[6] When temporal modifiers attach to past participle verb phrases, however, the constituent ordering principle of this book requires modifiers to follow the verb phrases, as in (4.158).[7] This rules out unacceptable sentences like (4.159), where *at 5:00 pm* precedes the *entered sector 2*.

(4.158) BA737 had [[entered sector 2] at 5:00 pm].
(4.159) *BA737 had [at 5:00 pm [entered sector 2]].

This approach causes (4.160) to receive only (4.161), because *at 5:00 pm* can modify only the whole *BA737 had entered sector 2*; it cannot modify just *entered sector 2*, because of the intervening *BA737 had*. In (4.161), 5:00 pm is a reference time (Section 2.5.5) where the entrance had already occurred. In contrast, (4.162) receives both (4.161) and (4.163), because in that case *at 5:00 pm* can modify either the whole *BA737 had entered sector 2* or only *entered sector 2*. In (4.163), 5:00 pm is the time of the entrance.

(4.160) At 5:00 pm [BA737 had entered sector 2].

(4.161) $Part[5{:}00pm, fv^v] \land$
$At[fv^v, Past[e1^v, Perf[e2^v, enter(ba737, sector2)]]]$

(4.162) BA737 had entered sector 2 at 5:00 pm.

(4.163) $Part[5{:}00pm, fv^v] \land$
$Past[e1^v, Perf[e2^v, At[fv^v, enter(ba737, sector2)]]]$

The fact that (4.160) does not receive (4.163) does not seem to be a disadvantage, because in (4.160) the reading of (4.163) seems unlikely, or at least much more unlikely than in (4.162).

4.14 Temporal subordinate clauses

This section discusses the treatment of temporal subordinate clauses (Section 2.10), focusing on clauses introduced by *while*. The treatment of clauses introduced by *before* and *after* is very similar.

As with temporal adverbials, clauses introduced by *while* are treated as temporal modifiers of finite sentences or past participle verb phrases. Also, as with prepositions introducing period adverbials, *while* is given two signs. The first one, shown in (4.164), is similar to (4.123): it introduces an *End* operator, it causes an aspectual shift to point, and can be used only with culminating activity main clauses. The second one is the same as (4.164), except that it does not introduce an *End* operator, it preserves the aspectual class of the main clause, and can be used with main clauses of any aspectual class. In both cases, *while* requires as its complement a finite sentence whose aspect must not be consequent state; this agrees with Table 2.6 on page 56, which does not allow the aspectual class of the *while* clause to be consequent state.

(4.164)
$$\begin{bmatrix} \text{PHON} & \langle \textit{while} \rangle \\ \text{SS} \mid \text{L} & \begin{bmatrix} \text{CAT} & \begin{bmatrix} \text{HEAD} & \begin{bmatrix} \text{MOD} & \text{S}\begin{bmatrix}\text{VFORM } \textit{fin}\end{bmatrix}{:}\boxed{2} \lor \\ & \text{VP}\begin{bmatrix}\text{VFORM } \textit{psp}\end{bmatrix}{:}\boxed{2} \\ \text{MOD} \mid \text{L} \mid \text{CAT} \mid \text{ASPECT} & \textit{culmact} \end{bmatrix} \\ \text{SPR} & \langle\rangle \\ \text{SUBJ} & \langle\rangle \\ \text{COMPS} & \langle \text{S}\begin{bmatrix}\text{VFORM} & \textit{fin} \\ \text{ASPECT} & \neg \textit{cnsq\_state}\end{bmatrix}{:}\boxed{1}\rangle \\ \text{ASPECT} & \textit{point} \end{bmatrix} \\ \text{CONT} & {}_{\textit{at\_op}}\begin{bmatrix} \text{TIME\_SPEC} & \boxed{1} \\ \text{MAIN\_PSOA} & {}_{\textit{end}}\begin{bmatrix}\text{MAIN\_PSOA} & \boxed{2}\end{bmatrix} \end{bmatrix} \end{bmatrix} \\ \text{QSTORE} & \{\} \end{bmatrix}$$

The $\boxed{1}$ in (4.164) refers to the CONT of the sign of the complement of *while*, i.e., of the subordinate clause. Assuming that *to land* is a culminating activity verb, the two *while* signs cause (4.165) to receive (4.166) and (4.167). (4.166) requires the landing to have simply been completed during the inspection, while (4.167) requires the landing to have both started and been completed during the inspection.

(4.165) UK160 landed while J. Adams was inspecting BA737.

(4.166) $At[Past[e1^v, inspecting(ja, ba737)],$
$End[Past[e2^v, Culm[landing(occr^v, uk160)]]]]$

(4.167) $At[Past[e1^v, inspecting(ja, ba737)],$
$Past[e2^v, Culm[landing(occr^v, uk160)]]]$

Since *while* clauses are treated as temporal modifiers, the ordering arrangements of Section 4.13 apply to *while* clauses as well. Hence, *while* clauses can either precede or follow finite sentences, as in (4.168) and (4.169).

(4.168) UK160 arrived while J. Adams was inspecting BA737.

(4.169) While J. Adams was inspecting BA737, UK160 arrived.

One problem with the treatment of *while* clauses is that it maps (4.170) to (4.171), which requires the inspection to have been completed. This does not agree with Table 2.6 on page 56, according to which any requirement that the situation of a culminating activity sentence must have been reached is cancelled when the sentence is used as a *while* clause. To overcome this problem, the post-processing stage, to be discussed in Section 4.17, removes any *Culm* operators that are within first arguments of *At* operators. This removes the *Culm* of (4.171), generating a formula that no longer requires the inspection to have been completed.

(4.170) UK160 departed while J. Adams inspected BA737.

(4.171) $At[Past[e1^v, Culm[inspecting(ja, ba737)]],$
$Past[e2^v, [actl\_depart(uk160)]]]$

4.15 Interrogatives

So far, this chapter has considered mainly assertions, like (4.172). The reader is reminded that assertions are treated semantically as yes/no questions; for example, (4.172) is taken to have the same meaning as (4.173). We will now examine how the HPSG version of this book handles questions, like (4.173)–(4.178).

(4.172) Tank 2 was empty.
(4.173) Was tank 2 empty?
(4.174) Did J. Adams inspect BA737?
(4.175) Which tank was empty?
(4.176) Who inspected BA737?

(4.177) What did J. Adams inspect?
(4.178) When did J. Adams inspect BA737?

Yes/no questions, like (4.173) and (4.174), constitute no particular problem. HPSG's schemata allow auxiliary verbs to be used in sentence-initial positions, and cause (4.173) to receive the same formula as (4.179); the formula is shown in (4.180). In both (4.173) and (4.179), the same lexical signs are used (punctuation is ignored). Similar comments apply to (4.174) and (4.181), which are mapped to (4.182).

(4.179) Tank 2 was empty.
(4.180) $Past[e^v, empty(tank2)]$
(4.181) J. Adams did inspect BA737.
(4.182) $Past[e^v, Culm[inspecting(occr^v, ja, ba737)]]$

The interrogative *which* is treated syntactically as a determiner of non-predicative noun phrases. The sign of *which* is the same as the sign of *a* and *the*, shown in (4.61), except that it introduces an interrogative quantifier rather than an existential one. For example, (4.175) is analysed syntactically in the same way as (4.183). However, the formula of (4.175), shown in (4.185), contains an additional interrogative quantifier, unlike the formula of (4.183), which is shown in (4.184). (The existential quantifier of the *a* determiner is removed during the extraction of (4.184) from the sign of (4.183), as discussed in Section 4.6. It is assumed here that *tank* does not introduce an *Ntense* operator.)

(4.183) A tank was empty.
(4.184) $tank(tk^v) \land Past[e^v, empty(tk^v)]$
(4.185) $?tk^v\ tank(tk^v) \land Past[e^v, empty(tk^v)]$

The interrogative *who* is treated syntactically as a non-predicative noun phrase, whose sign, shown in (4.186), introduces an interrogative quantifier. (4.176) is analysed syntactically in the same way as (4.187). The sign of *who*, however, gives rise to an interrogative quantifier in the formula of (4.176), shown in (4.189), which is not present in the formula of (4.187), shown in (4.188). The interrogative *what* is treated similarly.

(4.186)
$$\begin{bmatrix} \text{PHON} & \langle \textit{who} \rangle \\ \text{SS} \mid \text{L} & \begin{bmatrix} \text{CAT} & \begin{bmatrix} \text{HEAD} & {}_{\textit{noun}}\begin{bmatrix}\text{PRD} & - \end{bmatrix} \\ \text{SPR} & \langle\rangle \\ \text{SUBJ} & \langle\rangle \\ \text{COMPS} & \langle\rangle \end{bmatrix} \\ \text{CONT} & {}_{\textit{nom\_obj}}\begin{bmatrix} \text{INDEX} & {}_{\textit{person\_ent}}\begin{bmatrix}\text{TVAR} & + \end{bmatrix} \boxed{1} \\ \text{RESTR} & \{\} \end{bmatrix} \end{bmatrix} \\ \text{QSTORE} & \left\{ {}_{\textit{quant}}\begin{bmatrix} \text{DET} & \textit{interrog} \\ \text{RESTIND} & \boxed{1} \end{bmatrix} \right\} \end{bmatrix}$$

(4.187) J. Adams inspected BA737.
(4.188) $Past[Culm[inspecting(occr^v, ja, ba737)]]$
(4.189) $?wh^v\ Past[Culm[inspecting(occr^v, wh^v, ba737)]]$

The HPSG version of this book also admits questions like (4.190), although they are unacceptable in most contexts. (4.190) is licensed by the same syntactic analysis that allows (4.191), and receives the same formula as (4.192).

(4.190) ?Did J. Adams inspect which flight?
(4.191) Did J. Adams inspect a flight?
(4.192) Which flight did J. Adams inspect?

Questions like (4.192), where the interrogative refers to the object of the verb, are treated using HPSG's unbounded dependencies mechanisms, namely the SLASH feature (Pollard & Sag 1994).[8] Roughly speaking, (4.192) is analysed as a form of (4.190), where the object *which flight* has moved to the beginning of the question; see Pollard and Sag (1994) for more details.[9]

Questions with multiple interrogatives can also be handled. For example, (4.193) receives (4.194); (4.193) is parsed in the same way as (4.195). Unfortunately, the same mechanisms admit ungrammatical questions like (4.196), which is treated as a version of (4.193) where the *what* complement has moved to the beginning of the sentence; (4.196) receives (4.194).

(4.193) Who inspected what.
(4.194) $?w1^v\ ?w2^v\ Past[e^v, Culm[inspecting(occr^v, w1^v, w2^v)]]$
(4.195) J. Adams inspected BA737.
(4.196) *What who inspected.

The interrogative *when* of (4.197) is treated as a temporal adverbial modifier of finite sentences. (4.199) shows the sign of *when* that is used in (4.197). (4.199) causes (4.197) to receive (4.198).

(4.197) When was tank 2 empty?

(4.198) $?_{mxl} w^v \; Past[e^v, empty(tank2)]$

(4.199)

$$\left[\begin{array}{ll} \mathrm{PHON} & \langle \textit{when} \rangle \\ \mathrm{SS} \mid \mathrm{L} & \left[\begin{array}{ll} \mathrm{CAT} & \left[\begin{array}{ll} \mathrm{HEAD} & \left[\begin{array}{ll} \mathrm{MOD} & \mathrm{S}\left[\mathrm{VFORM}\ \textit{fin}\right]:\boxed{1} \\ \mathrm{MOD} \mid \mathrm{L} \mid \mathrm{CAT} \mid \mathrm{ASPECT} & \boxed{2} \end{array}\right] \\ \mathrm{SPR} & \langle\rangle \\ \mathrm{SUBJ} & \langle\rangle \\ \mathrm{COMPS} & \langle\rangle \\ \mathrm{ASPECT} & \boxed{2} \end{array}\right] \\ \mathrm{CONT} & \boxed{1} \end{array}\right] \\ \mathrm{QSTORE} & \left\{\left[\begin{array}{ll} \mathrm{DET} & \textit{interrog\_mxl} \\ \mathrm{RESTIND} & \left[\begin{array}{ll} \mathrm{INDEX} & \textit{temp\_ent}\left[\mathrm{TVAR}\ +\right] \\ \mathrm{RESTR} & \{\} \end{array}\right] \end{array}\right]\right\} \end{array}\right]$$

(4.199) introduces a $?_{mxl}$ quantifier whose variable does not appear elsewhere in the formula; for example, w^v in (4.198). The post-processing stage, to be discussed in Section 4.17, replaces the variables of $?_{mxl}$ quantifiers by variables that appear as first arguments of *Past* or *Perf* operators. In (4.198), this would replace w^v by e^v, generating a formula that asks for the maximal past periods where tank 2 was empty.

There is also a second sign for the interrogative *when*, shown in (4.202), which is used in habitual questions like (4.200). In (4.200), *when* is taken to play the same role as *at 5:00 pm* in (4.201), i.e., it is treated as the prepositional phrase complement of the habitual *depart*, which has moved to the beginning of the sentence via the unbounded dependencies mechanisms.

(4.200) When does BA737 depart (habitually)?

(4.201) Does BA737 depart (habitually) at 5:00 pm?

(4.202)
$$
\left[\begin{array}{ll}
\text{PHON} & \langle \textit{when} \rangle \\
\text{SS}\,|\,\text{L} & \left[\begin{array}{ll}
\text{CAT} & \left[\begin{array}{ll} \text{HEAD} & {}_{\textit{prep}}\left[\text{PRD}\ \ -\right] \\ \text{SPR} & \langle\rangle \\ \text{SUBJ} & \langle\rangle \\ \text{COMPS} & \langle\rangle \end{array}\right] \\
\text{CONT} & {}_{\textit{nom\_obj}}\left[\begin{array}{ll} \text{INDEX} & {}_{\textit{gappy\_partng}}\left[\text{TVAR}\ \ +\right] \\ \text{RESTR} & \{\} \end{array}\right]\boxed{1}
\end{array}\right] \\
\text{QSTORE} & \left\{\left[\begin{array}{ll} \text{DET} & \textit{interrog} \\ \text{RESTIND} & \boxed{1} \end{array}\right]\right\}
\end{array}\right]
$$

In the simple past (4.203), both the habitual and the non-habitual homonym of *to depart* can be used. The corresponding signs of the verb are (4.146) and (4.147); the habitual homonym requires a prepositional phrase complement, while the non-habitual homonym requires no complement. Hence, *when* can be either a prepositional phrase complement of the habitual *depart*, as in (4.202), or a temporal modifier of the non-habitual sentence *did BA737 depart*, as in (4.199). This gives rise to (4.204) and (4.205), which correspond to the habitual and non-habitual readings of (4.203), respectively. The w^v of (4.205) would be replaced by e^v during the post-processing.

(4.203) When did BA737 depart?
(4.204) $?w^v\ Past[e^v, hab\_departs\_at(ba737, w^v)]$
(4.205) $?_{mxl}w^v\ Past[e^v, actl\_depart(ba737)]$

4.16 Multiple temporal modifiers

Sentences with multiple temporal modifiers pose some problems for the English to TOP mapping that has been presented so far. This section discusses these problems, along with possible solutions. The proposed solutions are only tentative, however, and they have not been incorporated into the prototype NLITDB of Chapter 6.

Both preceding and trailing temporal modifiers. Temporal modifiers are allowed to either precede or follow finite sentences (Section 4.13). When a finite sentence is modified by both a preceding and a trailing temporal modifier, as in (4.206), two parses are generated: one where the *trailing* modifier is attached first to the sentence, as in (4.207), and one where the *preceding* modifier is attached first, as in (4.209). In most cases, this generates two semantically equivalent formulae; in (4.206), these are (4.208) and (4.210).

(4.206) Yesterday BA737 was at gate 2 for two hours.
(4.207) Yesterday [[BA737 was at gate 2] for two hours.]
(4.208) $At[yesterday, For[hour^c, 2, Past[e^v, located\_at(ba737, gate2)]]]$
(4.209) [Yesterday [BA737 was at gate 2]] for two hours.
(4.210) $For[hour^c, 2, At[yesterday, Past[e^v, located\_at(ba737, gate2)]]]$

One way to solve this problem would be to allow preceding modifiers to be attached to the sentence only after all trailing modifiers have been attached to it. This can be achieved by modifying the constituent ordering principle of Section 4.13, disallowing temporal modifiers to follow constituents that have already been modified by preceding temporal modifiers. A mechanism to mark constituents as having been modified by preceding temporal modifiers would also be needed.

Multiple temporal modifiers and anaphora. Another problem is that a question like (4.211) is mapped to (4.212). (It is assumed here that *flight* does not introduce an *Ntense* operator.) The problem with (4.212) is that it requires the flight to have arrived on 2/11/1995 and after an *arbitrary* 5:00 pm minute; for example, after the 5:00 pm minute of 1/11/1995. In effect, this causes the *after 5:00 pm* to be ignored.

(4.211) Which flight arrived after 5:00 pm on 2/11/1995?
(4.212) $?fl^v\ flight(fl^v) \land Part[5{:}00pm^g, fv^v] \land$
$At[2/11/1995, After[fv^v, Past[e^v, arrive(fl^v)]]]$

This is another case where temporal anaphora resolution mechanisms (Section 2.12) are needed. In (4.211), the *on 2/11/1995* adverbial provides a strongly salient period, that can be used to anchor the particular 5:00 pm minute that the user has in mind.

Culminating activity with both punctual and period adverbial. A further problem appears when a culminating activity is modified by both a punctual and a period adverbial. Unlike what one would expect, (4.213) and (4.214) do not receive equivalent TOP formulae. (It is assumed here that *to repair* is classified as culminating activity verb. Similar problems arise with punctual adverbials and temporal subordinate clauses.)

(4.213) J. Adams repaired fault 2 at 5:00 pm on 2/11/1995.
(4.214) J. Adams repaired fault 2 on 2/11/1995 at 5:00 pm.

In (4.213), the punctual adverbial *at 5:00 pm* modifies the culminating activity sentence *J. Adams repaired fault 2*. Following Table 2.2 on page 46, the aspectual class of the resulting sentence becomes point, and two formulae are generated: one where the repair *starts* at 5:00 pm, and one where it is *completed* at 5:00 pm. The period adverbial *on 2/11/1995* then modifies the point expression *J. Adams repaired fault 2 at 5:00 pm*. This leads to (4.215) and (4.216). (The first reading is easier to accept in *J. Adams inspected BA737 at 5:00 pm on 2/11/1995.*)

(4.215) $Part[5{:}00pm^g, fv^v] \land At[2/11/1995, At[fv^v,$
$Begin[Past[e^v, Culm[repairing(occr^v, ja, fault2)]]]]]$
(4.216) $Part[5{:}00pm^g, fv^v] \land At[2/11/1995, At[fv^v,$
$End[Past[e^v, Culm[repairing(occr^v, ja, fault2)]]]]]$

Before considering (4.214), it should be noted that (4.213) also demonstrates why punctual adverbials are taken to trigger an aspectual shift to point (Section 2.9.1). Without this shift, the aspectual class of *J. Adams repaired fault 2 at 5:00 pm* would be culminating activity, and the *on* signs of Section 4.11.2 would lead to the additional redundant formulae of (4.217) and (4.218), which are equivalent to (4.215) and (4.216), respectively.

(4.217) $Part[5{:}00pm^g, fv^v] \land At[2/11/1995, End[At[fv^v,$
$Begin[Past[e^v, Culm[repairing(occr^v, ja, fault2)]]]]]]$
(4.218) $Part[5{:}00pm^g, fv^v] \land At[2/11/1995, End[At[fv^v,$
$End[Past[e^v, Culm[repairing(occr^v, ja, fault2)]]]]]]$

In (4.214), *J. Adams repaired fault 2* is first modified by the period adverbial *on 2/11/1995*. Two formulae, shown in (4.219) and (4.220), are generated. (4.219) requires the repair to simply reach its completion on 2/11/1995, while (4.220) requires the repair to both start and reach its completion on 2/11/1995. In the first case, where (4.219) is generated, the aspectual class of the resulting sentence becomes point, while in the other case, where (4.220) is produced, the aspectual class remains culminating activity (Table 2.3 on page 50).

(4.219) $At[2/11/1995,$
$End[Past[e^v, Culm[repairing(occr^v, ja, fault2)]]]]$
(4.220) $At[2/11/1995,$
$Past[e^v, Culm[repairing(occr^v, ja, fault2)]]]$

In the case of (4.219), the *at* signs of Section 4.11.1 cause (4.214) to be mapped to (4.221), while with (4.220), they lead to (4.222) and (4.223).

(4.221) $\mathit{Part}[\mathit{5{:}00pm}^g, \mathit{fv}^v] \wedge \mathit{At}[\mathit{fv}^v, \mathit{At}[\mathit{2/11/1995}, \mathit{End}[\mathit{Past}[e^v, \mathit{Culm}[\mathit{repairing}(\mathit{occr}^v, \mathit{ja}, \mathit{fault2})]]]]]$

(4.222) $\mathit{Part}[\mathit{5{:}00pm}^g] \wedge \mathit{At}[\mathit{fv}^v, \mathit{Begin}[\mathit{At}[\mathit{2/11/1995}, \mathit{Past}[e^v, \mathit{Culm}[\mathit{repairing}(\mathit{occr}^v, \mathit{ja}, \mathit{fault2})]]]]]$

(4.223) $\mathit{Part}[\mathit{5{:}00pm}^g] \wedge \mathit{At}[\mathit{fv}^v, \mathit{End}[\mathit{At}[\mathit{2/11/1995}, \mathit{Past}[e^v, \mathit{Culm}[\mathit{repairing}(\mathit{occr}^v, \mathit{ja}, \mathit{fault2})]]]]]$

Hence, (4.213) receives two formulae, (4.215) and (4.216), while (4.214) receives three, (4.221)–(4.223). (4.221) is equivalent to (4.216). Unlike what one might expect, however, (4.222) is not equivalent to (4.215). (4.222) requires a past period that covers exactly the whole repair, from start to completion, to fall within 2/11/1995, and the beginning of that period to fall within some 5:00 pm minute. This means that the repair must start at 5:00 pm on 2/11/1995, as in (4.215); but it also means that the repair must reach its completion within 2/11/1995, which is not a requirement in (4.215). Also, unlike what one might expect, (4.223) is not equivalent to (4.216) and (4.221). It requires the repair to reach its completion at 5:00 pm on 2/11/1995, as in (4.216) and (4.221), but it also requires the repair to start within 2/11/1995, which is not a requirement in (4.216) and (4.221).

The formulae of (4.215) and (4.216) seem to capture the readings of both (4.213) and (4.214) better than those of (4.221)–(4.223). Hence, we would like (4.214) to be treated as (4.213). A tentative solution is to adopt some preprocessing mechanism that would reorder the temporal modifiers, so that punctual adverbials are always attached to sentences before period adverbials. This would reverse the order of *on 2/11/1995* and *at 5:00 pm* in (4.214), transforming it into (4.213).

Culminating activity and multiple period adverbials. A final problem is that a sentence like (4.224), where a culminating activity is modified by two period adverbials, receives three formulae, shown in (4.225)–(4.227). It turns out that (4.226) is equivalent to (4.227), and hence one of the two should be eliminated.

(4.224) J. Adams repaired fault 2 in June in 1992.

(4.225) $\mathit{Part}[\mathit{june}^g, j^v] \wedge \mathit{At}[1992, \mathit{At}[j^v, \mathit{End}[\mathit{Past}[e^v, \mathit{Culm}[\mathit{repairing}(\mathit{occr}^v, \mathit{ja}, \mathit{fault2})]]]]]$

(4.226) $\mathit{Part}[\mathit{june}^g, j^v] \wedge \mathit{At}[1992, \mathit{End}[\mathit{At}[j^v, \mathit{Past}[e^v, \mathit{Culm}[\mathit{repairing}(\mathit{occr}^v, \mathit{ja}, \mathit{fault2})]]]]]$

(4.227) $Part[june^g, j^v] \wedge At[1992, At[j^v,$
$Past[e^v, Culm[repairing(occr^v, ja, fault2)]]]]$

A period adverbial combining with a culminating activity can either insert an *End* operator and cause an aspectual shift to point, or insert no *End* operator and leave the aspectual class unchanged (Section 4.11.2). In the case where (4.225) is generated, *in June* inserts an *End* operator and changes the aspectual class to point. Period adverbials combining with points do not insert *End* operators, and hence when *in 1992* is then attached, no second *End* operator can be inserted. When (4.226) and (4.227) are generated, *in June* does not insert an *End* operator, and the aspectual class remains culminating activity. The *in 1992* can then insert an *End* operator, as in (4.226), or not, as in (4.227). (4.227) requires the whole of the repair to be located within the June of 1992, while (4.225) requires only the completion point of the repair to be located within that time; the two formulae seem to capture the most natural readings of (4.224). (4.226) requires the whole of the repair to be located within a June, and the completion point of the repair to fall within 1992. This is equivalent to requiring the whole of the repair to fall within the June of 1992; i.e., (4.226) is equivalent to (4.227), and one of the two should be eliminated.

One way to address this problem would be to allow period adverbials to insert *End* operators and trigger an aspectual shift to point only when attaching to constituents that have not been modified already by other period adverbials; this requires some mechanism to flag constituents as having been modified by period adverbials.

4.17 Post-processing

During the parsing each English question is mapped to an HPSG sign; or multiple signs, if the parser understands the question to be ambiguous. A TOP formula is extracted from each resulting sign, as discussed in Section 4.6. The extracted formulae then undergo an additional post-processing phase, which is a collection of minor transformations, discussed below, that cannot be carried out easily during the parsing.

Removing Culm operators. The TOP formula that is extracted from the sign of (4.228) is shown in (4.229). As discussed in Sections 2.9.3 and 4.11.3, (4.229) does not represent correctly (4.228), because it requires the taxiing to have been completed, whereas the *for* adverbial cancels that implication. To express correctly (4.228), the *Culm* operator of (4.229) must be removed.

(4.228) BA737 taxied to gate 2 for five minutes.
(4.229) $For[minute^c, 5, Past[e^v, Culm[taxiing\_to(ba737, gate2)]]]$

A first solution would be to remove during the post-processing any *Culm* operator that is within the scope of a *For* operator. The problem with this approach is that duration *in* adverbials also introduce *For* operators (Section 4.11.3), but unlike *for* adverbials they do not cancel the implication that the completion must have been reached. For example, the formula extracted from the sign of (4.230) is also (4.229). In this case, (4.229) is a correct rendering of (4.230), and the *Culm* operator should not be removed. To overcome this problem, the prototype NLITDB of Chapter 6 attaches to each *For* operator a flag showing whether it was introduced by a *for* or an *in* adverbial. Only *For* operators introduced by *for* adverbials cause *Culm* operators within their scope to be removed.

(4.230) BA737 taxied to gate 2 in five minutes.

The post-processing also removes any *Culm* operator from within the first argument of an *At* operator. As explained in Section 4.14, this is needed to express correctly *while* clauses.

Variables of $?_{mxl}$ *quantifiers.* As noted in Section 4.15, before the post-processing the variables of interrogative-maximal quantifiers do not occur elsewhere in their formulae. For example, (4.232) and (4.234) are extracted from the signs of (4.231) and (4.233), respectively. In both formulae, w^v occurs only immediately after the $?_{mxl}$ quantifier.

(4.231) When was J. Adams a manager?
(4.232) $?_{mxl}w^v\, Past[e^v, manager(ja)]$
(4.233) When while BA737 was circling was runway 2 open?
(4.234) $?_{mxl}w^v\, At[Past[e1^v, circling(ba737)], Past[e2^v, open(runway2)]]$

During the post-processing, the variables of interrogative-maximal quantifiers are replaced by variables that appear as first arguments of *Past* or *Perf* operators, excluding *Past* and *Perf* operators that are within first arguments of *At*, *Before*, or *After* operators. In (4.232), this causes w^v to be replaced by e^v. The resulting formula asks for the maximal past periods where J. Adams was a manager. Similarly, the w^v of (4.234) is replaced by $e2^v$. The resulting formula asks for the maximal past periods $e2^v$, such that runway 2 was open at $e2^v$, and $e2^v$ is a subperiod of a period $e1^v$ where BA737 was circling. In (4.234), w^v cannot be replaced by $e1^v$, because $Past[e1^v, circling(ba737)]$ is within the first argument of an *At*.

Past and *Perf* operators located within first arguments of *At*, *Before*, or *After* operators are excluded, to avoid interpreting *when* as referring to the time where the situation of a subordinate clause held (formulae that express subordinate clauses end up within first arguments of *At*, *Before*, or *After* operators). Time-asking questions always refer to the situation of the main clause. For example, (4.233) cannot be asking for maximal periods where BA737 was circling that subsume periods where runway 2 was open; this would be the meaning of (4.234) if w^v were replaced by $e1^v$.

When the main clause is in the past perfect, the variable of $?_{mxl}$ can be replaced by either the first argument of the main clause's *Past* operator, or the first argument of the main clause's *Perf* operator. (4.236), for example, shows the formula that is extracted from the sign of (4.235). The post-processing generates two formulae: one where w^v is replaced by $e1^v$, and one where it is replaced by $e2^v$. The first one asks for what Section 2.9.1 called the 'consequent period', i.e., the period that starts at the end of the inspection; readings of this kind look unlikely, and should probably be blocked. The second reading asks for the time of the actual inspection.

(4.235) When had J. Adams inspected BA737?

(4.236) $?_{mxl} w^v \; Past[e1^v, Perf[e2^v, Culm[inspecting(occr^v, ja, ba737)]]]$

Ntense operators. As noted in Section 4.9.1, when extracting TOP formulae from signs, if an *Ntense* operator is encountered and the sign contains no definite indication that the first argument of the *Ntense* should be *now**, the argument becomes a variable in the extracted formula. That variable does not occur elsewhere in the extracted formula. Assuming, for example, that the *queen* introduces an *Ntense* operator, the formula extracted from the sign of (4.237) is (4.238); the t^v of the *Ntense* does not occur elsewhere in (4.238).

(4.237) The queen was in Rome.

(4.238) $Ntense[t^v, queen(q^v)] \wedge Past[e1^v, located\_at(q^v, rome)]$

During the post-processing, variables appearing as first arguments of *Ntense* operators give rise to multiple formulae, where the first arguments of the *Ntense* operators are replaced by *now** or by first arguments of *Past* or *Perf* operators. In (4.238), for example, the post-processing generates two formulae: one where t^v is replaced by *now** (queen at the speech time), and one where t^v is replaced by e^v (queen when in Rome).

In (4.240), which is the formula extracted from the sign of (4.239), there is no *Past* or *Perf* operator, and hence t^v can only become *now**. Indeed, the *queen* in (4.239) most probably refers to the queen of the speech time.

(4.239) The queen is in Rome.

(4.240) $Ntense[t^v, queen(q^v)] \wedge Pres[located\_at(q^v, rome)]$

In (4.242), which is extracted from the sign of (4.241), the post-processing leads to three formulae, where t^v is replaced by *now** (queen at speech time), $e2^v$ (queen during the visit), or $e1^v$ (queen at a reference time after the visit).

(4.241) The queen had visited Rome.

(4.242) $Ntense[t^v, queen(q^v)] \wedge Past[e1^v, Perf[e2^v, visiting(q^v, rome)]]$

4.18 Summary

This chapter has shown how HPSG can be used to translate English questions submitted to an NLITDB to appropriate TOP formulae. During the parsing, each question receives one or more HPSG signs, from which TOP formulae are extracted. The extracted formulae then undergo an additional post-processing phase, which leads to formulae that capture the semantics of the original English questions.

Several modifications were made to HPSG for the purposes of this book. The main modifications were the following. (i) HPSG features and sorts intended to account for phenomena not examined in this book (e.g., pronouns, relative clauses, number agreement) were dropped. (ii) The quantifier storage mechanism of HPSG was replaced by a more primitive one, that does not allow quantifiers to be unstored during the parsing; the semantics principle was modified accordingly. (iii) An ASPECT feature was added, along with a principle that controls its propagation. (iv) The possible values of CONT and QSTORE were modified, to represent TOP expressions rather than situation-theory constructs. (v) A hierarchy of world-entity types was mounted under the *ind* sort; this is used to disambiguate sentences, and to block semantically ill-formed ones. (vi) New lexical signs and lexical rules were introduced to cope with temporal linguistic mechanisms. Apart from these modifications, the HPSG version of this book follows closely Pollard and Sag (1994).

Notes

1. This book follows the approach of Section 8.5.1 of Pollard and Sag's book (1994), whereby the RELATION feature is dropped, and its role is taken up by the sort of the feature structure.

2. In Pollard and Sag (1994), *nom_obj* has the subsorts *npro* (non-pronoun) and *pron* (pronoun). These subsorts are not used in this book.

3. In Pollard and Sag (1994), the signs of proper names involve *naming* relations, and CONTEXT and BACKGROUND features, which are not used in this book.

4. Apart from the *remove_ntense*, (4.77) is essentially the same as Borsley's 'predicative NP lexical rule', as discussed by Pollard and Sag (1994: 360f).

5. Pollard and Sag do not provide much information on determiners of predicative noun phrases. They seem to acknowledge, however, that they have to be treated differently from determiners of non-predicative noun phrases (1994: 360f).

6. An alternative approach is to allow temporal modifiers to participate in unbounded dependency constructions, as discussed by Pollard and Sag (1994: 176–181).

7. Constituent ordering restrictions are enforced in the ALE grammar of the prototype NLITDB in a rather ad hoc manner, which involves partitioning the *synsem* sort into *pre_mod_synsem* and *post_mod_synsem*, and using feature structures from the two subsorts as values of MOD to signal that the modifier can only precede or follow the modified constituent. This idea was borrowed from a grammar written by Suresh Manandhar.

8. Pollard and Sag also reserve a QUE feature, which is intended to be used in the treatment of interrogatives, but its exact role is left unspecified. They point to Ginzburg (1995a; 1995b; 1995c), where QUE is used in a general theory of interrogatives, which aims to address issues beyond the scope of this book. QUE is not used in this book.

9. The prototype NLITDB of Chapter 6 uses the traceless analysis of unbounded dependencies, presented in Chapter 9 of Pollard and Sag's book (1994).

CHAPTER 5

From TOP to TSQL2

"Time is money."

5.1 Introduction

This chapter shows how TOP formulae can be mapped systematically to appropriate expressions of a temporal database language. As already discussed in Chapter 1, numerous temporal extensions of the SQL database language and the relational model have been proposed. This book adopts TSQL2 (Snodgrass 1995), a temporal extension of SQL-92 (Melton & Simon 1993) that was designed by a committee of temporal database researchers and constitutes a good representative of the various extensions that have been proposed. After introducing TSQL2, a set of provably correct translation rules will be presented, which can transform systematically every TOP formula into an appropriate TSQL2 query that preserves the semantics of the TOP formula.

5.2 An introduction to TSQL2

This section introduces TSQL2 and the version of the relational model on which TSQL2 is based. Some additional related definitions, which will be used in following sections, will also be given.

5.2.1 The traditional relational model

As explained in Section 1.5, the traditional relational model stores information in relations, which can be thought of as tables. For example, *salaries* below is a relation showing the current salaries of a company's employees. It has two *attributes*, intuitively columns, *employee* and *salary*. The *tuples* of a relation correspond to the rows of the table; for example, *salaries* has three tuples.

salaries	
employee	*salary*
J. Adams	17000
T. Smith	19000
G. Papas	14500

A set-theoretic definition of relations will be adopted (Ullman 1988). A set of attributes $\mathcal{D}_A$ is assumed; for example, *employee* and *salary* above are elements of $\mathcal{D}_A$. A *relation schema* is an ordered tuple of one or more attributes, such as $\langle employee, salary \rangle$. A set of *domains* $\mathcal{D}_D = \{D_1, \ldots, D_{n_D}\}$ is also assumed. Each element D_i of $\mathcal{D}_D$ is itself a set; for example, D_1 may contain all the possible string values, D_2 all the positive integers, etc. Each attribute is assigned a domain, and $D(A)$ denotes the domain of attribute A. D on its own refers to the *universal domain*, the union of all $D_i \in \mathcal{D}_D$.

A *relation* over a relation schema $R = \langle A_1, A_2, \ldots, A_n \rangle$ is a subset of $D(A_1) \times D(A_2) \times \cdots \times D(A_n)$, where $\times$ denotes the cartesian product. That is, a relation over R is a set of tuples of the form $\langle v_1, v_2, \ldots, v_n \rangle$, where $v_1 \in D(A_1)$, $v_2 \in D(A_2), \ldots, v_n \in D(A_n)$. In each tuple $\langle v_1, v_2, \ldots, v_n \rangle$, v_1 is the *attribute value* of A_1, v_2 is the attribute value of A_2, etc. The universal domain D is the set of all the possible attribute values. Assuming, for example, that *employee*, *salary* $\in \mathcal{D}_A$, that D_1 and D_2 are as in the previous paragraph, and that *employee* and *salary* are assigned D_1 and D_2, respectively, r below is a relation over $\langle employee, salary \rangle$; r is a mathematical representation of *salaries* above. On its own, the term 'relation' will be used to refer to a relation over any relation schema.

$$r = \{\langle J.\ Adams, 17000 \rangle, \langle T.\ Smith, 19000 \rangle, \langle G.\ Papas, 14500 \rangle\}$$

The *arity* of a relation over R is the number of attributes in R; for example, the arity of r is 2. The *cardinality* of a relation is the number of tuples it contains; the cardinality of r is 3. A *relational database* is a set of relations; more elaborate definitions are possible, but this is sufficient for our purposes.

For simplicity, it will be assumed that every element of the universal domain D denotes an object in the modelled world, i.e., an object in TOP's *OBJS* (Section 3.4). The term 'object in the world' is used with a very general meaning that includes non-material objects, such as qualifications of employees, salaries, etc. It is also assumed that a function $f_D : D \mapsto OBJS$ is available, which maps each element v of D to the world object denoted by v. f_D reflects the semantics assigned to the attribute values by the people who use the database. In practice, an element of D may denote different world objects when used as the value of different attributes; for example, 15700 may denote a salary when used as the value of *salary*, and a part of an engine when used as the value of an attribute *part_no*. Hence, more strictly the value of f_D should also depend on the attribute where the element of D is used, i.e., it should be a function $f_D : D \times \mathcal{D}_A \mapsto OBJS$. For simplicity, this detail will be overlooked.

It will also be assumed that f_D is 1-1 (injective), i.e., that every element of D denotes a *different* world object. Again, in practice f_D may not be 1-1, as the database may use two different attribute values (e.g., *dpt*3 and *sales_dpt*) to refer to the same world object. Although the TOP to TSQL2 mapping can be formulated without assuming that f_D is 1-1, this assumption will allow us to bypass some uninteresting details. We will also assume that f_D is surjective, i.e., that for every $o \in OBJS$, there is a $v \in D$, such that $f_D(v) = o$. Then, since f_D is both 1-1 and surjective, the inverse mapping f_D^{-1} is also a function, and f_D^{-1} is also 1-1 and surjective.

5.2.2 TSQL2's model of time

Although stated in different terms in the TSQL2 definition (Snodgrass 1995), in effect TSQL2 models time as consisting of *chronons*, which are the shortest units of time that can be represented in the database. Depending on the TSQL2 implementation, chronons may correspond to nanoseconds, minutes, days, etc.[1] It also follows from the TSQL2 definition that chronons are ordered by a binary precedence relation, and have the properties of transitivity, irreflexivity, linearity, left and right boundedness, and discreteness, as in TOP (Section 3.3). This allows us to use chronons as TOP's time-points, and use the two terms interchangeably. The definitions of *PERIODS*, *PERIODS** and *INSTANTS* in TSQL2, then, are as in TOP.

A *temporal element* is a non-empty, but not necessarily convex, set of time-points. Let *TELEMS* be the set of all temporal elements; then $PERIODS \subseteq TELEMS$. For every $l \in TELEMS$, $mxlpers(l)$ is the set of the *maximal periods* of l, defined as follows:

$$mxlpers(l) \stackrel{def}{=} \{p \subseteq l \mid p \in PERIODS \text{ and } \text{for no } p' \in PERIODS,\ p' \subseteq l \text{ and } p \sqsubset p'\}$$

This extends the definition of maximal periods of Section 3.3.

TSQL2 supports multiple *granularities*. A granularity can be thought of as a complete partitioning of TOP (Section 3.4), and a *granule* is an element of the complete partitioning. A lattice is used in TSQL2 to capture relations between granularities; for example, a year-granule contains month-granules, etc. The finest available granularity is *INSTANTS*, also called the *granularity of chronons*. TSQL2 allows periods and temporal elements to be specified at any granularity. For example, one may specify that the first day of a period is 25/11/1995, and the last day is 28/11/1995. If the granularity of chronons is finer than the granularity of days, the exact chronons (time-points) within 25/11/1995 and 28/11/1995 where the period starts and ends are unknown. For simplicity, in this book all periods and temporal elements will be specified at the granularity of chronons. Granularities other than *INSTANTS* will be used only to express durations, as explained below.

TSQL2 uses the term *interval* to refer to a duration (Section 3.3). An interval is a number of consecutive granules of some particular granularity; for example, two day-granules or five minute-granules.

5.2.3 The BCDM version of the relational model

TSQL2 is based on a temporal extension of the relational model called BCDM (Snodgrass 1995). Apart from the relations of the standard relational model (Section 5.2.1), which are called *snapshot relations* in TSQL2, BCDM also provides *valid-time relations*, *transaction-time relations*, and *bitemporal relations*. Transaction-time and bitemporal relations are not used in this book (Section 1.5), and will not be discussed further. Valid-time relations are similar to snapshot relations, except that they have a special extra attribute, called the *implicit attribute*, which shows the times at which the information of each tuple is true in the world. A special domain $D_T \in \mathcal{D}_D$ is assumed, such that for every $v_t \in D_T$, $f_D(v_t) \in TELEMS$; this assumes that $TELEMS \subseteq OBJS$. D_T is the domain of the implicit attribute.

A *valid-time relation* r over a relation schema $R = \langle A_1, \dots, A_n \rangle$ is a subset of $D(A_1) \times \cdots \times D(A_n) \times D_T$. $A_1, \dots, A_n$ are the *explicit attributes* of r. The notation $\langle v_1, \dots, v_n; v_t \rangle$ will be used to refer to tuples of valid-time relations. If r is as above and $\langle v_1, \dots, v_n; v_t \rangle \in r$, then $v_1 \in D(A_1), \dots, v_n \in D(A_n)$, and $v_t \in D_T$; $v_1, \dots, v_n$ are the *values* of the explicit attributes, while v_t is the value of the implicit attribute and the *time-stamp* of the tuple. In snapshot relations, all attributes count as explicit.

TSQL2 actually distinguishes between *state* valid-time relations and *event* valid-time relations, which are intended to model situations that have duration or are instantaneous, respectively. This distinction seems particularly interesting, because it appears to capture some facets of the aspectual taxonomy of Chapter 2. Unfortunately, it is also an unclear and ill-defined feature of TSQL2. The time-stamps of state and event valid-time relations are said to denote temporal elements and instant sets, respectively, where temporal elements are defined as unions of periods, and instant sets as sets of chronons (Snodgrass 1995:314). This distinction is problematic, however, because a union of periods is a union of convex sets of chronons, i.e., simply a set of chronons; hence, one cannot distinguish between unions of periods and sets of chronons. It has also been argued elsewhere that TSQL2 does not allow specifying whether a computed valid-time relation should be state or event (Androutsopoulos, Ritchie, & Thanisch 1995a). Given these problems, this book does not use the distinction between state and event valid-time relations; alternative mechanisms will be introduced instead in the following sections. The time-stamps of all valid-time relations are taken to denote temporal elements, with temporal elements being sets of chronons.

Assuming that the domains of *employee* and *salary* are as in Section 5.2.1, *val_salaries* below is a valid-time relation over ⟨*employee, salary*⟩, shown in its tabular form. The double vertical line separates the explicit attributes from the implicit one. The elements of D_T, i.e., the values of the implicit attribute, are non-atomic (Snodgrass 1995, Chapter 10). Each $v_t \in D_T$ is in turn a set, whose elements denote the chronons that belong to the temporal element represented by v_t. For example, $\{c_1^1, c_2^1, c_3^1, \ldots, c_{n_1}^1\}$ in the first tuple for J. Adams is an element of D_T, and $c_1^1, c_2^1, c_3^1, \ldots, c_{n_1}^1$ represent the chronons where the salary of J. Adams was 17000.

val_salaries		
employee	*salary*	
J. Adams	17000	$\{c_1^1, c_2^1, c_3^1, \ldots, c_{n_1}^1\}$
J. Adams	18000	$\{c_1^2, c_2^2, c_3^2, \ldots, c_{n_2}^2\}$
J. Adams	18500	$\{c_1^3, c_2^3, c_3^3, \ldots, c_{n_3}^3\}$
T. Smith	19000	$\{c_1^4, c_2^4, c_3^4, \ldots, c_{n_4}^4\}$
T. Smith	21000	$\{c_1^5, c_2^5, c_3^5, \ldots, c_{n_5}^5\}$

When depicting valid-time relations, their time-stamps will often be replaced by higher-level descriptions of the temporal elements they denote. That is, *val_salaries* will be shown as in (5.1), meaning that the time-stamp of the first tuple represents a temporal element of two maximal periods, 1/1/1992 to 12/6/1992 and 8/5/1994 to 30/10/1994. Here, *now* refers to the current chronon, and it is assumed that chronons correspond to days.

(5.1)

val_salaries		
employee	*salary*	
J. Adams	17000	[1/1/1992, 12/6/92] ∪ [8/5/1994, 30/10/94]
J. Adams	18000	[13/6/1992, 7/5/1994] ∪ [31/10/1994, *now*]
T. Smith	21000	[15/6/1992, *now*]

Two tuples $\langle v_1^1, \ldots, v_n^1; v_t^1 \rangle$ and $\langle v_1^2, \ldots, v_n^2; v_t^2 \rangle$ are *value-equivalent* iff $v_1^1 = v_1^2$, $\ldots$, $v_n^1 = v_n^2$. A valid-time relation is *coalesced* iff it contains no value-equivalent tuples. BCDM requires all valid-time relations to be coalesced (Snodgrass 1995:188). For example, (5.2) is not allowed, because its first and third tuples are value-equivalent. For reasons that will be explained in later sections, this requirement is dropped in this book, and coalescing is made optional. This is not an unprecedented approach; for example, ATSQL (Section 1.5) also provides optional coalescing.

(5.2)

employee	*salary*	
J. Adams	17000	[1/1/1992, 12/6/1992]
J. Adams	18000	[13/6/1992, 7/5/1994]
J. Adams	17000	[8/5/1994, 30/10/1994]
J. Adams	18000	[31/10/1994, *now*]
T. Smith	21000	[15/6/1992, *now*]

Before moving on to a description of the actual TSQL2 language, let us define some additional notation that will prove useful in following sections:

- Let D_P be the subset of all elements of D_T that denote periods ($PERIODS \subseteq TELEMS$).[2]
- Let us also assume that there is a special value $v_\varepsilon \in D$, that is used to denote the empty set. For example, a TSQL2 expression that computes the intersection of two non-overlapping periods evaluates to v_ε.[3] The notation D_P^* will be used to refer to $D_P \cup \{v_\varepsilon\}$.
- Let $VREL_P$ be the set of valid-time relations whose time-stamps are all elements of D_P; i.e., all the time-stamps denote periods.
- Let $NVREL_P$ be the set of relations $r \in VREL_P$ with the following property: if $\langle v_1, \ldots, v_n; v_t^1 \rangle \in r$, $\langle v_1, \ldots, v_n; v_t^2 \rangle \in r$, and $f_D(v_t^1) \cup f_D(v_t^2) \in PERIODS$, then $v_t^1 = v_t^2$. This ensures that in every $r \in NVREL_P$, there is no pair of different value-equivalent tuples whose time-stamps v_t^1 and v_t^2 denote overlapping or adjacent periods, because if the periods of v_t^1 and v_t^2 overlap or are adjacent, their union is also a period, and then $v_t^1 = v_t^2$. Intuitively,

the relations of $NVREL_P$ are normalised, in the sense that their tuples are time-stamped by the maximal possible periods.

- Let *SREL* be the set of all snapshot relations.
- For every $n \in \{1, 2, 3, \dots\}$, let $VREL_P(n)$ be the set of all relations in $VREL_P$ with n explicit attributes. Similarly, $NVREL_P(n)$ and $SREL(n)$ contain all the relations of $NVREL_P$ and *SREL*, respectively, with n explicit attributes. To simplify the proofs in the rest of this chapter, the empty relation is included in all $VREL_P(n)$, $NVREL_P(n)$, and $SREL(n)$, for every n.

5.2.4 The TSQL2 language

Let us now turn to the actual TSQL2 language, focusing on the facilities of the language that will be used in this book. As already noted, TSQL2 is an extension of SQL-92 (Melton & Simon 1993). For the benefit of readers not familiar with SQL-92, at some points below the corresponding functionality of SQL-92 will be introduced first, where applicable, followed by the TSQL2 extensions.

SELECT statements. Roughly speaking, SQL-92 queries consist of three clauses: a `SELECT`, a `FROM`, and a `WHERE` clause, as shown in the query of (5.3). The term *`SELECT` statement* will be used to refer to the whole of a SQL-92 or TSQL2 query.

(5.3)
```
SELECT DISTINCT sal.salary
FROM salaries AS sal, managers AS mgr
WHERE mgr.manager = 'J. Adams'
  AND sal.employee = mgr.managed
```

Assuming that *salaries* and *managers* are as shown, (5.3) generates the third relation below.

(5.3)

salaries	
employee	*salary*
J. Adams	17000
T. Smith	18000
G. Papas	14500
B. Hunter	17000
K. Kofen	16000

managers	
manager	*managed*
J. Adams	*G. Papas*
J. Adams	*B. Hunter*
J. Adams	*J. Adams*
T. Smith	*K. Kofen*
T. Smith	*T. Smith*

(result)
salary
17000
14500

The query in (5.3) generates a snapshot one-attribute relation that contains the salaries of all employees managed by J. Adams. The `FROM` clause of (5.3) shows that the query operates on the *salaries* and *managers* relations. The `sal` and `mgr` are *correlation names*. They can be thought of as variables ranging over the tuples of *salaries* and *managers*, respectively. The optional `WHERE` clause imposes restrictions on the possible combinations of tuple-values of `sal` and `mgr`. In every combination, the *manager* value of `mgr` must be *J. Adams*, and the *managed* value of `mgr` must be the same as the *employee* value of `sal`. For example, ⟨*J. Adams*, *G. Papas*⟩ and ⟨*G. Papas*, 14500⟩ is an acceptable combination of `mgr` and `sal` values, respectively, while ⟨*J. Adams*, *G. Papas*⟩ and ⟨*B. Hunter*, 17000⟩ is not. In SQL-92 and TSQL2, correlation names are optional, and relation names can be used instead (e.g., `managers.manager`). To simplify the definitions in following sections, however, this book treats correlation names as mandatory.

The `SELECT` clause specifies the contents of the resulting relation. In (5.3), it specifies that the resulting relation should have only one attribute, and that for each acceptable combination of `sal` and `mgr` values, the corresponding tuple of the resulting relation should contain the *salary* value of `sal`'s tuple. The `DISTINCT` keyword in (5.3) causes duplicates of tuples to be removed from the resulting relation. Without the `DISTINCT`, the result of (5.3) would contain two identical tuples ⟨17000⟩, deriving from the tuples of J. Adams and B. Hunter in *salaries*, which is against the set-theoretic definition of relations of this book (Sections 5.2.1 and 5.2.3). To ensure that relations contain no duplicates, in this book `SELECT` statements always have a `DISTINCT` keyword in their `SELECT` clauses.

TSQL2 allows `SELECT` statements to operate on valid-time relations as well. A `SNAPSHOT` keyword in the `SELECT` statement indicates that the resulting relation is snapshot. When the resulting relation is valid-time, the `SELECT` clause specifies the values of the explicit attributes, and an additional `VALID` clause specifies the time-stamps. TSQL2 provides defaults for the case where the `VALID` clause is absent, but they will not be used in this book. Assuming that *val_salaries* is as in (5.1), (5.4) returns (5.5).

(5.4)
```
SELECT DISTINCT sal.employee, sal.salary
VALID PERIOD(BEGIN(VALID(sal)), END(VALID(sal)))
FROM val_salaries AS sal
```

(5.5)

employee	*salary*	
J. Adams	17000	[1/1/1992, 30/10/1994]
J. Adams	18000	[13/6/1992, *now*]
T. Smith	21000	[15/6/1992, *now*]

The VALID keyword is used both to start a VALID-clause and to refer to the time-stamp of a tuple. In (5.4), VALID(sal) refers to the time-stamp of sal's tuple, i.e., to the time-stamp of a tuple from *val_salaries*. The BEGIN(VALID(sal)) refers to the first chronon of the temporal element represented by that time-stamp, and END(VALID(sal)) to the last chronon.[4] The PERIOD function generates a period that starts at the chronon of its first argument, and ends at the chronon of its second argument.

Literals. TSQL2 provides PERIOD, INTERVAL, and TIMESTAMP literals, all discussed below. PERIOD literals specify periods. For example, PERIOD '[March 3, 1995 - March 20, 1995]' is a literal that specifies a period at the granularity of days. If chronons are finer than days, the assumption in TSQL2 is that the exact chronons within March 3 and March 20 where the period starts and ends are unknown (Section 5.2.2). In this book, PERIOD literals that refer to granularities other than that of chronons are treated as abbreviations for literals that refer to the granularity of chronons. The denoted period contains all the chronons that fall within the granules specified by the literal. For example, if chronons correspond to minutes, PERIOD '[March 3, 1995 - March 20, 1995]' is an abbreviation for PERIOD '[00:00 March 3, 1995 - 23:59 March 20, 1995]'.

TSQL2 allows different *calendars* to be used. Most Western countries use the Gregorian calendar, a corrected form of the Julian calendar, but other calendars, like the Chinese, Hebrew, Indian or Hijri, are also used around the world (Snodgrass 2000). The strings that can appear between the quotes of PERIOD literals depend on the available calendars and the selected formatting options. The convention is that the boundaries are separated by a dash, and that the first and last characters of the quoted string are square or round brackets, depending on whether the boundaries are to be included or not, respectively. This book also assumes that PERIOD 'today' can be used, provided that chronons are at least as fine as days, to refer to the period that covers all the chronons of the present day.

TIMESTAMP literals specify chronons. (The use of 'TIMESTAMP' in this case is unfortunate: these literals specify time-points, not time-stamps of valid-time relations, which denote temporal-elements). Only the following special TIMESTAMP literals are used in this book: TIMESTAMP 'beginning', TIMESTAMP 'forever', TIMESTAMP 'now'. These refer to the beginning of time, the end of time, and the present chronon, respectively.

An example of an INTERVAL literal is INTERVAL '5' DAY, which specifies a duration of five consecutive day-granules. The available granularities depend on the calendars that are active, but the granularities of years, months, days, hours, minutes, and seconds are supported by default. Intervals can also be used to shift periods or chronons towards the past or the future. For example, `PERIOD '[1991 - 1995]' + INTERVAL '1' YEAR` is the same as `PERIOD '[1992 - 1996]'`, and assuming that chronons correspond to minutes, `PERIOD(TIMESTAMP 'beginning', TIMESTAMP 'now' - INTERVAL '1' MINUTE)` specifies the period that covers all the chronons from the beginning of time up to, but not including, the current chronon.

Other TSQL2 functions. The `INTERSECT` function computes the intersection of two sets of chronons.[5] For example, `INTERSECT(PERIOD '[May 1, 1995 - May 10, 1995]', PERIOD '[May 3, 1995 - May 15, 1995]')` is the same as `PERIOD '[May 3, 1995 - May 10, 1995]'`. If the intersection is the empty set, `INTERSECT` returns v_ε (Section 5.2.3).

The `CONTAINS` keyword checks if a chronon belongs to a temporal element. For example, if *val_salaries* is as in (5.1), (5.6) generates a snapshot relation showing the current salary of each employee. `CONTAINS` can also be used to check if a temporal element (set of chronons) is a subset of another temporal element.

(5.6)
```
SELECT DISTINCT SNAPSHOT sal.employee, sal.salary
FROM val_salaries AS sal
WHERE VALID(sal) CONTAINS TIMESTAMP 'now'
```

The `PRECEDES` keyword checks if a chronon or temporal element strictly precedes another chronon or temporal element: $expr_1$ `PRECEDES` $expr_2$ is true iff all the chronons of $expr_1$ precede ($\prec$) all the chronons of $expr_2$.[6] For example, `PERIOD '[1/6/1995 - 21/6/1995]' PRECEDES PERIOD '[24/6/1995 - 30/6/1995]'` is true.

Embedded `SELECT` statements. TSQL2 and SQL-92 allow embedded `SELECT` statements to be used in the `FROM` clause, in the same way that relation names are used, as demonstrated in (5.7).

(5.7)
```
SELECT DISTINCT SNAPSHOT sal2.salary
FROM ( SELECT DISTINCT sal1.salary
       VALID VALID(sal1)
       FROM val_salaries AS sal1
     ) AS sal2
WHERE sal2.salary > 17500
```

Assuming that *val_salaries* is as in (5.1), the embedded `SELECT` statement above simply drops the *employee* attribute of *val_salaries*, generating (5.8). Hence, `sal2` ranges over the tuples of (5.8). (5.7) produces a one-attribute snapshot relation that includes only salaries greater than 17500.

(5.8)

salary	
17000	[1/1/1992, 12/6/1992] ∪ [8/5/1994, 30/10/1994]
18000	[13/6/1992, 7/5/1994] ∪ [31/10/1994, *now*]
21000	[15/6/1992, *now*]

Partitioning units. In TSQL2, relation names and `SELECT` statements embedded in the `FROM` clause can be followed by *partitioning units*.[7] These are not related in any way to TOP's partitionings of the time-axis (Section 3.4), but relate to the handling of value-equivalent tuples (Section 5.2.3). Two of TSQL2's partitioning units will be used in this book, `(ELEMENT)` and `(PERIOD)`, and two additional partitioning units will be introduced in Section 5.3 to support some facets of this book's aspectual taxonomy. The `(ELEMENT)` partitioning unit was actually dropped in the latest version of TSQL2 (Snodgrass 1995), but for reasons that will be explained below it is still used in this book.

The `(ELEMENT)` partitioning unit merges value-equivalent tuples. For example, if *rel1* is the relation of (5.9), (5.10) generates the coalesced relation of (5.11).

(5.9)

rel1		
employee	*salary*	
J. Adams	17000	[1986, 1988]
J. Adams	17000	[1987, 1990]
J. Adams	17000	[1992, 1994]
G. Papas	14500	[1988, 1990]
G. Papas	14500	[1990, 1992]

(5.10)

```
SELECT DISTINCT r1.employee, r1.salary
VALID VALID(r1)
FROM rel1(ELEMENT) AS r1
```

(5.11)

employee	*salary*	
J. Adams	17000	[1986, 1990] ∪ [1992, 1994]
G. Papas	14500	[1988, 1992]

The effect of (ELEMENT) on a valid-time relation r is captured by the *coalesce* function:

$$coalesce(r) \stackrel{def}{=} \{\langle v_1, \ldots, v_n; v_t\rangle \mid \langle v_1, \ldots, v_n; v'_t\rangle \in r \text{ and}$$
$$f_D(v_t) = \bigcup_{\langle v_1,\ldots,v_n;v''_t\rangle \in r} f_D(v''_t)\}$$

The (ELEMENT) partitioning unit has no effect on already coalesced valid-time relations. Hence, in the latest BCDM and TSQL2 versions (Snodgrass 1995), where all valid-time relations are coalesced (Section 5.2.3), (ELEMENT) is redundant, and this is probably why it was dropped. In this book, however, where valid-time relations are not necessarily coalesced, (ELEMENT) plays an important role.

The (PERIOD) partitioning unit intuitively breaks each tuple of a valid-time relation into value-equivalent tuples, each corresponding to a maximal period of the temporal element of the original time-stamp. Assuming, for example, that *rel2* is the relation of (5.11), (5.12) generates (5.13).

(5.12)
```
SELECT DISTINCT r2.employee, r2.salary
VALID VALID(r2)
FROM rel2(PERIOD) AS r2
```

(5.13)

employee	*salary*	
J. Adams	17000	[1986, 1990]
J. Adams	17000	[1992, 1994]
G. Papas	14500	[1988, 1992]

As shown in the example above, (PERIOD) may generate non-coalesced relations. This is mysterious in the latest BCDM version (Snodgrass 1995), where non-coalesced valid-time relations are not allowed. The assumption seems to be that although non-coalesced valid-time relations are not allowed, during the execution of SELECT statements temporary non-coalesced valid-time relations may be generated. Any resulting valid-time relations, however, are again coalesced automatically at the end of the statement's execution. (5.13) would be coalesced automatically at the end of the execution of (5.12), cancelling in this particular example the effect of (PERIOD). In the TSQL2 version of this book, no automatic coalescing takes place.

To preserve the spirit of (PERIOD) in the BCDM version of this book, where valid-time relations are not necessarily coalesced, it will be assumed that (PERIOD) operates on a coalesced copy of the original relation. Intuitively, (PE-

RIOD) first causes (5.9) to become (5.11), and then generates (5.13). More formally, the effect of (PERIOD) on a valid-time relation r is captured by the *pcoalesce* function:

$$pcoalesce(r) \stackrel{def}{=} \{\langle v_1, \ldots, v_n; v_t \rangle \mid \langle v_1, \ldots, v_n; v'_t \rangle \in coalesce(r) \text{ and } f_D(v_t) \in mxlpers(f_D(v'_t))\}$$

5.3 Modifications to TSQL2

We have already encountered some of the modifications to TSQL2 that this book introduces. The main changes were the following: (a) non-coalesced valid-time relations were admitted; (b) the distinction between state and event valid-time relations was abandoned; (c) the (ELEMENT) partitioning unit was re-introduced; and (d) the semantics of the (PERIOD) partitioning unit was enhanced to reflect the fact that non-coalesced valid-time relations are allowed. This section discusses some additional TSQL2 modifications that will be adopted in this book, along with the motivation for introducing them.

5.3.1 Referring to explicit attributes by number

In the TSQL2 version of this book, reference to explicit attributes is made by using numbers corresponding to the order of the explicit attributes in the relation schema (Section 5.2.1). For example, if the relation schema of *val_salaries* is ⟨*employee*, *salary*⟩, *employee* is the first explicit attribute and *salary* the second one; (5.14) would be used instead of (5.15). To refer to the implicit attribute, one still uses the VALID keyword.

(5.14)
```
SELECT DISTINCT sal.2
VALID VALID(sal)
FROM val_salaries AS sal
```

(5.15)
```
SELECT DISTINCT sal.salary
VALID VALID(sal)
FROM val_salaries AS sal
```

Referring to explicit attributes by number simplifies the TOP to TSQL2 translation, because there is no need to keep track of the attribute names of resulting relations. This is not an essential modification of TSQL2, and it could be removed by developing additional attribute-tracking mechanisms.

5.3.2 Additional partitioning units

Two new partitioning units (Section 5.2.4) will be assumed in the TSQL2 version of this book: `(SUBPERIOD)` and `(NOSUBPERIOD)`. The `(SUBPERIOD)` partitioning unit is intended to be used with relations from $VREL_P$ (Section 5.2.3). Its effect on a relation r is captured by the *subperiod* function:

$$subperiod(r) \stackrel{def}{=} \{\langle v_1, \ldots, v_n; v_t \rangle \mid \langle v_1, \ldots, v_n; v'_t \rangle \in r \text{ and } f_D(v_t) \sqsubseteq f_D(v'_t)\}$$

For each tuple $\langle v_1, \ldots, v_n; v'_t \rangle \in r$, the resulting relation contains many value-equivalent tuples of the form $\langle v_1, \ldots, v_n; v_t \rangle$, one for each subperiod $f_D(v_t)$ of $f_D(v'_t)$. Assuming, for example, that chronons correspond to years, and that *rel* is the relation of (5.16), (5.17) returns the relation of (5.18).

(5.16)

J. Adams	17000	[1992, 1993]
G. Papas	14500	[1988, 1990]
G. Papas	14500	[1990, 1991]

(5.17)
```
SELECT DISTINCT r.1, r.2
VALID VALID(r)
FROM rel(SUBPERIOD) AS r
```

(5.18)

J. Adams	17000	[1992, 1993]
J. Adams	17000	[1992, 1992]
J. Adams	17000	[1993, 1993]
G. Papas	14500	[1988, 1990]
G. Papas	14500	[1988, 1988]
G. Papas	14500	[1988, 1989]
G. Papas	14500	[1989, 1989]
G. Papas	14500	[1989, 1990]
G. Papas	14500	[1990, 1990]
G. Papas	14500	[1990, 1991]
G. Papas	14500	[1991, 1991]

The first three tuples of (5.18) correspond to the first tuple of (5.16). The following six tuples correspond to the first tuple of G. Papas in (5.16). The remaining two tuples of (5.18) derive from the second tuple of G. Papas in (5.16); the tuple for the subperiod [1990, 1990] has already been included. Notice that `(SUBPERIOD)` does not coalesce the original relation before generating the result, which is why there is no tuple for G. Papas time-stamped by [1988, 1991] in (5.18).

Obviously, the cardinality of the resulting relation can be very large, especially if chronons are very fine (e.g., seconds). Provided that the cardinality of the original relation is finite, however, the cardinality of the resulting relation is never infinite. Given that time is discrete, linear, and bounded, any period p is a finite set of chronons (time-points), and it has at most a finite number of subperiods. Hence, for any tuple in the original relation whose time-stamp represents a period p, there will be at most a finite number of tuples in the resulting relation whose time-stamps represent subperiods of p. It should also be stressed that the representation of the resulting relation above is only intended to demonstrate the functionality of `(SUBPERIOD)` at the conceptual level. At the physical level, more compact representations would have to be used, as it would be very inefficient to store individually all the tuples of the resulting relation.[8] It remains to be examined if efficient physical-level representations of this type exist, an issue that will not be addressed in this book. Alternatively, it may be possible to obtain the functionality of `(SUBPERIOD)` using other database language constructs; this, however, does not seem to be the case with TSQL2.

During the TOP to TSQL2 translation, every TOP formula will be mapped to a valid-time relation whose time-stamps denote the event-time periods where the formula is true. Since not all TOP formulae are homogeneous (Section 3.6), it does not suffice to include in the relation only the *maximal* event-time periods where the formula is true, which is why non-coalesced relations are allowed. On the other hand, there will be cases where we know only the maximal event-time periods of a *homogeneous* formula, and we need to ensure that the corresponding relation also contains all the subperiods of the maximal periods; this is where the `(SUBPERIOD)` partitioning unit is needed. This point will become clearer in Section 5.11.

The `(NOSUBPERIOD)` partitioning unit cancels, roughly speaking, the effect of `(SUBPERIOD)`. It is intended to be used with relations from $VREL_P$, and its effect on a valid-time relation r is captured by the following function:

$$nosubperiod(r) \stackrel{def}{=} \{\langle v_1, \ldots, v_n; v_t\rangle \in r \mid \text{there is no } \langle v_1, \ldots, v_n; v'_t\rangle \in r \text{ such that } f_D(v_t) \sqsubset f_D(v'_t)\}$$

In other words, `(NOSUBPERIOD)` eliminates any tuple $\langle v_1, \ldots, v_n; v_t\rangle$, for which there is a value-equivalent tuple $\langle v_1, \ldots, v_n; v'_t\rangle$, such that $f_D(v_t) \sqsubset f_D(v'_t)$. Applying `(NOSUBPERIOD)` to (5.18) generates (5.16). Notice that, unlike `(PE-`

RIOD), (NOSUBPERIOD) does not coalesce tuples time-stamped by adjacent periods. Applying (PERIOD) to (5.18) would have generated (5.19).

(5.19)

J. Adams	17000	[1992, 1993]
G. Papas	14500	[1988, 1991]

5.3.3 Calendric relations

As mentioned in Section 5.2.4, TSQL2 allows different calendars to be used; for example, Gregorian, Hijri, etc. Calendar definitions for TSQL2 are provided by the database administrator, the DBMS vendor, or third parties (Snodgrass 1995, Section 3.2). Among other things, TSQL2 calendar definitions specify the meanings of strings within the quotes of temporal literals, and the available granularities. In this book, it will be assumed that TSQL2 calendar definitions also provide *calendric relations*. Calendric relations behave like ordinary relations in the database, except that they contain information about the calendars, and cannot be updated. In the case of the Gregorian calendar, for example, it will be assumed that the following calendric relation is available. (It is assumed here that chronons are finer than minutes.)

gregorian						
year	*month*	*dnum*	*dname*	*hour*	*minute*	
…	…	…	…	…	…	…
1994	*Sept*	4	*Sun*	00	00	$\{c_{n_1}, \ldots, c_{n_2}\}$
1994	*Sept*	4	*Sun*	00	01	$\{c_{n_3}, \ldots, c_{n_4}\}$
…	…	…	…	…	…	…
1995	*Dec*	5	*Tue*	21	35	$\{c_{n_5}, \ldots, c_{n_6}\}$
…	…	…	…	…	…	…

The relation above means that the first minute (00:00) of September 4th 1994, which was a Sunday, covers exactly the period that starts at the chronon c_{n_1} and ends at the chronon c_{n_2}. Similarly, the period that starts at c_{n_3} and ends at c_{n_4} is the second minute (00:01) of September 4th 1994. Of course, the cardinality of *gregorian* is very large, though not infinite: time in TSQL2 is bounded, and hence there is at most a finite number of minute-granules. Again, it is important to realise that although *gregorian* behaves like a normal relation, it does not need to be physically present in the database. Its tuples can be computed dynamically, whenever they are needed, using some algorithm specified by the calendar definition. Other calendric relations may list the periods that correspond to seasons (spring-periods, summer-periods, etc.), special days (e.g., Easter days), etc.

Calendric relations like *gregorian* can be used to construct relations that represent the periods of TOP's partitionings (Section 3.4). For example, (5.20) constructs a one-attribute snapshot relation, which contains all the time-stamps of *gregorian* that correspond to 21:36-minutes. The resulting relation represents all the periods of the gappy partitioning of 21:36-minutes.

(5.20)
```
SELECT DISTINCT SNAPSHOT VALID(greg)
FROM gregorian AS greg
WHERE greg.5 = 21 AND greg.6 = 36
```

Similarly, (5.21) generates a one-attribute snapshot relation that represents the periods of the gappy partitioning of Sundays. The embedded `SELECT` statement generates a valid-time relation of one explicit attribute, whose value is *Sun* in all tuples. The time-stamps of this relation are all the time-stamps of *gregorian* that fall within Sundays; there are many tuples for each Sunday. The `(PERIOD)` coalesces tuples that correspond to the same Sunday, leading to a single period-denoting time-stamp for each Sunday. These time-stamps become the attribute values of the relation generated by the overall (5.21).

(5.21)
```
SELECT DISTINCT SNAPSHOT VALID(greg2)
FROM ( SELECT DISTINCT greg1.4
       VALID VALID(greg1)
       FROM gregorian AS greg1
       WHERE greg1.4 = 'Sun'
     )(PERIOD) AS greg2
```

It has been argued elsewhere (Androutsopoulos, Ritchie, & Thanisch 1995a) that calendric relations constitute a necessary addition to TSQL2, and that unless appropriate calendric relations are available, it is not possible to formulate TSQL2 queries for questions involving counts, existential, or universal quantification over day-names, month names, season-names, etc., like the ones in (5.22)–(5.24).

(5.22) Which technicians were at some site on a Sunday?
(5.23) Which technician was at Glasgow Central on every Monday in 1994?
(5.24) On how many Sundays was J. Adams at Glasgow Central in 1994?

5.3.4 Other minor changes

This section discusses some remaining minor TSQL2 modifications, which will allow us to bypass uninteresting details in the TOP to TSQL2 mapping.

The INTERVAL *function.* TSQL2 provides a function `INTERVAL` that accepts a period-denoting expression as its argument, and returns an interval reflecting the duration of the period. The assumption seems to be that the resulting interval is specified at whatever granularity the period is specified. For example, `INTERVAL(PERIOD '[1/12/1995 - 3/12/1995]')` is the same as `INTERVAL '3' DAY`. In this book, all periods are specified at the granularity of chronons, and if chronons correspond to minutes, `PERIOD '[1/12/1995 - 3/12/1995]'` is an abbreviation for `PERIOD '[00:00 1/12/1995 - 23:59 3/12/1995]'` (Section 5.2.4). Hence, the results of `INTERVAL` are always specified at the granularity of chronons. When translating from TOP to TSQL2, however, there are cases where we want the results of `INTERVAL` to be specified at other granularities.

The TSQL2 mechanisms for converting intervals from one granularity to another are obscure. To avoid these mechanisms, an additional version of the `INTERVAL` function is used in this book. If $expr_1$ is a TSQL2 expression that specifies a period p, and $expr_2$ is the TSQL2 name (e.g., `DAY`, `MONTH`) of a granularity G, then `INTERVAL(`$expr_1$`,` $expr_2$`)` specifies an interval of n granules (periods) of G, where n is as follows: if there are k consecutive granules $g_1, \ldots, g_k$ in G, such that $g_1 \cup \ldots \cup g_k = p$, then $n = k$; otherwise, $n = 0$. For example, `INTERVAL(PERIOD '[May 1, 1995 - June 30, 1995]', MONTH)` is the same as `INTERVAL '2' MONTH`, because the period covers exactly two consecutive month-granules. In contrast, `INTERVAL(PERIOD '[May 1, 1995 - June 15, 1995]', MONTH)` is the same as `INTERVAL '0' MONTH`, i.e., zero duration, because there is no union of consecutive month-granules that covers exactly the specified period.

Correlation names used in the FROM *clause that defines them.* The syntax of TSQL2 and SQL-92 does not allow a correlation name to be used in `SELECT` statements embedded in the same `FROM` clause that defines the correlation name. For example, (5.25) is not allowed, because the embedded `SELECT` statement uses `r1`, which is defined by the same `FROM` clause that contains the embedded `SELECT` statement.

(5.25)
```
SELECT ...
VALID VALID(r1)
FROM rel1 AS r1,
     ( SELECT ...
       VALID VALID(r2)
       FROM rel2 AS r2
       WHERE VALID(r1) CONTAINS VALID(r2)
     ) AS r3
WHERE ...
```

The term *definition of a correlation name* α, will be used in this book to refer to a TSQL2 expression '`AS α`' that associates α with a relation. For example, in (5.25) the definition of `r1` is the `AS r1`.[9] A correlation name α is *defined by a* `FROM` *clause* ξ, if ξ contains the definition of α, and this definition is not within an embedded `SELECT` statement of ξ. For example, in (5.25) the `r2` is defined by the `FROM rel2 AS r2`, not by the `FROM rel1 AS r1, ( ... ) AS r3`.

The TSQL2 version of this book allows correlation names to be used in `SELECT` statements embedded in the `FROM` clauses that define them, provided that the definitions of the correlation names precede the embedded `SELECT` statements. (5.25) is acceptable, because the definition of `r1` precedes the embedded `SELECT` statement where `r1` is used. In contrast, (5.26) is not acceptable, because the definition of `r1` follows the embedded `SELECT` statement where `r1` is used.

(5.26)
```
SELECT ...
VALID VALID(r1)
FROM ( SELECT ...
       VALID VALID(r2)
       FROM rel2 AS r2
       WHERE VALID(r1) CONTAINS VALID(r2)
     ) AS r3,
     rel1 AS r1
WHERE ...
```

The intended semantics of statements like (5.25) should be easy to see: when evaluating the embedded `SELECT` statement, `VALID(r1)` represents the timestamp of a tuple from `rel1`. The restriction that the definition of the correlation name must precede the embedded `SELECT` statement is imposed to make this modification easier to implement. The modification simplifies the translation of formulae of the form $At[\varphi_1, \varphi_2]$, $Before[\varphi_1, \varphi_2]$, and $After[\varphi_1, \varphi_2]$; see Section 5.11 and Appendix A.

Equality checks and different domains. In many cases, using the equality operator (=) with TSQL2 or SQL-92 expressions that refer to values from different domains (Section 5.2.1) leads to run-time errors. If, for example, the domain of the first explicit attribute of `rel` is the set of all integers, `r.1` in (5.27) stands for an integer. TSQL2 and SQL-92 do not allow integers to be compared to strings; consequently, a run-time error would be generated.

(5.27)
```
SELECT DISTINCT SNAPSHOT r.2
FROM rel AS r
WHERE r.1 = 'J. Adams'
```

In other cases, for example when a real number is compared to an integer, type conversions take place before the comparison. To bypass uninteresting details, this book assumes that no type conversions occur when the equality operator is used. The equality holds iff both of the arguments refer to the same element of the universal domain D, and no error occurs if the arguments refer to values from different domains. In the example of (5.27), `r.1 = 'J. Adams'` is not satisfied, because `r.1` refers to an integer, and integers are different from strings. Consequently, in the TSQL2 version of this book (5.27) generates the empty relation; no errors occur.

Partitioning units at top-level SELECT statements. TSQL2 does not allow partitioning units to follow `SELECT` statements that are not embedded in other `SELECT` statements. For example, (5.28) on its own is unacceptable.

(5.28)
```
( SELECT DISTINCT r1.1, r1.2
  VALID VALID(r1)
  FROM rel AS r1
)(PERIOD)
```

Statements like (5.28) can be easily rectified by embedding them in other `SELECT` statements, as in (5.29).

(5.29)
```
SELECT DISTINCT r2.1, r2.2
VALID VALID(r2)
FROM ( SELECT DISTINCT r1.1, r1.2
       VALID VALID(r1)
       FROM rel AS r1
     )(PERIOD) AS r2
```

To avoid introducing uninteresting layers in the mapping from TOP to TSQL2, the TSQL2 version of this book allows partitioning units to follow non-embedded `SELECT` statements, as in (5.28), assuming that they generate the same relations as the corresponding rectified queries. For uniformity, standalone SELECT statements enclosed in brackets, as in (5.30), are also allowed; the enclosing brackets are simply to be ignored.

(5.30)
```
( SELECT DISTINCT r1.1, r1.2
  VALID VALID(r1)
  FROM rel AS r1)
```

5.4 Additional TSQL2 terminology

This section defines some additional terminology, which will be used to refer to TSQL2 constructs or their denotations during the formulation of the TOP to TSQL2 mapping.

Column reference. A *column reference* is an expression of the form $\alpha.i$ or VALID(α), where α is a correlation name and $i \in \{1, 2, 3, \ldots\}$. For example, the sal.2 and VALID(sal) in (5.14) are column references.

Binding context. A SELECT statement Σ is a *binding context* for a column reference $\alpha.i$ or VALID(α) iff:

- the column reference is part of Σ,
- α is defined (in the sense of Section 5.3.4) by the topmost FROM clause of Σ, and
- the column reference is not in the topmost FROM clause of Σ; or it is in the topmost FROM clause of Σ, but the definition of α precedes the column reference.

The term *topmost FROM clause of* Σ refers to the single FROM clause of Σ that does not appear in any SELECT statement embedded in Σ; for example, the topmost FROM clause of (5.31) is the FROM (...) AS r3, tab1 AS r1.

(5.31)
```
SELECT DISTINCT r1.1, r3.2
VALID VALID(r1)
FROM ( SELECT DISTINCT SNAPSHOT r2.1, r2.2
       FROM tab2 AS r2
       WHERE VALID(r2) CONTAINS VALID(r1)
     ) AS r3,
     tab1 AS r1
WHERE r1.1 = 'J. Adams'
```

We will often have to distinguish between individual *occurrences* of column references. For example, (5.31) is a binding context for the occurrence of VALID(r1) in the VALID clause, because that occurrence is part of (5.31), r1 is defined by the topmost FROM clause of (5.31), and the occurrence of VALID(r1) is not in the topmost FROM clause of (5.31). However, (5.31) is not a binding context for the occurrence of VALID(r1) in the embedded SELECT statement, because that occurrence is in the topmost FROM clause, and it does not follow the definition of r1. In contrast, (5.32) *is* a binding context for the VALID(r1) in the embedded SELECT statement, because the definition of r1 precedes that occurrence of VALID(r1).

(5.32)
```
SELECT DISTINCT r1.1, r3.2
VALID VALID(r1)
FROM tab1 AS r1,
       ( SELECT DISTINCT SNAPSHOT r2.1, r2.2
         FROM tab2 AS r2
         WHERE VALID(r2) CONTAINS VALID(r1)
       ) AS r3
WHERE r1.1 = 'J. Adams'
```

In both (5.31) and (5.32), the overall SELECT statement is not a binding context for r2.1, r2.2, and VALID(r2), because r2 is not defined by the topmost FROM clause of the overall SELECT statement. The embedded SELECT statement of (5.31) and (5.32), however, *is* a binding context for r2.1, r2.2, and VALID(r2).

Free column reference. An occurrence of a column reference $\alpha.i$ or VALID(α) is a *free* in a TSQL2 expression ξ, iff:

- the occurrence of the column reference is part of ξ, and
- there is no SELECT statement in ξ, possibly being the whole ξ, which is a binding context for the occurrence of the column reference.

The VALID(r1) of the embedded SELECT statement of (5.31) is free in (5.31), because there is no binding context for that occurrence in (5.31). In contrast, the VALID(r1) of the VALID clause of (5.31) is not free in (5.31), because (5.31) is a binding context for that occurrence. The VALID(r2) of (5.31) is not free in (5.31), because the embedded SELECT statement is a binding context for it.

A correlation name α *has a free column reference in* a TSQL2 expression ξ, iff there is an occurrence of a column reference $\alpha.i$ or VALID(α) in ξ which is free. For every TSQL2 expression ξ, $fcn(\xi)$ is the set of all correlation names that have a free column reference in ξ. For example, if ξ is (5.31), $fcn(\xi) = \{$`r1`$\}$.

There must be no free column references in the overall `SELECT` statements that are submitted to the TSQL2 (or SQL-92) interpreter, though there may be free column references in their embedded `SELECT` statements. Hence, it is important to prove that the TOP to TSQL2 mapping generates TSQL2 code with this property.

Value expression. A value expression is a TSQL2 expression that normally evaluates to elements of the universal domain D. The meaning of 'normally' will be explained when defining the *eval* function below. For example, `'J. Adams'`, `VALID(sal)`, and `INTERSECT(PERIOD '[1993 - 1995]', PERIOD '[1994 - 1996]')` are all value expressions.

Assignment to correlation names. An assignment to correlation names is a function g^{db} that maps every TSQL2 correlation name to a possible tuple of a snapshot or valid-time relation. G^{db} is the set of all possible assignments to correlation names. If α is a correlation name, $\langle v_1, v_2, \dots \rangle$ is a possible tuple of a snapshot or valid-time relation, and $g^{db} \in G^{db}$, then $(g^{db})^{\alpha}_{\langle v_1, v_2, \dots \rangle}$ is the same as g^{db}, except that it assigns $\langle v_1, v_2, \dots \rangle$ to α.

The eval function. For every TSQL2 `SELECT` statement or value expression ξ, and every $st \in PTS$ and $g^{db} \in G^{db}$, $eval(st, \xi, g^{db})$ is the relation (if ξ is a `SELECT` statement) or the element of D (if ξ is a value expression) that is generated when the TSQL2 interpreter evaluates ξ in the following way:

– st is taken to be the current chronon (time-point).
– Every free column reference of the form $\alpha.i$ is treated as a value expression that evaluates to v_i, where v_i is the value of the i-th explicit attribute in $g^{db}(\alpha)$.
– Every free column reference of the form `VALID(`α`)` is treated as a value expression that evaluates to v_t, where v_t is the time-stamp of $g^{db}(\alpha)$.

If ξ cannot be evaluated in this way, for example if ξ contains a free column reference of the form $\alpha.4$ and $g^{db}(\alpha) = \langle v_1, v_2, v_3 \rangle$, then $eval(st, \xi, g^{db})$ returns the special value *error*; it is assumed that $error \notin D$. A value expression ξ *normally*, but not always, evaluates to an element of D, because when errors arise $eval(st, \xi, g^{db}) = error \notin D$; otherwise $eval(st, \xi, g^{db}) \in D$.

Strictly speaking, *eval* should also have as its argument the database against which ξ is evaluated. For simplicity, however, we will omit this argument.

Finally, if $fcn(\xi) = \emptyset$, i.e., if ξ contains no free column references, then $eval(st, \xi, g^{db})$ does not depend on g^{db}, in which case the notation $eval(st, \xi)$ will be used.

5.5 Adjustments in TOP and additional TOP terminology

This section discusses some adjustments that are made to the TOP formulae before translating them to TSQL2, and introduces some additional TOP terminology that will be useful in the remainder of this chapter.

Part, At, Before, and After opertors. In the formulae that are generated by the English to TOP mapping of Chapter 4, each $Part[\sigma, \beta]$ operator is conjoined with a subformula that is, or contains, an expression of the form $At[\beta, \varphi]$, $Before[\beta, \varphi]$, or $After[\beta, \varphi]$, where $\sigma \in PARTS$, $\varphi \in YNFORMS$, $\beta \in VARS$, and β is the same variable in all of the expressions. For example, (5.33) is mapped to (5.34), and the reading of (5.35) where Monday is the time when the tank was empty is mapped to (5.36).

(5.33) Tank 2 was empty on a Monday.

(5.34) $Part[monday^g, mon^v] \land At[mon^v, Past[e^v, empty(tank2)]]$

(5.35) Tank 2 had been empty on a Monday.

(5.36) $Part[monday^g, mon^v] \land$
$Past[e1^v, Perf[e2^v, At[mon^v, empty(tank2)]]]$

The mapping from TOP to TSQL2 of this chapter uses a slightly different version of TOP, where the $Part[\sigma, \beta]$ expressions are merged with the corresponding $At[\beta, \varphi]$, $Before[\beta, \varphi]$, or $After[\beta, \varphi]$ expressions, and $Part[\sigma, \beta]$, $At[\beta, \varphi]$, $Before[\beta, \varphi]$, and $After[\beta, \varphi]$ are no longer yes/no formulae. For example, (5.34) and (5.36) become (5.37) and (5.38), respectively.

(5.37) $At[monday^g, mon^v, Past[e^v, empty(tank2)]]$

(5.38) $Past[e1^v, Perf[e2^v, At[monday^g, mon^v, empty(tank2)]]]$

The semantics of $At[\sigma, \beta, \varphi]$, $Before[\sigma, \beta, \varphi]$, and $After[\sigma, \beta, \varphi]$ follow; f is f_{gparts} if $\sigma \in GPARTS$, and f_{cparts} if $\sigma \in CPARTS$. As with the TOP version of Chapter 3 (Section 3.2), β must not occur within φ. This is needed to prove the correctness of the TOP to TSQL2 translation process.

– $\|At[\sigma, \beta, \varphi]\|^{st,et,lt,g} = T$ iff $g(\beta) \in f(\sigma)$ and $\|\varphi\|^{st,et,lt \cap g(\beta),g} = T$.

– $\|Before[\sigma, \beta, \varphi]\|^{st,et,lt,g} = T$ iff
  $g(\beta) \in f(\sigma)$ and $\|\varphi\|^{st,et,lt \cap [t_{first}, minpt(\|\beta\|^g)),g} = T$.
– $\|After[\sigma, \beta, \varphi]\|^{st,et,lt,g} = T$ iff
  $g(\beta) \in f(\sigma)$ and $\|\varphi\|^{st,et,lt \cap (maxpt(\|\beta\|^g), t_{last}],g} = T$.

The TOP version of Chapter 3 is more convenient for the English to TOP mapping, while the version of this chapter simplifies the TOP to TSQL2 translation. In the prototype NLITDB of Chapter 6, the conversion between the two TOP versions is performed during the post-processing of the TOP formulae (Section 4.17).

The TOP to TSQL2 translator also assumes that in any expression of the form $At[\kappa, \varphi]$, $Before[\kappa, \varphi]$ or $After[\kappa, \varphi]$ ($\kappa \in CONS$, $\varphi \in YNFORMS$), $f_{cons}(\kappa) \in PERIODS$. The definitions of Section 3.10 are more liberal: they allow $f_{cons}(\kappa) \notin PERIODS$, in which case the denotation of the expression is always F. In practice, however, the formulae that are generated by the English to TOP mapping always use κ to denote a period.

Corners. For every $\varphi \in YNFORMS$, $\ulcorner\varphi\urcorner$, pronounced *corners* φ, is the tuple $\langle \tau_1, \ldots, \tau_n \rangle$, where $\tau_1, \ldots, \tau_n$ are all the constants that are used as arguments of predicates in φ, and all the variables that occur in φ, in the same order that they appear in φ. If a constant occurs more than once as a predicate argument in φ, or if a variable occurs more than once in φ, there are multiple τ_is in $\ulcorner\varphi\urcorner$ for that constant or variable. If $\ulcorner\varphi\urcorner = \langle \tau_1, \ldots, \tau_n \rangle$, the *length* of $\ulcorner\varphi\urcorner$ is n. For example, if:

$$\varphi = Ntense[t^v, woman(p^v)] \wedge At[1999, Past[e^v, manager\_of(p^v, sales)]]$$

then $\ulcorner\varphi\urcorner = \langle t^v, p^v, e^v, p^v, sales \rangle$, and the length of $\ulcorner\varphi\urcorner$ is 5.

5.6 Linking the TOP model to the database

The answer to an English question submitted at a time-point *st* (speech time) must report the denotation $\|\varphi\|^{M,st}$ of the corresponding TOP formula φ (Section 3.6). $\|\varphi\|^{M,st}$ follows from the semantics of TOP, provided that the model *M*, which provides all the necessary information about the modelled world, has been defined. In an NLIDB, the only source of information about the world is the database.[10] Hence, *M* has to be defined in terms of information in the database. This mainly involves defining the functions f_{cons}, f_{pfuns}, f_{culms}, f_{cparts}, and f_{gparts}, which are parts of M (Section 3.4), in terms of the database.

The functions above show how certain basic TOP expressions (e.g., constants, predicates, and partitioning names) relate to the modelled world. In this chapter, they will be defined in terms of another set of functions, h_{cons}, h_{pfuns}, h_{culms}, h_{cparts}, and h_{gparts}, respectively, and f_D (Section 5.2.1). Roughly speaking, the h functions map basic TOP expressions to database constructs, and f_D maps the attribute values of these constructs to world objects (Figure 5.1). The h functions will in turn be defined in terms of a third set of functions, h'_{cons}, h'_{pfuns}, h'_{culms}, h'_{cparts}, and h'_{gparts}, respectively, and *eval* (Section 5.4). The h' functions map basic TOP expressions to TSQL2 expressions, and *eval* maps TSQL2 expressions to database constructs.

After defining the h' functions, one could compute $\|\varphi\|^{M,st}$ using a reasoning system, which would contain inference rules encoding the semantics of TOP, and which would use the path from basic TOP expressions to TSQL2 expressions, database constructs, and the modelled world in Figure 5.1 to compute any necessary values of f_{cons}, f_{pfuns}, f_{culms}, f_{cparts}, and f_{gparts}. That is, only basic TOP expressions would be translated into TSQL2, and the DBMS would be used only to evaluate the TSQL2 translations of these expressions. The rest of the processing to compute $\|\varphi\|^{M,st}$ would be carried out by the reasoning system.

This book adopts an alternative approach, which exploits the capabilities of the DBMS to a larger extent and requires no additional reasoning system. Building upon the h' functions, which translate only basic TOP expressions to TSQL2, a method to translate any TOP formula into TSQL2 will be developed (Figure 5.2). The resulting TSQL2 code will then be executed by the DBMS, generating a relation that represents, via an interpretation function, $\|\varphi\|^{M,st}$. It can

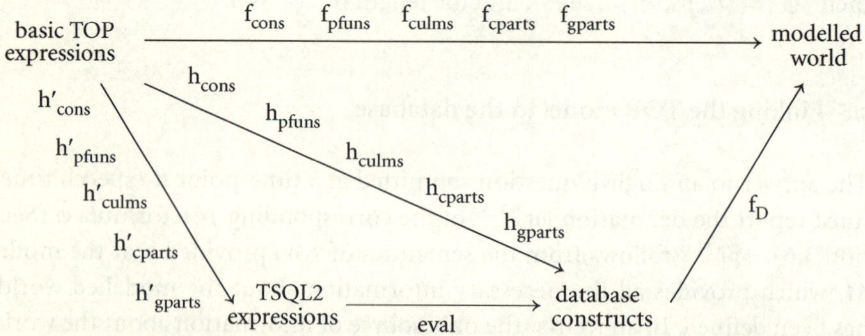

Figure 5.1 From basic TOP expressions to the modelled world

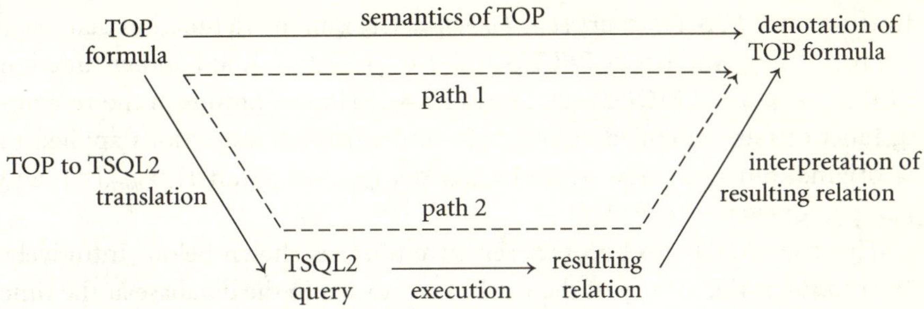

Figure 5.2 From TOP formulae to their denotations

be proven formally that this approach indeed generates $\|\varphi\|^{M,st}$, i.e., that paths 1 and 2 of Figure 5.2 lead to the same result. Central parts of this proof will be presented in later sections; the full details can be found in the thesis on which this book is based (Androutsopoulos 1996).

It should be noted at this point that, to the best of the author's knowledge, the semantics of TSQL2 was never defined formally. That is, the behaviour of the various TSQL2 expressions has been defined using only textual descriptions and examples, as opposed to specifying mathematically the data that the expressions generate when TSQL2 code is executed. Hence, the reader may wonder how it is possible to prove formally that the TOP to TSQL2 mapping is correct, if the semantics of the target language is not defined formally. To sidestep this deficiency, when a need arises to refer formally to the data that a TSQL2 expression generates, this book and the thesis on which it is based first specify formally, using set-theoretic notions, what the author understands to be the result of the TSQL2 expression, based on the available TSQL2 documentation. Although this does not rule out the risk of misunderstanding the intended functionality of some TSQL2 expressions, it clarifies the author's interpretation of the TSQL2 documentation, and the functionality that corresponding expressions in other database languages would have to provide if another database language were to be used instead of TSQL2.

There is one further complication: the values of f_{cons}, f_{pfuns}, f_{culms}, f_{cparts}, and f_{gparts} will ultimately be obtained by evaluating TSQL2 expressions. A TSQL2 expression, however, may generate different results when evaluated at different times; for example, as a result of database updates. Hence, the functions must be made sensitive to the speech time *st*, as explained below.

First, f_{cons} becomes a function $PTS \mapsto (CONS \mapsto OBJS)$, instead of $CONS \mapsto OBJS$. This allows the world objects that are assigned to TOP constants via f_{cons} to be different at different time-points *st*. Similarly, f_{pfuns} becomes a function over *PTS*. For every $st \in PTS$, $f_{pfuns}(st)$ is in turn a function that maps each pair $\langle \pi, n \rangle$, where $\pi \in PFUNS$ and $n \in \{1, 2, 3, \ldots\}$, to another function $(OBJS)^n \mapsto pow(PERIODS)$ (cf. Section 3.4). The definitions of the remaining functions are modified accordingly, and whatever restrictions applied to the original functions now apply to $f_{cons}(st)$, $f_{pfuns}(st)$, $f_{culms}(st)$, $f_{cparts}(st)$, and $f_{gparts}(st)$, for every $st \in PTS$.

The TOP model also becomes sensitive to *st*, as shown below. Intuitively, $M(st)$ contains the history of the world as recorded in the database at the time when the question is submitted (*st*). The answer to an English question submitted at *st* must now report the denotation $\|\varphi\|^{M(st),st}$ of the corresponding TOP formula φ.

$$M(st) = \langle OBJS, f_{cons}(st), f_{pfuns}(st), f_{culms}(st), f_{gparts}(st), f_{cparts}(st) \rangle$$

If the database supports both valid and transaction time (Section 1.5), it is possible to answer questions based on the history that was recorded in the database at non-present time-points *t*, by reporting $\|\varphi\|^{M(t),st}$ instead of $\|\varphi\|^{M(st),st}$.

5.7 The *h* functions

Let us now define h_{cons}, h_{pfuns}, h_{culms}, h_{cparts}, and h_{gparts}, i.e., the functions that map basic TOP expressions to database constructs (Figure 5.1). The values of these functions will ultimately be obtained by evaluating TSQL2 expressions at *st*; hence their definitions must be sensitive to *st*.

h_{cons}. This is a function $PTS \mapsto (CONS \mapsto D)$. For every $st \in PTS$, $h_{cons}(st)$ is in turn a function that maps each TOP constant to an attribute value that represents the same world-entity. For example, $h_{cons}(st)$ could map the TOP constant *sales_department* to the string attribute value *Sales Department*, and the constant *today* to the element of D_P ($D_P \subseteq D$) that denotes the day-period which contains *st*.

h_{pfuns}. This is a function over *PTS*. For every $st \in PTS$, $h_{pfuns}(st)$ is in turn a function over $PFUNS \times \{1, 2, 3, \ldots\}$, such that for every $\pi \in PFUNS$ and $n \in \{1, 2, 3, \ldots\}$, $h_{pfuns}(st)(\pi, n) \in NVREL_P(n)$ (Section 5.2.3). $h_{pfuns}(st)$ is intended to map every TOP predicate of functor π and arity n to a relation that shows for which arguments of the predicate and at which maximal periods the situation represented by the predicate is true. The relation draws information from the history that is recorded in the database at st. For example, if $circling(ba737)$ represents the situation where BA737 is circling, and if according to the history that is recorded in the database at st, p is a maximal period where BA737 was circling, then $h_{pfuns}(st)(circling, 1)$ must contain a tuple $\langle v; v_t \rangle$, such that $f_D(v) = f_{cons}(ba737)$ and $f_D(v_t) = p$.

h_{culms}. This is also a function over PTS. For every st, $h_{culms}(st)$ is in turn a function over $PFUNS \times \{1, 2, 3, \dots\}$, such that for every π and n, $h_{culms}(st)(\pi, n) \in SREL(n)$ (Section 5.2.3). Intuitively, h_{culms} plays the same role as f_{culms} (Section 3.4). In practice, h_{culms} is consulted only for predicates that describe situations with inherent climaxes. $h_{culms}(st)$ maps each TOP predicate of functor π and arity n to a relation that shows for which predicate arguments the situation of the predicate reaches its climax at the latest time-point where the situation is ongoing, according to the history recorded in the database at st.

For example, if $inspecting(ja, ba737)$ represents a situation where BA737 is being inspected by J. Adams, then $h_{pfuns}(st)(inspecting, 2)$ is a relation in $NVREL_P(2)$ and $h_{culms}(st)(inspecting, 2)$ a relation in $SREL(2)$. If the history that is recorded in the database at st shows that the maximal periods where J. Adams was inspecting BA737 are $p_1, \dots, p_j$, then $h_{pfuns}(st)(inspecting, 2)$ contains the tuples $\langle v_1, v_2; v_t^1 \rangle, \dots, \langle v_1, v_2; v_t^j \rangle$, where $f_D(v_1) = f_{cons}(ja)$, $f_D(v_2) = f_{cons}(ba737)$, and $f_D(v_t^1) = p_1, \dots, f_D(v_t^j) = p_j$. Let us assume that p is the latest maximal period among $p_1, \dots, p_j$. Then, $h_{culms}(st)(inspecting, 2)$ contains $\langle v_1, v_2 \rangle$ iff according to the history recorded in the database at st, the inspection of BA737 by J. Adams reaches its completion at the end of p.

h_{gparts}. This is a function over PTS. For every st, $h_{gparts}(st)$ is in turn a function that maps every element of $GPARTS$ to an $r \in SREL(1)$, such that the set $S = \{f_D(v) \mid \langle v \rangle \in r\}$ is a gappy partitioning. $h_{gparts}(st)$ is intended to map each TOP gappy partitioning name σ_g to a one-attribute snapshot relation r, whose attribute values represent the periods of the gappy partitioning S that is assigned to σ_g. For example, $h_{gparts}(st)$ could map $monday^g$ to a one-attribute snapshot relation whose attribute values denote all the Monday-periods.

h_{cparts}. This is similar to h_{gparts}, except that it is used with complete partitioning names. It is a function over PTS. For every st, $h_{cparts}(st)$ is in turn a function that maps every element of $CPARTS$ to an $r \in SREL(1)$, such that the set $S = \{f_D(v) \mid \langle v \rangle \in r\}$ is a complete partitioning. For example, $h_{cparts}(st)$ could map

day^c to a one-attribute snapshot relation whose attribute values denote all the day-periods.

5.8 The TOP model in terms of database concepts

The TOP model can now be defined in terms of database concepts as discussed below (see also Sections 3.4 and 5.6). A mapping f_D between the universal domain D and TOP's $OBJS$ is assumed, as in Section 5.2.1.

f_{cons}. For every $st \in PTS$ and $\kappa \in CONS$, $f_{cons}(st)(\kappa) \stackrel{def}{=} f_D(h_{cons}(st)(\kappa))$. $h_{cons}(st)$ is a function $CONS \mapsto D$, and f_D is a function $D \mapsto OBJS$. Hence, $f_{cons}(st)$ is a function $CONS \mapsto OBJS$, as required by Sections 3.4 and 5.6.

f_{pfuns}. For $st \in PTS$, $\pi \in PFUNS$, $n \in \{1, 2, 3, \ldots\}$, $o_1, \ldots, o_n \in OBJS$:

$$f_{pfuns}(st)(\pi, n)(o_1, \ldots, o_n) \stackrel{def}{=} \{f_D(v_t) \mid \langle f_D^{-1}(o_1), \ldots, f_D^{-1}(o_n); v_t\rangle \in h_{pfuns}(st)(\pi, n)\}$$

That is, $f_D(v_t)$ is a maximal period where the situation that involves the entities $o_1, \ldots, o_n$ is ongoing iff v_t is the time-stamp of a tuple in $h_{pfuns}(st)(\pi, n)$ that corresponds to $o_1, \ldots, o_n$. The definition of h_{pfuns} guarantees that $h_{pfuns}(st)(\pi, n) \in NVREL_P(n)$, which implies that $f_{pfuns}(st)(\pi, n)(o_1, \ldots, o_n)$ is a set of periods. According to Sections 3.4 and 5.6, it must also be the case that if $p_1, p_2 \in f_{pfuns}(st)(\pi, n)(o_1, \ldots, o_n)$ and $p_1 \cup p_2 \in PERIODS$, then $p_1 = p_2$. f_{pfuns}, as defined above, has this property. The proof follows.

Let us assume that p_1 and p_2 are as above, but $p_1 \neq p_2$. Let $v_t^1 = f_D^{-1}(p_1)$ and $v_t^2 = f_D^{-1}(p_2)$, i.e., $f_D(v_t^1) = p_1$ and $f_D(v_t^2) = p_2$. Since $p_1 \neq p_2$ and f_D^{-1} is 1-1 (Section 5.2.1), $f_D^{-1}(p_1) \neq f_D^{-1}(p_2)$, i.e., $v_t^1 \neq v_t^2$. Then, by the definition of f_{pfuns} above, $h_{pfuns}(st)(\pi, n)$ contains the value-equivalent tuples $\langle f_D^{-1}(o_1), \ldots, f_D^{-1}(o_n); v_t^1\rangle$ and $\langle f_D^{-1}(o_1), \ldots, f_D^{-1}(o_n); v_t^2\rangle$, where $f_D(v_t^1) \cup f_D(v_t^2) \in PERIODS$. This, however, implies that $v_t^1 = v_t^2$, because $h_{pfuns}(st)(\pi, n) \in NVREL_P(n)$ (Section 5.7), which is not true. Hence, it cannot be the case that $p_1 \neq p_2$, which implies that $p_1 = p_2$.

f_{culms}. For $st \in PTS$, $\pi \in PFUNS$, $n \in \{1, 2, 3, \ldots\}$, $o_1, \ldots, o_n \in OBJS$:

$$f_{culms}(st)(\pi, n)(o_1, \ldots, o_n) \stackrel{def}{=} \begin{cases} T, & \text{if } \langle f_D^{-1}(o_1), \ldots, f_D^{-1}(o_n) \rangle \\ & \quad \in h_{culms}(st)(\pi, n) \\ F, & \text{otherwise} \end{cases}$$

That is, the situation that involves $o_1, \ldots, o_n$ reaches its climax at the end of the latest maximal period where the situation is ongoing iff there is a tuple in $h_{culms}(st)(\pi, n)$ that corresponds to $o_1, \ldots, o_n$. The definition of h_{culms} guarantees that $h_{culms}(st)(\pi, n) \in SREL(n)$.

f_{gparts}. For every $st \in PTS$ and $\sigma_g \in GPARTS$, $f_{gparts}(st)(\sigma_g) \stackrel{def}{=} \{f_D(v) \mid \langle v \rangle \in h_{gparts}(st)(\sigma_g)\}$. The definition of h_{gparts} guarantees that $f_{gparts}(st)(\sigma_g)$ is always a gappy partitioning. Similar comments apply to f_{cparts} below.

f_{cparts}. For every $st \in PTS$ and $\sigma_c \in CPARTS$, $f_{cparts}(st)(\sigma_c) \stackrel{def}{=} \{f_D(v) \mid \langle v \rangle \in h_{cparts}(st)(\sigma_c)\}$.

5.9 The h' functions

We can now examine in more detail the h' functions, i.e., the functions that map basic TOP expressions to TSQL2 expressions (Figure 5.1), and how the h functions of Section 5.7 can be defined in terms of the h' functions. It is assumed that the exact definitions of the h' functions are provided in each application domain by the configurer of the NLITDB (Section 1.2).

h'_{cons}. This function maps every TOP constant κ to a TSQL2 value expression ξ, such that $fcn(\xi) = \emptyset$, and for every $st \in PTS$, $eval(st, \xi) \in D$. ξ is intended to represent the same world object as κ. For example, h'_{cons} could map the TOP constant *sales_department* to the TSQL2 value expression `'Sales Department'`, and the TOP constant *yesterday* to `PERIOD 'today' - INTERVAL '1' DAY`. In practice, the values of h'_{cons} need to be defined only for TOP constants that are used in the particular application domain. The values of h'_{cons} for other constants are not used, and can be chosen arbitrarily. Similar comments apply to h'_{pfuns}, h'_{culms}, h'_{gparts}, and h'_{cparts}.

The h_{cons} function can then be defined in terms of h'_{cons}. For every $st \in PTS$ and $\kappa \in CONS$:

$$h_{cons}(st)(\kappa) \stackrel{def}{=} eval(st, h'_{cons}(\kappa))$$

The restrictions on h'_{cons} above guarantee that $eval(st, h'_{cons}(\kappa)) \in D$. Hence, $h_{cons}(st)$ is a function $CONS \mapsto D$, as required by Section 5.7.

h'_{pfuns}. This is a function over $PFUNS \times \{1, 2, 3, \ldots\}$. The value of the function is always a TSQL2 SELECT statement Σ, such that $fcn(\Sigma) = \emptyset$, and for every $st \in PTS$, $eval(st, \Sigma) \in NVREL_P(n)$. For every $\pi \in PFUNS$ and $n \in \{1, 2, 3, \ldots\}$, $h'_{pfuns}(\pi, n)$ is intended to be a SELECT statement that generates the relation to which $h_{pfuns}(st)$ maps π and n, i.e., the relation that shows for which arguments and at which maximal periods the situation described by $\pi(\tau_1, \ldots, \tau_n)$ is true.

The h_{pfuns} function can then be defined in terms of h'_{pfuns}. For every $st \in PTS$, $\pi \in PFUNS$, and $n \in \{1, 2, 3, \ldots\}$:

$$h_{pfuns}(st)(\pi, n) \stackrel{def}{=} eval(st, h'_{pfuns}(\pi, n))$$

The restrictions on h'_{pfuns} above ensure that $h_{pfuns}(st)(\pi, n) \in NVREL_P(n)$, as required by Section 5.7.

Let us assume, for example, that $manager(\tau)$ means that τ is a manager, and that *manager_of* is the relation of $NVREL_P(2)$ in (5.39) that shows the maximal periods where somebody is the manager of a department. (To save space, the names of the explicit attributes will often be omitted. References to explicit attributes are made by number, as in Section 5.3.1.)

(5.39)

J. Adams	*sales*	[1/5/1993, 31/12/1994]
J. Adams	*personnel*	[1/1/1995, 31/3/1995]
J. Adams	*research*	[5/9/1995, 31/12/1995]
T. Smith	*sales*	[1/1/1995, 7/5/1995]
...	...	...

Then, $h'_{pfuns}(manager, 1)$ could be defined to be (5.40), which generates (5.41). The embedded SELECT statement of (5.40) discards the second explicit attribute of *manager_of*, and the (PERIOD) coalesces tuples that correspond to the same employees, generating one tuple for each maximal period.

(5.40)
```
SELECT DISTINCT mgr2.1
VALID VALID(mgr2)
FROM ( SELECT DISTINCT mgr1.1
       VALID VALID(mgr1)
       FROM manager_of AS mgr1
     )(PERIOD) AS mgr2
```

(5.41)

J. Adams	[1/5/1993, 31/3/1995]
J. Adams	[5/9/1995, 31/12/1995]
T. Smith	[1/1/1995, 7/5/1995]
...	...

h'_{culms}. This is a function over $PFUNS \times \{1, 2, 3, \ldots\}$. The value of the function is always a TSQL2 SELECT statement Σ, such that $fcn(\Sigma) = \emptyset$, and for every $st \in PTS$, $eval(st, \Sigma) \in SREL(n)$. For every $\pi \in PFUNS$ and $n \in \{1, 2, 3, \ldots\}$, $h'_{culms}(\pi, n)$ is intended to be a SELECT statement that generates the relation to which $h_{culms}(st)$ maps π and n, i.e., the relation that shows for which arguments of $\pi(\tau_1, \ldots, \tau_n)$ the situation of the predicate reaches its climax at the end of the latest maximal period where it is ongoing.

The h_{culms} function is then defined in terms of h'_{culms} as follows. For every $st \in PTS$, $\pi \in PFUNS$, and $n \in \{1, 2, 3, \ldots\}$:

$$h_{culms}(st)(\pi, n) \stackrel{def}{=} eval(st, h'_{culms}(\pi, n))$$

The restrictions on h'_{culms} above guarantee that $h_{culms}(st)(\pi, n) \in SREL(n)$, as required by Section 5.7.

In the airport application, for example, $inspecting(\tau_1, \tau_2, \tau_3)$ means that an occurrence τ_1 of an inspection of τ_3 by τ_2 is ongoing. An *inspections* relation is available, and it has the form shown below:

inspections				
code	*inspector*	*inspected*	*status*	
i158	*J. Adams*	*UK160*	*complete*	[9:00*am* 1/5/1995, 9:45*am* 1/5/1995] ∪ [10:10*am* 1/5/1995, 10:25*am* 1/5/1995]
i160	*J. Adams*	*UK160*	*incomplete*	[11:00*pm* 2/7/1995, 1:00*am* 3/7/1995] ∪ [6:00*am* 3/7/1995, 6:20*am* 3/7/1995]
i205	*T. Smith*	*BA737*	*complete*	[8:00*am* 16/11/1995, 8:20*am* 16/11/1995]
i214	*T. Smith*	*BA737*	*incomplete*	[8:10*am* 14/2/1996, *now*]

The first tuple above shows that J. Adams started to inspect UK160 at 9:00 am on 1/5/1995, and continued the inspection up to 9:45 am. He resumed the inspection at 10:10 am, and completed the inspection at 10:25 am on the same day. The *status* shows whether or not the inspection reaches its completion at the last time-point of the time-stamp. The inspection of the second tuple was ongoing from 11:00 pm on 2/7/1995 to 1:00 am on 3/7/1995, and from 6:00 am to 6:20 am on 3/7/1995, without reaching its completion. The inspection of the last tuple started at 8:10 am on 14/2/1996 and is still ongoing. Each inspection is assigned a unique inspection code, stored as the value of the *code* attribute. The inspection codes are useful to distinguish, for example, J. Adams' inspection of UK160 on 1/5/1995 from that on 2-3/7/1995 (Section 3.16). $h'_{pfuns}(inspecting, 3)$ and $h'_{culms}(inspecting, 3)$ are defined to be (5.42) and (5.43), respectively, which causes $h_{pfuns}(st)(inspecting, 2)$ and $h_{culms}(st)(inspecting, 2)$ to be (5.44) and (5.45), respectively.

(5.42)
```
SELECT DISTINCT insp.1, insp.2, insp.3
VALID VALID(insp)
FROM inspections(PERIOD) AS insp
```

(5.43)
```
SELECT DISTINCT SNAPSHOT icmp.1, icmp.2, icmp.3
FROM inspections AS icmp
WHERE icmp.4 = 'complete'
```

(5.44)

i158	*J. Adams*	*UK160*	[9:00*am* 1/5/1995, 9:45*am* 1/5/1995]
i158	*J. Adams*	*UK160*	[10:10*am* 1/5/1995, 10:25*am* 1/5/1995]
i160	*J. Adams*	*UK160*	[11:00*pm* 2/7/1995, 1:00*am* 3/7/1995]
i160	*J. Adams*	*UK160*	[6:00*am* 3/7/1995, 6:20*am* 3/7/1995]
i205	*T. Smith*	*BA737*	[8:00*am* 16/11/1995, 8:20*am* 16/11/1995]
i214	*T. Smith*	*BA737*	[8:10*am* 14/2/1996, *now*]

(5.45)

i158	*J. Adams*	*UK160*
i205	*T. Smith*	*BA737*

h'_{gparts}. This is a function that maps every TOP gappy partitioning name σ_g to a TSQL2 SELECT statement Σ, such that $fcn(\Sigma) = \emptyset$, and for every $st \in PTS$, it is true that $eval(st, \Sigma) \in SREL(1)$ and $\{f_D(v) \mid \langle v \rangle \in eval(st, \Sigma)\}$ is a gappy partitioning. $h'_{gparts}(\sigma_g)$ is intended to generate the relation to which $h_{gparts}(st)$ maps σ_g, i.e., the relation that represents the members of the gappy partitioning. Assuming, for example, that the *gregorian* calendric relation of Section 5.3.3 is available, $h'_{gparts}(sunday^g)$ could be (5.21).

The h_{gparts} function is then defined in terms of h'_{gparts}. For every $st \in PTS$ and $\sigma_g \in GPARTS$:

$$h_{gparts}(st)(\sigma_g) \stackrel{def}{=} eval(st, h'_{gparts}(\sigma_g))$$

h'_{cparts}. It is assumed that for each complete partitioning used in the TOP formulae, there is a corresponding TSQL2 granularity (Section 5.2.2). h'_{cparts} is a function that maps each TOP complete partitioning name to an ordered pair $\langle \gamma, \Sigma \rangle$, where γ is the name of the corresponding TSQL2 granularity and Σ is a SELECT statement that returns a relation representing the periods of the partitioning. More precisely, it must be the case that $fcn(\Sigma) = \emptyset$, and for every $st \in PTS$, $eval(st, \Sigma) \in SREL(1)$ and $\{f_D(v) \mid \langle v \rangle \in eval(st, \Sigma)\}$ is a complete partitioning. For example, if the *gregorian* relation of Section 5.3.3 is available, h'_{cparts} could map day^c to $\langle$DAY, $\Sigma\rangle$, where Σ is (5.46). (5.46) returns a one-attribute snapshot relation whose attribute values denote all the day-periods. The γ, in this case DAY, is used when translating formulae of the form $For[\sigma_c, \nu_{qty}, \varphi]$; see Section 5.11 and Appendix A.

(5.46)
```
SELECT DISTINCT SNAPSHOT VALID(greg2)
FROM ( SELECT DISTINCT greg1.4
       VALID VALID(greg1)
       FROM gregorian AS greg1
     )(PERIOD) AS greg2
```

The h_{cparts} function is then defined in terms of h'_{cparts} as follows. For every $st \in PTS$ and $\sigma_c \in CPARTS$, if $h'_{cparts}(\sigma_c) = \langle \gamma, \Sigma \rangle$, then:

$$h_{cparts}(st)(\sigma_c) \stackrel{def}{=} eval(st, \Sigma)$$

5.10 Formulation of the translation problem

Let us now specify formally what we want the TOP to TSQL2 translation process to achieve. The *interp* function, defined below, will allow us to interpret the relations that the resulting TSQL2 queries generate. For every $\varphi \in FORMS$ and every relation r:

(5.47)
$$interp(r, \varphi) \stackrel{def}{=} \begin{cases} T, \text{ if } \varphi \in YNFORMS \text{ and } r \neq \emptyset \\ F, \text{ if } \varphi \in YNFORMS \text{ and } r = \emptyset \\ \{\langle f_D(v_1), \ldots, f_D(v_n) \rangle \mid \langle v_1, \ldots, v_n \rangle \in r\}, \\ \quad \text{if } \varphi \in WHFORMS \end{cases}$$

Assuming that φ is translated to a `SELECT` statement that generates r, $interp(r, \varphi)$ shows how to interpret r. If $\varphi \in YNFORMS$, i.e., if the user has submitted a yes/no question, then an non-empty r signals that an affirmative answer should be generated; otherwise, if r is empty, the answer must be negative. If $\varphi \in WHFORMS$, i.e., if the user's question contained interrogatives (e.g., *who?*, *when?*), the answer should report all the tuples of world objects that correspond to the tuples of r.

A translation function *tr* is needed, which will map every $\varphi \in FORMS$ to a TSQL2 `SELECT` statement $tr(\varphi)$, such that for every $st \in PTS$, (5.48) and (5.49) hold.

(5.48) $fcn(tr(\varphi)) = \emptyset$
(5.49) $interp(eval(st, tr(\varphi)), \varphi) = \|\varphi\|^{M(st),st}$

As discussed in Section 3.6, each reading of an English question is mapped to a TOP formula φ. The answer for each reading must report $\|\varphi\|^{M(st),st}$. If *tr* satisfies (5.49), then $\|\varphi\|^{M(st),st}$ can be computed as $interp(eval(st, tr(\varphi)), \varphi)$ by letting the DBMS execute $tr(\varphi)$.

The *tr* function will be defined in terms of an auxiliary function *trans*. This is a function of two arguments, $\varphi \in FORMS$ and λ, where λ is a TSQL2 value expression (Section 5.4). The value of *trans* is always a TSQL2 `SELECT` statement Σ.

$$trans(\varphi, \lambda) = \Sigma$$

A set of translation rules, to be discussed in Section 5.11, specifies the Σ values of *trans* for different forms of φ. The λ corresponds to TOP's *lt*. When *trans* is invoked for the first time, via *tr*, as will be explained below, λ is set to `PERIOD(TIMESTAMP 'beginning', TIMESTAMP 'forever')` to reflect the fact that TOP's *lt* is initially set to *PTS*, i.e., the whole time-axis (Section 3.6). Recursive calls to *trans* may then follow to translate subformulae of φ. When calling *trans* recursively, λ may represent a period that does not cover the whole time-axis, to reflect the fact that already encountered TOP operators may have narrowed *lt*.

We can now define the top-level *tr* function as follows, where λ_{init} stands for `PERIOD(TIMESTAMP 'beginning', TIMESTAMP 'forever')`.

(5.50) $tr(\varphi) \stackrel{def}{=} trans(\varphi, \lambda_{init})$

Since λ_{init} contains no correlation names, $fcn(\lambda_{init}) = \emptyset$, which implies that $eval(st, \lambda_{init}, g^{db})$ does not depend on g^{db}. λ_{init} always evaluates to the element of D_P that represents the period that covers the whole time-axis. Therefore, Lemma 5.1 below holds.

Lemma 5.1 *$fcn(\lambda_{init}) = \emptyset$, and for every $st \in PTS$, $eval(st, \lambda_{init}) \in D_P$ and $f_D(eval(st, \lambda_{init})) = PTS$.*

Using (5.50), we can rewrite (5.48) and (5.49) as (5.51) and (5.52), respectively. The translation rules, which specify the values of *trans*, must ensure that for every $\varphi \in FORMS$ and $st \in PTS$, (5.51) and (5.52) hold. The thesis on which this book is based (Androutsopoulos 1996) proves that the translation rules of Section 5.11 satisfy Theorems 5.1 and 5.2; and it will be shown below that the two theorems imply (5.51) and (5.52).

(5.51) $fcn(trans(\varphi, \lambda_{init})) = \emptyset$
(5.52) $interp(eval(st, trans(\varphi, \lambda_{init})), \varphi) = \|\varphi\|^{M(st),st}$

In effect, Theorems 5.1 and 5.2 can be used as entry points for anybody wishing to add new translation rules. The theorems are proven separately for each translation rule, and for each new translation rule, one has to guarantee that Theorems 5.1 and 5.2 still hold.

Theorem 5.1 *If* $\varphi \in WHFORMS$, $st \in PTS$, $trans(\varphi, \lambda_{init}) = \Sigma$, *and the total number of interrogative and interrogative-maximal quantifiers in* φ *is n, then:*

1. $fcn(\Sigma) = \emptyset$
2. $eval(st, \Sigma) \in SREL(n)$
3. $\{\langle f_D(v_1), \ldots, f_D(v_n)\rangle \mid \langle v_1, \ldots, v_n\rangle \in eval(st, \Sigma)\} = \|\varphi\|^{M(st),st}$

That is, if the user's question contains interrogatives, the resulting TSQL2 query contains no free column references, and it evaluates to a snapshot relation with as many attributes as the interrogatives, whose tuples represent $\|\varphi\|^{M(st),st}$.

Theorem 5.2 *If* $\varphi \in YNFORMS$, $st \in PTS$, λ *is a* TSQL2 *expression*, $g^{db} \in G^{db}$, $eval(st, \lambda, g^{db}) \in D_P^*$, $\ulcorner\varphi\urcorner = \langle\tau_1, \ldots, \tau_n\rangle$, *and* $trans(\varphi, \lambda) = \Sigma$, *then:*

1. $fcn(\Sigma) \subseteq fcn(\lambda)$
2. $eval(st, \Sigma, g^{db}) \in VREL_P(n)$
3. $\langle v_1, \ldots, v_n; v_t\rangle \in eval(st, \Sigma, g^{db})$ *iff for some* $g \in G$:
   $\|\tau_1\|^{M(st),g} = f_D(v_1), \ldots, \|\tau_n\|^{M(st),g} = f_D(v_n)$ *and*
   $\|\varphi\|^{M(st),st,f_D(v_t),f_D(eval(st,\lambda,g^{db})),g} = T$

That is, the TSQL2 query that is generated when the user submits a yes/no question φ contains no correlation names with free column references, apart from correlation names in *fcn*(λ). Furthermore, if $\ulcorner\varphi\urcorner = \tau_1, \ldots, \tau_n$, i.e., if $\tau_1, \ldots, \tau_n$ are all the constants in predicate argument positions and all the variables in φ, the resulting TSQL2 query generates a valid-time relation of n explicit attributes, whose time-stamps denote periods. In each tuple of the relation, the values of the explicit attributes and the time-stamp correspond to denotations of $\tau_1, \ldots, \tau_n$ and an *et*, such that $\|\varphi\|^{M(st),st,et,lt,g} = T$, for some $g \in G$, where *lt* is the element of $PERIODS^*$ represented by λ.

Let us now prove that Theorems 5.1 and 5.2 imply (5.51) and (5.52), for every $st \in PTS$ and $\varphi \in FORMS$; i.e., that *trans* has the desired properties.

Proof of (5.51). Since $FORMS = WHFORMS \cup YNFORMS$, it is either the case that $\varphi \in WHFORMS$ or $\varphi \in YNFORMS$. In both cases, (5.51) holds:

- If $\varphi \in WHFORMS$, then by Theorem 5.1, $fcn(trans(\varphi, \lambda_{init})) = \emptyset$; i.e., (5.51) holds.
- If $\varphi \in YNFORMS$, then by Theorem 5.2 and Lemma 5.1, it is true that $fcn(trans(\varphi, \lambda_{init})) \subseteq fcn(\lambda_{init}) = \emptyset$; i.e., (5.51) holds.

Proof of (5.52). Again, it will either be the case that $\varphi \in WHFORMS$ or $\varphi \in YNFORMS$. If $\varphi \in WHFORMS$, by Theorem 5.1 the following is true:

$$\{\langle f_D(v_1), \ldots, f_D(v_n)\rangle \mid \langle v_1, \ldots, v_n\rangle \in eval(st, trans(\varphi, \lambda_{init}))\} = \|\varphi\|^{M(st),st}$$

Then, by the definition of *interp*, (5.52) holds.

It remains to prove (5.52) for $\varphi \in YNFORMS$. Let $\ulcorner\varphi\urcorner = \langle \tau_1, \ldots, \tau_n\rangle$. By Lemma 5.1, for every $g^{db} \in G^{db}$, $eval(st, \lambda_{init}, g^{db}) = eval(st, \lambda_{init}) \in D_P$ and $f_D(eval(st, \lambda_{init})) = PTS$. Also, by (5.51), $eval(st, trans(\varphi, \lambda_{init}), g^{db})$ does not depend on g^{db}. Then, from Theorem 5.2 we get (5.53) and (5.54).

(5.53) $eval(st, trans(\varphi, \lambda_{init})) \in VREL_P(n)$

(5.54) $\langle v_1, \ldots, v_n; v_t\rangle \in eval(st, trans(\varphi, \lambda_{init}))$ iff for some $g \in G$:
$\|\tau_1\|^{M(st),g} = f_D(v_1), \ldots, \|\tau_n\|^{M(st),g} = f_D(v_n)$ and
$\|\varphi\|^{M(st),st,f_D(v_t),PTS,g} = T$

Since $\varphi \in YNFORMS$, by the definition of *interp* the left-hand side of (5.52) has the following values:

$$\begin{cases} T, & \text{if } eval(st, trans(\varphi, \lambda_{init})) \neq \emptyset \\ F, & \text{if } eval(st, trans(\varphi, \lambda_{init})) = \emptyset \end{cases}$$

Also, the definition of $\|\varphi\|^{M(st),st}$ for $\varphi \in YNFORMS$ (Section 3.6) implies that the right-hand side of (5.52) has the following values:

$$\begin{cases} T, & \text{if for some } g \in G \text{ and } et \in PERIODS,\ \|\varphi\|^{M(st),st,et,PTS,g} = T \\ F, & \text{otherwise} \end{cases}$$

Hence, to complete the proof of (5.52), it is enough to prove (5.55):

(5.55) $eval(st, trans(\varphi, \lambda_{init})) \neq \emptyset$ iff
for some $g \in G$ and $et \in PERIODS$, $\|\varphi\|^{M(st),st,et,PTS,g} = T$

We first prove the forward direction of (5.55). If $eval(st, trans(\varphi, \lambda_{init})) \neq \emptyset$, by (5.53) $eval(st, trans(\varphi, \lambda_{init}))$ contains at least a tuple of the form $\langle v_1, \ldots, v_n; v_t\rangle$; i.e., (5.56) is true. (5.56) and (5.54) imply that for some $g \in G$, (5.57) holds.

(5.56) $\langle v_1, \ldots, v_n; v_t \rangle \in eval(st, trans(\varphi, \lambda_{init}))$

(5.57) $\|\varphi\|^{M(st),st,f_D(v_t),PTS,g} = T$

The definition of *VREL*$_P$, (5.53), and (5.56) imply that $f_D(v_t) \in PERIODS$. Let $et = f_D(v_t)$. Then, (5.57) becomes (5.58), where $g \in G$ and $et = f_D(v_t) \in PERIODS$. The forward direction of (5.55) has been proven.

(5.58) $\|\varphi\|^{M(st),st,et,PTS,g} = T$

We now prove the backwards direction of (5.55). We assume that $g \in G$, $et \in PERIODS$, and $\|\varphi\|^{M(st),st,et,PTS,g} = T$. Let $v_t = f_D^{-1}(et)$, which implies that $et = f_D(v_t)$; then (5.59) holds. Let us also set $v_1 = f_D^{-1}(\|\tau_1\|^{M(st),g}), \ldots, v_n = f_D^{-1}(\|\tau_n\|^{M(st),g})$; then (5.60) also holds.

(5.59) $\|\varphi\|^{M(st),st,f_D(v_t),PTS,g} = T$

(5.60) $\|\tau_1\|^{M(st),g} = f_D(v_1), \ \ldots, \ \|\tau_n\|^{M(st),g} = f_D(v_n)$

The assumption that $g \in G$, (5.60), (5.59), and (5.54) imply (5.61), which in turn implies that $eval(st, trans(\varphi, \lambda_{init})) \neq \emptyset$. The backwards direction of (5.55) has been proven, which concludes the proof of (5.52).

(5.61) $\langle v_1, \ldots, v_n; v_t \rangle \in eval(st, trans(\varphi, \lambda_{init}))$

5.11 The translation rules

The values of *trans* are specified by translation rules of two kinds: (a) base, non-recursive, rules that specify $trans(\varphi, \lambda)$ when φ is an atomic formula or a formula of the form $Culm[\pi(\tau_1, \ldots, \tau_n)]$; and (b) recursive rules that specify $trans(\varphi, \lambda)$ in all other cases by calling other translation rules to process subformulae of φ. This section attempts to convey the intuitions behind the design of the translation rules, and to illustrate the functionality of some representative rules. The full set of the rules can be found in Appendix A, and a proof that they satisfy Theorems 5.1 and 5.2 can be found in the thesis on which this book is based (Androutsopoulos 1996).

Translation rule for predicates. The reader is reminded that in the case of a yes/no formula φ, with $\ulcorner\varphi\urcorner = \langle \tau_1, \ldots, \tau_n \rangle$, the aim is for the resulting SELECT statement to return a relation in $VREL_P(n)$ that shows all the combinations of event times *et* and denotations of $\tau_1, \ldots, \tau_n$ for which φ is satisfied. In each tuple $\langle v_1, \ldots, v_n; v_t \rangle$, v_t represents *et*, while $v_1, \ldots, v_n$ correspond to the values of $\tau_1, \ldots, \tau_n$. The translation rule for predicates is as follows.

$$trans(\pi(\tau_1, \ldots, \tau_n), \lambda) \stackrel{def}{=}$$

```
( SELECT DISTINCT α.1, α.2, ... , α.n
  VALID VALID(α)
  FROM (h'_pfuns(π, n))(SUBPERIOD) AS α
  WHERE ...
    AND ...
    ⋮
    AND λ CONTAINS VALID(α))
```

The dots in the WHERE clause stand for all the strings in $S_1 \cup S_2$:

$$S_1 = \{\text{“}\alpha.i = h'_{cons}(\tau_i)\text{”} \mid i \in \{1, 2, 3, \ldots, n\}, \tau_i \in CONS\}$$

$$S_2 = \{\text{“}\alpha.i = \alpha.j\text{”} \mid i, j \in \{1, 2, 3, \ldots, n\},\ i < j,\ \tau_i = \tau_j, \tau_i, \tau_j \in VARS\}$$

It is assumed that whenever the translation rule is invoked, a new correlation name α is used (e.g., `t354`, `t355`, …), which has never been used before and which is obtained by calling a generator of correlation names. The use of the generator means that *trans* is strictly speaking not a pure function, since the same π and $\tau_1, \ldots, \tau_n$ lead to slightly different `SELECT` statements whenever $trans(\pi(\tau_1, \ldots, \tau_n), \lambda)$ is computed: each time the resulting statement contains a different α.

Let us consider, for example, the predicate *inspecting*(*i*158, *ja*, *uk*160). According to Section 3.6, $\|inspecting(i158, ja, uk160)\|^{M(st),st,et,lt,g} = T$ iff $et \sqsubseteq lt$ and $et \sqsubseteq p$, where:

$$p \in f_{pfuns}(st)(inspecting, 3)(\|i158\|^{M(st),g}, \|ja\|^{M(st),g}, \|uk160\|^{M(st),g})$$

Let us assume that $h'_{pfuns}(inspecting, 3)$ and $h_{pfuns}(st)(inspecting, 3)$ are as in (5.42) and (5.44), respectively, that h'_{cons} maps *i*158, *ja*, and *uk*160 to `'i158'`, `'J. Adams'`, and `'UK160'`, respectively, and that λ, the TSQL2 expression that corresponds to *lt* is `PERIOD '[9:00am 1/5/1995 - 9:30pm 1/5/1995]'`. By the definition of f_{pfuns} (Section 5.8):

$$f_{pfuns}(st)(inspecting, 3)(\|i158\|^{M(st),g}, \|ja\|^{M(st),g}, \|uk160\|^{M(st),g}) = \{p_1, p_2\}$$

where p_1 and p_2 are the periods of the first two tuples of (5.44). The denotation of *inspecting*(*i*158, *ja*, *uk*160) is *T* for all the *et*s that are both subperiods of p_1 or p_2 and also subperiods of *lt*.

The translation rule above maps *inspecting*(*i*158, *ja*, *uk*160) to (5.62), where h'_{pfuns}(*inspecting*, 3) is the query of (5.42), which returns (5.44).

(5.62)
```
( SELECT DISTINCT t1.1, t1.2, t1.3
  VALID VALID(t1)
  FROM (h'_pfuns(inspecting, 3)) (SUBPERIOD) AS t1
  WHERE t1.1 = 'i158'
    AND t1.2 = 'J. Adams'
    AND t1.3 = 'UK160'
    AND PERIOD '[9:00am 1/5/1995 - 9:30pm 1/5/1995]'
          CONTAINS VALID(t1))
```

(5.62) returns (5.63), where the time-stamps correspond to all the subperiods of p_1 and p_2 that are also subperiods of *lt*.

(5.63)

*i*158	*J. Adams*	*UK160*	[9:00*am* 1/5/1995, 9:30*pm* 1/5/1995]
*i*158	*J. Adams*	*UK160*	[9:10*am* 1/5/1995, 9:15*pm* 1/5/1995]
*i*158	*J. Adams*	*UK160*	[9:20*am* 1/5/1995, 9:25*pm* 1/5/1995]
...	...	...	...

In other words, the time-stamps of (5.63) represent correctly all the *ets* where the denotation of *inspecting*(*i*158, *ja*, *uk*160) is *T*. In this example, all the predicate arguments are constants. Hence, there can be no variation in the values of the arguments, and the values of the explicit attributes in (5.63) are the same in all the tuples. When some of the predicate arguments are variables, however, the values of the corresponding explicit attributes are not necessarily fixed.

The S_2 constraints in the WHERE clause of the translation rule are needed when the predicate contains the same variable in more than one argument position. In those cases, S_2 requires the attributes that correspond to the argument positions where the variable appears to have the same values. S_2 contains redundant constraints when some variable appears in more than two argument positions. For example, in $\pi(\beta, \beta, \beta)$, with $\beta \in VARS$, S_2 requires the tuples $\langle v_1, v_2, v_3; v_t \rangle$ of the resulting relation to satisfy $v_1 = v_2$, $v_1 = v_3$, and $v_2 = v_3$; the third constraint is redundant, because it follows from the others. The prototype NLITDB of Chapter 6 employs a slightly more complex definition of S_2 that does not generate redundant constraints of this type. Similar comments apply to the rule for $Culm[\pi(\tau_1, \ldots, \tau_n)]$ below, and the rules for conjunction, $At[\varphi_1, \varphi_2]$, $Before[\varphi_1, \varphi_2]$, and $After[\varphi_1, \varphi_2]$ in Appendix A.

Translation rule for $Culm[\pi(\tau_1, \ldots, \tau_n)]$. Formulae of this form are translated using the following rule.

$trans(Culm[\pi(\tau_1, \ldots, \tau_n)], \lambda) \stackrel{def}{=}$

```
( SELECT DISTINCT α1.1, α1.2, ... , α1.n
  VALID PERIOD(BEGIN(VALID(α1)), END(VALID(α1)))
  FROM (h'_pfuns(π, n))(ELEMENT) AS α1, (h'_culms(π, n)) AS α2
  WHERE α1.1 = α2.1
    AND α1.2 = α2.2
      ⋮
    AND α1.n = α2.n
    AND ...
      ⋮
    AND λ CONTAINS PERIOD(BEGIN(VALID(α1)), END(VALID(α1))))
```

Whenever the rule is used, α_1 and α_2 are two new different correlation names, which have never been used before, obtained by calling the correlation names generator. The dots after $\alpha_1.n = \alpha_2.n$ in the WHERE clause stand for all the strings in $S_1 \cup S_2$, where S_1 and S_2 are as in the translation rule for predicates, except that α is now α_1.

The rule for $Culm[\pi(\tau_1, \ldots, \tau_n)]$ is similar to that for $\pi(\tau_1, \ldots, \tau_n)$. The resulting SELECT statement returns an element of $VREL_P(n)$ that shows the *ets* and the values of the predicate arguments for which the denotation of $Culm[\pi(\tau_1, \ldots, \tau_n)]$ is T. In the case of $Culm[\pi(\tau_1, \ldots, \tau_n)]$, however, the generated relation contains only tuples $\langle v_1, \ldots, v_n; v_t \rangle$ for which $\langle v_1, \ldots, v_n \rangle$ appears in $h_{culms}(st)(\pi, n)$, the relation returned by $h'_{culms}(\pi, n)$. This captures the requirement that the situation of $\pi(\tau_1, \ldots, \tau_n)$ must reach its climax at the latest time-point where it is ongoing. Also, $h_{pfuns}(st)(\pi, n)$ is coalesced using (ELEMENT). This causes all the tuples of $h_{pfuns}(st)(\pi, n)$ that refer to the same situation to be merged into one tuple, time-stamped by a temporal element that is the union of all the periods where the situation is ongoing. Let us refer to this coalesced version of $h_{pfuns}(st)(\pi, n)$ as r. α_1 ranges over the tuples of r, while α_2 over the tuples of $h_{culms}(st)(\pi, n)$. The relation returned by $trans(Culm[\pi(\tau_1, \ldots, \tau_n)], \lambda)$ contains all the tuples $\langle v_1, \ldots, v_n; v_t \rangle$, such that for some $\langle v_1, \ldots, v_n; v'_t \rangle \in r$, v_t represents the period that starts at the beginning of the temporal element of v'_t and ends at the end of that temporal element, $\langle v_1, \ldots, v_n \rangle \in h_{culms}(st)(\pi, n)$, and v_t's period is a subperiod of λ's, i.e., $et \sqsubseteq lt$. S_1 and S_2 play the same role as in the translation rule for predicates.

As an example, let us consider the case where $h'_{pfuns}(inspecting, 3)$ and $h'_{culms}(inspecting, 3)$ are (5.42) and (5.43), respectively, with their results being (5.44) and (5.45), and that λ = `PERIOD '[1/5/1995 - 18/11/1995]'`. The translation rule above maps *Culm*[*inspecting*(*occr*^{v}, *person*^{v}, *flight*^{v})] to (5.64), which returns (5.65).

(5.64)
```
( SELECT DISTINCT t1.1, t1.2, t1.3
  VALID PERIOD(BEGIN(VALID(t1)), END(VALID(t1)))
  FROM (h'_pfuns(inspecting, 3))(ELEMENT) AS t1,
       (h'_culms(inspecting, 3)) AS t2
  WHERE t1.1 = t2.1
    AND t1.2 = t2.2
    AND t1.3 = t2.3
    AND PERIOD '[1/5/1995 - 18/11/1995]' CONTAINS
        PERIOD(BEGIN(VALID(t1)), END(VALID(t1))))
```

In (5.65), there is, correctly, no tuple for the incomplete inspection *i*160. There is also no tuple for *i*214, because that inspection is also incomplete and it is not located within λ's period. Finally, (5.65) does not contain tuples for the subperiods of [9:00am 1/5/1995, 10:25am 1/5/1995] and [8:00am 16/11/1995, 8:20am 16/11/1995]. This is in accordance with the semantics of *Culm* (Section 3.9), which allows *Culm*[*inspecting*(*occr*^{v}, *ja*, *ba*737)] to be true only at *ets* that cover entire inspections, from start to completion.

(5.65)

*i*158	*J. Adams*	*UK160*	[9:00*am* 1/5/1995, 10:25*am* 1/5/1995]
*i*205	*T. Smith*	*BA737*	[8:00*am* 16/11/1995, 8:20*am* 16/11/1995]

Translation rule for Past[β, φ]. All the other translation rules for yes/no formulae are recursive. For example, *Past*[β, φ′] is translated using the following rule.

$$trans(Past[\beta, \varphi'], \lambda) \stackrel{def}{=}$$

```
( SELECT DISTINCT VALID(α), α.1, α.2, ..., α.n
  VALID VALID(α)
  FROM trans(φ', λ') AS α)
```

The λ′ stands for `INTERSECT(λ, PERIOD(TIMESTAMP 'beginning', TIMESTAMP 'now' - INTERVAL '1' χ))`, χ is the TSQL2 name of the granularity of chronons (e.g., `DAY`), and *n* is the length of ⌜φ′⌝. Whenever the rule is used, α is a new correlation name, which has never been used before.

The rule for $Past[\beta, \varphi']$ calls recursively *trans* to translate φ'. φ' is translated with respect to λ', i.e., the intersection of the period of the original λ with the period that covers all the time up to, but not including, the present chronon. This reflects the semantics of the *Past* operator (Section 3.8), which narrows lt to $lt \cap [t_{first}, st)$. The relation returned by $trans(Past[\beta, \varphi'], \lambda)$ is the same as that of $trans(\varphi', \lambda')$, except that it contains an additional explicit attribute that corresponds to the β of $Past[\beta, \varphi']$. The values of that attribute are the same as the corresponding time-stamps, i.e., they represent *et*. This reflects the semantics of $Past[\beta, \varphi']$, that requires the value of β to be *et*.

Translation rule for $At[\kappa, \varphi']$. As a further example, $At[\kappa, \varphi']$, with $\kappa \in CONS$, is translated using the following rule, where λ' stands for the expression `INTERSECT(`λ, $h'_{cons}(\kappa)$`)`.

$$trans(At[\kappa, \varphi'], \lambda) \stackrel{def}{=} trans(\varphi', \lambda')$$

The translation of $At[\kappa, \varphi']$ is the same as the translation of φ', but φ' is translated with respect to λ', which represents the intersection of λ's period with that of κ. This reflects the semantics of $At[\kappa, \varphi']$ (Section 3.10). There are separate rules for $At[\sigma_c, \beta, \varphi']$, $At[\sigma_g, \beta, \varphi']$, and $At[\varphi_1, \varphi_2]$, where $\sigma_c \in CPARTS$, $\sigma_g \in GPARTS$, $\varphi', \varphi_1, \varphi_2 \in YNFORMS$ (see Appendix A).

Translation rule for $?\beta_1 \ldots ?\beta_k\ \varphi'$. Let us now consider the translation rules for wh-formulae, starting from formulae of the form $?\beta_1 \ldots ?\beta_k\ \varphi'$, where $\varphi' \in YNFORMS$. These are processed using the following rule.

$$trans(?\beta_1 \ldots ?\beta_k\ \varphi', \lambda_{init}) \stackrel{def}{=}$$
```
( SELECT DISTINCT SNAPSHOT α.ω1, ..., α.ωk
  FROM trans(φ',λinit) AS α)
```

Whenever the rule is used, α is a new correlation name, which has never been used before. Assuming that $\ulcorner\varphi'\urcorner = \langle\tau_1, \ldots, \tau_n\rangle$, for every $i \in \{1, 2, 3, \ldots, \kappa\}$:

$$\omega_i = min(\{j \mid j \in \{1, 2, 3, \ldots, n\} \text{ and } \tau_j = \beta_i\})$$

That is, ω_i is the index of the first position in $\langle\tau_1, \ldots, \tau_n\rangle$ from left to right where β_i appears. The rules for wh-formulae define $trans(\varphi, \lambda)$ only for $\lambda = \lambda_{init}$, as they are invoked only with this value of λ.

Intuitively, the translation of $?\beta_1 \ldots ?\beta_k\ \varphi'$ must return a snapshot relation whose tuples represent $\|?\beta_1 \ldots ?\beta_k\ \varphi'\|^{M(st),st}$. That is, the tuples must represent all the possible combinations of denotations assigned to $\beta_1, \ldots, \beta_k$ by any

$g \in G$, such that for some $et \in PERIODS$, $\|\varphi'\|^{M(st),st,et,PTS,g} = T$ (Section 3.6). By Theorem 5.2, the relation returned by $trans(\varphi', \lambda_{init})$ in the translation rule is a valid-time relation whose tuples show all the possible *ets* and denotations of $\tau_1, \ldots, \tau_n$ for which $\|\varphi'\|^{M(st),st,et,PTS,g} = T$. The syntax of TOP (Section 3.2) guarantees that $\beta_1, \ldots, \beta_k$ appear within φ'. This in turn guarantees that $\beta_1, \ldots, \beta_k$ appear among $\tau_1, \ldots, \tau_n$, i.e., the relation of $trans(\varphi', \lambda_{init})$ contains attributes for $\beta_1, \ldots, \beta_k$. Hence, to find all the possible combinations of denotations of $\beta_1, \ldots, \beta_k$ for which $\|\varphi'\|^{M(st),st,et,PTS,g} = T$ for some *et*, we simply need to pick, to 'project' in relational terms, from the relation of $trans(\varphi', \lambda_{init})$ the attributes that correspond to $\beta_1, \ldots, \beta_k$. If a β_i occurs more than once in φ', there will be several attributes for it, all with identical values. The translation rule picks the leftmost of those attributes.

Let us consider, for example, the wh-formula of (5.67), which is generated when (5.66) is submitted.

(5.66) Who inspected what?

(5.67) $?w1^v \; ?w2^v \; Past[e^v, Culm[inspecting(occr^v, w1^v, w2^v)]]$

In this case, $\varphi' = Past[e^v, Culm[inspecting(occr^v, w1^v, w2^v)]]$ and $\ulcorner\varphi'\urcorner = \langle e^v, occr^v, w1^v, w2^v\rangle$. Let us assume that $trans(\varphi', \lambda_{init})$ returns (5.68), i.e., that (5.68) shows all the possible combinations of *ets* and denotations that can be assigned by some $g \in G$ to e^v, $occr^v$, $w1^v$, and $w2^v$, such that $\|\varphi'\|^{M(st),st,et,PTS,g} = T$. In every tuple, the time-stamp is the same as the value of the first explicit attribute, because the semantics of the *Past* operator requires the value of e^v, which is represented by the first explicit attribute, to be set to *et*, which is represented by the time-stamp. To save space, the time-stamps of (5.68) are ommitted.

(5.68)

[9:00*am* 1/5/1995, 3:00*pm* 1/5/1995]	*i*158	*J. Adams*	*UK*160	...
[10:00*am* 4/5/1995, 11:30*am* 4/5/1995]	*i*165	*J. Adams*	*BA*737	...
[7:00*am* 16/11/1995, 7:30*am* 16/11/1995]	*i*204	*T. Smith*	*UK*160	...

To generate the snapshot relation that represents $\|?w1^v \; ?w2^v \; \varphi'\|^{M(st),st}$, we simply need to project the leftmost explicit attributes of (5.68) that correspond to $w1^v$ and $w2^v$. The leftmost positions where $w1^v$ and $w2^v$ appear in $\ulcorner\varphi'\urcorner$ are the third and fourth ones. The resulting TSQL2 query is shown in (5.69); it generates (5.70).

(5.69) (SELECT DISTINCT SNAPSHOT t1.3, t1.4
FROM $trans(Past[e^v, Culm[inspecting(occr^v, w1^v, w2^v)]], \lambda_{init})$ AS t1)

(5.70)

J. Adams	*UK*160
J. Adams	*BA*737
T. Smith	*UK*160

Translation rule for $?_{mxl}\beta_1\ ?\beta_2\ \ldots\ ?\beta_k\ \varphi'$. Wh-formulae of this form, where $\varphi' \in YNFORMS$, are translated using the following rule.

$trans(?_{mxl}\beta_1\ ?\beta_2\ \ldots\ ?\beta_k\ \varphi', \lambda_{init}) \stackrel{def}{=}$

```
( SELECT DISTINCT SNAPSHOT VALID(α2), α2.2, α2.3, ..., α2.k
  FROM ( SELECT DISTINCT 'dummy', α1.ω2, α1.ω3, ..., α1.ωk
         VALID α1.ω1
         FROM trans(φ', λinit) AS α1
       )(NOSUBPERIOD) AS α2)
```

Whenever the rule is used, α_1 and α_2 are two different new correlation names, that have never been used before. Assuming that $\ulcorner\varphi'\urcorner = \langle\tau_1, \ldots, \tau_n\rangle, \omega_1, \ldots, \omega_k$ are as in the rule for $?\beta_1\ \ldots\ ?\beta_k\ \varphi$.

Let us consider, for example, the wh-formula of (5.72), which is generated when (5.71) is submitted. In this case, $\varphi' = Past[e^v, circling(w^v)]$ and $\ulcorner\varphi'\urcorner = \langle e^v, w^v\rangle$.

(5.71) What circled when?

(5.72) $?_{mxl}e^v\ ?w^v\ Past[e^v, circling(w^v)]$

(5.73)

[5:02*pm* 22/11/1995, 5:17*pm* 22/11/1995]	*BA*737	...
[5:05*pm* 22/11/1995, 5:15*pm* 22/11/1995]	*BA*737	...
[5:07*pm* 22/11/1995, 5:13*pm* 22/11/1995]	*BA*737	...
...	...	...
[4:57*pm* 23/11/1995, 5:08*pm* 23/11/1995]	*BA*737	...
[4:59*pm* 23/11/1995, 5:06*pm* 23/11/1995]	*BA*737	...
[5:01*pm* 23/11/1995, 5:04*pm* 23/11/1995]	*BA*737	...
...	...	...
[8:07*am* 22/11/1995, 8:19*am* 22/11/1995]	*UK*160	...
[8:08*am* 22/11/1995, 8:12*am* 22/11/1995]	*UK*160	...
[8:09*am* 22/11/1995, 8:10*am* 22/11/1995]	*UK*160	...
...	...	...

Let us also assume that $trans(Past[e^v, circling(w^v)], \lambda_{init})$ returns (5.73), i.e., that (5.73) shows all the *ets* and values of e^v and w^v for which the denotation of

Past$[e^v, circling(w^v)]$ is *T*. As a result of the semantics of the *Past* operator, the values of the first explicit attribute, which correspond to e^v, are the same as the time-stamps, which correspond to *et*. To save space, the time-stamps are omitted. For example, BA737 was circling from 5:02 pm to 5:17 pm on 22/11/1995, and from 4:57 pm to 5:08 pm on 23/11/1995. (5.73) also contains tuples for the subperiods of these periods, because $circling(w^v)$, like all TOP predicates, is homogeneous (Section 3.6).

The embedded `SELECT` statement of $trans(?_{mxl}\beta_1\ ?\beta_2\ \ldots\ ?\beta_k\ \varphi', \lambda_{init})$ becomes (5.74). The `'dummy'` means that the first explicit attribute of the resulting relation should have that string as its value in all the tuples. This is needed for $k = 1$, where the `SELECT` clause of the embedded statement would otherwise specify no explicit attributes, which is not allowed in TSQL2.

(5.74)
```
( SELECT DISTINCT 'dummy', t1.2
  VALID t1.1
  FROM trans(Past[e^v, circling(w^v)], λ_init) AS t1)
```

The result of (5.74) is shown in (5.75). The time-stamps of (5.75) are the values of the first explicit attribute of (5.73), i.e., they correspond to e^v. The `(NOSUBPERIOD)` of the translation rule then removes from (5.75) any tuples that do not correspond to maximal periods, and (5.75) becomes (5.76).

(5.75)

dummy	*BA*737	[5:02*pm* 22/11/1995, 5:17*pm* 22/11/1995]
dummy	*BA*737	[5:05*pm* 22/11/1995, 5:15*pm* 22/11/1995]
dummy	*BA*737	[5:07*pm* 22/11/1995, 5:13*pm* 22/11/1995]
...	...	...
dummy	*BA*737	[4:57*pm* 23/11/1995, 5:08*pm* 23/11/1995]
dummy	*BA*737	[4:59*pm* 23/11/1995, 5:06*pm* 23/11/1995]
dummy	*BA*737	[5:01*pm* 23/11/1995, 5:04*pm* 23/11/1995]
...	...	...
dummy	*UK*160	[8:07*am* 22/11/1995, 8:19*am* 22/11/1995]
dummy	*UK*160	[8:08*am* 22/11/1995, 8:12*am* 22/11/1995]
dummy	*UK*160	[8:09*am* 22/11/1995, 8:10*am* 22/11/1995]
...	...	...

(5.76)

dummy	*BA*737	[5:02*pm* 22/11/1995, 5:17*pm* 22/11/1995]
dummy	*BA*737	[4:57*pm* 23/11/1995, 5:08*pm* 23/11/1995]
dummy	*UK*160	[8:07*am* 22/11/1995, 8:19*am* 22/11/1995]

The overall (5.72) is mapped to (5.77), which generates (5.78). (5.78) represents the denotation of (5.72) w.r.t. $M(st)$ and st, i.e., it shows the pairs of maximal past circling periods and the corresponding flights.

(5.77)
```
( SELECT DISTINCT SNAPSHOT VALID(t2), t2.2
  FROM ( SELECT DISTINCT 'dummy', t1.2
         VALID t1.1
         FROM trans(Past[e^v, circling(w^v)], λ_init) AS t1
       )(NOSUBPERIOD) AS t2)
```

(5.78)

[5:02*pm* 22/11/1995, 5:17*pm* 22/11/1995]	*BA*737
[4:57*pm* 23/11/1995, 5:08*pm* 23/11/1995]	*BA*737
[8:07*am* 22/11/1995, 8:19*am* 22/11/1995]	*UK*160

5.12 Optimising the generated TSQL2 code

The generated TSQL2 code is often verbose, in the sense that it can often be shortened and still return the same results. Figure 5.3, for example, shows the code that is generated for (5.80), if chronons correspond to minutes. (5.80) expresses the reading of (5.79) where the inspection must have both started and been completed on the previous day.

(5.79) Who inspected UK160 yesterday?

(5.80) $?w^v\ At[yesterday, Past[e^v, Culm[inspecting(occr^v, w^v, uk160)]]]$

It is assumed here that $h'_{pfuns}(inspecting, 3)$ and $h'_{culms}(inspecting, 3)$ are (5.42) and (5.43), respectively. The embedded `SELECT` statements of Figure 5.3 that are associated with `t1` and `t2` are (5.42) and (5.43). The embedded `SELECT` statement that is associated with `t3` is generated by the translation rule for $Culm[\pi(\tau_1, \ldots, \tau_n)]$. It returns a relation whose explicit attributes show all the combinations of codes, inspectors, and inspected objects that correspond to complete inspections. The time-stamps of this relation represent periods that cover whole inspections, from start to completion. The `CONTAINS` constraint in the `WHERE` clause admits only tuples whose time-stamps are subperiods of lt. The *At* has narrowed lt to its intersection with the previous day (`PERIOD 'today' - INTERVAL '1' DAY)`), and the *Past* has narrowed lt further to its intersection with $[t_{first}, st)$ (`PERIOD(TIMESTAMP 'beginning', TIMESTAMP 'now' - INTERVAL '1' MINUTE)`). The embedded `SELECT` statement that is associated with `t4` is generated by the translation rule

```
(SELECT DISTINCT SNAPSHOT t4.3
 FROM (SELECT DISTINCT VALID(t3), t3.1, t3.2, t3.3
       VALID VALID(t3)
       FROM (SELECT DISTINCT t1.1, t1.2, t1.3
             VALID PERIOD(BEGIN(VALID(t1)), END(VALID(t1)))
             FROM (SELECT DISTINCT insp.1, insp.2, insp.3
                   VALID VALID(insp)
                   FROM inspections(PERIOD) AS insp
                   )(ELEMENT) AS t1,
                  (SELECT DISTINCT SNAPSHOT
                   icmp.1, icmp.2, icmp.3
                   FROM inspections AS icmp
                   WHERE icmp.4 = 'complete') AS t2
             WHERE t1.1 = t2.1 AND t1.2 = t2.2
               AND t1.3 = t2.3 AND t1.3 = 'UK160'
               AND INTERSECT(INTERSECT(
                    PERIOD(TIMESTAMP 'beginning',
                           TIMESTAMP 'forever'),
                    PERIOD 'today' - INTERVAL '1' DAY),
                    PERIOD(TIMESTAMP 'beginning',
                           TIMESTAMP 'now' -
                           INTERVAL '1' MINUTE))
                   CONTAINS
                    PERIOD(BEGIN(VALID(t1)), END(VALID(t1)))
             ) AS t3
       ) AS t4)
```

Figure 5.3 Example of generated TSQL2 code

for *Past*[β, φ′] (Section 5.11). It returns the same relation as the statement that is associated with `t3`, except that the relation of `t4`'s statement has an additional explicit attribute that corresponds to the first argument of *Past*. In each tuple, the value of this extra attribute is the same as the time-stamp (*et*). The topmost `SELECT` clause projects only the third explicit attribute of the relation returned by `t4`'s statement (this attribute corresponds to w^v of (5.80)).

The code of Figure 5.3 could be shortened in several ways. For example, `t4`'s statement simply adds an extra attribute for the first argument of *Past*. In this particular case, this extra attribute is not used, because (5.80) contains no interrogative quantifier for that argument. Hence, `t4`'s statement could be replaced by `t3`'s; the topmost `SELECT` clause would also have to become SE-

```
(SELECT DISTINCT SNAPSHOT t1.2
 FROM (SELECT DISTINCT insp.1, insp.2, insp.3
      VALID VALID(insp)
      FROM inspections(PERIOD) AS insp
      )(ELEMENT) AS t1,
      (SELECT DISTINCT SNAPSHOT icmp.1, icmp.2, icmp.3
      FROM inspections AS icmp
      WHERE icmp.4 = 'complete') AS t2
 WHERE t1.1 = t2.1 AND t1.2 = t2.2
   AND t1.3 = t2.3 AND t1.3 = 'UK160'
   AND INTERSECT(
        PERIOD 'today' - INTERVAL '1' DAY,
        PERIOD(TIMESTAMP 'beginning',
              TIMESTAMP 'now' - INTERVAL '1' MINUTE))
      CONTAINS
        PERIOD(BEGIN(VALID(t1)), END(VALID(t1)))
```

Figure 5.4 Shortened TSQL2 code

LECT DISTINCT SNAPSHOT t3.2. One could also drop the top-level SELECT statement, and replace the SELECT clause of t3's statement with SELECT DISTINCT SNAPSHOT t1.2 removing the VALID clause. Furthermore, the intersection of the whole time-axis (PERIOD(TIMESTAMP 'beginning', TIMESTAMP 'forever')) with any period p is simply p. Hence, one of the two INTERSECTs in Figure 5.3 can be omitted. The resulting code is shown in Figure 5.4.

Although DBMSs typically employ optimisation techniques, that would be able to carry out at least some of the simplifications above, long queries can confuse generic DBMS optimisers, causing them to produce inefficient code. Hence, it would be interesting to examine if optimisations like the ones discussed above could be automated and integrated into the framework of this book as an additional layer between the TOP to TSQL2 translator and the DBMS. This issue, however, will not be explored in this book.

5.13 Related work

Various mappings from forms of logic to and from relational algebra or relational calculus (Ullman 1988; van Gelder & Topor 1991; Abiteboul, Herr, & den

Bussche 1999), from logic programming languages to SQL (Lucas 1988; Draxler 1991), and from meaning representations generated by NLIDBS to SQL (Lowden et al. 1991; Androutsopoulos 1992; Androutsopoulos, Ritchie, & Thanisch 1993; Rayner 1993) have been studied in the past. This section discusses briefly a mapping proposed by Böhlen et al. (1996), which has influenced the TOP to TSQL2 translation method of this chapter; see also Chomicki et al. (2001).

Böhlen et al. study the relation between a subset of TSQL2 and a form of temporal logic, hereafter called TL, that provides the temporal operators • (previous), ∘ (next), **since**, and **until**. TL is point-based, in the sense that its formulae are evaluated with respect to single time-points. TL also assumes that time is discrete. Roughly speaking, $\bullet\varphi$ is true at a time-point t iff φ is true at the time-point immediately before t. Similarly, $\circ\varphi$ is true at t iff φ is true at the time-point immediately after t. φ_1 **since** φ_2 is true at t iff there is some t' before t, such that φ_2 is true at t', and for every t'' between t' and t, φ_1 is true at t''. Similarly, φ_1 **until** φ_2 is true at t iff there is some t' after t, such that φ_2 is true at t', and for every t'' between t and t', φ_1 is true at t''.

Various other TL operators are also defined, but these are all definable in terms of •, ∘, **since**, and **until**. For example, ♦φ is equivalent to *true* **since** φ; *true* is a special formula that is true at all time-points. In effect, ♦φ is true at t if there is a t' before t, and φ is true at t'. For example, (5.81) and (5.83) can be expressed as (5.82) and (5.84), respectively.

(5.81) BA737 departed (at some past time).
(5.82) ♦*depart*(*ba737*)
(5.83) Tank 2 has been empty (all the time) since BA737 departed.
(5.84) *empty*(*tank2*) **since** *depart*(*ba737*)

Böhlen et al. provide rules that translate from TL to TSQL2. (They also show how to translate from a subset of TSQL2 back to TL, but this direction is irrelevant here.) The underlying ideas are very similar to those of this chapter. Roughly speaking, there are non-recursive rules for atomic formulae, and recursive rules for non-atomic formulae. For example, the translation rule for φ_1 **since** φ_2 calls recursively the translation algorithm to translate φ_1 and φ_2. The result is a SELECT statement, that contains two embedded SELECT statements corresponding to φ_1 and φ_2. Devising rules to map from TL to TSQL2 is much easier than in the case of TOP, because TL formulae are evaluated with respect to only one time-parameter, as opposed to TOP's *st*, *et*, and *lt* parameters; furthermore, TL is point-based, whereas TOP is period-based (Section 3.1), and it provides only four temporal operators whose semantics are very simple.

It should be noted, however, that TOP and TL were designed for very different purposes. TL is interesting from a theoretical temporal-logic point of view (van Benthem 1991; Abiteboul, Herr, & den Bussche 1999). The mapping from TL to TSQL2 and the reverse mapping from a fragment of TSQL2 to TL are parts of a study of the relative expressiveness of the two languages. The existence of a mapping from TL to TSQL2 shows that TSQL2 is at least as expressive as TL. The reverse is not true; i.e., full TSQL2 is more expressive than TL, as shown by Böhlen et al.

In contrast, TOP was not designed to study expressiveness issues, but to facilitate the mapping from English questions with temporal expressions to meaning representations. Chapter 4 showed how to translate systematically from a fragment of English questions to TOP. No such systematic translation has been shown to exist in the case of TL, and it is not at all obvious how temporal English questions, e.g., containing progressive and perfect tenses, temporal adverbials, or temporal subordinate clauses, could be mapped systematically to appropriate TL formulae.

Although the study of expressiveness issues is beyond the scope of this book, it can be noted that the TOP to TSQL2 translation of this chapter implies that TSQL2 is at least as expressive as TOP, because every TOP formula can be mapped to an appropriate TSQL2 query. The reverse is not true: it is easy to think of TSQL2 queries, e.g., queries that report the cardinalities of sets, that cannot be expressed in TOP. Finally, neither TOP nor TL can be said to be more expressive than the other, as there are English sentences that can be expressed in TL but not TOP, and vice-versa. For example, the TL formula (5.84) expresses (5.83), a sentence that cannot be expressed in the current version of TOP. On the other hand, the TOP formula (5.86) expresses (5.85), but there does not seem to be any way to express (5.85) in TL.

(5.85) Tank 2 was empty for two hours.

(5.86) $For[hour^c, 2, Past[e^v, empty(tank2)]]$

5.14 Summary

This chapter has shown how TOP formulae can be translated into TSQL2, a temporal extension of SQL-92. When configuring the NLITDB for a new application domain, certain mappings from basic TOP expressions, like constants and predicate functors, to the corresponding TSQL2 expressions need to be provided (the h' functions). Once this information has been provided, any TOP formula can be transformed automatically into an appropriate TSQL2 query. The transformation is carried out by a set of translation rules, which comprises base rules for TOP predicates and other simple formulae, and rules that process more complex formulae by invoking recursively other rules to translate subformulae. A representative sample of translation rules was examined in detail; the full set of rules can be found in Appendix A.

The translation process is provably correct, in the sense that the resulting TSQL2 code generates relations that represent the denotations of the original TOP formulae. Formal machinery was introduced to capture the exact properties that the translation rules must satisfy for the translation process to be correct, along with an overview of the proof of their correctness. The full proof can be found in the thesis this book is based on.

Some modifications to TSQL2 had to be made to facilitate the mapping from TOP to TSQL2. Most of them are rather minor, and where introduced to avoid uninteresting details or obscure points in the definition of TSQL2. The most significant modifications were: (a) calendric relations, which is a necessary addition regardless of natural language issues, (b) allowing non-coalesced valid-time relations, and (c) the `(SUBPERIOD)` partitioning unit. It remains to be examined if the latter can be supported efficiently at the physical level, or if its functionality can be obtained in terms of other database language constructs. Further work is also needed to optimise the generated TSQL2 code.

The TOP to TSQL2 translation process of this chapter has been influenced by the mapping from temporal logic to TSQL2 of Böhlen et al. (1996). TOP and the logic of Böhlen et al., however, were designed for very different purposes. The mapping of Böhlen et al. is also much simpler than the TOP to TSQL2 one.

Notes

1. TSQL2 distinguishes between *valid-time chronons*, *transaction-time chronons*, and *bitemporal chronons*. Since transaction time is ignored in this book (Section 1.5), transaction-time and bitemporal chronons are not used here, and 'chronon' refers to valid-time chronons.

2. The TSQL2 book (Snodgrass 1995) seems to adopt a different approach, where D_P and D_T are separate domains. There is no significant difference between the two approaches.

3. The TSQL2 book (Snodgrass 1995, Table 8.3) implies that v_ε is the special 'null' value, which has several roles in SQL. Here, it is assumed that a special value v_ε exists, whose only purpose is to denote the empty set.

4. The TSQL2 book (Snodgrass 1995, Section 30.5) allows BEGIN and END to be used only with periods. There seems to be no reason for this limitation, and in this book BEGIN and END are allowed to be used with any temporal element.

5. It is unclear in the TSQL2 book if the arguments of INTERSECT can only be periods or if temporal elements are allowed as well (Snodgrass 1995, Sections 8.3.3 and 30.14). This book adopts the latter choice. Similar comments apply to the CONTAINS and PRECEDES keywords (Snodgrass 1995, Sections 8.3.6 and 32.4).

6. The TSQL2 book (Snodgrass 1995, Section 8.3.6) specifies the functionality of PRECEDES only when its arguments are chronons or periods. The extension to temporal elements follows naturally.

7. Section 30.3 of the TSQL2 book (Snodgrass 1995) allows partitioning units to follow only relation names, not embedded SELECT statements, in the FROM clause. However, other TSQL2 documentation (Snodgrass et al. 1994d, queries Q.1.2.2, Q.1.2.5, Q.1.7.6), shows partitioning units following embedded SELECT statements in FROM clauses, and there seems to be no reason to disallow this.

8. In that respect, SUBPERIOD is similar to Lorentzos' FOLD and UNFOLD operators (Lorentzos & Johnson 1988).

9. In SELECT statements that contain other embedded SELECT statements, multiple definitions of the same correlation name may be present, and there are rules that determine the scope of each definition. We do not need to worry about such cases, however, because the generated TSQL2 code of this book never contains multiple definitions of the same correlation name.

10. This is not entirely true in the framework of this book, as there is also a type hierarchy of world entities in the HPSG grammar (Section 4.2).

CHAPTER 6

The prototype NLITDB

"Time works wonders."

6.1 Introduction

To demonstrate that the theoretical framework of this book is workable, it was used to implement a prototype NLITDB, the source code of which accompanies this book.* This chapter describes the architecture of the prototype NLITDB, provides some information on how the modules of the system were implemented, and explains which extensions would have to be made if the prototype were to be used in real-life applications. A more detailed description of the hypothetical airport database (Chapter 2) is also given, followed by sample questions from the airport domain and the corresponding output of the prototype NLITDB.

6.2 Architecture of the prototype NLITDB

Figure 6.1 shows the architecture of the prototype NLITDB. For simplicity, the prototype does not include a preprocessor (cf. Figure 1.2 on page 6). As we will see in later sections, this has the consequence that English questions have to be typed in a slightly awkward format, as lists of Prolog atoms, imitating the output of a preprocessor.

Each English question is first parsed using the HPSG grammar of Chapter 4, generating an HPSG sign. Multiple signs are generated for questions that the parser understands to be ambiguous. A TOP formula is then extracted from each sign, as discussed in Section 4.6, and each extracted formula undergoes the post-processing of Section 4.17; this may generate multiple formulae from the same original formula. As discussed in Chapter 1, this book does not address dialogue management or anaphora resolution issues; hence, the role of

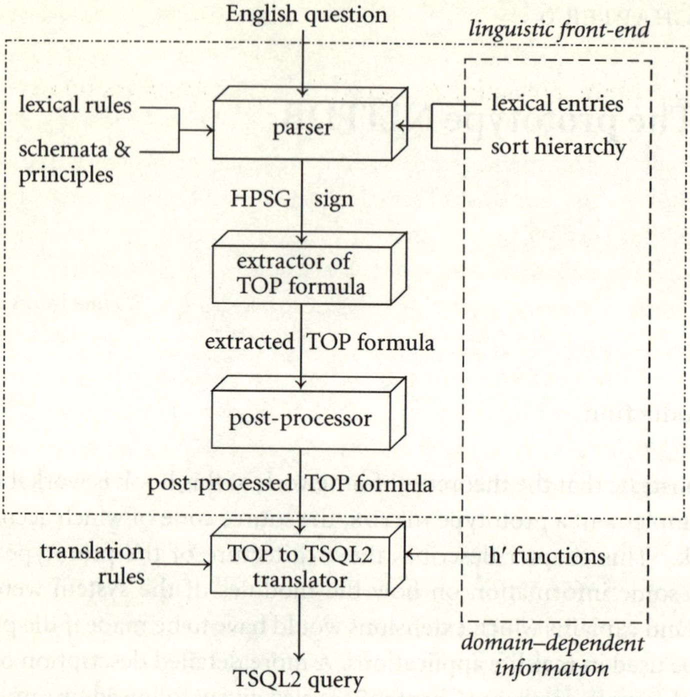

Figure 6.1 Architecture of the prototype NLITDB

the post-processor is much simpler than in a fully-fledged NLIDB, which is why it has no access to a discourse history or the ontology (cf. Figure 1.2).

Each of the formulae that are generated at the end of the post-processing captures what the NLITDB understands to be a possible reading of the English question. Many fully-fledged NLIDBS use preference measures to guess the most likely reading, or generate unambiguous English paraphrases of the various readings asking the user to select one (Section 1.2). No such mechanism is present in the prototype NLITDB. All the formulae that are generated at the end of the post-processing are translated into TSQL2, and the NLITDB prints all the resulting TSQL2 queries along with the corresponding TOP formulae. In a real-life system, the TSQL2 queries would be executed by the DBMS to retrieve the information requested by the user. As discussed in Section 1.5, however, the prototype NLITDB is not linked to a DBMS, which means that the TSQL2 queries are currently not executed.

6.3 Implementation

The HPSG version of Chapter 4 was coded in the formalism of ALE (Carpenter 1992; Carpenter & Penn 2001).[1] ALE can be thought of as a grammar-development environment. It provides a chart parser, which is the one used in the prototype NLITDB, and a formalism that can be used to write unification grammars that employ feature structures. Coding the HPSG version of Chapter 4 in ALE's formalism proved straightforward. ALE's formalism allows one to specify grammar rules, lexical entries, lexical rules, a hierarchy of sorts of feature structures, and definite constraints; the latter are similar to Prolog rules, except that the predicate arguments are feature structures. The schemata and principles of the HPSG version of Chapter 4 were coded using ALE grammar rules and definite constraints. HPSG's lexical signs, lexical rules, and sort hierarchy were coded using ALE's lexical entries, lexical rules, and sort hierarchy, respectively.

The ALE grammar rules and definite constraints that encode the HPSG schemata and principles are domain-independent (Figure 6.1); i.e., they require no modifications when the NLITDB is configured for a new application. The lexical rules of the prototype NLITDB are also intended to be domain-independent, though their morphology parts need to be extended to cover arbitrary verbs and nouns. The lexical entries of the system that correspond to function words (e.g., determiners, prepositions) or names of months, days, etc. are domain-independent, but the configurer of the NLITDB needs to provide lexical entries for the open-class words, namely nouns, adjectives, and non-auxiliary verbs, of the application domain (e.g., *flight*, *open*, *to land*). The largest part of the NLITDB's sort hierarchy is also domain-independent; however, two parts of it need to be modified when the system is configured for a new domain: the hierarchy of entity types that is mounted under *ind* (Figure 4.4 on page 116), and the subsorts of *predicate* that correspond to the TOP predicates of the domain (Figure 4.1 on page 113).

The module that extracts TOP formulae from HPSG signs was implemented using Prolog rules and ALE definite constraints. It operates as discussed in Section 4.6, and generates TOP formulae written as Prolog terms; for example, (6.1) is written as (6.2). The Prolog notation of (6.2) is also used in the formulae that are passed to the TOP to TSQL2 translator, and in the output of the NLITDB.

(6.1) $?x1^v \; Ntense[x3^v, president(x1^v)] \wedge Past[x2^v, located\_at(x1^v, gate2)]$

(6.2)
```
interrog(x1^v, and( ntense(x3^v, president(x1^v)),
                    past(x2^v, located_at(x1^v, gate2))))
```

The post-processor's code is a rather straightforward implementation in Prolog of the manipulations discussed in Section 4.17, including the TOP conversions of Section 5.5. The module that translates from TOP to TSQL2 is an equally straightforward implementation in Prolog of the translation rules of Chapter 5.

6.4 Extensions for real-life applications

The prototype NLITDB is only intended to demonstrate that the mappings from English to TOP and from TOP to TSQL2 of Chapters 4 and 5, respectively, are implementable. Consequently, it is a rather minimal system, that would have to be extended in several ways if it were to be used in real-life applications.

We have already discussed the need for a *preprocessor* (Section 1.2), that would decompose the English questions into tokens, and would identify and normalise expressions such as dates, times, and proper names. Since no preprocessor is currently present, questions have to be typed as Prolog lists of atoms, as in (6.3), with multi-token expressions (e.g., *J. Adams*, *5:00 pm*) merged into single atoms (e.g., `j_adams`, `pm5_00`).

(6.3) `[was,ba737,circling,at,pm5_00]`

For demonstration purposes, the lexicon of the prototype NLITDB contains some entries for proper names, such as names of flights and persons, as well as sample entries for times and dates (e.g., *5:00 pm*, *1/1/1991*). In real-life applications, however, proper names and expressions like times and dates cannot usually be included in the lexicon, because they are too many or they are not known in advance. Instead, they would be identified during the preprocessing, and the corresponding lexicon entries would be generated on the fly based on appropriate templates.

The post-processor would also have to be enhanced for real-life applications, in order to be able to handle *anaphoric expressions* (Sections 1.2 and 2.12) and *quantifier scoping*. The latter refers to cases where the meaning representation contains both universal and existential quantifiers, with the relative scope of the quantifiers being unclear. For example, ignoring temporal issues, (6.4) can be represented in first-order predicate logic as (6.5) or (6.6). According to (6.5), where the existential quantifier has wider scope, all the gates were inspected by the same guard; in contrast, in (6.6) each gate may have been inspected by a different guard.

(6.4) A guard inspected every gate.
(6.5) $\exists x\ (guard(x) \wedge \forall y\ (gate(y) \rightarrow inspect(x, y)))$
(6.6) $\forall y\ (gate(y) \rightarrow \exists x\ (guard(x) \wedge inspect(x, y)))$

Although in (6.4) both scopings seem plausible, often one of the possible scopings is more natural, and heuristics can be used to identify it; see Chapter 8 of Alshawi et al. (1992). In this book, words that introduce universal quantifiers were deliberately excluded from the linguistic coverage (Section 2.13). This leaves only existential quantification, and sidesteps quantifier scoping, because when all the quantifiers are existential ones, their relative scope does not matter. (In TOP, existential quantification is expressed using free variables. There are also interrogative and interrogative-maximal quantifiers, but these are in effect existential ones, with the additional side-effect of including the values of their variables in the answer.)

An additional inferencing layer may also be necessary between the post-processor and the TOP to TSQL2 translator. This is needed when some TOP predicates cannot be mapped directly to relations computed from the information in the database. The *doctor on board* problem (Rayner 1993) is a well-known example of such a case. Let us consider (6.7), which would be mapped to the TOP formula (6.8). It is assumed here that *doctor* and *ship* introduce predicates of the form $doctor(\tau_1)$ and $ship(\tau_2)$, respectively, and that the predicative preposition *on* introduces a predicate of the form $located\_on(\tau_3, \tau_4)$, with $\tau_1, \ldots, \tau_4 \in TERMS$. For simplicity, it is assumed that *doctor* and *ship* do not introduce *Ntense* operators (Section 4.9.1).

(6.7) Is there a doctor on some ship?
(6.8) $doctor(d^v) \wedge ship(s^v) \wedge Pres[located\_on(d^v, s^v)]$

To apply the TOP to TSQL2 translation method of Chapter 5, $doctor(\tau_1)$ has to be mapped to a valid-time relation, computed from information in the database, that shows when τ_1 was a doctor. Similarly, $ship(\tau_2)$ has to be mapped to a relation showing the ships that existed at each time, and $located\_on(\tau_3, \tau_4)$ to a relation showing when the entity denoted by τ_3 was on the entity denoted by τ_4. The database, however, may contain only the relation *doctor_on_board* below, which does not show the times when particular people were doctors, when ships existed, or when particular doctors where on the various ships. The relation simply shows the times when some (any) doctor was on each ship. Consequently, $doctor(\tau_1)$, $ship(\tau_2)$, and $located\_on(\tau_3, \tau_4)$ cannot be mapped to appropriate relations, and the translation method of Chapter 5 cannot be used.

If, however, $doctor\_on\_ship(\tau_5)$ is true at event times where the entity denoted by τ_5 is a ship and a doctor of that time is on that ship, (6.8) is equivalent to (6.9).

(6.9) $Pres[doctor\_on\_ship(s^v)]$

Unlike (6.8), in (6.9) there is enough information in the database to map $doctor\_on\_ship(\tau_5)$ to an appropriate relation: the predicate can be mapped to the *doctor_on_board* relation. Hence, the TOP to TSQL2 translation method of Chapter 5 can be applied to (6.9), and the answer to (6.7) can be found by evaluating the resulting TSQL2 code.

doctor_on_board	
ship	
Vincent	[8:30*am* 22/1/1996 – 11:45*am* 22/1/1996] ∪ [3:10*pm* 23/1/1996 – 5:50*pm* 23/1/1996] ∪ [9:20*am* 24/1/1996 – 2:10*pm* 24/1/1996]
Invincible	[8:20*am* 22/1/1996 – 10:15*am* 22/1/1996] ∪ [1:25*pm* 23/1/1996 – 3:50*pm* 23/1/1996]
...	...

The problem is that (6.7) cannot be mapped directly to (6.9), because the English to TOP mapping of Chapter 4 generates (6.8). We need to convert (6.8), whose predicates are introduced by the lexical entries of nouns, prepositions, etc., to (6.9), whose predicates are chosen to correspond to relations computed from the database. An inference module could be used to carry out this conversion (Alshawi et al. 1992; Rayner 1993). Roughly speaking, this would be an inference module between the post-processor and the TOP to TSQL2 translator, that would use domain-dependent conversion rules. (6.10) is a simplistic example of such a rule; it allows any formula of the form $doctor(\tau_1) \wedge ship(\tau_2) \wedge Pres[located\_on(\tau_1, \tau_2)]$ to be replaced by $Pres[doctor\_on\_ship(\tau_2)]$.

(6.10) $doctor(\tau_1) \wedge ship(\tau_2) \wedge Pres[located\_on(\tau_1, \tau_2)] \equiv Pres[doctor\_on\_ship(\tau_2)]$

The rule of (6.10) would license the conversion of (6.8) into (6.9). In practice, the rules would have to be written in a more complex pattern-matching formalism, to allow them to apply to broader sets of formulae.

To these extensions, one has to add the need to tailor the linguistic coverage to the characteristics of the target range of applications, possibly in conjunction with robust parsing and error recovery techniques (Sections 1.2 and 2.1), and the need for a response generator (Section 1.2); throughout the book, we have identified several cases where a generator of cooperative responses would be particularly useful. Configuration tools could also be added, to help people that are not familiar with the internals of the NLITDB port the system to new applications; see Androutsopoulos and Ritchie (2000), and Chapter 11 of Alshawi et al. (1992) for related discussion.

6.5 The airport database

Let us now consider in more detail the hypothetical airport database (Section 2.4.5) for which the prototype NLITDB is currently configured.

The database contains nineteen relations, all valid-time and coalesced (Section 5.2.3). Figure 6.2 shows the names and explicit attributes of the relations. For simplicity, it is assumed that the values of all the explicit attributes are strings. It is also assumed that chronons correspond to minutes, and that the *gregorian* calendric relation of Section 5.3.3 is available. Let us first consider the *runways* relation, which has the following form.

gates(gate, availability)
runways(runway, availability)
queues(queue, runway)
servicers(servicer)
inspectors(inspector)
sectors(sector)
flights(flight)
tanks(tank, content)
norm_departures(flight, norm_dep_time, norm_dep_gate)
norm_arrivals(flight, norm_arr_time, norm_arr_gate)
norm_servicer(flight, servicer)
flight_locations(flight, location)
circling(flight)
inspections(code, inspector, inspected, status)
services(code, servicer, flight, status)
boardings(code, flight, gate, status)
landings(code, flight, runway, status)
takeoffs(code, flight, runway, status)
taxiings(code, flight, origin, destination, status)

Figure 6.2 Relations of the airport database

runways		
runway	*availability*	
runway1	*open*	[8:00*am* 1/1/1996, 7:30*pm* 3/1/1996] ∪ [6:00*am* 4/1/1996, 2:05*pm* 8/1/1996] ∪ ...
runway1	*closed*	[7:31*pm* 3/1/1996, 5:59*am* 4/1/1996] ∪ [2:06*pm* 8/1/1996, 5:45*pm* 8/1/1996] ∪ ...
runway2	*open*	[5:00*am* 1/1/1996, 9:30*pm* 9/1/1996] ∪ ...
runway2	*closed*	[9:31*pm* 9/1/1996, 10:59*am* 10/1/1996] ∪ ...

The *availability* values are always *open* or *closed*. There are two tuples for each runway: one showing the times when the runway was open, and one showing the times when it was closed. If a runway did not exist at some time, both tuples of that runway exclude that time from their time-stamps. The *gates* relation is similar. Its *availability* values are always *open* or *closed*, and there are two tuples for each gate, showing the times when the gate was open or closed, respectively.

Runways used for landings or take-offs have queues, where flights wait until they are given permission to enter the runway. The *queues* relation lists the names of the queues that exist at various times, along with the runways the queues lead to. The *servicers* relation shows the names of the servicing companies that existed over time. The *inspectors, sectors*, and *flights* relations are similar. The *tanks* relation shows the contents of each tank over time; for example, *water*, *foam*, or *empty* if the tank was empty.

Each outgoing flight is assigned a normal departure time and gate (Section 2.4.5); these are recorded in *norm_departures* as shown below. From 9:00 am on 1/1/1992 to 5:30 pm on 9/9/1995 BA737 normally departed each day from gate 2 at 2:05 pm. (For simplicity, it is assumed here that all flights are daily.) At 5:31 pm on 9/9/1995, the normal departure time of BA737 was changed to 2:20 pm, while the normal departure gate remained gate 2. No further change to the normal departure time or gate of BA737 was made since then.

norm_departures			
flight	*norm_dep _time*	*norm_dep _gate*	
BA737	2:05*pm*	*gate2*	[9:00*am* 1/1/1992, 5:30*pm* 9/9/1995]
BA737	2:20*pm*	*gate2*	[5:31*pm* 9/9/1995, *now*]

Similarly, each incoming flight is assigned a normal arrival time and gate, recorded in *norm_arrivals*. Flights are also assigned normal servicers, i.e., companies that normally service the flights whenever they arrive or depart; this information is stored in *norm_servicer*. The *flight_locations* relation shows the location of each flight over time. Possible *location* values are the names of airspace sectors, gates, runways, or queues of runways. The *circling* relation shows the flights that were circling at each time.

As discussed in Section 2.4.5, flights, gates, and runways are occasionally inspected. The *inspections* relation was discussed in Section 5.9. It shows the inspection code, inspector, inspected object, status (completed or not), and time of each inspection. The *services*, *boardings*, *landings*, *takeoffs*, and *taxiings* relations are very similar; they provide information about actual services, boardings, landings, take-offs, and taxiings from one location (*origin*) to another (*destination*). Each service, boarding, landing, take-off, or taxiing is assigned a unique code, stored in the *code* attribute. The *status* attribute shows if the climax is reached at the latest time-point of the time-stamp. The values of the *origin* and *destination* attributes of *taxiings* are names of gates, runways, and queues.

Apart from relations, a temporal database would in practice also contain time-sensitive *integrity constraints* (Gertz & Lipeck 1995; Wijsen 1995; Snodgrass 2000). There would be, for example, a constraint saying that if the *circling* relation shows a flight as circling at some time, the *flights* relation must show that flight as existing at the same time. The integrity constraints of the airport database will not be discussed, as they are not directly relevant to the topic of this book.

6.6 Sample questions and output

Let us now examine sample questions from the airport domain, along with the corresponding output of the prototype NLITDB. The questions are chosen to demonstrate that the NLITDB is a faithful implementation of the theory presented in the previous chapters. The questions are not intended to be, and are probably not, representative of the questions that real users might use in the airport domain; see related comments on Wizard of Oz experiments in Sections 1.2 and 2.1.

The user submits questions using the `nli` Prolog predicate, as illustrated below. The system first reports the generated HPSG sign.

```
?- nli([which,flight,left,sector3,at,pm5_00,yesterday]).

HPSG Sign:
(phrase,
 qstore:(ne_set_quant,
```

```
          elt:(det:exists,
               restind:(index:(_10148,
                               minute_ent,
                               tvar:plus),
                        restr:(ne_set_psoa,
                               elt:(part,
                                    part_var:_10148,
                                    partng:pm5_00),
                               elts:e_set))),
          elts:(ne_set_quant,
                elt:(det:interrog,
                     restind:(index:(_10486,
                                     flight_ent,
                                     tvar:plus),
                              restr:(ne_set_psoa,
                                     elt:(flight,
                                          arg1:_10486),
                                     elts:e_set))),
                elts:e_set)),
  synsem:(synsem,
          loc:(cat:(aspect:point,
                    comps:e_list,
                    head:(aux:minus,
                          inv:minus,
                          mod:none,
                          prd:minus,
                          vform:fin),
                    spr:e_list,
                    subj:e_list),
               cont:(at_op,
                     main_psoa:(at_op,
                                main_psoa:(past,
                                           et_handle:(temp_ent,
                                                      tvar:plus),
                                           main_psoa:(leave_something,
                                                      arg1:_10486,
                                                      arg2:sector3)),
                                time_spec:_10148),
                     time_spec:yesterday)),
          nonloc:(inherited:slash:e_set,
                  to_bind:slash:e_set)))
```

The sign above is written in ALE's notation. The sign is of sort *phrase*, i.e., it corresponds to a phrase rather than a single word, and it has the features QSTORE and SYNSEM. The *ne_set_quant* value of QSTORE stands for a non-empty set of quantifiers. Its ELT feature describes the first element of that set, which is an existential quantifier. The quantifier ranges over a TOP variable, represented by an HPSG index of sort *minute_ent* (Figure 4.4 on page 116) whose TVAR is + (Section 4.3). The ELT value represents the TOP-like expression $\exists x2^v$ $Part[pm5\_00^g, x2^v]$. The Prolog variable `_10148` corresponds to the index of the quantifier; i.e., it plays the same role as the boxed numbers (e.g., 1, 2) in the HPSG formalism of Chapter 4. The ELTS value describes the rest of the set of quantifiers, using in turn an ELT feature, which corresponds to the second element of the overall set, and an ELTS feature, which describes the remainder of the set, in this case the empty set. The second element of the overall set represents the TOP expression $?x1^v$ $flight(x1^v)$. In the airport application, the lexical entries of non-predicative nouns do not introduce *Ntense* operators (Section 4.9.1); this generates appropriate readings in most cases. This is why no *Ntense* operator is present in the second quantifier of the sign. The effect of *Ntense* operators can be seen in the case of non-predicative adjectives, that do introduce *Ntenses*, as will be shown in later examples. The features of SYNSEM are as in Chapter 4. The CONT value above stands for $At[yesterday, At[x2^v, Past[x3^v, leave\_something(x1^v, sector3)]]]$.

The overall formula is then extracted from the HPSG sign, and is printed as a Prolog term:

```
TOP formula extracted from HPSG sign:
interrog(x1^v,
          and(part(pm5_00^g, x2^v),
              and(flight(x1^v),
                  at(yesterday,
                     at(x2^v,
                        past(x3^v,
                             leave_something(x1^v, sector3)))))))
```

The Prolog term above stands for:

$$?x1^v\ Part[pm5\_00^g, x2^v] \land flight(x1^v) \land \\ At[yesterday, At[x2^v, Past[x3^v, leave\_something(x1^v, sector3)]]]$$

The extracted formula then goes through the post-processor (Sections 4.17, 5.5), which eliminates the *Part* operator, adding the $pm5\_00^g$ as an extra argument to the corresponding *At* operator:

```
TOP formula after post-processing:
interrog(x1^v,
          and(flight(x1^v),
              at(yesterday,
                 at(pm5_00^g, x2^v,
                    past(x3^v,
                         leave_something(x1^v, sector3))))))
```

The Prolog term above stands for:

(6.11) $$?x1^v\ flight(x1^v) \land At[yesterday, \\ At[pm5\_00^g, x2^v, Past[x3^v, leave\_something(x1^v, sector3)]]]$$

The post-processed formula is then translated to TSQL2:

```
TSQL2 query:

(SELECT DISTINCT SNAPSHOT t8.1
 FROM (SELECT DISTINCT t6.1, t7.1, t7.2, t7.3, t7.4
    VALID VALID(t6)
    FROM (SELECT DISTINCT t1.1
          VALID VALID(t1)
          FROM (SELECT DISTINCT fl.1
                VALID VALID(fl)
                FROM flights(PERIOD) AS fl
               )(SUBPERIOD) AS t1
          WHERE PERIOD(TIMESTAMP 'beginning', TIMESTAMP 'forever')
                CONTAINS VALID(t1)
         ) AS t6,
         (SELECT DISTINCT t2.1, t5.1, t5.2, t5.3
          VALID VALID(t5)
          FROM (SELECT DISTINCT SNAPSHOT VALID(cp2)
                FROM gregorian AS cp2
                WHERE cp2.5 = '17' AND cp2.6 = '00'
               ) AS t2,
               (SELECT DISTINCT VALID(t4), t4.1, t4.2
                VALID VALID(t4)
                FROM (SELECT DISTINCT t3.1, t3.2
                      VALID VALID(t3)
                      FROM (SELECT DISTINCT flocs.1, flocs.2
                            VALID PERIOD(END(VALID(flocs)),
                                         END(VALID(flocs)))
                            FROM flight_locations(PERIOD) AS flocs
                           )(SUBPERIOD) AS t3
                      WHERE t3.2 = 'sector3'
                        AND INTERSECT(
                              INTERSECT(t2.1,
                                INTERSECT(
                                   PERIOD(TIMESTAMP 'beginning',
                                          TIMESTAMP 'forever'),
                                   PERIOD 'today' - INTERVAL '1' DAY)),
                              PERIOD(TIMESTAMP 'beginning',
                                     TIMESTAMP 'now' -
                                       INTERVAL '1' MINUTE))
                            CONTAINS VALID(t3)
                     ) AS t4
               ) AS t5
         ) AS t7
    WHERE t6.1 = t7.3
      AND VALID(t6) = VALID(t7)
   ) AS t8
)
```

The expression SELECT DISTINCT fl.1... FROM flights(PERIOD) AS fl that starts in the sixth line of the TSQL2 code is the SELECT statement to which h'_{pfuns} maps predicates of the form *flight*(τ_1). It returns a relation that shows the flights that existed at each time. The SELECT statement that is associated with the correlation name `t6` is the result of applying the translation rule for predicates (Section 5.11) to the *flight*($x1^v$) of (6.11). The `WHERE PERIOD(TIMESTAMP 'beginning', TIMESTAMP 'forever') CONTAINS VALID(t1)` corresponds to the restriction that *et* must fall within *lt*. (At this point, no constraint has been imposed on *lt*, and hence it covers the whole time-axis.) This `WHERE` clause has no effect, and could be removed during an optimisation phase (Section 5.12).

The expression `SELECT DISTINCT flocs.1 ... flight_locations(PERIOD) AS flocs` that starts in the 23rd line of the TSQL2 code is the `SELECT` statement to which h'_{pfuns} maps predicates of the form *leave_something*(τ_1, τ_2). This statement generates a relation that shows, for each flight and location, the end-points of the maximal periods where the flight was at that location. The broader `SELECT` statement that is associated with `t4` is the result of applying the translation rule for predicates to the *leave_something*($x1^v$, *sector3*) of (6.11). `VALID(t3)` is the leaving-time, which has to fall within *lt*. The three nested `INTERSECT`s represent constraints that have been imposed on the localisation time: the *Past* operator requires *lt* to be a subperiod of $[p_{first}, st)$ (i.e., a subperiod of `TIMESTAMP 'beginning', TIMESTAMP 'now' - INTERVAL '1' MINUTE`), the *At*[$pm5\_00^g$, ...] requires *lt* to be a subperiod of a 5:00pm-period (`t2.1` ranges over 5:00pm-periods), and *At*[*yesterday*, ...] requires *lt* to be a subperiod of the previous day (`PERIOD 'today' - INTERVAL '1' DAY`).

The `SELECT` statement that is associated with `t5` is generated by the translation rule for *Past* (Section 5.11), and the `SELECT` statement that is associated with `t7` is introduced by the translation rule for *At*[$\sigma_g, \beta, \varphi'$] (Section A.1.15). (The *At*[*yesterday*, ...] of (6.11) does not introduce its own `SELECT` statement, it only restricts *lt*; see the translation rule for *At*[κ, φ'] in Section 5.11.) The `SELECT` statement that is associated with `t8` is introduced by the translation rule for conjunction (Section A.1.3). It requires the attribute values that correspond to the $x1^v$ arguments of *flight*($x1^v$) and *leave_something*($x1^v$, *sector*3), and the event times where the two predicates are true to be identical. Finally, the top-level `SELECT` statement is introduced by the translation rule for $?\beta_1 \ldots ?\beta_k\ \varphi'$ (Section 5.11). It returns a snapshot relation that contains the attribute values corresponding to $x1^v$, i.e., the flights.

In the following examples we will concentrate on the generated TOP formulae, ignoring the HPSG signs and the TSQL2 code. The sample questions also serve as a recapitulation of the linguistic coverage of this book.

Progressives of state verbs. As noted in Section 2.5.3, no attempt is made to block progressive forms of state verbs. The progressive forms of these verbs are taken to have the same meanings as the corresponding non-progressive ones. This causes the two questions below to receive the same TOP formula.

```
?- nli([which,tanks,contain,water]).

TOP formula after post-processing:
interrog(x1^v,
        and(tank(x1^v),
            pres(contains(x1^v, water))))

?- nli([which,tanks,are,containing,water]).

TOP formula after post-processing:
[same formula as above]
```

Habituals and simple present. There are two lexical entries for the base form of *to service*, one for the habitual homonym, and one for the non-habitual one. The habitual entry introduces the predicate functor *hab_servicer_of* and classifies the base form as state. The non-habitual entry introduces the functor *actl_servicing* and classifies the base form as culminating activity. The simple present lexical rule (Section 4.7.1) generates a simple present lexical entry only for the habitual homonym, whose base form is state. Hence, the *services* below is treated as the simple present of the habitual homonym, not as the simple present of the non-habitual homonym, and only a formula that contains the *hab_servicer_of* functor is generated. This captures the fact that the question can only have a habitual meaning; it cannot refer to a servicer that is actually servicing BA737 at the present. The reader is reminded that the scheduled-to-happen reading of the simple present is ignored in this book (Section 2.5.1).

```
?- nli([which,servicer,services,ba737]).

TOP formula after post-processing:
interrog(x1^v,
        and(servicer(x1^v),
            pres(hab_servicer_of(x1^v, ba737))))
```

Habituals and progressives. In contrast, the present participle lexical rule (Section 4.7.1) generates progressive entries for both the non-habitual (culminating activity base form) and the habitual (state base form) homonyms. This gives rise to two formulae, one involving the *actl_servicing* functor (the servicer must be servicing BA737 at the present), and one involving the *hab_servicer_of* functor (the servicer must be the current normal servicer of BA737). The $x2^v$ in the first formula is an occurrence identifier (Section 3.16). The habitual reading of the second formula seems less likely in this case.

```
?- nli([which,servicer,is,servicing,ba737]).

TOP formula after post-processing:
interrog(x1^v,
         and(servicer(x1^v),
             pres(actl_servicing(x2^v, x1^v, ba737))))

TOP formula after post-processing:
interrog(x1^v,
         and(servicer(x1^v),
             pres(hab_servicer_of(x1^v, ba737))))
```

Habituals and temporal complements. There are also different lexical entries for the habitual and actual *to depart*. The habitual entry introduces the functor *hab_dep_time*, requires a complement introduced by *at* that specifies the habitual departure time, and classifies the base form as state. The non-habitual entry introduces the functor *actl_depart*, requires no complement, and classifies the base form as point. In the following question, this leads to two formulae: one where the habitual departure time of each reported flight must have been 5:00 pm at some time in 1993, and one where each reported flight must have actually departed at least once at 5:00 pm in 1993. In the habitual reading, *at 5:00 pm* is the complement that specifies the habitual departure time, while in the actual reading, it is a temporal modifier that introduces an *At* operator (Section 4.11.1).

```
?- nli([which,flights,departed,at,pm5_00,in,y1993]).

TOP formula after post-processing:
interrog(x1^v,
         and(flight(x1^v),
             at(y1993,
                at(pm5_00^g, x2^v,
                   past(x3^v,
                        actl_depart(x1^v))))))

TOP formula after post-processing:
interrog(x1^v,
         and(flight(x1^v),
             at(y1993,
                past(x2^v,
                     hab_dep_time(x1^v, pm5_00)))))
```

Simple present with non-states. The first question below receives no parse, because *to circle* is classified as an activity verb (there is no habitual state homonym in this case), and the simple present lexical rule does not generate simple present lexical entries for activity verbs. In contrast, the present participle lexical rule does generate progressive entries for activity verbs. This causes the second question below to be mapped to the formula one would expect. The failure to parse the first question is justified, in the sense that the question seems to be asking about flights that have some circling habit, and the NLITDB has no access to information of this kind. A more cooperative response, however, is needed.

```
?- nli([does,ba737,circle]).

  **No (more) parses.

?- nli([is,ba737,circling]).

TOP formula after post-processing:
pres(circling(ba737))
```

Culminating activity with period adverbial. Following the arrangements of Section 4.11.2, in the following question where a culminating activity combines with a period adverbial, two formulae are generated: one where the inspection must have simply been completed on 1/5/1992, and one where the whole inspection, from start to completion, must have been carried out on 1/5/1992. The first reading seems unlikely in this example, though as discussed in Section 2.9.2, there are sentences where the first reading is the intended one.

```
?- nli([who,inspected,uk160,on,d1_5_92]).

TOP formula after post-processing:
interrog(x1^v,
        at(d1_5_92,
            end(past(x2^v,
                        culm(inspecting(x3^v, x1^v, uk160))))))

TOP formula after post-processing:
interrog(x1^v,
        at(d1_5_92,
            past(x2^v,
                    culm(inspecting(x3^v, x1^v, uk160)))))
```

Culminating activity with both punctual and period adverbial. In the following question, the punctual adverbial *at 5:00 pm* combines with a culminating activity. According to Section 2.9.1, two readings arise: one where the taxiing starts at 5:00 pm, and one where it finishes at 5:00 pm. In both cases, the punctual adverbial causes the aspect of *which flight taxied to gate 2* to become point. That point sentence then combines with the period adverbial *yesterday*. According to Section 2.9.2, the instantaneous situation of the point phrase, i.e., the start or end of the taxiing, must occur within the period of the adverbial. This leads to two formulae: one where the taxiing starts at 5:00 pm on the previous day, and one where the taxiing finishes at 5:00 pm on the previous day. The formulae capture the most likely readings of the question. Unfortunately, if the order of *at 5:00 pm* and *yesterday* is reversed, the generated formulae are not equivalent to the ones below; see the discussion in Section 4.16.

```
?- nli([which,flight,taxied,to,gate2,at,pm5_00,yesterday]).

TOP formula after post-processing:
interrog(x1^v,
         and(flight(x1^v),
             at(yesterday,
                at(pm5_00^g, x2^v,
                   end(past(x3^v,
                            culm(taxiing_to(x4^v, x1^v, gate2))))))))

TOP formula after post-processing:
interrog(x1^v,
         and(flight(x1^v),
             at(yesterday,
                at(pm5_00^g, x2^v,
                   begin(past(x3^v,
                              culm(taxiing_to(x4^v, x1^v, gate2))))))))
```

Past perfect of point verb and punctual adverbial. In the sentence below, which is treated as a yes/no question, the treatment of past perfects and punctual adverbials of Section 4.11.1 allows *at 5:00 pm* to modify either the verb phrase *left gate 2*, or the entire *BA737 had left gate 2*. This gives rise to two TOP formulae: one where 5:00 pm is the time when BA737 left gate 2, and one where 5:00 pm is a reference time at which BA737 had already left gate 2. The two formulae capture the most likely readings of the sentence.

```
?- nli([ba737,had,left,gate2,at,pm5_00]).

TOP formula after post-processing:
past(x2^v,
     perf(x3^v,
          at(pm5_00^g, x1^v,
             leave_something(ba737, gate2))))

TOP formula after post-processing:
at(pm5_00^g, x1^v,
   past(x2^v,
        perf(x3^v,
             leave_something(ba737, gate2))))
```

Past perfect of culminating activity verb and punctual adverbial. Similarly, in the following question, the *at 5:00 pm* is allowed to modify either the verb phrase *taken off*, or the entire *BA737 had taken off*. In the first case, the verb phrase still has the aspectual class of the base form, i.e., culminating activity. According to Section 2.9.1, 5:00 pm is the time where the taking off was completed or started; the second reading seems unlikely in this particular example. The two readings are captured by the first and second formulae below, respectively. In the case where *at 5:00 pm* modifies the entire *BA737 had taken off*, the *had* has already caused the aspect of the sentence to become consequent state. Then, according to Section 2.9.1, 5:00 pm is simply a time-point where the situation of the sentence (having departed) holds. This reading is captured by the third formula.

```
?- nli([ba737,had,taken,off,at,pm5_00]).

TOP formula after post-processing:
past(x2^v,
     perf(x3^v,
          at(pm5_00^g, x1^v,
             end(culm(taking_off(x4^v, ba737))))))

TOP formula after post-processing:
past(x2^v,
     perf(x3^v,
          at(pm5_00^g, x1^v,
             begin(culm(taking_off(x4^v, ba737))))))

TOP formula after post-processing:
at(pm5_00^g, x1^v,
   past(x2^v,
        perf(x3^v,
             culm(taking_off(x4^v, ba737)))))
```

Both preceding and trailing temporal modifiers. The first question below receives the formula one would expect. As discussed in Section 4.16, in the second question below the grammar of Chapter 4 allows two parses: one where *yesterday* attaches to *BA737 was circling for two hours*, and one where it attaches to *BA737 was circling*. The two parses give rise to different, but semantically equivalent, formulae.

```
?- nli([ba737,was,circling,for,two,hours,yesterday]).

TOP formula after post-processing:
at(yesterday,
   for(hour^c, 2,
       past(x1^v,
            circling(ba737))))

?- nli([yesterday,ba737,was,circling,for,two,hours]).

TOP formula after post-processing:
[same formula as above]
```

```
TOP formula after post-processing:
for(hour^c, 2,
    at(yesterday,
       past(x1^v,
            circling(ba737))))
```

Temporal modifier between verb and complement. The following example reveals a problem in the current treatment of temporal modifiers. The HPSG version of this book (Section 4.11) allows temporal modifiers to attach only to finite sentences, i.e., finite verb forms that have already combined with their subjects and complements, or past participle verb phrases, i.e., past participles that have combined with all their complements but not their subjects. In both cases, the temporal modifier is attached after the verb has combined with all of its complements. English temporal modifiers typically appear either at the beginning or the end of the sentence, not between the verb and its complements, and hence requiring temporal modifiers to attach after the verb has combined with its complements is in most cases not a problem. However, in the following question, which native English speakers seem to find acceptable, the temporal modifier (*for two hours*) is between the verb (*queued*) and its complement (*for runway2*). Therefore, the temporal modifier cannot attach to the verb after the verb has combined with its complement, and the system fails to parse the sentence. In contrast, *UK160 queued for runway 2 for two hours*, where the temporal modifier follows the complement, is parsed without problems.

```
?- nli([uk160,queued,for,two,hours,for,runway2]).

  **No (more) parses.
```

Culm operators and 'for' duration adverbials. As explained in Section 4.17, the post-processor removes *Culm* operators from the scope of *For* operators introduced by *for* adverbials; this is demonstrated in the following example. The *for* adverbial introduces a `for_remove_culm` pseudo-operator; this can be thought of as a *For* operator with a flag attached to it, which signals that *Culm* operators within its scope must be removed. The post-processor removes the *Culm* operator, and replaces the `for_remove_culm` with an ordinary *For* operator.

```
?- nli([which,flight,boarded,for,two,hours]).

TOP formula extracted from HPSG sign:
interrog(x1^v,
         and(flight(x1^v),
             for_remove_culm(hour^c, 2,
                             past(x2^v,
                                  culm(boarding(x3^v, x1^v))))))
```

```
TOP formula after post-processing:
interrog(x1^v,
        and(flight(x1^v),
            for(hour^c, 2,
                past(x2^v,
                     boarding(x3^v, x1^v)))))
```

Culm operators and 'in' duration adverbials. Duration adverbials introduced by *in* contribute *For* operators that carry no flags to remove enclosed *Culm* operators. In the following question, this leads to a formula that, correctly, requires the boarding to have been completed.

```
?- nli([which,flight,boarded,in,two,hours]).

TOP formula after post-processing:
interrog(x1^v,
        and(flight(x1^v),
            for(hour^c, 2,
                past(x2^v,
                     culm(boarding(x3^v, x1^v))))))
```

Present perfect. As explained in Section 2.5.4, the present perfect is treated semantically in exactly the same way as the simple past. This causes the two questions below to receive the same formula.

```
?- nli([which,flight,has,been,at,gate2,for,two,hours]).

TOP formula after post-processing:
interrog(x1^v,
        and(flight(x1^v),
            for(hour^c, 2,
                past(x2^v,
                     located_at(x1^v, gate2)))))

?- nli([which,flight,was,at,gate2,for,two,hours]).

TOP formula after post-processing:
[same formula as above]
```

Temporal verbs. As discussed in Section 2.6, when *finished* combines with a culminating activity, the situation must have reached its completion. In contrast, with *stopped* the situation must have simply stopped, without necessarily reaching its completion. This difference is captured in the two formulae below by the existence or absence of a *Culm* operator.

```
?- nli([j_adams,finished,inspecting,uk160,at,pm5_00]).

TOP formula after post-processing:
at(pm5_00^g, x1^v,
   past(x2^v,
        end(culm(inspecting(x3^v, j_adams, uk160)))))

?- nli([j_adams,stopped,inspecting,uk160,at,pm5_00]).

TOP formula after post-processing:
at(pm5_00^g, x1^v,
   past(x2^v,
        end(inspecting(x3^v, j_adams, uk160))))
```

Non-predicative adjectives and Ntense operators. In the airport domain, non-predicative adjectives, like *closed* below, introduce *Ntense* operators. In the question below, the formula that is extracted from the HPSG sign contains an *Ntense* operator whose first argument is a variable. As explained in Section 4.17, this leads to two different formulae after the post-processing, one where *closed* refers to the present, and one where *closed* refers to the time of the verb tense.

```
?- nli([was,any,flight,on,a,closed,runway,yesterday]).

TOP formula extracted from HPSG sign:
and(flight(x1^v),
    and(and(ntense(x2^v, closed(x3^v)),
            runway(x3^v)),
        at(yesterday,
           past(x4^v,
                located_at(x1^v, x3^v)))))

**Post processing of TOP formula generated 2 different
formulae.

TOP formula after post-processing:
and(flight(x1^v),
    and(and(ntense(now, closed(x3^v)),
            runway(x3^v)),
        at(yesterday,
           past(x4^v,
                located_at(x1^v, x3^v)))))

TOP formula after post-processing:
and(flight(x1^v),
    and(and(ntense(x4^v, closed(x3^v)),
            runway(x3^v)),
        at(yesterday,
           past(x4^v,
                located_at(x1^v, x3^v)))))
```

Ntense operator and 'currently'. In the following question, the *currently* clarifies that *closed* refers to the present. The *Ntense* in the formula that is extracted from the HPSG sign has *now** as its first argument, and the post-processing has no effect.

```
?- nli([was,any,flight,on,a,currently,closed,runway,yesterday]).

TOP formula extracted from HPSG sign:
and(flight(x1^v),
    and(and(ntense(now, closed(x2^v)),
            runway(x2^v)),
        at(yesterday,
           past(x3^v,
                located_at(x1^v, x2^v)))))
```

Ntense operator and present tense. In the following question, the verb tense refers to the present, and hence *closed* can only refer to a currently closed runway. The post-processor generates only one formula, where the first argument of *Ntense* is *now**.

```
?- nli([is,any,flight,on,a,closed,runway]).

TOP formula extracted from HPSG sign:

and(flight(x1^v),
    and(and(ntense(x2^v, closed(x3^v)),
            runway(x3^v)),
        pres(located_at(x1^v, x3^v))))

TOP formula after post-processing:

and(flight(x1^v),
    and(and(ntense(now, closed(x3^v)),
            runway(x3^v)),
        pres(located_at(x1^v, x3^v))))
```

Predicative adjectives. Predicative adjectives do not introduce *Ntense* operators (Section 4.10); TOP predicates introduced by these adjectives always end up within the operator(s) of the verb tense. This captures the fact that predicative adjectives always refer to the time of the verb tense.

```
?- nli([was,gate2,open,on,monday]).

TOP formula after post-processing:
at(monday^g, x1^v
   past(x2^v,
        open(gate2)))
```

Proper names as predicative noun phrases. For reasons explained in Section 4.9.2, the system fails to parse sentences that contain proper names or names of days, months, etc. when they are used as predicative noun phrases, as in the first two questions below. Other predicative noun phrases pose no problem, as illustrated in the third question below.

```
?- nli([d1_1_91,was,a,monday]).

  **No (more) parses.

?- nli([ba737,is,uk160]).

  **No (more) parses.

?- nli([ba737,is,a,flight]).

TOP formula after post-processing:
pres(flight(ba737))
```

Multiple interrogatives. Multiple interrogative words can be handled, as demonstrated below.

```
?- nli([which,flight,is,at,which,gate]).

TOP formula after post-processing:
interrog(x1^v,
        interrog(x2^v,
                and(gate(x1^v),
                    and(flight(x2^v),
                        pres(located_at(x2^v, x1^v))))))
```

Subordinate clause and adverbial. The first question below reveals another case where two semantically equivalent TOP formulae are generated; see also Section 4.16. The grammar of Chapter 4 allows *yesterday* to attach to either *BA737 was circling* or to the whole *did any flight leave a gate while BA737 was circling*, leading to two HPSG signs from which the equivalent formulae are generated. In contrast, in the second question below, *yesterday* cannot attach to *BA737 was circling*, because the intervening *while* causes the subordinate clause to be treated as an adverbial, and *yesterday* cannot attach to another adverbial; hence, only one formula is generated.

```
?- nli([did,any,flight,leave,a,gate,while,ba737,was,circling,yesterday]).

TOP formula after post-processing:
and(flight(x1^v),
    and(gate(x2^v),
        at(at(yesterday,
              past(x3^v,
                   circling(ba737))),
           past(x4^v,
                leave_something(x1^v, x2^v)))))
```

```
TOP formula after post-processing:
and(flight(x1^v),
    and(gate(x2^v),
        at(yesterday,
           at(past(x3^v,
                   circling(ba737)),
              past(x4^v,
                   leave_something(x1^v, x2^v))))))

?- nli([did,any,flight,leave,a,gate,yesterday,while,ba737,was,circling]).

TOP formula after post-processing:
and(flight(x1^v),
    and(gate(x2^v),
        at(past(x3^v,
                circling(ba737)),
           at(yesterday,
              past(x5^v,
                   leave_something(x1^v, x2^v))))))
```

Progressive state subordinate clause introduced by 'before' or 'after'. In the questions below, the subordinate clause is a progressive state that modifies a point sentence (*to arrive* is a point verb in the airport domain). Following Section 2.10.2, the formula of the first question requires the flights to have arrived before a time-point where BA737 started to board. In the second question, Section 2.10.2 allows two readings: the flights must have arrived after a time-point where BA737 started or stopped boarding; the generated formulae capture these readings.

```
?- nli([which,flights,arrived,before,ba737,was,boarding]).

TOP formula after post-processing:
interrog(x1^v,
         and(flight(x1^v),
             before(past(x2^v,
                         boarding(x3^v, ba737)),
                    past(x4^v,
                         actl_arrive(x1^v)))))

?- nli([which,flights,arrived,after,ba737,was,boarding]).

TOP formula after post-processing:
interrog(x1^v,
         and(flight(x1^v),
             after(begin(past(x2^v,
                              boarding(x3^v, ba737))),
                   past(x4^v,
                        actl_arrive(x1^v)))))
```

```
TOP formula after post-processing:
interrog(x1^v,
        and(flight(x1^v),
            after(past(x2^v,
                       boarding(x3^v, ba737)),
                  past(x4^v,
                       actl_arrive(x1^v)))))
```

Consequent state subordinate clause introduced by 'before' or 'after'. In the next two questions, the subordinate clause is a consequent state. According to Section 2.10.2, in the first question the flights must have arrived before the situation of the subordinate clause (having boarded) began, i.e., before BA737 finished boarding. In the second question, the flights must have arrived after the situation of the subordinate clause began, i.e., after BA737 finished boarding. These readings are captured by the generated formulae.

```
?- nli([which,flights,arrived,before,ba737,had,boarded]).

TOP formula after post-processing:
interrog(x1^v,
        and(flight(x1^v),
            before(past(x2^v,
                        perf(x3^v,
                             culm(boarding(x4^v,
                                           ba737)))),
                   past(x5^v,
                        actl_arrive(x1^v)))))

?- nli([which,flights,arrived,after,ba737,had,boarded]).

TOP formula after post-processing:
interrog(x1^v,
        and(flight(x1^v),
            after(begin(past(x2^v,
                             perf(x3^v,
                                  culm(boarding(x4^v,
                                                ba737))))),
                  past(x5^v,
                       actl_arrive(x1^v)))))
```

Culminating activity subordinate clause introduced by 'before' or 'after'. Below, the subordinate clause is a culminating activity. Following Section 2.10.2, in the first question the flights must have arrived before a time-point where BA737 finished or started to board. In the second question, the flights must have arrived after a time-point where BA737 finished boarding. The generated formulae capture these readings.

```
?- nli([which,flights,arrived,before,ba737,boarded]).

TOP formula after post-processing:
interrog(x1^v,
         and(flight(x1^v),
             before(end(past(x2^v,
                             culm(boarding(x3^v, ba737)))),
                    past(x4^v,
                         actl_arrive(x1^v)))))

TOP formula after post-processing:
interrog(x1^v,
         and(flight(x1^v),
             before(past(x2^v,
                         culm(boarding(x3^v, ba737))),
                    past(x4^v,
                         actl_arrive(x1^v)))))

?- nli([which,flights,arrived,after,ba737,boarded]).

TOP formula after post-processing:
interrog(x1^v,
         and(flight(x1^v),
             after(past(x2^v,
                        culm(boarding(x3^v, ba737))),
                   past(x4^v,
                        actl_arrive(x1^v)))))
```

Interrogative 'when' and subordinate clause introduced by 'while'. The question below combines a *when* interrogative and a subordinate clause introduced by *while*. The generated formula asks for maximal past circling-periods of BA737 that fall within maximal past periods where UK160 was located at gate 2.

```
?- nli([when,while,uk160,was,at,gate2,was,ba737,circling]).

TOP formula after post-processing:
interrog_mxl(x3^v,
             at(past(x2^v,
                     located_at(uk160, gate2)),
                past(x3^v,
                     circling(ba737))))
```

Interrogative 'when' and habituals. The first question below receives two formulae, one for actual past departures, and one for habitual past departure times; the latter reading is easier to accept if an adverbial like *in 1992* is attached. In the second question, only a formula for the habitual reading is generated, because the simple present lexical rule (Section 4.7.1) does not generate a simple present lexical entry for the non-habitual *to depart*.

```
?- nli([when,did,ba737,depart]).

TOP formula after post-processing:
interrog_mxl(x2^v,
             past(x2^v,
                  actl_depart(ba737)))

TOP formula after post-processing:
interrog(x1^v,
         past(x2^v,
              hab_dep_time(ba737, x1^v)))

?- nli([when,does,ba737,depart]).

TOP formula after post-processing:
interrog(x1^v,
         pres(hab_dep_time(ba737, x1^v)))
```

6.7 Performance

The prototype NLITDB was developed for demonstration purposes, and its code is not optimised for speed. Nevertheless, improvements that have been made to ALE over recent years (Carpenter & Penn 2001) and the availability of faster computers have had a very significant impact on the prototype's speed compared to the performance figures that were reported in the thesis on which this book is based (Androutsopoulos 1996).[2] On a Pentium III PC at 730 MHz with 256 MB RAM, none of the questions above requires more than a couple of seconds to map to TSQL2, including the time to print the HPSG signs, TOP formulae and TSQL2 code; loading and compiling the source code takes approximately 10 seconds.

6.8 Summary

To demonstrate that the theoretical framework of this book is workable, it was used to implement a prototype NLITDB, using Prolog and ALE. The source code of the prototype is freely available, and it is currently configured for a hypothetical airport database. A number of sample questions were used in this chapter to demonstrate that the prototype behaves according to the theory of the previous chapters.

The architecture of the system is currently minimal. Apart from tailoring the linguistic coverage, additional mechanisms for preprocessing, robust parsing, anaphora resolution, quantifier scoping, response generation, and possibly inferencing would have to be added if the system were to be used in real-life applications.

Notes

* The code can be downloaded from:
`http://www.aueb.gr/users/ion/nlitdb_book/`

1. The prototype NLITDB currently uses ALE version 3.2.1 and SWI Prolog version 5.0.1, which are freely available for both Unix and Windows platforms. Instructions on how to obtain ALE and SWI Prolog are included in the files of the prototype NLITDB.

2. See also Flickinger et al. (2000) for related work on efficient processing with HPSG.

CHAPTER 7

Related work and directions for further research

"Times change and we with time."

7.1 Introduction

The previous chapters have established a theoretical framework for constructing NLITDBS, which is intended to serve as a starting point for developers of NLITDBS and as a basis for further research. The framework consists of a semantic analysis of a range of English temporal mechanisms (Chapter 2), a formal meaning representation language, TOP, that can represent the semantics of these mechanisms (Chapter 3), a temporally enhanced HPSG grammar that maps English questions containing the supported mechanisms to appropriate TOP expressions (Chapter 4), and a set of translation rules that turn TOP expressions into suitable TSQL2 queries (Chapter 5). A prototype NLITDB, intended to demonstrate that the framework is implementable, is also available (Chapter 6). This chapter examines how the framework of this book relates to work on NLITDBS that has been carried out by other researchers, and concludes with proposals for further research.

7.2 Related work on NLITDBs

This section discusses prominent work on NLITDBS that has been carried out by Moens (1987), Clifford (1990), and Nelken (2001). Information about other work on NLITDBS (Bruce 1972; De, Pan, & Whinston 1985; Hafner 1985; Mays 1986; Spenceley 1989) can be found in the thesis on which this book is based (Androutsopoulos 1996).

7.2.1 Moens

Moens' work on temporal linguistic phenomena (Moens 1987; Moens & Steedman 1988) has been highly influential in the area of tense and aspect theories; some ideas from Moens' work were mentioned in Chapter 2. As an application of his theory, Moens also developed a simplistic NLITDB (Moens 1987; Moens 1988). This is mainly intended to illustrate his tense and aspect theory, rather than constitute a detailed exploration of issues related to NLITDBS. Hence, the system is based on a very limited, and largely undocumented, DCG grammar (Pereira & Warren 1980) that maps English questions to Prolog expressions, and additional Prolog rules that evaluate the resulting expressions against the Prolog database. There is no clear notion of a meaning representation language, and the Prolog database is required to record information according to an idiosyncratic temporal database model. Nevertheless, Moens' system is interesting in that it demonstrates how additional time-related information, that is normally not included in temporal databases, can be useful when processing English questions; this is discussed in the following paragraphs.

Apart from purely temporal information, i.e., information showing when various events took place, Moens' database model also stores information about what he calls *episodes*. According to Moens, an episode is a sequence of 'contingently' related events. The term 'contingency' seems to have two possible meanings: it may denote a consequence relation (event A was a consequence of event B), or it may refer to events that constitute preparatory steps towards the satisfaction of a common goal. Moens argues that contingency information of this kind is necessary, if certain time-related linguistic mechanisms are to be handled appropriately. For example, as discussed in Section 2.5.4, the English present perfect often carries the implication that some consequence of the past situation holds at the present. The contingency information in Moens' database allows the possible consequences to be identified. In a similar manner, if landing is viewed as an instantaneous situation comprising only the timepoint where the plane touches down, the progressive *BA737 was landing* can be thought of as asserting that a preparatory step of the landing was in progress; again, the contingency information in Moens' database allows the preparatory steps to be identified.

Although Moens argues convincingly that contingency information plays an important role in temporal linguistic mechanisms, it is often difficult to see how information of this kind can be used in practical NLITDBS. For example, it is difficult to represent explicitly in the database all the consequences of each event. Furthermore, even if all the consequences of each event are represented, it is difficult to figure out which consequence the user has in mind when using the present perfect; see also the discussion in Section 2.5.4. Representing and reasoning about the preparatory steps of each event is equally challenging. Consequently, the framework of this book does not employ contingency information.

Moen's database model is also interesting in that it provides some support for imprecise temporal information. One may know, for example, that two events A and B occurred, and that B was a consequence of A, without knowing the precise times when A and B occurred. Information of this kind can be stored in Moens' database, because in his database model events are not necessarily associated with times. One can store events A and B as a sequence of contingently related events without assigning them specific times; here 'contingency' would denote consequence. Note, however, that if there is no contingency relation between A and B, and their exact times are unknown, the database model does not allow the temporal order of A and B to be stored. Although there has been research on imprecise temporal information in databases (Brusoni, Console, & Terenziani 1995; Koubarakis 1995), most of the work on temporal databases assumes that events are assigned specific times. To remain compatible with this work, the framework of this book has made the same assumption.

7.2.2 Clifford

Clifford (1988; 1990) defined a temporal version of the relational database model, and showed how a fragment of English questions involving time can be mapped systematically to logical expressions whose semantics are defined in terms of a database structured according to his model. Clifford's approach is notable in that both the semantics of the English fragment and of the temporal database are defined within a common model-theoretic framework, based on Montague semantics (Dowty, Wall, & Peters 1981).

Clifford extended the syntactic coverage of Montague's PTQ grammar to allow questions, past, present, and future verb forms, and some temporal adverbials and temporal subordinate clauses. In terms of syntactic coverage of time-related phenomena, Clifford's grammar is similar to the grammar of Chapter 4. Both grammars support yes/no questions, questions introduced by *who*, *what*, and *which*, time-asking questions introduced by *when*, questions with multiple interrogatives (e.g., *Who inspected what on 1/1/1991?*), and assertions, which are treated as yes/no questions. Clifford's grammar allows simple future verb forms, which are not covered by the grammar of Chapter 4, but it does not allow progressive or perfect forms, which are partially covered by the grammar of this book. The two grammars allow similar temporal adverbials (e.g., *in 1991*, *before 3/5/1990*, *yesterday*), though there are adverbials that are supported by Clifford's grammar but not the grammar of this book (e.g., *never*, *always*), and adverbials that are covered by the grammar of this book but not Clifford's (e.g., *for five hours*, *in two days*). Both grammars support only three kinds of temporal subordinate clauses, introduced by *while*, *before*, and *after*, respectively.

Despite the similarities in the syntactic coverage, however, Clifford assigns to temporal linguistic mechanisms semantics that are generally much shallower than the semantics of this book. Most notably, he does not employ any form of aspectual taxonomy. As discussed in Chapter 2, the distinction between aspectual classes pertains to the semantics of most of the English temporal mechanisms. Without an aspectual taxonomy, important semantic differences cannot be captured; for example, the fact that the simple past of a culminating activity verb normally implies that the climax was reached, while the simple past of a point, state, or activity verb carries no such implication; the fact that a punctual adverbial typically has an inchoative or terminal meaning with a culminating activity, but an interjacent meaning with a state; or the fact that the simple present of non-state verbs is typically used with a habitual meaning. The aspectual taxonomy of this book allowed us to capture many distinctions of this kind, which cannot be accounted for in Clifford's framework. Particular care was also taken in this book to explain clearly which temporal linguistic mechanisms are supported, which simplifications were introduced in their semantics, and which phenomena remain to be considered; see Table 2.9 on page 70 for a summary. This information is difficult to obtain in Clifford's work.

Following the Montague tradition, Clifford employs an intensional higher order language, called IL$_s$, to represent the meanings of English questions. His grammar comprises a set of syntactic rules, that determine the syntactic structure of each sentence, and a set of semantic rules that map syntactic structures to expressions of IL$_s$. For example, (7.1) is mapped to the IL$_s$ expression of (7.2).

(7.1) When did Liz manage Peter?

(7.2) $\lambda i_1 [[i_1 < i] \wedge \exists y[EMP'_*(i_1)(Peter) \wedge MGR'(i_1)(y) \wedge y(i_1) = Liz \wedge AS\_1(Peter, y)]]$

Unlike TOP, IL$_s$ is point-based; i.e., the truth of an IL$_s$ formula is always evaluated with respect to a time-point, rather than an a period (cf. Section 3.1). In (7.2), $EMP'_*(i_1)(Peter)$ means that Peter must be an employee at the time-point i_1. $MGR'(i_1)(y)$ means that y must be a partial function from time-points to managers, defined for at least the time-point i_1. $AS\_1(Peter, y)$ requires y to represent the history of Peter's managers; i.e., the value $y(i_1)$ of y at each time-point i_1 must be the manager of Peter at that time-point. The $y(i_1) = Liz$ requires the manager of Peter at i_1 to be Liz. Finally, i is the present time-point, and $i_1 < i$ means that i_1 must precede i. Roughly speaking, the λ at the beginning of (7.2) plays the role of an interrogative quantifier: it indicates that all the possible values of i_1 are to be reported, such that i_1 precedes the present time-point, Peter is an employee at i_1, and Peter's manager at i_1 is Liz. As in the case of TOP, the syntax and semantics of IL_s are clearly defined, which constitutes a significant improvement over earlier work on NLITDBS (Bruce 1972; De, Pan, & Whinston 1985; Moens 1987).

In Clifford's version of the relational model, called HRDM (Historical Relational Database Model), attribute values are not necessarily atomic. They can also be sets of symbols that denote time-points, or partial functions from symbols that denote time-points to atomic values. This is illustrated in the *emprel* relation below.[1]

emprel				
EMP	*MGR*	*DEPT*	*SAL*	*lifespan*
Peter	$\begin{bmatrix} S2 \rightarrow Elsie \\ S3 \rightarrow Liz \end{bmatrix}$	$\begin{bmatrix} S2 \rightarrow Hardware \\ S3 \rightarrow Linen \end{bmatrix}$	$\begin{bmatrix} S2 \rightarrow 30K \\ S3 \rightarrow 35K \end{bmatrix}$	$\{S2, S3\}$
Liz	$\begin{bmatrix} S2 \rightarrow Elsie \\ S3 \rightarrow Liz \end{bmatrix}$	$\begin{bmatrix} S2 \rightarrow Toy \\ S3 \rightarrow Hardware \end{bmatrix}$	$\begin{bmatrix} S2 \rightarrow 35K \\ S3 \rightarrow 50K \end{bmatrix}$	$\{S2, S3\}$
Elsie	$\begin{bmatrix} S1 \rightarrow Elsie \\ S2 \rightarrow Elsie \end{bmatrix}$	$\begin{bmatrix} S1 \rightarrow Toy \\ S2 \rightarrow Toy \end{bmatrix}$	$\begin{bmatrix} S1 \rightarrow 50K \\ S2 \rightarrow 50K \end{bmatrix}$	$\{S1, S2\}$

The relation above shows that, for example, at the time-point *S2* the manager of Peter was Elsie, while at *S3* his manager was Liz. Similarly, at *S2* and *S3* Peter worked in the hardware and linen departments, respectively. The *lifespan* of each tuple shows the time-points the tuple carries information for. HRDM provides additional time-stamps, not shown here, to cope with cases where the structure of the database changes (Section 1.5).

Clifford shows how the semantics of IL$_s$ expressions can be defined in terms of an HRDM database; for example, how the semantics of (7.2) can be defined in terms of information in *emprel*. This corresponds to the link that has to be established between TOP's model and the underlying BCDM database (Section 5.6). Clifford also defines a temporal version of relational algebra (Ullman 1988), a theoretical database query language that DBMSs often use internally to represent the operations that need to be carried out to satisfy the user's requests. The answer to (7.1) can be found using (7.3), which is an expression in Clifford's algebra.

(7.3) $\omega(\sigma\text{-}WHEN_{EMP=Peter,MGR=Liz}(emprel))$

The expression $\sigma\text{-}WHEN_{EMP=Peter,MGR=Liz}(emprel)$ generates a single-tuple relation, shown below as *emprel2*, that carries the information of Peter's tuple from *emprel*, restricted to the times when his manager was Liz. The ω operator returns a set of symbols that denote all the time-points for which there is information in the relation-argument of ω. In our example, (7.3) returns {*S3*}.

emprel2

EMP	*MGR*	*DEPT*	*SAL*	*lifespan*
Peter	[*S3* → *Liz*]	[*S3* → *Linen*]	[*S3* → *35K*]	{*S3*}

Clifford (1990:170) outlines an algorithm for mapping IL$_s$ expressions to appropriate expressions of his relational algebra. The description of the algorithm, however, is very sketchy and informal, and there is no proof that the algorithm is correct; i.e., that the generated relational algebra expressions preserve the semantics of the IL$_s$ expressions. In contrast, the TOP to TSQL2 mapping of this book is defined rigorously, and it is provably correct (Chapter 5). Furthermore, it should be pointed out that Clifford's database model, although well defined, is very far away from the current ANSI recommendations on how to support time in SQL (Section 1.5), unlike TSQL2 and its underlying BCDM database model. Finally, it is unclear if Clifford's overall theory was ever used to implement a prototype NLITDB; in contrast, the prototype of this book is publicly available, as discussed in Chapter 6.

7.2.3 Nelken

Nelken's work (2001) covers an interesting range of topics related to the semantics of questions, including issues such as the equivalence of questions, or the relation between a question and the declarative sentences that constitute possible answers to it.[2] In this section we will focus on the, relatively independent, part of Nelken's work that considers English questions to temporal databases. This is particularly interesting, because it refers to, and at some points criticises, the framework of this book, as it was presented in the thesis on which the book is based.

In terms of linguistic coverage, Nelken focuses on temporal adverbials, rather than issues related to the tense and aspect of verbs. His treatment of temporal adverbials, which is based on the theory of Pratt and Francez (2001), is particularly strong in sentences with multiple temporal modifiers. In Section 4.16, for example, we considered cases where it would be desirable for the order of temporal modifiers to be reversed, transforming (7.4) to (7.5), so that the punctual adverbial is attached to the sentence before the period adverbial.

(7.4) J. Adams repaired fault 2 on 2/11/1995 at 5:00 pm.
(7.5) J. Adams repaired fault 2 at 5:00 pm on 2/11/1995.

Building upon the theory of Pratt and Francez, Nelken proposes mechanisms that first generate semantic representations for all the possible orderings of the adverbials, and then reject inappropriate orderings using world knowledge constraints. Nelken (2001:89) illustrates these mechanisms with (7.6), where, at the semantics level, the universal quantifier of *during every month* must be placed within the scope of the existential quantifier of *one year*, as if *during every month* were attached to the sentence before *one year*; in Nelken's semantic representation, this forces the universal quantifier to range over the months of a particular year.

(7.6) John worked in marketing one year during every month.

The alternative scoping, whereby John worked in marketing for a year within each month, is rejected by world knowledge constraints that indicate that months are parts of years. Temporal subordinate clauses are treated in a similar manner; Nelken provides examples with clauses introduced by *before* and *after*. Unlike the framework of this book, Nelken's work (2001:75) also covers relative clauses (Section 2.13).

Nelken's framework is also interesting in that it covers quantification and negation, issues that were not considered in this book (Section 2.13). Nelken (2001:77) points out that queries involving quantification or negation are easier to formulate in natural language than in formal query languages, like SQL, or graphical user interfaces, as argued by Copestake and Sparck Jones (1990).

Therefore, supporting quantification and negation in NLITDBS is particularly important.

Unlike the framework of this book, Nelken's work essentially ignores issues related to the tense and aspect of verbs. Only simple past questions are considered, and all the verbs are treated as if they were states. Nelken (2001:75) claims that the use of aspectual distinctions in NLITDBS is questionable for two reasons. First, some aspectual distinctions, which may be prevalent in everyday language use, seem irrelevant to NLITDBS; he uses the imperfective paradox (Section 1.3) as an example of a fine distinction which he claims is of unclear practical interest in NLITDBS. Second, Nelken argues that handling aspectual distinctions requires a more complex data model than those currently adopted in temporal databases; he points to the occurrence identifiers of this book (Section 3.16) and the information in the database that shows if a situation has reached its inherent climax (Section 5.9) as examples of linguistically motivated additions to data models, which are unlikely to be supported by the temporal databases community. Nelken also points to TSQL2's distinction between state and event relations as a further example of a distinction related to aspectual classes that was not adopted by subsequent work on temporal databases. As discussed in Section 5.2.3, however, this was an ill-defined feature of TSQL2, which is probably why it was not adopted in subsequent work.

As already noted in the discussion of Clifford's work (Section 7.2.2), Chapter 2 has shown that the distinction between aspectual classes pertains to the semantics of most of the English temporal mechanisms, and that without an aspectual taxonomy, important semantic differences cannot be captured. Hence, although Nelken's first claim above may be justified in particular database applications where all the modelled situations are viewed as states, it cannot be easily accepted in the general case, at least not without appropriate Wizard of Oz studies (Section 1.2). Regarding Nelken's second claim above, the particular examples that he mentions do not seem to require modifications to the commonly used temporal database models. In fact, when modelling situations that are viewed as culminating activities, like the inspections or services of the airport domain (Sections 2.4.5 and 6.5), it seems natural to include in the database an additional attribute that distinguishes the occurrences of the situations (e.g., an inspection identifier acting as a key), as well as information that shows the status of the situation (completed or not); it would be surprising if real-world databases did not include this information. Nelken, however, is right in the sense that this book has introduced some additional features to TSQL2 to support its tense and aspect theory (Section 5.3). Although some of the additional features may prove difficult to support in forthcoming temporal

DBMSs, mostly the (SUBPERIOD) partitioning unit (Section 5.3.2), identifying cases where additional support is desirable from the underlying DBMS is useful, since it provides feedback to researchers working on temporal databases.

As in the framework of this book, Nelken adopts a two-stage mapping from English to database language, whereby English questions are initially mapped to an intermediate meaning representation language. Nelken uses a two-sorted first-order logic, called L_{Allen}, as his intermediate language.[3] L_{Allen} includes Allen's (1983) operators, which can express all the possible relations between two periods. For example, ignoring some details, (7.7) is represented in L_{Allen} as (7.8).

(7.7) Did John work in marketing?

(7.8) $\exists j_0\ (work(john, marketing, j_0) \wedge j_{past} \supseteq j_0 \wedge i \bigcirc j_0)$

Unlike TOP, L_{Allen} does not use Priorean-style temporal operators (Section 1.4). Instead, each predicate has an extra period-denoting argument, j_0 in the case of $work(john, marketing, j_0)$, and relations between the various periods are represented explicitly using Allen's operators. The extra argument of the predicates corresponds to TOP's event time, except that it always denotes a *maximal* period where the corresponding situation was true. j_{past} denotes the period that covers all the past time, and i, called the 'time of interest', corresponds to TOP's localisation time. $j_{past} \supseteq j_0$ requires a maximal period where John worked in marketing to fall entirely within the past, and $i \bigcirc j_0$ requires that maximal period to overlap the time of interest. As with TOP's localisation time, i can in principle be used to limit the time of the verb's tense to a contextually salient period (Section 3.17).

In a similar manner, Nelken (2001: 85) treats nouns that introduce situations, e.g., *recession*, *construction*, as contributing a period that is required to fall within the time of interest. It would be interesting to investigate if this approach can be incorporated in the framework of this book (cf. Section 2.7). Non-temporal nouns introduce predicates with a similar time-denoting argument. For example, (7.9) is represented in L_{Allen} by (7.10), where j_1 is the time when d was a department; i.e., j_1 plays the role of $j1^v$ in the corresponding TOP formula, shown in (7.11).

(7.9) Which departments did John work in?

(7.10) $\exists j_1\ (department(d, j_1)) \wedge$
$\exists j_0\ (work(john, d, j_0) \wedge j_{past} \supseteq j_0 \wedge i \bigcirc j_0)$

(7.11) $?d^v\ Ntense[j1^v, department(d^v)] \wedge Past[e^v, working(john, d^v)]$

Nelken, however, uses the extra time-denoting argument of non-temporal nouns only as a placeholder for future work on temporal anaphora; he always applies an existential quantifier on it, as shown in (7.10). In contrast, Section 4.9.1 has provided some mechanisms that force the variable of the *Ntense* operator in (7.11) to point to either the speech time or the time of the verb's tense.

It should be noted that, apart from the differences that derive from the lack of aspectual taxonomy, Nelken's semantics of the English temporal mechanisms are often different from the semantics of this book. For example, unlike the corresponding TOP formula, shown in (7.12), (7.8) leads to a negative answer if there is only one maximal period where John worked in marketing, and that period does not fall entirely in the past; i.e., if John still works in marketing. In contrast, the answer is affirmative if John still works in marketing, but also worked in marketing during another maximal period that is located entirely in the past. The TOP formula of (7.12) seems to be closer to the meaning of (7.7); it simply requires John to have worked in marketing during some past time, regardless of whether or not he still works in marketing.

(7.12) *Past*[e^v, *working*(*john*, *marketing*)]

Similar comments can be made for Nelken's semantics of *before* and *after*. For example, in subordinate clauses introduced by *after*, like *after John worked in marketing*, Nelken's semantics requires the situation of the main clause to take place after the *end* of a maximal period of the subordinate clause; in our example, after the end of a maximal period where John worked in marketing. As we saw in Section 2.10.2, however, there are cases where the situation of the main clause must be allowed to take place after the *beginning* of a maximal period of the subordinate clause, as in (7.13).

(7.13) Which flights departed after runway 2 was open?

For the mapping from English to L_{Allen}, Nelken employs Type-Logical Grammar (Morrill 1994; Carpenter 1998), a version of Categorial Grammar (McGee Wood 1993). Nelken (2001:76–77, 108–109) argues that using Type-Logical Grammar simplifies the construction of the meaning representation, because the resulting formulae can be read off directly from the root node of the parse tree. In contrast, a separate extraction step (Section 4.6) is needed in the HPSG grammar of Chapter 4 to recover the TOP formulae from the resulting HPSG signs; though admittedly less elegant, this does not seem to constitute a significant disadvantage.

Turning to his temporal database model and language, Nelken adopts ATSQL as supported by TIMEDB (Section 1.5). Nelken's database model is very similar to the database model of this book; following Section 5.3.3, Nelken (2000b:1077) also includes calendric relations. The main difference between the two models is that Nelken's valid-time relations, including intermediate relations generated during the evaluation of database queries, are automatically coalesced (cf. Section 5.2.3). In effect, the time-stamps of Nelken's tuples show only the maximal periods of the corresponding situations; this is largely a consequence of the fact that all the situations are viewed as states, which endows them with the homogeneity property (Sections 3.6 and 5.3.2). As with the framework of this book, Nelken focuses on valid time, ignoring transaction time (Section 1.5); the same holds for Moens and Clifford (Sections 7.2.1 and 7.2.2).

Nelken's mapping from L_{Allen} to ATSQL is a temporal extension of previously proposed techniques for translating from first-order predicate logic to SQL (van Gelder & Topor 1991; Abiteboul, Hull, & Vianu 1995).[4] Nelken (2001:95) rightly points out that his mapping is much simpler than the corresponding mapping from TOP to TSQL2 of Chapter 5. Much of the simplicity of Nelken's mapping is due to the fact that L_{Allen} remains very close to traditional first-order predicate logic, by treating time as an extra argument of predicates and by expressing directly the relations between the various periods using Allen's operators. In contrast, TOP employs Priorean-style operators (Section 1.4), each intended to correspond roughly to a temporal mechanism of English; consequently, there is a large number of operators, often with complex semantics, and this gives rise to a large number of often complicated translation rules. On the other hand, TOP's operators lead to more compact formulae, where the semantic contribution of each temporal linguistic mechanism is easier to see; compare, for example, (7.8) to (7.12). This is particularly useful when studying or extending the mapping from English to meaning representation, especially in sentences with aspectual distinctions, perfect tenses, or subordinate clauses, where the L_{Allen} expressions would be very difficult to comprehend.

One way to combine in the framework of this book the benefits of the two approaches is to introduce a second meaning representation language, say BOT, between TOP and the database language. BOT would be similar to L_{Allen}, and hence the mapping from BOT to database language would be straightforward, as in Nelken's work. For each TOP operator, a corresponding translation rule to BOT would be provided; since BOT would be a form of logic, this would be simpler than defining a translation rule for all the way from TOP to the database language, making it easier to add new TOP operators for new temporal linguistic mechanisms. This approach has already been explored to some extent elsewhere (Androutsopoulos 2000). Its disadvantage is that one has to define and cope with two separate meaning representation languages.

To demonstrate his theory, Nelken has also built a prototype NLITDB, based on Carpenter's Type-Logical Grammar Theorem Prover.[5] Roughly speaking, the latter plays the same role as ALE in the system of Chapter 6. Like the prototype of this book, Nelken's NLITDB adopts a simple pipeline architecture, and would have to be extended with several additional modules if it were to be used in real-life applications; for example, modules for anaphora resolution and co-operative responses. Nelken's prototype is linked to TIMEDB (Section 1.5), and, hence, the generated ATSQL queries can be evaluated against a database, unlike the prototype of Chapter 6.

7.3 Directions for further research

Let us now turn to possible extensions to the work of this book. Most of the extensions have already been mentioned in previous parts of the book, and, hence, this section will be rather brief, pointing to relevant previous sections where appropriate. The author hopes that the discussion below may offer to researchers and students wishing to work in the area of NLITDBS ideas for research projects.

Linguistic coverage. Although the theoretical framework of this book covers an interesting range of temporal linguistic mechanisms, there are still many time-related linguistic phenomena that it does not support (Table 2.9 on page 70), and one could explore how some of them could be handled. As discussed in Sections 1.2 and 2.1, this could be performed in conjunction with Wizard of Oz experiments, to determine the phenomena that are most prevalent in the target range of applications. From a theoretical point of view, temporal anaphoric phenomena (Section 2.12) are among those that seem more interesting. It would also be particularly interesting to explore if the linguistic coverage of the framework can be tailored to be easily explainable in the form of a controlled language (Section 1.2). Another interesting direction would be to develop a corresponding theoretical framework for a language other than English, and investigate the degree to which components of this book's framework, e.g., TOP or the aspectual taxonomy of Chapter 2, can be reused.

Response generation and paraphrases. The framework of this book provides no response generation facilities (Section 1.2). We have encountered several cases where cooperative responses would be beneficial (Sections 2.5.1, 2.5.2, 2.5.3, 2.6, 2.9.2, 2.9.3, 2.10.1, 2.10.2, 3.10, and 6.6), and, hence, it would be particularly interesting to investigate how the framework of this book could be extended to generate responses of this kind. Facilities to paraphrase ambiguous English questions in order to show their possible meanings would also be useful, as discussed in Sections 1.2 and 6.2.

A second meaning representation language. As discussed in Section 7.2.3, introducing a second meaning representation language, which would be closer to traditional first-order predicate logic, between TOP and the database language could simplify the mapping from TOP to database language, and make it easier to introduce new TOP operators for new temporal linguistic mechanisms. It would be interesting to explore this direction, possibly along the lines that have been suggested elsewhere (Androutsopoulos 2000).

Database language and prototype DBMS. Although TSQL2 is a good representative of the various temporal extensions to SQL that have been proposed, the SQL/Temporal part of the new SQL:1999 standard (Section 1.5) is expected to differ from TSQL2 in many ways. Therefore, it would be particularly interesting to investigate how the framework of this book could be modified to generate queries in SQL:1999, once the standardisation of SQL/Temporal has been completed. Another strand of work could investigate how the prototype NLITDB of Chapter 6 could be modified to generate ATSQL queries; this would allow it to be linked to the add-ons for commercial DBMSs that support ATSQL (Section 1.5). Along with an appropriate tailoring of the linguistic coverage, as discussed above, this would pave the way for usability tests (Bell & Rowe 1992; Dekleva 1994; King 1996; Sparck Jones & Galliers 1996). For real-life applications, it would also be useful to consider how the resulting database queries could be optimised, as discussed in Section 5.12.

7.4 Summary

This chapter has discussed work on NLITDBs by Moens, Clifford, and Nelken, as well as possible extensions to the work of this book.

Although Moens' work on temporal linguistic phenomena has been highly infuential in tense and aspect theories, his prototype NLITDB is rather simplistic in terms of grammar, lacks a clearly defined meaning representation language, and assumes an idiosyncratic temporal database model. Nevertheless, Moens' NLITDB is interesting in that it demonstrates how additional information about episodes, that is normally not included in temporal databases, can be useful when processing English questions. The work of Clifford and Nelken is closer to the framework of this book, in the sense that they both adopt more principled grammars, and clearly defined meaning representation languages and temporal database models.

In terms of syntactic coverage of temporal mechanisms, the framework of this book is similar to Clifford's. The semantics that Clifford assigns to these mechanisms, however, are much shallower, and they ignore aspectual distinctions. Clifford's database model is also very far away from the current ANSI recommendations on how to support time in SQL, the mapping from meaning representation to database language is sketchy, and it is unclear if the theory was ever used to implement a prototype NLITDB. In contrast, both Nelken's and the theory of this book are accompanied by prototype NLITDB implementations.

Nelken adopts ATSQL, which is closer to the current ANSI recommendations than TSQL2 is. This has the additional benefit that ATSQL is supported by add-ons for commercial DBMSs, and, hence, the database language queries that his prototype generates can be evaluated against a database, unlike the prototype of this book. In terms of linguistic coverage, Nelken focuses on temporal adverbials, rather than issues related to the tense and aspect of verbs. Nelken's work covers some phenomena that were ignored or not considered in full detail in this book, like quantification, negation, and multiple temporal adverbials. On the other hand, as in Clifford's work, the semantics that Nelken assigns to temporal linguistic mechanisms are often shallower than the semantics of this book, and this is often a consequence of the fact that he ignores aspectual distinctions. Nelken's mapping from meaning representation to database language is much simpler than the corresponding mapping of this book. Although this can be partly attributed to the lack of aspectual distinctions, it is also a consequence of the fact that Nelken's meaning representation language is closer to traditional first-order predicate logic than TOP is. Similar benefits could be obtained in the framework of this book by introducing a second meaning representation language, similar to Nelken's, between TOP and the database language.

Other possible extensions to the work of this book include extensions to the linguistic coverage, possibly in conjunction with Wizard of Oz experiments to determine the linguistic phenomena that are most prevalent in the target range of applications. Temporal anaphoric phenomena are among those that seem most interesting to investigate, and the same holds for mechanisms to generate cooperative responses and paraphrases of the user's questions. It would also be interesting to develop a corresponding theoretical framework for a language other than English, investigating the degree to which the work of this book can be reused. Additional work can be carried out on the database side, to replace TSQL2 by ATSQL or the forthcoming SQL standard for temporal queries, to link the prototype NLITDB to a DBMS, and to optimize the database queries that the NLITDB generates.

Notes

1. The discussion here refers to the latest version of HRDM (Clifford 1990), as opposed to an earlier version (Clifford & Warren 1983).

2. See also Nelken and Francez (1999a; 1999b; 2000a; 2000b; 2001a; 2001b).

3. According to Nelken, L_{Allen} is an augmented version of a language with the same name defined by Toman (1996).

4. Nelken actually shows how L_{Allen} expressions can be translated to a form of temporal relational algebra (Böhlen, Jensen, & Snodgrass 2000), but the expressions of the algebra map directly to ATSQL expressions, and his prototype NLITDB uses the corresponding ATSQL expressions.

5. See `http://www.colloquial.com/tlg/`.

References

Abiteboul, S., Herr, L., & Van den Bussche, J. (1999). Temporal connectives versus explicit timestamps to query temporal databases. *Journal of Computer and System Sciences, 58*(1), 54–68.

Abiteboul, S., Hull, R., & Vianu, V. (1995). *Foundations of Databases.* Addison-Wesley.

Alexandersson, J. (Ed.). (1999). *Proceedings of the Workshop on Knowledge and Reasoning in Practical Dialogue Systems, 16th International Joint Conference on Artificial Intelligence.* Stockholm, Sweden.

Allen, J. (1995). *Natural Language Understanding* (2nd edition). Benjamin/Cummings.

Allen, J. F. (1983). Maintaining knowledge about temporal intervals. *Communications of the ACM, 26*(11), 832–843.

Allen, J. F. (1984). Towards a general theory of action and time. *Artificial Intelligence, 23,* 123–154.

Alshawi, H. (Ed.). (1992). *The Core Language Engine.* MIT Press.

Alshawi, H., Carter, D., Crouch, R., Pulman, S., Rayner, M., & Smith, A. (1992). CLARE – a contextual reasoning and cooperative response framework for the core language engine. Final report, SRI International.

Androutsopoulos, I. (1992). Interfacing a natural language front-end to a relational database. Master's thesis, Department of Artificial Intelligence, University of Edinburgh, U.K.

Androutsopoulos, I. (1996). A Principled Framework for Constructing Natural Language Interfaces to Temporal Databases. Ph.D. thesis, Department of Artificial Intelligence, University of Edinburgh, U.K.

Androutsopoulos, I. (2000). Temporal meaning representations in a natural language front-end. In M. Gergatsoulis & P. Rondogiannis (Eds.), *Intensional Programming II – Proceedings of the 12th International Symposium on Languages for Intensional Programming* (pp. 197–213). Athens, Greece. World Scientific.

Androutsopoulos, I. & Aretoulaki, M. (2002). Natural language interaction. In R. Mitkov (Ed.), *Handbook of Computational Linguistics.* Oxford University Press. Forthcoming.

Androutsopoulos, I. & Dale, R. (2000). Selectional restrictions in HPSG. In *Proceedings of the 18th International Conference on Computational Linguistics* (pp. 15–20). Saarbrücken, Germany.

Androutsopoulos, I. & Ritchie, G. D. (2000). Database interfaces. In R. Dale, H. Moisl, & H. Somers (Eds.), *Handbook of Natural Language Processing,* Chapter 9 (pp. 209–240). Marcel Dekker.

Androutsopoulos, I., Ritchie, G. D. & Thanisch, P. (1993). An efficient and portable natural language query interface for relational databases. In P. W. Chung, G. Lovegrove, & M. Ali (Eds.), *Proceedings of the 6th International Conference on Industrial and Engineering Applications of Artificial Intelligence and Expert Systems* (pp. 327–330). Edinburgh, U.K. Gordon and Breach.

Androutsopoulos, I., Ritchie, G. D., & Thanisch, P. (1995a). Experience using TSQL2 in a natural language interface. In J. Clifford & A. Tuzhilin (Eds.), *Recent Advances in Temporal Databases – Proceedings of the International Workshop on Temporal Databases* (pp. 113–132). Zurich, Switzerland. Springer-Verlag.

Androutsopoulos, I., Ritchie, G. D., & Thanisch, P. (1995b). Natural language interfaces to databases – an introduction. *Natural Language Engineering, 1*(1), 29–81.

Androutsopoulos, I., Ritchie, G. D., & Thanisch, P. (1998). Time, tense and aspect in natural language database interfaces. *Natural Language Engineering, 4*(3), 229–276.

Barros, F. A., & De Roeck, A. (1994). Resolving anaphora in a portable natural language front end to a database. In *Proceedings of the 4th Conference on Applied Natural Language Processing* (pp. 119–124). Stuttgart, Germany.

Bates, M., Bobrow, R., Ingria, R., & Stallard, D. (1994). The Delphi natural language understanding system. In *Proceedings of the 4th Conference on Applied Natural Language Processing* (pp. 132–137). Stuttgart, Germany.

Bell, J. E., & Rowe, L. A. (1992). An exploratory study of ad hoc query languages to databases. In *Proceedings of the 8th International Conference on Data Engineering* (pp. 606–6130). Tempe, Arizona.

Bernsen, N. O., Dybkjaer, H., & Dybkjaer L. (1998). *Designing Interactive Speech Systems – from First Ideas to User Testing*. Springer-Verlag.

Blackburn, P., Gardent, C., & de Rijke, M. (1994). Back and forth through time and events. In D. M. Gabbay (Ed.), *Proceedings of the First International Conference on Temporal Logic* (pp. 225–237). Bonn, Germany. Springer-Verlag.

Böhlen, M., Jensen, C. S., & Snodgrass, R. T. (2000). Temporal statement modifiers. *ACM Transactions on Database Systems, 25*(4), 407–456.

Böhlen, M. H., Chomicki, J., Snodgrass, R. T., & Toman, D. (1996). Querying TSQL2 databases with temporal logic. In P. M. G. Apers, M. Bouzeghoub, & G. Gardarin (Eds.), *Proceedings of the International Conference on Extended Database Technology* (pp. 325–341). Avignon, France.

Böhlen, M. H., Snodgrass, R. T., & Soo, M. D. (1996). Coalescing in temporal databases. In T. M. Vijayaraman, A. P. Buchmann, C. Mohan, & N. L. Sarda (Eds.), *Proceedings of the 22th International Conference on Very Large Data Bases* (pp. 180–191). Mumbai, India.

Brent, M. R. (1990). A simplified theory of tense representations and constraints on their composition. In *Proceedings of the 28th Annual Meeting of the Association for Computational Linguistics* (pp. 119–126). Pittsburgh, Pennsylvania.

Briscoe, T. (1997). Robust parsing. In R. Cole, J. Mariani, H. Uszkoreit, G. B. Varile, A. Zaenen, A. Zampolli, & V. Zue (Eds.), *Survey of the State of the Art in Human Language Technology*, Chapter 3.7 (pp. 121–123). Cambridge University Press and Giardini.

Bruce, B.C. (1972). A model for temporal references and its application in a question answering program. *Artificial Intelligence, 3*, 1–25.

Brusoni, V., Console, L., & Terenziani, P. (1995). Extending temporal relational databases to deal with imprecise and qualitative information. In J. Clifford & A. Tuzhilin (Eds.), *Recent Advances in Temporal Databases – Proceedings of the International Workshop on Temporal Databases* (pp. 3–22). Zurich, Switzerland. Springer-Verlag.

Carpenter, B. (1992). *The Logic of Typed Feature Structures.* Cambridge University Press.

Carpenter, B. (1998). *Type-Logical Semantics.* MIT Press.

Carpenter, B., & Penn, G. (2001). The Attribute Logic Engine – user's guide. Version 3.2.1.

Chomicki, J., Toman, D., & Böhlen, M. H. (2001). Querying ATSQL databases with temporal logic. *ACM Transactions on Database Systems, 26*(2), 145–178.

CLAW. (2000). *Proceedings of the 3rd International Workshop on Controlled Language Applications.* Seattle, Washington.

Clifford, J. (1988). Natural language querying of historical databases. *Computational Linguistics, 14*(4), 10–34.

Clifford, J. (1990). *Formal Semantics and Pragmatics for Natural Language Querying.* Cambridge University Press.

Clifford, J., & Warren, D. S. (1983). Formal semantics for time in databases. *ACM Transactions on Database Systems, 8*(2), 215–254.

Cole, R., Mariani, J., Uszkoreit, H., Varile, G. B., Zaenen, A., Zampolli, A., & Zue, V. (Eds.). (1997). *Survey of the State of the Art in Human Language Technology.* Cambridge University Press and Giardini.

Comrie, B. (1976). *Aspect.* Cambridge University Press.

Comrie, B. (1985). *Tense.* Cambridge University Press.

Cooper, R., Mukai, K., & Perry, J. (Eds.). (1990). *Situation Theory and Its Applications.* Center for the Study of Language and Information, Stanford.

Copestake, A., & Sparck Jones, K. (1990). Natural language interfaces to databases. *The Knowledge Engineering Review, 5*(4), 225–249.

Crouch, R. S., & Pulman, S. G. (1993). Time and modality in a natural language interface to a planning system. *Artificial Intelligence, 63*, 265–304.

Dahlbäck, N., Jönsson, A., & Ahrenberg, L. (1993). Wizard of Oz studies – why and how. *Knowledge-Based Systems, 6*(4), 258–266.

Dale, R., Moisl, H., & Somers, H. (Eds.). (2000). *Handbook of Natural Language Processing.* Marcel Dekker.

Dalrymple, M. (1988). The interpretation of tense and aspect in English. In *Proceedings of the 26th Annual Meeting of the Association for Computational Linguistics* (pp. 68–74). Buffalo, New York.

Davidson, J., & Kaplan, S. J. (1983). Natural language access to data bases: Interpreting update requests. *Computational Linguistics, 9*(2), 57–68.

De, S., Pan, S., & Whinston, A. B. (1985). Natural language query processing in a temporal database. *Data and Knowledge Engineering, 1*, 3–15.

De Roeck, A. N., & Lowden, B. G. T. (1986). Generating English paraphrases from formal relational calculus expressions. In *Proceedings of the 11th International Conference on Computational Linguistics* (pp. 581–583). Bonn, Germany.

Dekleva, S. M. (1994). Is natural language querying practical? *Data Base* (pp. 24–36).

Dowty, D. R. (1977). Toward a semantic analysis of verb aspect and the English 'imperfective' progressive. *Linguistics and Philosophy, 1*, 45–77.

Dowty, D. R. (1982). Tenses, time adverbs, and compositional semantic theory. *Linguistics and Philosophy, 5*, 23–55.

Dowty, D. R. (1986). The effects of aspectual class on the temporal structure of discourse: Semantics or pragmatics? *Linguistics and Philosophy, 9*, 37–61.

Dowty, D. R., Wall, R. E., & Peters, S. (1981). *Introduction to Montague Semantics*. D. Reidel.

Draxler, C. (1991). Accessing Relational and Higher Databases through Database Set Predicates in Logic Programming Languages. Ph.D. thesis, Department of Computer Science, University of Zurich, Switzerland.

Dutoit, T. (1997). *An Introduction to Text-to-Speech Synthesis*. Kluwer.

Enc, M. (1986). Towards a referential analysis of temporal expressions. *Linguistics and Philosophy, 9*, 405–426.

Epstein, S. S. (1985). Transportable Natural Language Processing Through Simplicity – the PRE System. *ACM Transactions on Office Information Systems, 3*(2), 107–120.

Flickinger, D., Oepen, S., Tsujii, J., & Uszkoreit, H. (Eds.). (2000). Special issue on efficient processing with HPSG: Methods, systems, evaluation. *Natural Language Engineering, 6*(1).

Gabbay, D. M., Hodkinson, I., & Reynolds, M. (1994). *Temporal Logic: Mathematical Foundations and Computational Aspects*, volume 1. Oxford University Press.

Gabbay, D. M., Reynolds, M. A., & Finger, M. (2000). *Temporal Logic: Mathematical Foundations and Computational Aspects*, volume 2. Oxford University Press.

Gazdar, G., & Mellish, C. (1989). *Natural Language Processing in Prolog – An Introduction to Computational Linguistics*. Addison-Wesley.

Gertz, M., & Lipeck, U. W. (1995). Temporal integrity constraints in temporal databases. In J. Clifford & A. Tuzhilin (Eds.), *Recent Advances in Temporal Databases – Proceedings of the International Workshop on Temporal Databases* (pp. 77–92). Zurich, Switzerland. Springer-Verlag.

Gibbon, D., Moore, R., & Winski, R. (1997). *Handbook of Standards and Resources for Spoken Language Systems*. Mouton de Gruyter.

Ginzburg, J. (1995a). *Questions, Queries, and Facts: A Semantics and Pragmatics for Interrogatives*. Cambridge University Press.

Ginzburg, J. (1995b). Resolving questions, I. *Linguistics and Philosophy, 18*(5), 459–427.

Ginzburg, J. (1995c). Resolving questions, II. *Linguistics and Philosophy, 18*(6), 567–609.

Hafner, C.D. (1985). Semantics of temporal queries and temporal data. In *Proceedings of the 23rd Annual Meeting of the Association for Computational Linguistics* (pp. 1–8). Chicago, Illinois.

Harper, M. P., & Charniak, E. (1986). Time and tense in English. In *Proceedings of the 24th Annual Meeting of the Association for Computational Linguistics* (pp. 3–9). New York, NY.

Hinrichs, E. (1986). Temporal anaphora in discourses of English. *Linguistics and Philosophy, 9*, 63–82.

Hinrichs, E. W. (1988). Tense, quantifiers, and contexts. *Computational Linguistics, 14*(2), 3–14.

Hirschberg, J., Kamm, C., & Walker, M. (Eds.). (1997). *Proceedings of the Workshop on Interactive Spoken Dialog Systems – Bringing Speech and NLP Together*. 35th Annual Meeting of the Association for Computational Linguistics and 8th Conference of the European Chapter of the Association for Computational Linguistics. Madrid, Spain.

Hirst, G. (1981). *Anaphora in Natural Language Understanding: A Survey*. Springer-Verlag.

Hobbs, J. R. (1986). Resolving pronoun references. In B. J. Grosz, K. Sparck Jones, & B. L. Webber (Eds.), *Readings in Natural Language Processing* (pp. 339–352). Morgan Kaufmann.

Hwang, C. H., & Schubert, K. (1994). Interpreting tense, aspect and time adverbials: A compositional, unified approach. In D. M. Gabbay & H. J. Ohlbach (Eds.), *Proceedings of the First International Conference on Temporal Logic* (pp. 238–264). Bonn, Germany. Springer-Verlag.

Jelinek, F. (1997). *Statistical Methods for Speech Recognition*. MIT Press.

Jensen, C. S., Dyreson, C. E., Böhlen, M., Clifford, J., Elmasri, R., Gadia, S. K., Grandi, F., Hayes, P., Jajodia, S., Kaefer, W., Kline, N., Lorentzos, N., Mitsopoulos, Y., Montanari, A., Nonen, D., Peressi, E., Pernici, B., Roddick, J., Sarda, N. L., Scalas, M. R., Segev, A., Snodgrass, R. T., Soo, M. D., Tansel, A., Tiberio, P., & Wiederhold, G. (1998). A consensus glossary of temporal database concepts. In O. Etzion, S. Jajodia, & S. M. Sripada (Eds.), *Temporal Databases: Research and Practice* (pp. 367–405). Springer-Verlag.

Jurafsky, D., & Martin, J. H. (2000). *Speech and Language Processing – An Introduction to Natural Language Processing, Computational Linguistics, and Speech Recognition*. Prentice Hall.

Kameyama, M., Passonneau, R., & Poesio, M. (1993). Temporal centering. In *Proceedings of the 31st Annual Meeting of the Association for Computational Linguistics*. Columbus, Ohio.

Kamp, H., & Reyle, U. (1993). *From Discourse to Logic – Introduction to Modeltheoretic Semantics of Natural Language, Formal Logic and Discourse Representation Theory*. Kluer.

Kaplan, S. J. (1982). Cooperative responses from a portable natural language data base query system. *Artificial Intelligence, 19*, 165–187.

Kenny, A. (1963). *Action, Emotion and Will*. Routledge and K. Paul.

Kent, S. (1993). Modelling Events from Natural Language. Ph.D. thesis, Department of Computing, Imperial College of Science Technology and Medicine, University of London, U.K.

King, M. (1996). Evaluating natural language processing systems. *Communications of the ACM, 39*(1), 73–79.

Kline, N. (1993). An update of the temporal database bibliography. *ACM SIGMOD Record, 22*(4), 66–80.

Kobsa, A., & Wahlster, W. (Eds.). (1989). *User Models in Dialog Systems*. Springer-Verlag.

Koubarakis, M. (1995). Databases and temporal constraints: Semantics and complexity. In J. Clifford & A. Tuzhilin (Eds.), *Recent Advances in Temporal Databases – Proceedings of the International Workshop on Temporal Databases* (pp. 93–109). Zurich, Switzerland. Springer-Verlag.

Kowalski, R., & Sergot, M. (1986). A logic-based calculus of events. *New Generation Computing, 4*, 67–95.

Lappin, S., & Leass, H. (1994). An algorithm for pronominal anaphora resolution. *Computational Linguistics, 20*(4), 535–561.

Lascarides, A. (1988). A Formal Semantic Analysis of the Progressive. Ph.D. thesis, Centre for Cognitive Science, University of Edinburgh, U.K.

Lascarides, A., & Oberlander, J. (1993). Temporal connectives in a discourse context. In *Proceedings of the 6th Conference of the European Chapter of the Association for Computational Linguistics* (pp. 260–268). Utrecht, The Netherlands.

Lorentzos, N. A., & Johnson, R. G. (1988). Extending relational algebra to manipulate temporal data. *Information Systems, 13*(3), 289–296.

Lowden, B. G. T., Walls, B. R., De Roeck, A. N., Fox, C. J., & Turner, R. (1991). A formal approach to translating English into SQL. In M. S. Jackson & A. E. Robinson (Eds.), *Aspects of Databases – Proceedings of the 9th British National Conference on Databases* (pp. 110–127). Wolverhampton Polytechnic, England.

Lucas, R. (1988). *Database Applications Using Prolog*. Halsted Press.

LuperFoy, S., Nijholt, A., & Veldhuijzen van Zanten, G. (Eds.). (1996). *Dialogue Management in Natural Language Systems*, 11th Twente Workshop on Language Technology, Enschede, the Netherlands.

Mays, E. (1986). A temporal logic for reasoning about changing data bases in the context of natural language question-answering. In L. Kerschberg (Ed.), *Expert Database Systems – Proceedings of the First International Workshop* (pp. 559–578). Benjamin/Cummings.

McCarthy, J., & Hayes, P. J. (1969). Some philosophical problems from the standpoint of artificial intelligence. In *Machine Intelligence 4* (pp. 463–502). Edinburgh University Press.

McDermott, D. (1982). A temporal logic for reasoning about processes and plans. *Cognitive Science, 6*, 101–155.

McGee Wood, M. (1993). *Categorial Grammars*. Routledge.

McKenzie, E. (1986). Bibliography: Temporal databases. *ACM SIGMOD Record, 15*(4), 40–52.

McKenzie, E., & Snodgrass, R. (1990). Schema evolution and the relational algebra. *Information Systems, 15*(2), 207–232.

McKenzie, E., & Snodgrass, R. (1991). Evaluation of relational algebras incorporating the time dimension in databases. *ACM Computing Surveys, 23*(4), 501–543.

Melton, J., & Simon, A. R. (1993). *Understanding the New SQL: A Complete Guide*. Morgan Kaufmann.

Melton, J., Simon, A. R., & Gray, J. (2001). *SQL: 1999 – Understanding Relational Language Components*. Morgan Kaufmann.

Mitkov, R. (2002a). Anaphora resolution. In R. Mitkov (Ed.), *Handbook of Computational Linguistics*, Chapter 14. Oxford University Press. Forthcoming.

Mitkov, R. (Ed.). (2002b). *Handbook of Computational Linguistics*. Oxford University Press. Forthcoming.

Moens, M. (1987). Tense, Aspect and Temporal Reference. Ph.D. thesis, Centre for Cognitive Science, University of Edinburgh, U.K.

Moens, M. (1988). Temporal databases and natural language. In C. Rolland, F. Bodart, & M. Leonard (Eds.), *Proceedings of Working Conference on Temporal Aspects in Information Systems* (pp. 171–183). Sophia-Antipolis, France. Elsevier.

Moens, M., & Steedman, M. (1988). Temporal ontology and temporal reference. *Computational Linguistics, 14*(2), 15–28.

Morrill, G. V. (1994). *Type Logical Grammar – Categorial Logic of Signs.* Kluwer.

Mourelatos, A. P. D. (1978). Events, processes, and states. *Linguistics and Philosophy, 2*, 415–434.

Nelken, R. (2001). Questions, Time, and Natural Language Interfaces to Temporal Databases. Ph.D. thesis, Department of Computer Science, Technion, Israel.

Nelken, R., & Francez, N. (1999a). The algebraic semantics of questions. In *Proceedings of the Sixth Meeting on Mathematics of Language* (pp. 167–182). Orlando, Florida.

Nelken, R., & Francez, N. (1999b). A semantics for temporal questions. In G. J. M. Kruijf & R. T. Oehrle (Eds.), *Proceedings of the 5th Conference on Formal Grammar* (pp. 131–142). Utrecht, The Netherlands.

Nelken, R., & Francez, N. (2000a). A calculus for interrogatives based on their algebraic semantics. In A. Nijholt, D. Heylen, & G. Scollo (Eds.), *Proceedings of the 16th Twente Workshop on Language Technology and the 2nd Workshop on Algebraic Methods in Language Processing* (pp. 143–160). Iowa City, Iowa.

Nelken, R., & Francez, N. (2000b). Querying temporal databases using controlled natural language. In *Proceedings of the 18th International Conference on Computational Linguistics* (pp. 1076–1080). Saarbrücken, Germany.

Nelken, R., & Francez, N. (2001a). The algebraic semantics of interrogative NPs. *Grammars, 3*(2–3).

Nelken, R., & Francez, N. (2001b). Bilattices and the semantics of natural language questions. *Linguistics and Philosophy*. To appear.

Parsons, T. (1989). The progressive in English: Events, states and processes. *Linguistics and Philosophy, 12*, 213–241.

Parsons, T. (1990). *Events in the Semantics of English: A Study in Subatomic Semantics.* MIT Press.

Partee, B. H. (1984). Nominal and temporal anaphora. *Linguistics and Philosophy, 7*, 243–286.

Passonneau, R. J. (1988). A computational model of the semantics of tense and aspect. *Computational Linguistics, 14*(2), 44–60.

Pereira, F., & Warren, D. H. D. (1980). Definite clause grammars for language analysis – a survey of the formalism and a comparison with augmented transition networks. *Artificial Intelligence, 13*, 231–278.

Perrault, C. R., & Grosz, B. J. (1988). Natural language interfaces. In H. E. Shrobe (Ed.), *Exploring Artificial Intelligence* (pp. 133–172). Morgan Kaufmann.

Pirie, N., Crabtree, B., Crouch, R., Pulman, S., Moffat, D., Ritchie, G., & Tate, A. (1990). A natural language interface to an intelligent planning system – system documentation. Technical Paper 5, Department of Artificial Intelligence, University of Edinburgh.

Pollard, C., & Sag, I. A. (1987). *Information-Based Syntax and Semantics – Fundamentals*, volume 1. Center for the Study of Language and Information, Stanford.

Pollard, C., & Sag, I. A. (1994). *Head-Driven Phrase Structure Grammar*. University of Chicago Press and Center for the Study of Language and Information, Stanford.

Pratt, I., & Bree, D. S. (1995). An approach to the semantics of some English temporal constructions. In *Proceedings of the 17th Annual Conference of the Cognitive Science Society* (pp. 118–123). Pittsburgh, Pennsylvania. Lawrence Earlbaum Associates.

Pratt, I., & Francez, N. (2001). Temporal prepositions and temporal generalized quantifiers. *Linguistics and Philosophy, 24*(2), 187–222.

Prior, A. (1967). *Past, Present and Future*. Oxford University Press.

Rayner, Manny. (1993). Abductive Equivalential Translation and its Application to Natural Language Database Interfacing. Ph.D. thesis, Royal Institute of Technology and University of Stockholm, Sweden.

Reichenbach, H. (1947). *Elements of Symbolic Logic*. Collier-Macmillan.

Reiter, E., & Dale, R. (2000). *Building Applied Natural Language Generation Systems*. Cambridge University Press.

Richards, B., Bethke, I., van der Does, J., & Oberlander, J. (1989). *Temporal Representation and Inference*. Academic Press.

Ritchie, G. D. (1979). Temporal clauses in English. *Theoretical Linguistics, 6*(1), 87–115.

Shieber, S. M. (1986). *An Introduction to Unification-Based Approaches to Grammar*. Center for the Study of Language and Information, Stanford.

Singh, M., & Singh, M. P. (1992). Computing the temporal structure of events in natural language. In B. Neumann (Ed.), *Proceedings of the 10th European Conference on Artificial Intelligence* (pp. 528–532). Vienna, Austria. John Wiley.

Smith, C. S. (1986). A speaker-based approach to aspect. *Linguistics and Philosophy, 9*, 97–115.

Smith, C. S. (1997). *The Parameter of Aspect* (2nd edition). Kluwer.

Snodgrass, R. T. (Ed.). (1995). *The TSQL2 Temporal Query Language*. Kluwer.

Snodgrass, R. T. (2000). *Developing Time-Oriented Database Applications in SQL*. Morgan Kaufmann.

Snodgrass, R. T., Böhlen, M. H., Jensen, C. S., & Steiner, A. (1998). Transitioning temporal support in TSQL2 to SQL3. In O. Etzion & S. Sripada (Eds.), *Temporal Databases: Research and Practice* (pp. 150–194). Springer.

Soo, M. (1991). Bibliography on temporal databases. *ACM SIGMOD Record, 20*(1), 14–23.

Sparck Jones, K., & Galliers, J. R. (1996). *Evaluating Natural Language Processing Systems – An Analysis and Review*. Springer.

Spenceley, S. (1989). Imperatives and temporal question answering in an English language front-end. Master's thesis, Department of Artificial Intelligence, University of Edinburgh, U.K.

Sripada, S. M., Rosser, B. L., Bedford, J. M., & Kowalski, R. A. (1994). Temporal database technology for air traffic flow management. In *Proceedings of the First International Conference on Applications of Databases* (pp. 28–41). Vadstena, Sweden. Springer-Verlag.

Stallard, D., & Bobrow, R. (1993). The semantic linker – a new fragment combining method. In *Proceedings of the ARPA Workshop on Human Language Technology* (pp. 37–42). Princeton, New Jersey.

Stam, R., & Snodgrass, R. (1988). A bibliography on temporal databases. *IEEE Database Engineering, 7*(4), 231–239.

Stirling, L. (1985). Distributives, quantifiers and a multiplicity of events. In *Proceedings of the 2nd Conference of the European Chapter of the Association for Computational Linguistics* (pp. 16–24). Geneva, Switzerland.

Tansel, A., Clifford, J., Gadia, S. K., Jajodia, S., Segev, A., & Snodgrass, R. T. (1993). *Temporal Databases – Theory, Design, and Implementation*. Benjamin/Cummings.

Tennant, H. R., Ross, K. M., Saenz, M., Thompson, C. W., & Miller, J. R. (1983). Menu-based natural language understanding. In *Proceedings of the 21st Annual Meeting of the Association for Computational Linguistics* (pp. 151–158). Cambridge, Massachusetts.

ter Meulen, A. (1994). Situated reasoning with temporal anaphora. In D. M. Gabbay & H. J. Ohlbach (Eds.), *Proceedings of the First International Conference on Temporal Logic* (pp. 42–48). Bonn, Germany. Springer-Verlag.

Thomson, A. J., & Martinet, A. V. (1986). *A Practical English Grammar* (4th edition). Oxford University Press.

Toman, D. (1996). Point vs. interval-based query languages for temporal databases. In *Proceedings of the 15th ACM SIGACT-SIGMOD-SIGART Symposium on Principles of Database Systems* (pp. 58–67). Montreal, Canada.

Tsotras, V. J., & Kumar, A. (1996). Temporal database bibliography update. *ACM SIGMOD Record, 25*(1), 41–51.

Ullman, J. D. (1988). *Principles of Database and Knowledge-Base Systems*, volume 1. Computer Science Press.

van Benthem, J. (1991). *The Logic of Time – A Model-Theoretic Investigation into the Varieties of Temporal Ontology and Temporal Discourse* (2nd edn.). Kluwer.

van Gelder, A., & Topor, R. W. (1991). Safety and translation of relational calculus queries. *ACM Transactions on Database Systems, 16*(2), 235–278.

Vendler, Z. (1967). Verbs and times. In *Linguistics in Philosophy*, Chapter 4 (pp. 97–121). Cornell University Press.

Vila, L. (1994). A survey on temporal reasoning in Artificial Intelligence. *AI Communications, 7*(1), 4–28.

Vlach, F. (1993). Temporal adverbials, tenses and the perfect. *Linguistics and Philosophy, 16*, 231–283.

Webber, B. L. (1988). Tense as discourse anaphor. *Computational Linguistics, 14*(2), 61–73.

Wijsen, J. (1995). Design of temporal relational databases based on dynamic and temporal functional dependencies. In J. Clifford & A. Tuzhilin (Eds.), *Recent Advances in Temporal Databases – Proceedings of the International Workshop on Temporal Databases* (pp. 61–76). Zurich, Switzerland. Springer-Verlag.

Wu, Y., Jajodia, S., & Wang, X. S. (1998). Temporal database bibliography update. In O. Etzion, S. Jajodia, & S. M. Sripada (Eds.), *Temporal Databases: Research and Practice* (pp. 338–366). Springer-Verlag.

Yip, K. M. (1985). Tense, aspect and the cognitive representation of time. In *Proceedings of the 23rd Annual Meeting of the Association for Computational Linguistics* (pp. 18–26). Chicago, Illinois.

Index

The index points to pages that define or provide prominent information about the corresponding concepts. Entries written in lower case italics, e.g., *activity*, are HPSG sorts, except when followed by brackets, e.g., *coalesce*(), in which case they are function names. Entries in italics where only the first letter is in upper case, e.g., *After*, are TOP operators. Entries written in upper case italics, e.g., *AFORMS*, are names of sets. Entries in small capitals, e.g., ASPECT, are HPSG features. Entries in upper case typewriter font, e.g., `AND`, are SQL keywords. Entries in normal capitals, e.g., HPSG, are acronyms. All other symbols appear as in the main body of the book.

Symbols

A

B

Appendix A

TOP to TSQL2 translation rules

A.1 Translation rules for yes/no formulae

In the rules below, it is assumed that $\pi \in PFUNS$, $\tau_1, \ldots, \tau_n \in TERMS$, $\varphi', \varphi_1, \varphi_2 \in YNFORMS$, $\beta \in VARS$, $\kappa \in CONS$, $\sigma_c \in CPARTS$, $\sigma_g \in GPARTS$, $\nu_{qty} \in \{1, 2, 3, \ldots\}$, and that λ is a TSQL2 value expression. n, n_1, n_2 are the lengths of $\ulcorner\varphi\urcorner, \ulcorner\varphi_1\urcorner, \ulcorner\varphi_2\urcorner$, respectively. λ_{init} stands for `PERIOD(TIMESTAMP 'beginning', TIMESTAMP 'forever')`. χ is the TSQL2 name of the granularity of chronons (e.g., `DAY` if chronons correspond to days). $\alpha, \alpha_1, \alpha_2$ are new correlation names, which have never been used before, obtained by calling a generator of correlation names.

A.1.1 $\pi(\tau_1, \ldots, \tau_n)$

$trans(\pi(\tau_1, \ldots, \tau_n), \lambda) \stackrel{def}{=}$

```
( SELECT DISTINCT α.1, α.2, ... , α.n
  VALID VALID(α)
  FROM (h'_pfuns(π, n))(SUBPERIOD) AS α
  WHERE ...
     AND ...
       ⋮
     AND λ CONTAINS VALID(α))
```

The dots in the `WHERE` clause stand for all the strings in $S_1 \cup S_2$:

$$S_1 = \{\text{“}\alpha.i = h'_{cons}(\tau_i)\text{”} \mid i \in \{1, 2, 3, \ldots, n\}, \tau_i \in CONS\}$$
$$S_2 = \{\text{“}\alpha.i = \alpha.j\text{”} \mid i, j \in \{1, 2, 3, \ldots, n\},\ i < j,\ \tau_i = \tau_j, \tau_i, \tau_j \in VARS\}$$

A.1.2 $Culm[\pi(\tau_1, \ldots, \tau_n)]$

$trans(Culm[\pi(\tau_1, \ldots, \tau_n)], \lambda) \overset{def}{=}$

```
( SELECT DISTINCT α1.1, α1.2, ..., α1.n
  VALID PERIOD(BEGIN(VALID(α1)), END(VALID(α1)))
  FROM (h'pfuns(π, n))(ELEMENT) AS α1, (h'culms(π, n)) AS α2
  WHERE α1.1 = α2.1
    AND α1.2 = α2.2
     ⋮
    AND α1.n = α2.n
    AND ...
     ⋮
    AND λ CONTAINS PERIOD(BEGIN(VALID(α1)), END(VALID(α1))))
```

The dots after $\alpha_1.n = \alpha_2.n$ in the WHERE clause stand for all the strings in $S_1 \cup S_2$, where S_1 and S_2 are as in the translation rule for predicates, except that α is now α_1.

A.1.3 $\varphi_1 \wedge \varphi_2$

$trans(\varphi_1 \wedge \varphi_2, \lambda) \overset{def}{=}$

```
( SELECT DISTINCT α1.1, ..., α1.n1, α2.1, ..., α2.n2
  VALID VALID(α1)
  FROM trans(φ1, λ) AS α1, trans(φ2, λ) AS α2
  WHERE ...
    AND ...
     ⋮
    AND VALID(α1) = VALID(α2))
```

Assuming that $\ulcorner\varphi_1\urcorner = \langle\tau_1^1, \ldots, \tau_{n_1}^1\rangle$ and $\ulcorner\varphi_2\urcorner = \langle\tau_1^2, \ldots, \tau_{n_2}^2\rangle$, the dots in the WHERE clause are all the strings in S:

$$S = \{\text{“}\alpha_1.i = \alpha_2.j\text{”} \mid i \in \{1, \ldots, n_1\},\ j \in \{1, \ldots, n_2\}, \tau_i^1 = \tau_j^2,\ \tau_i^1, \tau_j^2 \in VARS\}$$

A.1.4 *Pres*[φ′]

trans(*Pres*[φ′], λ) $\stackrel{def}{=}$

```
( SELECT DISTINCT α.1, α.2, ... , α.n
  VALID VALID(α)
  FROM trans(φ′,λ) AS α
  WHERE VALID(α) CONTAINS TIMESTAMP 'now')
```

A.1.5 *Past*[β, φ′]

trans(*Past*[β, φ′], λ) $\stackrel{def}{=}$

```
( SELECT DISTINCT VALID(α), α.1, ... , α.n
  VALID VALID(α)
  FROM trans(φ′,λ′) AS α)
```

λ′ is the expression `INTERSECT(λ, PERIOD(TIMESTAMP 'beginning', TIMESTAMP 'now' - INTERVAL '1' χ))`.

A.1.6 *Perf*[β, φ′]

trans(*Perf*[β, φ′], λ) $\stackrel{def}{=}$

```
( SELECT DISTINCT VALID(α), α.1, ... , α.n
  VALID INTERSECT(λ, PERIOD(END(VALID(α)) + INTERVAL '1' χ,
                                 TIMESTAMP 'forever'))
  FROM trans(φ′,λinit) AS α
 )(SUBPERIOD)
```

A.1.7 *Ntense*[β, φ′]

trans(*Ntense*[β, φ′], λ) $\stackrel{def}{=}$

```
( SELECT DISTINCT VALID(α), α.1, ... , α.n
  VALID PERIOD(TIMESTAMP 'beginning', TIMESTAMP 'forever')
  FROM trans(φ′,λinit) AS α
 )(SUBPERIOD)
```

A.1.8 $Ntense[now^*, \varphi']$

$trans(Ntense[now^*, \varphi'], \lambda) \stackrel{def}{=}$

```
( SELECT DISTINCT α.1, ... , α.n
  VALID PERIOD(TIMESTAMP 'beginning', TIMESTAMP 'forever')
  FROM trans(φ', λ_init) AS α
  WHERE VALID(α) = PERIOD(TIMESTAMP 'now', TIMESTAMP 'now')
 )(SUBPERIOD)
```

A.1.9 $For[\sigma_c, \nu_{qty}, \varphi']$

$trans(For[\sigma_c, \nu_{qty}, \varphi'], \lambda) \stackrel{def}{=}$

```
( SELECT DISTINCT α.1, ... , α.n
  VALID VALID(α)
  FROM trans(φ', λ) AS α
  WHERE INTERVAL(VALID(α), γ) = INTERVAL 'ν_qty' γ)
```

γ is the first element of the pair $h'_{cparts}(\sigma_c) = \langle \gamma, \Sigma_c \rangle$ (Section 5.9).

A.1.10 $Begin[\varphi']$

$trans(Begin[\varphi'], \lambda) \stackrel{def}{=}$

```
( SELECT DISTINCT α.1, ... , α.n
  VALID PERIOD(BEGIN(VALID(α)), BEGIN(VALID(α)))
  FROM trans(φ', λ_init)(NOSUBPERIOD) AS α
  WHERE λ CONTAINS BEGIN(VALID(α)))
```

A.1.11 $End[\varphi']$

$trans(End[\varphi'], \lambda) \stackrel{def}{=}$

```
( SELECT DISTINCT α.1, ... , α.n
  VALID PERIOD(END(VALID(α)), END(VALID(α)))
  FROM trans(φ', λ_init)(NOSUBPERIOD) AS α
  WHERE λ CONTAINS END(VALID(α)))
```

A.1.12 $At[\kappa, \varphi']$

$trans(At[\kappa, \varphi'], \lambda) \stackrel{def}{=} trans(\varphi',$ `INTERSECT(λ, ` $h'_{cons}(\kappa)$`))`

A.1.13 *Before*$[\kappa, \varphi']$

$trans(Before[\kappa, \varphi'], \lambda) \stackrel{def}{=} trans(\varphi', \lambda')$

λ' is the expression `INTERSECT(`λ`, PERIOD(TIMESTAMP 'beginning', BEGIN(`$h'_{cons}(\kappa)$`) - INTERVAL '1' `χ`))`.

A.1.14 *After*$[\kappa, \varphi']$

$trans(After[\kappa, \varphi'], \lambda) \stackrel{def}{=} trans(\varphi', \lambda')$

λ' stands for the expression `INTERSECT(`λ`, PERIOD(END(`$h'_{cons}(\kappa)$`)) + INTERVAL '1' `χ`, TIMESTAMP 'forever'))`.

A.1.15 *At*$[\sigma_g, \beta, \varphi']$

$trans(At[\sigma_g, \beta, \varphi'], \lambda) \stackrel{def}{=}$

```
( SELECT DISTINCT α1.1, α2.1, ..., α2.n
  VALID VALID(α2)
  FROM (h'gparts(σg)) AS α1, trans(φ', INTERSECT(α1.1, λ)) AS α2)
```

A.1.16 *Before*$[\sigma_g, \beta, \varphi']$

$trans(Before[\sigma_g, \beta, \varphi'], \lambda) \stackrel{def}{=}$

```
( SELECT DISTINCT α1.1, α2.1, ..., α2.n
  VALID VALID(α2)
  FROM (h'gparts(σg)) AS α1, trans(φ', λ') AS α2)
```

λ' stands for `INTERSECT(PERIOD(TIMESTAMP 'beginning', BEGIN(`α_1`.1) - INTERVAL '1' `χ`), `λ`)`.

A.1.17 *After*$[\sigma_g, \beta, \varphi']$

$trans(After[\sigma_g, \beta, \varphi'], \lambda) \stackrel{def}{=}$

```
( SELECT DISTINCT α1.1, α2.1, ..., α2.n
  VALID VALID(α2)
  FROM (h'gparts(σg)) AS α1, trans(φ', λ') AS α2)
```

λ' is `INTERSECT(PERIOD(END(`α_1`.1) + INTERVAL '1' `χ`, TIMESTAMP 'forever'), `λ`)`.

A.1.18 $At[\sigma_c, \beta, \varphi']$

$trans(At[\sigma_c, \beta, \varphi'], \lambda) \stackrel{def}{=}$

```
( SELECT DISTINCT α1.1, α2.1, ... , α2.n
  VALID VALID(α2)
  FROM (Σc) AS α1, trans(φ',INTERSECT(α1.1, λ)) AS α2)
```

Σ_c is the second element of the pair $\langle \gamma, \Sigma_c \rangle = h'_{cparts}(\sigma_c)$ (Section 5.9).

A.1.19 $Before[\sigma_c, \beta, \varphi']$

$trans(Before[\sigma_c, \beta, \varphi'], \lambda) \stackrel{def}{=}$

```
( SELECT DISTINCT α1.1, α2.1, ... , α2.n
  VALID VALID(α2)
  FROM (Σc) AS α1, trans(φ',λ') AS α2)
```

λ' is `INTERSECT(PERIOD(TIMESTAMP 'beginning', BEGIN(α1.1) - INTERVAL '1' χ), λ)`, and Σ_c is the second element of the pair $\langle \gamma, \Sigma_c \rangle = h'_{cparts}(\sigma_c)$.

A.1.20 $After[\sigma_c, \beta, \varphi']$

$trans(After[\sigma_c, \beta, \varphi'], \lambda) \stackrel{def}{=}$

```
( SELECT DISTINCT α1.1, α2.1, ... , α2.n
  VALID VALID(α2)
  FROM (Σc) AS α1, trans(φ',λ') AS α2)
```

λ' is `INTERSECT(PERIOD(END(α1.1) + INTERVAL '1' χ, TIMESTAMP 'forever'), λ)`, and Σ_c is the second element of the pair $\langle \gamma, \Sigma_c \rangle = h'_{cparts}(\sigma_c)$.

A.1.21 $At[\varphi_1, \varphi_2]$

$trans(At[\varphi_1, \varphi_2], \lambda) \stackrel{def}{=}$

```
( SELECT DISTINCT α1.1, ... , α1.n1, α2.1, ... , α2.n2
  VALID VALID(α2)
  FROM trans(φ1,λinit)(NOSUBPERIOD) AS α1,
       trans(φ2,INTERSECT(VALID(α1),λ)) AS α2
  WHERE ...
   ⋮
    AND ... )
```

The dots in the `WHERE` clause are as in the translation rule for $\varphi_1 \wedge \varphi_2$.

A.1.22 $Before[\varphi_1, \varphi_2]$

$trans(Before[\varphi_1, \varphi_2], \lambda) \stackrel{def}{=}$

```
( SELECT DISTINCT α₁.1, ... , α₁.n₁ α₂.1, ... , α₂.n₂
  VALID VALID(α₂)
  FROM trans(φ₁,λ_init)(NOSUBPERIOD) AS α₁, trans(φ₂,λ') AS α₂
  WHERE ...
     ⋮
     AND ... )
```

λ' is the expression `INTERSECT(PERIOD(TIMESTAMP 'beginning', BEGIN(VALID(α1)) - INTERVAL '1' χ), λ)`. The dots in the `WHERE` clause are as in the translation rule for $At[\varphi_1, \varphi_2]$.

A.1.23 $After[\varphi_1, \varphi_2]$

$trans(After[\varphi_1, \varphi_2], \lambda) \stackrel{def}{=}$

```
( SELECT DISTINCT α₁.1, ... , α₁.n₁ α₂.1, ... , α₂.n₂
  VALID VALID(α₂)
  FROM trans(φ₁,λ_init)(NOSUBPERIOD) AS α₁, trans(φ₂,λ') AS α₂
  WHERE ...
     ⋮
     AND ... )
```

λ' stands for the expression `INTERSECT(PERIOD(END(VALID(α1)) + INTERVAL '1' χ, TIMESTAMP 'forever'), λ)`. The dots in the `WHERE` clause are as in the translation rule for $At[\varphi_1, \varphi_2]$.

A.2 Translation rules for wh-formulae

Below it is assumed that $\beta_1, \ldots, \beta_k \in VARS$, and that $\varphi' \in YNFORMS$, with $\ulcorner \varphi' \urcorner = \langle \tau_1, \ldots, \tau_n \rangle$. λ_{init} stands for `PERIOD(TIMESTAMP 'beginning', TIMESTAMP 'forever')`. $\alpha, \alpha_1, \alpha_2$ are new correlation names, which have never been used before, obtained by calling a generator of correlation names.

A.2.1 $?\beta_1 \ldots ?\beta_k\ \varphi'$

$trans(?\beta_1 \ldots ?\beta_k\ \varphi', \lambda_{init}) \stackrel{def}{=}$

```
( SELECT DISTINCT SNAPSHOT α.ω1, ... , α.ωk
  FROM trans(φ', λinit) AS α)
```

For every $i \in \{1, 2, 3, \ldots, \kappa\}$, $\omega_i = min(\{j \mid j \in \{1, 2, 3, \ldots, n\}$ and $\tau_j = \beta_i\})$.

A.2.2 $?_{mxl}\beta_1\ ?\beta_2 \ldots ?\beta_k\ \varphi'$

$trans(?_{mxl}\beta_1\ ?\beta_2 \ldots ?\beta_k\ \varphi', \lambda_{init}) \stackrel{def}{=}$

```
( SELECT DISTINCT SNAPSHOT VALID(α2), α2.2, α2.3, ... , α2.k
  FROM ( SELECT DISTINCT 'dummy', α1.ω2, α1.ω3, ... , α1.ωk
         VALID α1.ω1
         FROM trans(φ', λinit) AS α1
       )(NOSUBPERIOD) AS α2)
```

$\omega_1, \ldots, \omega_k$ are as in the translation rule for $?\beta_1 \ldots ?\beta_k\ \varphi'$.

In the series NATURAL LANGUAGE PROCESSING (NLP) the following titles have been published thus far, or are scheduled for publication:

1. BUNT, Harry and William BLACK (eds.): *Abduction, Belief and Context in Dialogue. Studies in computational pragmatics.* 2000.
2. BOURIGAULT, Didier, Christian JACQUEMIN and Marie-Claude L'HOMME (eds.): *Recent Advances in Computational Terminology.* 2001.
3. MANI, Inderjeet: *Automatic Summarization.* 2001.
4. MERLO, Paola and Suzanne STEVENSON (eds.): *The Lexical Basis of Sentence Processing: Formal, computational and experimental issues.* 2002.
5. JACKSON, Peter and Isabelle MOULINIER: *Natural Language Processing for Online Applications.* 2002.
6. ANDROUTSOPOULOS, Ion: *Exploring Time, Tense and Aspect in Natural Language Database Interfaces.* 2002.